Ecumenical Documents III

Towards
the Healing
of Schism

THE SEES OF ROME
AND CONSTANTINOPLE

Public statements and correspondence
between the Holy See and the
Ecumenical Patriarchate
1958–1984

---

edited and translated by
E.J. Stormon, SJ

Introduction by Thomas F. Stransky, CSP

PAULIST PR
New York   Ma

D1449576

Library of Congress Cataloging-in-Publication Data

Towards the healing of schism.

    Outgrowth of a translation of the earlier collection of documents edited by a joint Roman Catholic-Orthodox commission under title: Tomos agapis.
    1. Catholic Church—Relations—Orthodox Eastern Church—Sources. 2. Orthodox Eastern Church—Relations—Catholic Church—Sources. 3. Athēnagoras I, Ecumenical Patriarch of Constantinople, 1886–1972. 4. Paul VI, Pope, 1897–1978. I. Stormon, E. J. II. Tomos agapis. English.
BX324.3.T69 1987   281.9   87-15517
ISBN 0-8091-2910-8 (pbk.)

Published by Paulist Press
997 Macarthur Boulevard
Mahwah, New Jersey 07430

Printed and bound in the
United States of America

CONTENTS

PART I
From Silence to Dialogue

Nos 1–28   **10/7/1958–6/7/1963**

Pope John XXIII ... Patriarch Athenagoras I†
Sickness and death of Pope Pius XII (1–2) ■   Pages
Statements on Church unity and civil society by 27–45
Pope John XXIII and Patriarch Athenagoras (4–
5) ■ Visits by Monsignor Willebrands to
Istanbul (8–11, 15–17) ■ Possibility of
observer-delegates to Vatican Council II (12,
17–21) ■ Information about First Session
(23) ■ Death of Pope John XXIII (25, 28)

---

† Only the more striking events and subjects are indicated here and in the following
sections. For a complete list of documents see Chronological Table, p. 509.

PART II
Growth and Fruits of Dialogue

delegations for patronal feasts 1980 (416–418,
422–424) ■ Sixteenth centenary of First
Council of Constantinople (427, 433–436), and
1550th anniversary of Council of Ephesus
(428) ■ Attempted assassination of Pope John
Paul II (431, 438–440) ■ Exchanges of
delegations 1981 (437, 445–447); for 1982 (452–
454, 459–461) [References to Second Plenary
Session for Theological Dialogue, Munich, 30
June–6 July 1982, in 460–461]; for 1983 (466–
468, 472–474); Patriarchal Delegation in Rome
for feast of Sts. Peter and Paul 1984, following
Third Plenary Session for Theological Dialogue,
Crete, 30 May–8 June (479–481)

Appendixes

DEDICATION

To The Memory Of Two Great Religious Leaders
Pope Paul VI And The Ecumenical Patriarch Athenagoras I,
Who, "After Centuries Of Silence And Waiting,"
Came From The East And The West
To Meet On The Mount Of Olives,
And There Felt The Power Of An Ancient Love.
... Their Works Follow Them.

INTRODUCTION

Thomas F. Stransky
Paulist Fathers

In outlining those historical divisions "which affect the seamless robe of Christ," the 1964 *Decree on Ecumenism* of the Second Vatican Council uses the word *solutio*, "the dissolving," to describe the gradual estrangement "between the Eastern Patriarchates and the Roman See."[1]

Historians who sift through the dense history of centuries sketch causes and conditions for this dissolving process: geographical remoteness between East and West; dearth of personal contacts among hierarchs and other church leaders, who thus became suspicious abstractions; all too human rivalries over sees or jurisdictions; shifts in imperial powers and other political events which reinforced isolation and opposition; ritual, canonical and even theological differences which were often pushed to extremes; and the 1054 excommunications in the conflict between Patriarch Michael Cerularius and Cardinal Humbertus.

Later, other specific events quickened the estrangement: the sack of Constantinople during the Fourth Crusade (1204), the slaughter of Christians by Christians, the western takeover of eastern churches, and the establishment of a parallel Latin hierarchy in the Middle East. Even the Decree of Union at the Council of Florence (1453) was most fragile; within twenty years all the Eastern Churches had repudiated it.

In 1453 Mohammed II conquered Constantinople. This city of Eastern unity became the capital of the Ottoman Empire, and it so remained for over four hundred years. Within the century, the entire Christian East, except for Russia, was under Islamic sway; and most eastern Christians preferred the Sultan's rule to union with the West.

Western and eastern Christians did more than settle into their separate ways. Sisters and brothers of the same "household of God" (Eph 2:9) changed into strangers, even enemies. Worse, there was hardly a

---

1. *The Decree on Ecumenism*, N. 13, in *Doing the Truth in Charity*, Ecumenical Documents I, eds. Thomas F. Stransky and John B. Sheerin (Paulist Press, 1982), 27.

1

sign of suffering from the abnormality, indeed the sin. Schism became an accepted, unrepentant fact.

Then other Christian divisions arose, stemming from "the grave crisis in the West that began at the end of the Middle Ages" and led to the Reformation. "Many Communions, national or confessional, were separated from the Holy See" of Rome.[2]

The post-Reformation period in the West found Roman Catholic religious communities engaged in zealous missionary activities, also among the Christian peoples in the Middle East and in Slav countries. That work bore fruit in the rise of Catholic groups which retained Eastern rites and customs, eventually with their own hierarchy, in places even with a patriarchate. In the nineteenth century Protestant missionaries intensified their efforts in the Middle East to convert to their Communions both Orthodox and Roman Catholics. Such a situation soured even more the relations between eastern and western Christians, especially between the See of Rome and the See of Constantinople.

Yet during the nineteenth century popes and patriarchs attempted "dialogue at a distance," through a series of initiating papal encyclicals and responses from the patriarchate. The papal letters called for reunion, but union was clearly expressed as a "return to the See of Rome"; only one partner needed to move. The negative responses of patriarchs, also through their encyclicals, were understandably negative, attacking the assumed primacy of the bishops of Rome.[3]

On the occasion of the First Vatican Council (1869–70), Pope Pius IX issued an Apostolic Letter "to all the Bishops of the Churches of the Eastern Rite not in Communion with the Apostolic See." After strongly asserting papal prerogatives, he exhorted these bishops to come to the "General Synod, as your ancestors came to the Councils of Lyons and of Florence, in order that the conditions of our former love may be renewed, and the peace of our Fathers may be once more called to vigor, so that the light of desired union may shine brightly upon all. Thus may continual thanksgivings be ever offered up to the Father of Mercies by all his Saints, and especially those most glorious ancient Fathers and Doctors of the Eastern Churches, when from heaven they look down on the restoration and renewal of that union with the Apostolic See, the center of Catholic truth and unity. . . ."

2. *Ibid.,* NN. 13 and 19.
3. Two examples: in 1848 Pope Pius IX's *In Suprema Petri Apostoli Sede* and the response by Ecumenical Patriarch Anthimos VI, *The Encyclical of the Four Patriarchs of 1848;* in 1894 Pope Leo XIII's *Praeclara gratulationis* and Patriarch Anthimos's answer. Cf. George A. Maloney, *A History of Orthodox Theology since 1453* (Belmont, Mass.: Nordland, 1976), 189–190, 195–196.

The Letter had leaked to the press before the Ecumenical Patriarch received it. When Rome's Vicar Apostolic presented it to the Patriarch, the latter commented that he already knew the contents from the newspapers, and so he could already reply that its principles and claims were not acceptable to the Eastern Orthodox Church. Its attendance at the Council would only reopen old wounds. Furthermore, the Pope should have sent the letter to each of the patriarchs and synods, and asked them how, where and in what conditions they would agree to the assembling of a Council. The Patriarch returned the letter to the papal representative, unopened.[4]

After Vatican I, Orthodox studies sharpened the differences in polemics which focused on papal infallibility, the "Filioque" formula in the Creed, the Immaculate Conception of Mary, and the existence of Eastern Churches in communion with the Bishop of Rome.

Direct personal contacts between patriarchs and popes were nil, except for two "almosts." In 1883 metropolitan Joachim of Dercos, convalescing in Italy, had a cordial audience with Pope Leo XIII. The next year Joachim was elected Ecumenical Patriarch, and Leo XIII had his Apostolic Delegate in Turkey present his felicitations. But Joachim died prematurely, and further contacts, based on this personal acquaintance, did not develop.

Another "almost" occurred in March 1919. On his way to Paris to defend the civil rights of Christians in Asia Minor, the locum tenens of the Patriarchate, Dorotheus of Brassi, stopped in Rome with his entourage and respectfully prostrated before the tomb of St. Peter. On that visit, however, there was no contact between him and officials of the Holy See.

The post-World War I period witnessed an increased desire of the Patriarchate of Constantinople to enter into the fledgling ecumenical movement. In the spring of 1919, a deputation of five bishops from the Protestant Episcopal Church in the U.S.A. visited Europe and the Middle East in order to elicit support for a planning conference which would consider "questions touching the Faith and Order" of "all Christian Communions throughout the world which confess Our Lord Jesus Christ as God and Savior."[5] In the visit to the Holy Synod of Athens the delegation received formal acceptance of the invitation, and afterward Metropolitan Meletius of Athens asked the thirty-six year old deacon who was the Synod's secretary to learn English—

---

4. Cf. Dom Cuthbert Butler, *The Vatican Council, 1869–1870* (Westminster, Maryland: Newman, 1962), 74–75.

5. An initiative of the General Convention of the Protestant Episcopal Church, 19 October 1910. Cf. *Faith and Order Pamphlets, N. 1,* 12ff.

"essential for such ecumenical contacts." That deacon was Athenagoras, later Ecumenical Patriarch.[6]

The American delegation proceeded to Constantinople, met with the Synod, and received written positive support and the promise to send delegates to the proposed conference.[7]

In January 1920, before that preparatory Faith and Order conference was held, the Ecumenical Patriarchate had addressed a Letter to all "the Churches of Christ, wheresoever they be." It requested that the Churches, despite their doctrinal differences, should come closer to one another by "the removal and abolition of all mutual mistrust and bitterness" and in a frank exchange of Christian thought and love, "for the preparation and advancement of that blessed union which would be completed in the future in accordance with the will of God." The Churches should emulate the spirit of the League of Nations and have some organ *(koinonia)* of common expression and action.[8]

The Eastern Orthodox were participants in the first conferences of Life and Work (Stockholm, 1925) and of Faith and Order (Lausanne, 1927), and in their later meetings. At the opening of the first assembly of the World Council of Churches (Amsterdam, 1948), the only Orthodox members were Constantinople, Greece, and the Rumanian Church in America. Two months later, on 1 November 1948, Athenagoras was elected Ecumenical Patriarch, enthroned on 27 January 1949.

Patriarch Athenagoras was born Aristocles Spyrou, on 25 March 1886, in Vassilikon, a village in northern Greece, then under Turkish rule. He studied theology at Halki in Turkey, was ordained deacon in 1910, and for nine years was archdeacon at Monastir (now the Yugoslavian city of Bitolj). There, he recalled, "I had a wonderful experience of the love with which simple people are capable, of dialogue, and of my first contact with Christians in the Western Church. . . . In order to manage to communicate with the Catholics there, I became a pupil at the school of the Marian Brothers, using as an excuse that I wanted to perfect my French."[9]

---

6. According to Stelios Castanos de Médicis, *Athénagoras Ier: l'Apport de L'Orthodoxie à l'Oecuménisme* (Lausanne: Editions l'Age d'Homme, 1968), 14.

7. Cf., "Report of the Deputation to Europe and the East," *Faith and Order Pamphlet, N. 32.*

8. The entire text in *The Orthodox Churches in the Ecumenical Movement: Documents and Statements, 1902–1975,* ed. Constantine G. Patelos (Geneva: World Council of Churches, 1978), 40–43. The Letter requests of each Church "a statement of its own judgment and opinion." The Orthodox scholar, Olivier Clément, considers Pope John XXIII's Christmas Message of 1958 (cf. in this book, N. 4) "the response to the 1920 invitation." Cf. his *Dialogues avec le Patriarche Athénagoras* (Paris: Fayard, 1969), 332.

9. Cf. Demetrios Tsakonas, *A Man Sent by God. A Life of Patriarch Athenagoras*

Later, in his maiden sermon as Metropolitan of Corfu (1922–30), he preached: "Unfortunately came the divisions of the Churches. Christ wanted one indivisible Church; instead, the Church became divided into factions. One must not hide the truth. The Church, which should have been the House of God, the Mother of all Christians, often forsook these principles and embarked on petty struggles, on missions of hate and persecution, and abandoned the people to their own fate without lifting a finger to help those in need, to help those who were sick or those who had been thrown into prison." At Corfu, he recalled, "I was on very friendly terms with Catholics, and especially with their Archbishop Leonardo Printezzi, which in a sense was quite revolutionary in view of the prevailing attitudes and psychology of the Greek clergy. Printezzi and I used to go out for walks together, and we freely exchanged ideas and views."[10]

In 1930 Athenagoras was elected Archbishop of North and South America, with headquarters in New York City. In the United States he succeeded in bringing unity to a politically fragmented Greek community. He also gave his Church status and respect in a religiously pluralistic society. He noted, for example, that in 1947 he and Cardinal Richard Cushing of Boston embraced at a public event, and the widely publicized photograph had the title in one newspaper: "The first embrace between East and West."[11]

After eighteen years in the Americas, in 1948 he was elected the Ecumenical Patriarchate's 269th leader, under the name of Athenagoras I.

Until then, the Roman Catholic Church had officially remained aloof from active participation in the ecumenical movement and any of its institutions. That same U.S. Episcopal delegation which in April 1919 had obtained from the Ecumenical Patriarchate positive support for the Faith and Order planning conference, in May visited Pope Benedict XV (1914–22) and received a negative response.[12] Shortly after the first Faith and Order conference in 1927, Pope Pius XI (1922–39) promulgated *Mortalium Animos,* on "fostering religious union."

---

of Constantinople, translated from the Greek by George Angeloglou (Brookline, Mass.: Holy Cross Orthodox Press, 1977), 13–14.

10. *Ibid.,* 17, 15.

11. Aristide Panotis, *Les Pacificateurs: Jean XXIII–Athénagoras–Paul VI–Dimitrios* (Athens: Dragon, 1974), 58. This incident is part of a long tape recorded interview with the Patriarch. For details of Archbishop Athenagoras's ministry in the United States, cf. George Papaioannou, *From Mars Hill to Manhattan: The Greek Orthodox in America under Patriarch Athenagoras I* (Minneapolis: Light and Life, 1976).

12. For details of this visit, cf. Thomas F. Stransky, "A Basis beyond the Basis," *The Ecumenical Review* 37.2 (April 1985), 213–215.

Without any distinctions between the Eastern Churches and Protestant Communions, the See of Rome perceived the movement at that time to be subversive of the very foundations of the Catholic faith "by the desires of other Christians to treat the Catholic Church as one among many churches. . . . There is only one way in which the unity of Christians may be fostered, and that is by promoting the return to the one true Church of Christ of those who are separated from it; for from that one true Church they have in the past unhappily fallen away."[13]

As the ecumenical movement developed and matured, the Holy See shifted its evaluation and policy. A year after the World Council of Churches Assembly (1948), the Holy Office in the Roman Curia published *Ecclesia Sancta*. The Letter now positively evaluated the ecumenical movement "among those who are dissident from the Catholic Church" and "believe in Christ the Lord," as derived from "the inspiration of the Holy Spirit," and thus "for the children of the true Church a source of holy joy in the Lord." Other Christians do care deeply for church unity, and Catholics must take those efforts seriously, in charity and prayer. Under strict conditions, competent Catholics can participate in discussions "on faith and morals" with other Christians.[14]

But the more radical shift in the Roman Catholic Church's understanding of the ecumenical movement, of its own role in it, and of its restored recognition of the Orthodox Churches of the East as "sister churches" would have to await the death of Pius XII, the election of Angelo Roncalli as John XXIII, his convocation of the Second Vatican Council, and the solemn conciliar acts over the signatures of Pope Paul VI and the Council Fathers.

Angelo Roncalli was born in 1881 at Sotto il Monte, on the slopes of the Italian Alps. After his priestly ordination in 1910 he was the secretary to the bishop of Bergamo, and later an army chaplain in World War I. In 1921 he became the first national direction of missions, with an office in the Roman Curia's Congregation for the Propagation of the Faith.

Four years later, the Secretary of State, Cardinal Gasparri, appointed Roncalli to Sophia as the Holy See's Apostolic Visitor to Bulgaria. The vast majority of that nation's Christians were of the Bulgarian Orthodox Church, then in schism with Constantinople. The Roman Catholics were either of the Latin rite or of the Byzantine Slav rite. Cardinal Gasparri informed him that "the situation in Bulgaria is

13. *Acta Apostolicae Sedis (AAS)* XX (1928), 5–15.
14. *AAS* XLIV (1950), 142–147.

very confused. . . . Everyone seems to be fighting with everyone else, the Moslems and the Orthodox, the Greek Catholics and the Latins, and the Latins with each other. Could you go there and find out what's happening." Monsignor Roncalli soon discovered the cardinal's description to be an understatement.[15]

In Bulgaria, as part of his "mission of peace,"[16] Roncalli began his ecumenical apprenticeship in a ministry of sincere and selfless charity among the Orthodox laity, clergy and hierarchy. He took the initiative to visit the Ecumenical Patriarch in Constantinople, Basil III, on 25 March 1927. A month later he reflected on the visit in a letter: "What a great thing it is to understand and show compassion. . . . How times have changed! Catholics are impelled by charity to hasten the return of the brethren to the unity of the one fold. . . . By charity—this rather than by theological discussion." The language is still of "return," but the theme is charity.[17]

But it was during his twelve-year term as Apostolic Delegate to Turkey (1934–44) that Archbishop Roncalli got personally to know a far greater number of Orthodox laity and prelates in Turkey and in Greece. He attended the funeral of Ecumenical Patriarch Photius II (January 1936), and that same month first met with his successor, Benjamin, who later arranged for Roncalli's visit to the monasteries on Mount Athos in Greece.[18] During the grim years of World War II, in diplomacy and in humanitarian work, especially among numerous refugees, Roncalli remained faithful to what he wrote in his 1940 private journal—to be "above all nationalistic disputes." He saw his mission as "a teacher of mercy and truth . . . principles and exhortations from my lips and encouragement from my conduct in the eyes of all, Catholics, Orthodox, Turks and Jews."[19]

As the war was drawing to a close, Archbishop Roncalli preached on Pentecost in 1944 that we all can find plausible reasons for stressing

---

15. For details on this most complicated church situation in Bulgaria and Roncalli's diplomacy, cf. Peter Hebblethwaite, *John XXIII* (London: Chapman, 1984), 113–142.

16. His March 1925 retreat notes in Rome before leaving for Bulgaria. Pope John XXIII, *Journey of a Soul,* tr. Dorothy White (New York: McGraw-Hill, 1964), 204.

17. Letter to Signorina Coari, 9 May 1927. A year later, Basil III remarked, "If I live long enough, I will myself go to the Pope of Rome and beg him to have pity on the persecuted Church everywhere . . . and together we will fight the anti-Christ." Cf. Hebblethwaite, *op. cit.,* 123–124. O. Clément claims that Patriarch Basil said that on such a visit he would even ask the Pope to convoke a Council which would consider "the problem of union." *Op. cit.,* 415.

18. Vittore Ugo Righi details Roncalli's activities in wartime Turkey and Greece, *Papa Giovanni sulle rive del Bosforo* (Padua: Messagero, 1971); and Hebblethwaite, 166–198.

19. November 1940 retreat notes. Cf. *Journal of a Soul,* op. cit., 251, 250.

differences in race, religion, culture or education. Catholics in particular like to mark themselves off from others—"our Orthodox brothers, Protestants, Jews, Moslems, believers or non-believers." But "in the light of the Gospel and the Catholic principle this logic of division does not hold. Jesus came to break down all barriers; He died to proclaim universal brotherhood; the central point of His teaching is charity, that is, the love which binds all to Him as the elder brother, and binds us all with Him to the Father." The Delegate prayed for "an explosion of charity."[20]

Archbishop Roncalli left Turkey in late December 1944 for Paris, as the Apostolic Nuncio to DeGaulle's post-war France. In 1963 he became the Cardinal Patriarch of Venice.

Meanwhile, the new Ecumenical Patriarch Athenagoras wanted to have official relations with the papal representative to Turkey, in order to "continue what had been so well begun by Roncalli before the war," as he later reminisced. In early 1952 he finally met the Apostolic Delegate, Andrea Cassulo, at the Delegation. During the conversation, Cassulo had a heart attack and died two days later. "After that tragic event and until John XXIII's accession to the pontifical throne," Athenagoras observed, "there had been no marked evolution in the relations of the two Churches."[21]

The new evolution began on the occasions of Pius XII's death (9 October 1958) and the election of Angelo Roncalli as Pope John XXIII (28 October). Patriarch Athenagoras issued press communiqués, and the *Tomos Agapis,* the Book of Love, received its first two entries. Only in hindsight does one detect the surprising hand of God in his shaping the graced histories of Aristocles Spyrou and Angelo Roncalli in their ministry of reconciliation. Only in hindsight does one realize that in that autumn of 1958 the former dissolving of ecclesial relations between the Sees of Constantinople and of Rome, and their subsequent lonely isolations, began to give place to a dialogue of charity and truth—the common journey of sister Churches towards the healing of schism.

During Pope John's papacy neither letter nor telegram was exchanged between him and Patriarch Athenagoras; they communicated through intermediaries.

---

20. P. Hebblethwaite, *op. cit.,* 197.

21. Aristide Panotis, *op. cit.,* 92. Pierre Duprey recalls that the Patriarch "very clearly and concretely" expressed his desire to visit Pope Pius XII in a conversation with Duprey, in May 1954. Cf. his "La Théologie et le Rapprochement," in *Le service théologique dans l'Eglise. Mélanges offerts au Père Yves Congar* (Paris: Cerf, 1974), 45.

On 25 January 1959, three months into his pontificate, Pope John announced his intention to convoke "an Ecumenical Council for the Universal Church." He then envisaged the Council to be of service "not only for the spiritual good and joy of the Christian people but also an invitation to the separated communities to seek again that unity for which so many souls are longing in these days throughout the world."[22] The announcement perplexed also other Christians. Would this be a papal attempt to reunite all Christians in the fashion of the Second Council of Lyons (1274)—a common table, presided over by the Pope, at which "reunion formulae" could and would be signed?

Thus, initial Orthodox anxiety about Vatican II had been based on a lack of clarity about the ecumenical intention of Pope John, and on the memory of Pope Pius IX's overtures to the Orthodox Churches before the First Vatican Council. Within three months Patriarch Athenagoras took the initative of seeking a papal audience for his personal representative, the newly elected Archbishop of North and South America—His Eminence Iakovos. With no publicity, the meeting took place on 17 March 1959. This was the first visit to the Bishop of Rome of a delegate of the Ecumenical Patriarch since May 1547, when Metropolitan Mitrophanes of Caesaria, a delegate of Dionysius II, met with Pope Paul III (he later became Patriarch Mitrophanis III [1565–72]).[23]

Official records of the Patriarch's message and of the conversation between Archbishop Iakovos and Pope John are still not available. But the Pope gave assurance that he would not act unilaterally in his relations with the Patriarch. On April 16 his papal delegate to Turkey, Archbishop Giacomo Testa, in the name of John XXIII, visited Patriarch Athenagoras at the Phanar in Constantinople and briefed him on the Pope's hopes and intentions for the Council.[24]

In his first encyclical, *Ad Petri Cathedram* (29 June 1959), Pope John made it quite clear that he intended the Council to be one of internal renewal of the Roman Catholic Church. A year later, he instituted the Secretariat for Promoting Christian Unity (SPCU) which would enable "those who bear the name of Christians but are separated from this Apostolic See . . . to follow the work of the Council and to find more easily the path by which they may arrive at that unity for which Christ prayed."[25] He appointed the Jesuit biblical scholar,

---

22. *AAS* LI (1959), 69.
23. A. Panotis, *op. cit.*, 42.
24. Cf. S. Castanos de Medicis, *op. cit.*, 24.
25. *Superno Dei Nutu* (5 June, 1960), *AAS* LII (1960), 436.

Augustin Cardinal Bea, to be the SPCU president, and the Dutch ecumenist, Monsignor John Willebrands, as its secretary. Cardinal Bea immediately became the Pope's liaison-officer with the Patriarch, and Monsignor Willebrands would be the traveling envoy to negotiate the invitation to the Orthodox Churches for the participation of Delegated Observers to the sessions of Vatican II.[26] The first session convened on 11 October 1962.

Already in 1952 Patriarch Athenagoras had called for a Pan-Orthodox Great and Holy Council, and to prepare for that event the first Pan-Orthodox Conference was held on the island of Rhodes in late September 1961. So long in varying types of isolation from each other, primarily because of political situations, now all the Orthodox Churches, except Albania, were drawing together through their representatives. At Rhodes it was resolved that in future relations with other Christian Churches, the Orthodox would adopt a common stance.[27] On that principle, for example, relations with the Roman Catholic Church and its upcoming Council would be decided together, and not by individual Orthodox Churches on their own.

The first session of Vatican II surfaced the positive concern to articulate an ecclesiological understanding of the relationship between the Catholic Church and the Eastern Churches which were not in communion with the See of Rome, and to establish a common healing policy in its relations with them. These deliberations began to soften ecumenical fears among other Christians.

Then in June 1963, the Pope died, the one of whom Patriarch Athenagoras had often said, "There was a man sent by God whose name was John." Upon the election of Cardinal Montini as Pope Paul VI, the Church of Rome restored an ancient custom, long abandoned. It announced the election directly to all the heads of the Churches of the East (cf. N. 29). Three months later, just before the second Pan-Orthodox Conference was to convene, Pope Paul sent a handwritten letter to Patriarch Athenagoras (N. 33). The last letter of a Pope to a Patriarch had been in 1584, when Gregory XIII wrote to Jeremiah II about the reform of the calendar.[28]

---

26. Cf. Thomas F. Stransky, "The Foundation of the Secretariat for Promoting Christian Unity" (1960–1962), in *Vatican II by Those Who Were There,* ed. Alberic Stacpoole (London: Chapman, 1986), 62–87.

27. Encyclical of 12 February 1951, in *Orthodoxia* 26 (1951), 118–120. Cf. Pierre Duprey, "La conférence interorthodoxe de Rhodes," *Proche-Orient chrétien* XI (1961), 169–180, 351–378, esp. 367–371.

28. The entire texts of the letters, 1583–1584, in Vittorio Peri, *Due Dati, Un'unica Pasqua* (Milano: Vita e Pensiero, 1967), 240–253. O. Clement states that Archbishop Roncalli informed the Patriarchate of the election of Pius XII. *Op. cit.,* 332.

In his letter Pope Paul begged to "confide the past to the mercy of God," and held up, for the first time, "the gift of the same Baptism and the same Priesthood, in which the same Eucharist is celebrated." In his response, the Patriarch acknowledged that the "fellowship in love which was formerly strong in the bond of peace is now being renewed, through the Lord's grace, 'to the praise of His glory'" (N. 35). The Patriarchate had already published the papal letter in its official bulletin under the large headline, "The Two Sister Churches." This was the first modern use of an ancient expression to describe the relations between the Churches of Rome and of Constantinople, and it would enter the vocabulary of the Vatican Council.[29]

This papal letter and the patriarchal response not only displayed genuine charity and zealous concern for reconciliation, but they also provided the necessary ecclesiological foundation for the quick development of personal relations between the two leaders, especially through their meeting at Jerusalem three months later, with their common declaration. That meeting of "two pilgrims with eyes fixed on Christ," which culminated in the fraternal embrace on the Mount of Olives, remains an icon. It contains what it represents, it anticipates a promise. As the two imaged their encounter, it was "the sign and prelude of things to come" (N. 50).

After Pope Paul's first letter and before the opening of the second session of Vatican II, the second Pan-Orthodox Conference had accepted the principle of "a dialogue on an equal footing" with the Roman Catholic Church, and submitted the proposal to the heads of the autocephalous Churches. The 1964 Pan-Orthodox Conference renewed the desire for dialogue, but added that "an indispensable preparation and the creation of appropriate conditions would be necessary" by "the dialogue of charity." Each local Orthodox Church would be free to initiate such relationships in the conviction that "the present difficulties would eventually disappear."[30] Thus the Ecumenical Patriarchate, without directly involving the other Orthodox Churches, on its own behalf could intensify familial relations with the Church of Rome.

For example, because in 1962 the Orthodox Churches had not been unanimous in face of Rome's invitation for delegated observers

---

29. *Apostolos Andreas,* 6 November 1963. Cf. *Proche-Orient chrétien* XIII (1963), 336–337. In the *Decree on Ecumenism,* N. 14, the expression referred only to the relations between the Orthodox Churches. Then in 1967 Pope Paul VI called the Catholic and the Orthodox Churches "sister churches" (N. 176), and he and the Patriarch used it in their common declaration three months later (N. 195).

30. Cf. "La 3° conférence panorthodox de Rhodes," *Proche-Orient chrétien* XV (1965), 104.

to Vatican II, Patriarch Athenagoras sent a purely personal representative to the second session (1963). But now the Patriarchate could and did delegate official observers to the third and fourth sessions (1964, 1965).[31]

And the dialogue of charity had so progressed that at the closing of the Vatican Council, Patriarch Athenagoras and Pope Paul VI together could decide to "remove from the memory and from the midst of the Church the excommunications of 1054," and confidently pledge the two Churches to the dialogue between them which will lead to "the full communion of faith, of brotherly harmony, and of sacramental life, which obtained between them throughout the first thousand years of the life of the Church" (N. 127).

In the 1960s some western observers were calling these events "purely protocol gestures," without value insofar as they do not directly lead the Churches into the arena of "theology." Others, Orthodox, were fearful that the dialogue of charity would develop at the expense of the dialogue of truth; vague sentimentalism would hide the demands of dogma. Such criticisms, today more heard in conversations than seen in print, belittle both charity and truth.

In hindsight one can now see in the continuous flow of the pages of this book the clear reflection of the symbiosis of charity and truth, of ecclesial acts and truth. In 1971 Patriarch Athenagoras considered the experienced dialogue of charity already as a reversal of the path which had led to division, a reversal of alienation from mutual love (N. 286). Reciprocal love expressed in acts is already theological. Experience has already shown that there is, in the words of Metropolitan Meliton, "no clear, definitive, categorical division between the dialogue of charity and the theological dialogue."[32] Furthermore, in so

---

31. The Orthodox Churches of Russia and of Georgia had delegated observers to all four sessions of Vatican II. Alexandria also had observers at the third and fourth, and the patriarchates of Serbia and of Bulgaria at the fourth. For the listing of churches and names, cf. *Obsérvateurs-Délegués et Hôtes du Secrétariat* (Vatican Polyglot Press, 1965). Already before the first session, Patriarch Athenagoras stated in an interview for the Greek journal *To Vima* (Spring 1962) that he woud be willing to visit the Pope in Rome if John XXIII would reciprocate at the Phanar. Cf. O. Clément, *op. cit.*, 335.

32. His address to the fourth Pan-Orthodox Conference (June 1968). Entire text in *Proche-Orient chrétien* XVIII (1968), 359–361. In the dialogue, continued Meliton, "we discover that charity has acted not purely and simply as a sentimental and psychological factor, a creator of a suitable climate for the opening of a purely theological dialogue. Since charity is a theological virtue, it acts also as a theological element. It lays the foundation of the subsequent theological structure of dialogue between the two Churches." From his address to the fourth Pan-Orthodox Conference (8–15 June 1968), in *Proche-Orient chrétien* XVIII (1968), 359–361. It seems Metropolitan Meliton himself was the first to use the expression, "dialogue of charity," on 18 November 1964, while the par-

many of the key speeches, letters and declarations, the authors themselves assess the mutual growth of reconciliation in theological and ecclesiological language.

The experienced dialogue of charity did open the way to formal theological work. In November 1979, Patriarch Dimitrios I and Pope John Paul II jointly declared the opening of the official theological dialogue between the Catholic Church and the Orthodox local autocephalous Churches. Its aim: "an advance towards the reestablishment of full communion between the Catholic and Orthodox sister Churches" and "a contribution to the multiple dialogues that are pursuing their courses in the Christian world as it seeks its unity" (NN. 404, 406).

The seeking of unity is a process, and in three decades we have witnessed the beginnings of reconciliation. Between the Roman Catholic and Orthodox Churches, the ancient weight of negative attitudes, acts and symbols is beginning to be counterbalanced by an infant tradition of positive ones: from letters and statements of distant monologue to equal-to-equal personal dialogue; from mutual recrimination based on past events to mutual forgiveness with eyes toward the future; from a consciousness primarily of what divides to what already unites; from an almost fatalistic acceptance of division to a recognition of its scandal, then to the question, "Do we have a right to remain separated?"[33]

What is being done, though not yet by all and not yet everywhere, nevertheless is a symbol of Christian hope and a realistic direction for the future. Protocol becomes respectful Christian courtesy, courtesy develops into a dialogue of charity, and friendship provides the trustful milieu for theological dialogue and common missionary and pastoral concerns. In such experiences of "living out the truth in charity" (Eph 4:15), Christians rediscover the unity of the same household which God has given and wills to manifest in God's one mission to God's one world.

In *Towards the Healing of Schism,* the letters, common declarations and visits between Patriarchs and Popes, and between other church leaders of the two ancient sees, form "so many stones in the

---

ticipants in the third Pan-Orthodox Conference were on pilgrimage to Patras; for the first time more publicly, cf. N. 84. Cf. Pierre Duprey, "La Théologie et la Rapprochement," *op cit.,* 38–39. The expression took hold immediately (NN. 87, 88, 92, 93, 94, etc.).

33. Pope John Paul II: "It seems to me that the question we must ask ourselves is not so much whether we can reestablish full communion, but whether we still have the right to remain separated" (N. 402).

construction of the edifice of reconciliation and union in Christ of our Churches" (Patriarch Dimitrios I, N. 359). They are living stones, but not the only ones. If the hardened division between East and West had been the result of the gradual dissolving of relationships at all levels of the Churches' lives, one should not expect a quick reverse simply through high level visits and letters, declarations and theological dialogues. The long experience of isolation can cede only to parish, diocesan, and national "rediscoveries" in mutual trust and love and in common witness.

And such experiences should join all those rediscoveries in relations between all the Christian Communions which share in the one ecumenical movement. That movement is a gift of the Holy Spirit to our times, with an objective that "transcends human powers and gifts." Therefore, our hope is placed "entirely in the prayer of Christ for His Church, in the love of the Father for us, and in the power of the Holy Spirit."[34] We place our hope in "the One who has begun this good work in you and will carry it through to completion" (Phil 1:6), for "He who calls us is trustworthy, therefore He will do it" (1 Thes 5:24).

Pentecost Sunday, 1987

---

34. The concluding paragraph of the *Decree on Ecumenism*.

COMMENDATION

Archbishop Frank Little, D.D.,
of Melbourne, Australia

It was during a small ecumenical gathering of Catholics and Orthodox in Melbourne some years ago that the idea of making this book—or a first form of it—arose. Since 1958 important exchanges between the Vatican and the Orthodox Patriarchate of Constantinople had been taking place in then fairly recent times, and a record of them in the original languages, French and Greek, had been published by the partners to this dialogue under the Greek title *Tomos Agapis* (Volume of Charity). As the contents clearly marked an entirely new and most promising epoch in the relations, not merely of the two great sees of Rome and Constantinople, but by implication between Catholics and Orthodox all over the world, it seemed to our Melbourne gathering that the good news should be spread on a wider scale, and in the English language.

At my suggestion Father E. J. Stormon, S.J. of the Jesuit Theological College, Melbourne, with whose deep interest in the subject I had been long familiar, and who was known to possess the appropriate linguistic and literary skills, was invited to undertake the demanding task. Since then I have watched the work grow over the years, to eclipse the original limited plan, and become a complete record in accurate and easily readable English of the correspondence and other dealings between the central sees of the Catholic and Orthodox worlds, right up to a natural halting place on the threshold of the present time.

The translator has had the satisfaction of seeing his work taken up by the Paulist Press in the United States as a volume in its valuable series of documentary works on current ecumenical dialogues. This seems an admirable way of making available to a wide audience an absorbing account of how Catholic and Orthodox, in the persons of their highest representatives, are rediscovering themselves as "sister Churches," and after a centuries old estrangement are striving anew towards the sacramental communion which they had in earlier times. There is reason to think that these efforts, made on both sides under the influence of the Holy Spirit, will also have a stimulating and beneficient effect on the many men and women of good will in different parts of the world who are aspiring to a total Christian unity, with the preservation of their own authentic traditions—for this more inclusive unity is indeed the further aim of the present dialogue.

May I add that in this country Catholics and Orthodox alike take special pleasure in the fact that my friend, His Eminence Archbishop Stylianos, Greek Orthodox Primate of Australia, is Co-Chairman (with Cardinal John Willebrands, President of the Secretariat for Promoting Christian Unity) of the Joint Catholic-Orthodox Commission for Theological Dialogue, which has a vital role to play, under divine guidance, in preparing the way for future developments.

I heartily commend the present work, and wish it the wide readership which its important subject matter and attractive presentation call for.

COMMENDATION

Archbishop Stylianos
Primate of the Greek Orthodox Church in Australia

The publication of *Tomos Agapis* in an English translation must be greeted as an important theological event for the entire Christian world.

The contents of this volume which signifies the milestone of a new era in the relations between Orthodox and Roman Catholics should be - studied and known by all those Christians who are sincerely interested in the restoration of Christian Unity understood as a commonly shared *faith, love* and *hope.*

There is no greater obstacle in the way of restoring this long lost Christian Unity and communion than the unchristian mutilation of these major gifts of the Holy Spirit by Christians themselves. The three substantial dimensions of Christian Unity—namely, faith, love and hope—correspond to the triune God. This means that none of the three can be honored alone nor separated from the other two.

Since the restoration of Christian Unity concerns not only the leaders and theologians of the two Churches, but also the entire body of the faithful, one should carefully compare all actions and expressions of Christian life on both sides with the officially conducted statements and gestures.

Only through such moral sensitivity for coherence between theology and life may one hope that the ongoing theological dialogue of the two sister Churches will be crowned from above with the expected success.

Father E. J. Stormon, S.J. should be warmly congratulated for accomplishing the painstaking and huge task of such a translation.

TRANSLATOR'S FOREWORD

E.J. Stormon, S.J.

This book has grown by successive instalments out of what was first meant to be simply a translation of the earlier collection of documents edited by a joint Roman Catholic-Orthodox commission, and given the traditional Greek title of *Tomos Agapis* (Volume of Charity). In 1971 this work was beautifully produced by the Vatican Polyglot Press with accompanying photographs, and was brought out simultaneously at Rome and Istanbul in a bilingual edition, with French and Greek matching each other on opposite pages. The book indeed marked that epoch of the beginnings and astoundingly rapid growth of the "dialogue of charity" between the two Churches.

The documentation called for a much wider diffusion. Translations, also containing a few supplementary items, appeared in Spanish (*Biblioteca de Autores Cristianos,* Madrid 1973), in German (*Pro Oriente,* Vienna 1978), and in French (Cerf "Semeurs," Paris, 1984).

Obviously an English edition was also called for, but only later was an invitation to take this in hand directed to this writer. As I settled down to this often exacting and unexpectedly time consuming task, the closing date of the *Tomos* (1970) was being left further and further behind, and in the meantime interesting new developments in the dialogue of charity were taking place (including the decision to institute an official theological dialogue—the first in over five hundred years). It was imperative that this new material be incorporated in any new edition of the *Tomos Agapis.* From time to time the Vatican Secretariat for Promoting Christian Unity provided photocopies of the new correspondence.

But where to fix on a suitable halting point? In agreement with the publishers, it was decided that this should be the feast of Saints Peter and Paul, 29 June 1984, in preparation for which a delegation from the Orthodox Patriarchate of Constantinople had arrived in Rome, and where for the first time the proceedings were conducted in English. From this point onwards the center of interest was moving more and more to the theological dialogue, and at its term, this dialogue will need separate and special treatment.

The *Tomos Agapis* then has been extended to cover a further fourteen years, and the book has practically doubled in size. This English edition is meant to serve as a faithful record—the only one so far available in any language—of the exchanges between the sees of Rome and Constantinople from 1958 to mid-1984.

A documentary book of this size does not easily lend itself to being read from cover to cover. The reader might be well advised, after going though the earlier pages—and perhaps skipping lightly over minor telegrams—to settle down to some particular sections that most readily engage attention, and to work backwards and forwards from these, following the "meshing" of the documents. The table of contents, the list of communications, and the divisions of the book are meant to facilitate this kind of reading. My main hope, of course, and that of the Orthodox and Catholic friends who have encouraged me, is that the general tenor and perhaps much of the detail of what has been said and done on the highest levels in both Churches may find its echo among the much larger numbers of clergy and laity who instinctively desire fraternity and unity while remaining faithful to their own essential and loved traditions. There is indeed encouragement and inspiration to be had on a wide scale in seeing the steps taken by responsible and generous-minded leaders to heal the ancient schism in search of full fellowship or communion.

Now to more technical matters. The two main languages in these exchanges are French and Greek. French is the standard language on the Roman side. Even the Latin Bull *Ambulate in Dilectione* (7 December 1965) and the Brief *Anno Ineunte* (25 July 1967) seem to be based on the accompanying French texts. On the Orthodox side, Patriarch Athenagoras usually preferred French for his telegrams (presumably for alphabetic reasons), but his letters and formal statements are in Greek, as are most of the communications from his successor, Patriarch Dimitrios. The Doyen of the Holy Synod of the Patriarchate, Metropolitan Meliton, wrote his addresses in Greek, but read a French translation at papal audiences; I have translated from his original Greek drafts except where only the French had been preserved. The Popes' discourses to people assembled in St. Peter's Square (from which a few extracts are included) are in Italian, as are various speeches of Pope John Paul II reproduced in the *Osservatore Romano*. The original languages of the texts are indicated by the simple system of asterisks.

My ideal aim in the English renderings is that of most translators today, i.e., to get the real meaning and as much as possible of the "feeling" of the originals into a natural and easily flowing English which can exist in its own right. This demands some flexibility even with modern French, so close to our own English. The "archaistic" Greek, however, in which Patriarch Athenagoras couched his more formal communications, calls consistently for a more thorough type of transmutation if it is to deliver its message in current English. One has to let one's mind sink down into the meaning well beyond the outer fabric of phrase and sentence structure until these tend to dissolve, and then reform themselves in English style and sequence. I can only hope that in striving for ease and lucidity I have not sacrificed too many qualities inherent in the original, and indeed that something of the distinctive richness and flavor has survived. With few exceptions the Greek of the other Orthodox writers in this volume, while not without its own eloquence, is far nearer to modern usage and presents no special problem.

The numerous telegrams exchanged between Rome and Constantinople fall so little short of normal prose that it seems better to fill out the sentences slightly than to imitate the abbreviations. I have placed the rare elucidatory word or words within square brackets.

I have been more sparing of honorific titles ("Your Holiness," "Your Eminence," etc.) than are the original documents, except at the beginning and end of letters and at certain emphatic points; elsewhere the translation slips rapidly into the unobtrusive pronouns ("you," "he," etc.), without loss of respect, I hope, and with some gain of readability. In the interest of conciseness I have dispensed with the signatures to letters (since the writer's name is already given in the title), and with as much of the formal endings as seems feasible and proper in each case. Since I adopt the now common practice of using small initials for pronouns referring to God and Christ, it seems right to reduce the capitals in the Papal and Patriarchal "We" to lower case. Any ambiguities concerning the formal and ordinary uses of these pronouns should be sufficiently resolved by the context. Finally, I have had to do some very mild pruning among the traditional epithets "holy" (Church, desire, visit, etc.) and "beloved" (brother, etc.) on the few occasions when these, if all taken over, would have cluttered up the English or made it too cloying (effects which they do not have in the formal originals).

In the course of the editing, the number of footnotes has grown from the merest handful to something more considerable, since the publishers took the view, correctly I am sure, that most readers would appreciate a few biographical facts about personalities in the dialogue, brief explanations of lesser known allusions, and here and there basic information helpful to the reading of the text. The rule was that these notes were to be purely objective and exclusive of value judgments, and to fall far short of systematic commentary. The major role in all this was played by Father Thomas F. Stransky, C.S.P., who supplied many notes of his own and abridged, modified, or rephrased some of mine to meet editorial requirements. This involved many friendly discussions. While the final form of course often ended in a compromise, I am deeply and genuinely grateful for his fraternal collaboration. I thank him also for the introduction to this work, a contribution for which his years of service in the Roman Secretariat for Promoting Christian Unity and his general ecumenical experience and standing have singularly fitted him.

My greatest debt during the work of translation has been to Father Pierre Duprey of the White Fathers, who until 1985 was Under-Secretary of the above Secretariat (he is now Secretary). He was personally involved in many of the proceedings represented in this book. As one of the editors of the original *Tomos Agapis,* he, more than anyone else, understood the occasional difficulties of my task, and was more than generous in his encouragement and never-failing replies to my frequent questions. At my request he provided photocopies of the material by which I was able to bring the earlier *Tomos* up to date. In short, while I alone take responsibility for the translation and publication, it is hard to see how this book could have appeared without Father Duprey's constant support and faith in the enterprise. *Un grand merci, cher Père, de tout mon coeur!*

It would take too long to enumerate all the Catholic and Orthodox friends in Australia, whose good will and moral support have sustained me. Outstanding among these have been my own Archbishop, The Most Reverend Sir Frank Little of Melbourne, and the Greek Orthodox Primate of Australia, His Eminence the Most Reverend Archbishop Stylianos of Sydney. Both have also generously supplied the commendations found in the forefront of this book. I thank them for this further mark of their kindness.

Among the Orthodox clergy and laity of Melbourne with whom I have often experienced a sense of brotherhood, combined at times with personal affection, I must single out my friend of many years, the Very Reverend Archimandrite C. M. Boyazoglu, now the senior Greek Orthodox priest of Australia, to whom I owe it that my academic Greek was gradually transformed into a living tongue, though still far from the perfection and ease of his own. But on a level deeper than language we have together lived out the "dialogue of charity" to the point where our two traditions meet joyfully, and both nourish and are nourished by a close and confident personal friendship. *Eis polla ta eti, O phile mou!*

I must add, too, a tribute to my own community of the Jesuit Theological College, Melbourne. Its sensitivity and insight freed me from various tasks to attend to this one thing necessary. In particular I thank our secretary, Mrs. Leonie Hudson, who shared my labor of love by serenely and graciously typing out my text through what must have seemed its endless metamorphoses and revisions.

It remains to acknowledge permission to use quotations from a small array of Scriptural versions, each selected in turn to bring out a particular nuance, or to fit a special context. I have drawn on *The Common Bible* (William Collins Sons and Co., Ltd., London and New York), *The Jerusalem Bible* (1st ed., Darton, Longman and Todd, London; Doubleday and Company, Inc., New York), *The New English Bible* (Oxford and Cambridge University Presses), and *The New American Bible* (P. J. Kenedy and Sons, New York). I should like to thank the copyright holders in each case.

* * *

Original languages

* = French	A combination of asterisks (e.g., * **) indi-
** = Greek	cates that the original was drawn up in both
*** = Latin	the languages indicated, or that a text used for
**** = Italian	public purposes was based on a preceding
	draft (e.g., in French) which is also available.

PREFACE
TO 1971 *Tomos Agapis* 1958–1970 ** *

In recent years the Holy Spirit has given his Church the privilege of living through certain highly significant events which have a rich potential for the future, though this fact has not yet been properly grasped by all. These events have been prepared for, accompanied, and followed by all sorts of contacts and friendly relations. Letters, messages, and telegrams have been exchanged between the Churches of Rome and Constantinople, and addresses have been delivered by both Pope and Patriarch, and by representatives sent from one to the other.

The texts of these declarations give evidence of a common life which is being taken up again in increasing measure, and of a new awareness of unity and of our communion in the mystery of Christ. It seemed right that the record of these exchanges, many of which have been known so far only to a few, or have been inadequately appreciated, should be presented for the consideration of the Christian people at large. This is a necessary step, not only to ensure a wider dissemination of the documents, but to enable the Catholic and Ortho- dox peoples as a whole to share in this new experience, which is a rediscovery of one another. These are the grounds for publishing this volume containing the various exchanges between the Holy See and the Ecumenical Patriarchate over the last ten or more years.

The proposal for publication, made by the Doyen of the Holy Synod of the Ecumenical Patriarchate, during an exchange of views at the Phanar with the Secretary of the Secretariat for Christian Unity,† in December 1968, was immediately welcomed and adopted by the Patriarch Athenagoras and Pope Paul VI. It is due to the wish of both these last named that the book now appears.

Metropolitan of Chalcedon, Meliton
John Cardinal Willebrands‡

8 February 1971

---

†The Phanar is an ancient quarter of the city of Constantinople (the modern Istan- bul) in which the Ecumenical Patriarchate is situated. The name is often practically syn- onymous with the Patriarchate itself, as the Vatican is with the Holy See. The official title of this Curia office of the Holy See is *Secretariatus ad Christianorum Unitatem Fov- endam,* the Secretariat for Promoting Christian Unity.

‡Cf. below, footnotes 5 (p.31) and 23 (p.81).

PART I

From Silence to Dialogue

Nos 1–28   **October 7, 1958–
June 7, 1963**

Pope John XXIII . . . Patriarch Athenagoras I
Sickness and death of Pope Pius XII (1–2) ▪
Statements on Church unity and civil society by
Pope John XXIII and Patriarch Athenagoras (4–5) ▪
Visits by Monsignor Willebrands to Istanbul (8–11,
15–17) ▪ Possibility of observer-delegates to Vatican
Council II (12, 17–21) ▪ Information about First
Session (23) ▪ Death of Pope John XXIII (25, 28)

1. *7 October 1958*

Press Communication of Patriarch Athenagoras concerning the illness of Pope Pius XII**

It is with deep grief that His Holiness the Ecumenical Patriarch Athenagoras[1] has learnt of the grave illness with which His Holiness Pope Pius XII is stricken.[2]

Besides expressing his deep sympathy and concern, the Patriarch wishes to convey his wishes for the restoration to health—so important in this instance for all—of the venerable head of the Catholic Church.

2. *10 October 1958*

Press Communication of Patriarch Athenagoras on the death of Pope Pius XII**

His Holiness the Ecumenical Patriarch Athenagoras I has heard with profound sorrow of the death of His Holiness Pope Pius XII. He shares wholeheartedly in the deep mourning of the venerable Church of Rome, and prays that a worthy successor may be appointed in place of the late Pope.

3. *30 October 1958*

Press Communication of Patriarch Athenagoras on the election of Pope John XXIII**

It is with great pleasure that the Ecumenical Patriarch has been informed of the election of His Holiness, the New Pope of Rome, John

---

1. Aristoklis Spyrou, born in 1886 at Vassilikon in present-day Greece, was Metropolitan of Corfu (1922), then Archbishop of North and South America (1930). In 1948 he was elected Ecumenical Patriarch, under the name of Athenagoras I.

2. Eugenio Pacelli, born in 1876 at Rome and Secretary of State under Pope Pius XI, was elected his successor, 12 March, 1939. He chose the name Pius XII.

XXIII.[3] The Patriarch notes that, in his first message to the world, the Pope has expressed his desire for a coordination of the efforts now being made for the triumph of a true and lasting peace.

The human race, which has lived through these last decades in deep apprehension and is so anxious for peace, has received this news with much relief.

The Patriarch of Constantinople congratulates the Pope of Rome on his election, and prays that God may give him success, length of days, and strength in the fulfilment of his sacred mission.

4.   *Christmas 1958*

From the Christmas message of Pope John XXIII concerning Unity and Peace*

The commemoration of the birth of Christ unfailingly renews from year to year tidings of the same teaching, sounding ever the same note: Unity and Peace! Alas, human history is marked at its very beginnings by a story of bloodshed, of brother killed by brother. The law of love which the Creator imprinted in the heart of man was disrupted by *mala voluntas,* that evil will which forthwith led the human race along the road of injustice and disorder. Unity was broken, and nothing less than the intervention of the Son of God himself was called for: it was he who undertook through obedience to restore the sacred ties of the human family which had been so soon brought into jeopardy; and this he did at the cost of his own blood. The process of restoration is always going on: Jesus founded a Church, giving it the visible sign of unity, so that all peoples should be gathered together under its immense canopy stretching from sea to sea. Is there any reason why this unity of the Catholic Church, divinely directed in the first place to matters of the spiritual order, should not be brought to bear upon the reconciliation of different races and nations, especially since these too are committing themselves to the formation of a society marked by the laws of justice and brotherhood?

Here we come once more on the principle, already well known to believers, that the true service of God and his justice favors the development of civil society as a community of peoples and nations.

---

3. Angelo Roncalli, born in 1881 at Sotto il Monte (Bergamo) and Cardinal Archbishop of Venice, took the name John XXIII at his election, 28 October.

We still have fresh in mind the memory of a time, some decades ago now, when representatives of the Orthodox Churches (as they are commonly called) of the Near East, took up the cause of the union of civilized countries, in some cases with government support. They began with an agreement between Christian denominations differing in historical background and forms of worship. Unfortunately, more immediately pressing considerations of a tangible kind prevailed, and these, together with nationalistic interests, nullified excellent intentions which called for nothing but respect. The grievous problem of the broken unity in the heritage left by Christ is still a disturbing factor, and impedes even the very quest towards solution—a solution which itself can only be found after passing through grave difficulties and uncertainties.

However, we place our full confidence in God, and the sad awareness of this painful situation does not and will not bring to a halt our endeavor to meet the extremely kind and loving invitation of these separated brethren. They too bear the name of Christ on their foreheads, they too read his holy Gospel, and are open to the inspirations that spring from religious devotion and a charity that blesses and does good.

We remember the many utterances of our predecessors, from Pope Leo XIII to Pope Pius XII, including St. Pius X, Benedict XV, and Pope Pius XI, all of them worthy and glorious Pontiffs, who from the Chair of Peter have issued the invitation to unity. In view of this we take leave—but there is no point in using such weak language as this—let us say that we fully *intend* to carry out with humility and fervor the task towards which the words and example of Jesus summon us. He is the divine Good Shepherd who never ceases to direct our gaze towards the ripening harvests in the vast missionary fields: "These sheep too must I bring. . . . and there will be one fold and one Shepherd" (Jn 10:16). And in the midst of those prayers to his Father which were torn from him as with a groan in the last hours before his supreme sacrifice, he said: "May they all be one; as you, Father, are in me, and I in you, so also may they be one in us, that the world may believe that you have sent me" (Jn 17:21).

It is as we recall and harken to these profound and sublime words that peace begins to spread—that Christmas peace which is the peace of Christ. At the same time there is heard the sighing of souls and of whole peoples, the counterpart of every grace of heaven and earth. Without this peace the world is in agony, and when it is granted, as it was on that day when the angels of Bethlehem proclaimed it, it fills the mind and heart with vibrant joy.

5.　*1 January 1959*

New Year message of the Patriarch Athenagoras in reply to the
appeal for unity by Pope John XXIII**

This Holy, Apostolic and Ecumenical Throne, and we in our own
person, pray continually for the unity of all men, and we hail with joy
every sincere appeal for peace, from whatever source it may come, but
especially when it comes from such a Christian centre as that of
ancient Rome.

The distressing picture of humanity today, as it undergoes all sorts
of trials deriving from mutual incomprehension and the failure of one
people to live in peace with another, imposes on the leaders of the
Christian Churches a very pressing duty. This consists in a concerted
effort to make it quite clear to the contemporary world that technical
and scientific achievements are not enough to form an all-embracing
human civilization, if the spiritual, religious, and moral foundations
are not there—that is to say, if Christ himself, who is the author of
love, peace, and justice between people, is not there.

With a profound awareness of our responsibility, then, we declare
that we are sincerely ready, in accordance with the incessant prayers
and entreaties of our Orthodox Church for the peace of the whole
world, to add our positive cooperation on quite practical levels. This
can take place both within the wider inter-Church organizations in
which we already play our full part, and also within the context provided by our special contacts with the senior Church of the West. We
have in view the alleviation of the "distress of the nations, bewildered
for fear and dread of the things that are coming on the world" (cf. Lk
21:25–26), and a reinforcement of the hope of the human race in happier prospects for the future.

We regard it as all the more opportune, at a time like this, when
humanity is experiencing the birth of a new world, that we who have
been called by God to bear "the care and solicitude" of the millions of
the faithful of our churches, should come together on the subject of
this deep and imperative need of the peoples of the world to find relief
in a solution to the problems that now beset them.

Swayed as we are by such thoughts and dispositions, we came
indirectly to hear of the renewed appeal for the unity of the Churches
which Your Holiness recently made. This we greet with a fraternal welcome, seeing in it a clear understanding of the need for a combination
and fusion of the spiritual forces represented by the divinely founded
Church. We speak, to be sure, of the Church, not in the state of division and disagreement in which it has been for centuries past, and still

is, but in its desirable ideal unity, such as was envisaged and given by the Lord—and given, moreover, as a proof that the message of Christmas does not point to some summit of self-perfection and inaccessible virtue, but to a power which "lifts what is mortal to the likeness of the Perfect One."

For this reason we are convinced that every appeal for unity must be accompanied by those indispensable definite deeds and endeavors which would prove that intentions are meant to be fulfilled. Such a course would really bring us and the members of our Churches closer to the Lord, at least under present conditions on a practical basis, and this in a spirit of equality, justice, spiritual freedom, and mutual respect.

During this season of the Epiphany of Christ the Savior, which took place from out of the hallowed soil of the East, we regard ourselves as having grounds for the following hope and prayer. This is that, in common with the whole human race now turned in mind towards "the Prince of Peace and Father of the world to come" (Is 9:5), as he rises from the lands of dawn, the most holy Church of Rome, too, will turn in a brotherly spirit towards the East. This is what we desire and look for from the new Pope of Rome, John XXIII, who is personally so well known, loved, and respected in our parts. This request is one that finds an echo all over the world, and it betokens the dawn of a truly New Year in Christ.[4]

6. *6 December 1961*

Letter of Cardinal Augustin Bea[5] to Patriarch Athenagoras, thanking him for a present sent to Pope John XXIII and sending him three medals struck on the occasion of the 80th birthday of the Pope*

---

4. Four weeks later, on 25 January, 1959, Pope John XXIII announced his intention to convoke an "Ecumenical Council for the whole Church, not only for the spiritual good and joy of the Christian people but also to invite the separated Communities to seek again that unity for which so many souls are longing in these days throughout the world." *Acta Apostolicae Sedis* (hereafter *AAS*), 51 (1959), 69.

5. On Pentecost, 5 June, 1960, Pope John XXIII established the Secretariat for Promoting Christian Unity (hereafter, SPCU), which would enable "those who bear the name of Christian but are separated from this Apostolic See ... to follow the work of the Council and to find more easily the path by which they may arrive at the Unity Jesus Christ sought from His Heavenly Father with fervent prayers." *Superno Dei Nutu, AAS* 52 (1960), 436. The Pope appointed the German biblical scholar, Cardinal Augustin Bea, S.J., to be the SPCU President, and the Dutch theologian, Monsignor John Willebrands, its Secretary.

Your Holiness,

It is with very special pleasure that I send you, on behalf of His Holiness Pope John XXIII, the series of three medals which were struck on the occasion of his eightieth birthday.

The Sovereign Pontiff was deeply touched by your kind thought in sending him a souvenir of Istanbul by means of Archmandrite Andrew Scrima. He has asked me to thank you, and to tell you that these medals are the sign of his gratitude towards you.

For my own part, I am very happy to write to your venerable self, since for a long time past I have been following your efforts in the cause of Christian unity, a notable example of these being the Conference of Rhodes.

In view of the forthcoming feast of the Nativity of our great God and Savior, Jesus Christ, I offer you my best wishes, and pray that the grace of our Savior Jesus Christ, the fellowship of the Holy Spirit, and the love of God our Father may be with you.

In this spirit I ask Your Holiness to accept the expression of my fraternal and respectful charity in the Lord.

7.   *21 December 1961*

Letter of thanks of Metropolitan Maximos[6] to Cardinal Bea*

Your Eminence,

His Holiness the Ecumenical Patriarch Athenagoras I was very glad to receive the brotherly letter which you sent him on the sixth of this month, together with the set of three commemorative medals so thoughtfully forwarded on behalf of His Holiness Pope John XXIII on the occasion of his eightieth birthday.

I have special pleasure in carrying out the instructions given me by His Holiness the Patriarch, who wishes me to convey his deep feeling and warm thanks for the brotherly sentiments and the kind token of them on the part of His Holiness the Pope—a lover of Christian unity and worker in that cause. May the Lord God bless the efforts being made by the Church leaders with charity and in the spirit of Christ, by way of fulfilling the Lord's command "that they all may be one."

---

6. Since 1958 Metropolitan Maximos of Sardis had been President of the Commission for Ecumenical Affairs in the Synod of the Ecumenical Patriarchate of Constantinople, and was chairman of the First Pan-Orthodox Conference (Rhodes, 24 September–2 October, 1961). He died in 1986.

I count myself particularly happy to be able to tell you that the Christian sentiments expressed in your letter, and the kind and favorable judgment on the work which, through the grace of God, was carried out by the Pan-Orthodox Conference of Rhodes,[7] have been duly appreciated by His Holiness, who wishes me to send you his fervent thanks on this score also.

For quite some time past I have been following with great interest the work which you are carrying out so zealously in the important post which you hold in the Vatican. I am very glad indeed to have this opportunity of entering into contact with you now, and I pray from the bottom of my heart that the Lord who was born in a cave and laid in a manger may give you strength and bless you in the discharge of your great responsiblities.

I send on to Your Eminence the good wishes of His Holiness the Patriarch, as the great and holy feasts of the Christian world draw near, and I earnestly ask you to offer His Holiness Pope John XXIII my deepest feelings of respect.

8.   *27 February 1962*

Letter of Monsignor John Willebrands to Patriarch Athenagoras, thanking him for the Monsignor's first visit to the Phanar*

Your Holiness,

It is with my eyes and heart still full of what I saw and heard at Istanbul that I write to express my gratitude for the welcome given me by Your Holiness, and also by the venerable Metropolitans and members of the Patriarchal Curia.[8] This welcome went hand in hand with a hospitality of which I had already heard from others as one of the characteristics of the Christian East. I was able to have first-hand experience of this myself. I would ask your Holiness to be kind enough to accept herewith the full sum of my gratitude. All the more so, seeing that I was not merely won over by the welcome and hospitality, but was made the recipient of gifts prompted by your kindly thought.

---

7. The Conference had resolved that in future relations with other Christian Churches, the Orthodox would adopt a common policy.

8. On 25 December, 1961, Pope John formally convoked the Second Vatican Council, and hoped that other Christian Communions would be able to send to it "their own representatives who will make it possible for them to follow the Council proceedings more closely." The SPCU "will facilitate these contacts." *Humanae Salutis, AAS* 64 (1962), 1–13. Monsignor Willebrands visited the Ecumenical Patriarchate, then the Church of Greece in Athens, 14–20 February, 1962.

But beyond all this, I had the opportunity in my interviews with your venerable self to tell you how deeply moved I was at finding myself in a city which is inseparable from our common Christian heritage. My emotion at finding myself on a visit to "the Great Church" was increased by the paternal charity and trust which Your Holiness extended to me from the very first moment. The discussions which I had with all who assist you in your pastoral charge were always marked by the greatest sincerity and frankness. For this, too, I wish to express my deepest thanks.

It is my belief that the contacts and conversations which had such a happy beginning will continue, and I hope to make another visit after Easter.

His Eminence Cardinal Bea, to whom I have given a very detailed account of my stay, was very happy at what he heard, and intends to speak to the Holy Father on the subject. All those, too, who are interested in and are working for the drawing together of minds and hearts were delighted with me over this journey, which was ecumenical from so many points of view.

I thank Your Holiness once again, and would ask you to accept my deep and religious respect in Our Lord. It is with these sentiments that I have the honor of being the humble and devoted servant of Your Holiness.

9.   *28 February 1962*

Letter of Cardinal Bea to Patriarch Athenagoras, thanking him for the welcome given to Monsignor Willebrands*

Your Holiness,

It is a pleasant duty to thank you for the welcome which you so kindly gave the devoted Secretary of our Secretariat for Unity, Monsignor J. M. G. Willebrands, and also for the delightful souvenir which you sent me by his hands. In listening to the detailed account which he gave me of his time as your guest, I realized with what fatherly kindness and generosity you exercised this virtue of *philoxenia* [hospitality], which is one of the characteristics of the venerable Churches of the East.

I have received a faithful report of the discussions which Monsignor Willebrands had both with your venerable self and with their

Excellencies the Metropolitans of the Holy Synod, and the members of the Commission for Ecumenical Affairs.

I take pleasure in seeing in all this evidence of the constructive work in which we are together engaged in the quest for unity. A beginning has now been made, and I hope that other contacts and discussions will follow the course which Your Holiness has so wisely set.

May the liturgical season of Lent, so soon to begin, be for our Churches a time of prayer and reflection, helping us towards greater progress along the path of unity, which will be illuminated in a special way by the light of the Resurrection.

It is with this feeling of union in thought and prayer that I have the pleasure of expressing once more my deep veneration of Your Holiness, together with my fraternal affection in the Lord.

10. *12 April 1962*

Reply of Patriarch Athenagoras to Cardinal Bea**

His Eminence Cardinal Augustin Bea,
our beloved brother in Christ God,
grace and peace be to you from God.

With great joy we received your letter, dated 28 February this year, in which your beloved and much esteemed Eminence expressed your impressions of the visit recently made us by the Very Reverend Monsignor John Willebrands. We read this letter with pleasure both privately and before a session of our Holy Synod.

What you have to say in general terms about your desire for the *rapprochement* of the sister Churches and the restoration of unity in the Church moved us deeply, as it was bound to do, given the fact that we have repeatedly manifested our own readiness to do all in our power to contribute to this restoration.

Hence we warmly thank you for your courteous and brotherly letter, and for the initiative you have taken through having Monsignor Willebrands enter into communication with us. We pray that the chief Shepherd Christ, our God, may richly bless this approach, so happily begun in a spirit of Christian charity and mutual homage. We pray further that God may grant you many years of health and saving service, and remain with much charity and special regard.

Your Eminence's dear brother in Christ, . . .

11.   *12 April 1962*

Reply of Patriarch Athenagoras to Monsignor John Wille-brands*

To Monsignor Willebrands,
grace and peace from God.

We received and read with great pleasure in a session of our Holy and sacred Synod the letter which you wrote on 27 February and sent us after your return to Vatican City. In it you declare the feelings which came over you as a result of your visit to this historic city and to the Holy and Great Church of Christ here.

In thanking you for your letter, we wish to let you know that your visit and the reason that inspired it brought us great joy. This will be ours again if you make us another visit after the festive days of Holy Easter, as you indicate in your letter. We ask on your behalf the most powerful blessings of Christ. May his Resurrection fill you with grace and joy and heap endless mercy on you.

With fatherly affection, and with ardent prayer to God, . . .

12.   *18 April 1962*

Letter of Monsignor Willebrands to Patriarch Athenagoras about contacts with other Christian bodies to examine the possibility of having observers sent to the Second Vatican Council*

Confidential

Your Holiness,

It is with deep gratitude and keen pleasure that I call to mind again and again my visit to the venerable city of Constantinople, and in particular to your Holiness. This visit is not like a simple memory of the past, it is present to me as a living experience. The precious candle-holder which you gave me as a present reminds me of your great-heartedness, and recalls the spiritual conversation in which you brought out the present position of Christianity and the Lord's call to unity. Nor have I forgotten the courteous invitation which I received from His Excellency the Metropolitan Chrysostom of Myra to visit you again after Easter.

In the meantime I have visited other Christian bodies, calling particularly on His Grace the Archbishop of Canterbury, Dr. Ramsey, and the President of the Evangelical Church in Germany, Dr. Scharf, and I have attended a meeting of denominations from all over the world at Geneva, where I was able to explain that it is now possible to send observers to the Second Vatican Council.[9]

After the discussions with these various Christian bodies, I should like very much to make another visit to Your Holiness, and to give you more precise details about the observer-delegates to Vatican Council II. May I ask you to let me know at what time in May it would be most convenient for you to receive me?

Just now we are celebrating Holy Week, and we are preparing ourselves for the feast of the Resurrection of the Lord. On Holy Thursday His Eminence Cardinal Bea will be consecrated Bishop by the Holy Father in the Roman cathedral, the Basilica of San Salvatore, usually called St. John Lateran. The Cardinal is at the moment on retreat, and has asked me to convey to you his sincere wishes for a happy and radiant Easter. May I humbly add to his best wishes the assurance of my own prayers and my most respectful wishes for a blessed Easter full of every kind of grace.

13. *21 April 1962*

Telegram from Metropolitan Maximos to Cardinal Bea, asking him to convey to the Pope the Easter wishes of the Patriarch*

On the occasion of the light-bearing Resurrection of Christ, the feast of charity *par excellence*, following august instructions, I beg Your beloved Eminence kindly to convey to His Holiness Pope John of Rome, the brotherly greetings, cordial salutations, and Easter wishes of the Ecumenical Patriarch Athenagoras. These are sent also to Your Eminence.

---

9. Archbishop Michael Ramsey presided over the Lambeth Conference of Bishops (Anglican). Present at the Geneva meeting (3 April), besides Dr. W. A. Visser 't Hooft, General Secretary of the World Council of Churches, were representatives from the Lutheran World Federation, the World Presbyterian Alliance, the World Methodist Council, the Baptist World Alliance, the International Congregational Council, the World Convention of the Churches of Christ (Disciples), the World Society of Friends, the Old Catholic Church (Union of Utrecht), the Pentecostals, the Patriarchates of Constantinople and of Moscow.

14.   *5 May 1962*

Telegram from Cardinal Bea to Metropolitan Maximos, conveying the thanks and good wishes of Pope John to Patriarch Athenagoras*

His Excellency Maximos, Metropolitan of Sardis, Phanar,

Please let His Holiness Patriarch Athenagoras know that the Holy Father thanks him warmly for his good wishes, which he is happy to reciprocate.

I have the honor to add my own.

15.   *18 June 1962*

Letter of Cardinal Bea to Patriarch Athenagoras thanking him for the welcome which he gave to Monsignor Willebrands*

Your Holiness,

It is my pleasant duty to express, on behalf of His Holiness John XXIII, his warm gratitude for the gift which you so kindly sent him by means of Monsignor Willebrands.

This also gives me an opportunity for thanking you for the kind welcome which you extended to our devoted secretary on the occasion of his recent visit to the Great Church.[10] I like to think that these repeated contacts, with the blessing of the Lord, serve the cause of unity.

It is in this spirit that I take pleasure in assuring Your Holiness once again of my deep respect and in expressing my brotherly affection in Christ the Lord.

16.   *29 June 1962*

Letter of Patriarch Athenagoras to Cardinal Bea**

Your Eminence Cardinal Augustin Bea,
our beloved brother in Christ God,
grace and peace from God be with you.

---

10. From 13 May to 2 June, Monsignor Willebrands travelled to contact the "Non-Chalcedonian" Communions: the Coptic Church in Egypt, the Orthodox Church of Ethiopia, the Armenian Orthodox Church (Catholicate of Cilicia), and the Syrian Orthodox. On 1 June, he again visited Patriarch Athenagoras.

We were very happy to receive your letter of the 18th of this month in which you thanked us for the kind welcome given to the Very Reverend Monsignor Willebrands during his recent visit to us, and at the same time expressed your satisfaction with the contacts which he made.

May the Lord make charity abound, and may he direct all things to the good of the Church and the glory of his holy Name.

In thanking you for your letter, we embrace you in the Lord, and remain with fraternal charity and special respect.

Your venerated Eminence's dear brother in Christ, . . .

17.   *3 July 1962*

Letter of Monsignor Willebrands to Patriarch Athenagoras about invitations to send observer-delegates to Vatican Council II*

Your Holiness,

Feelings of gratitude and joy are still with me as I fondly remember my last and all too short visit to you on the 1st of last June. I then had the chance of explaining to you that for practical reasons we have been obliged to issue invitations [already] to the international organizations of the Reformation Churches concerning the sending of observer-delegates to the Second Vatican Council. For the same reasons we have also sent invitations to the non-Chalcedonian Churches (with the exception, however, of the Armenian Church).[11]

We shall be very happy to receive a response to the news that I was able earlier to communicate to the Church of Constantinople. This will enable us to take further steps.

It is with these prospects in view that I have the pleasure of expressing the feelings of deep veneration with which I am

Your Holiness' very humble and devoted servant, . . .

18.   *24 July 1962*

Letter of Cardinal Bea to Patriarch Athenagoras, in the name of Pope John XXIII, inviting him to send observer-delegates to the Second Vatican Council*

---

11. That is, the Catholicate of Etchmiadzin (Armenia); a year late it did receive and accept an invitation to the Second Session. The Armenian Catholicate of Cilicia (Antelias, Lebanon) received and accepted an invitation to the First Session.

Your Holiness,

In the name of His Holiness Pope John XXIII, who has shown so many tokens of good will towards Christians who are not in communion with the apostolic Holy See, our Secretariat, after the contacts made by its Secretary, Monsignor J. G. M. Willebrands, with Your Holiness and the authorities of the Patriarchate of Constantinople—and earlier by His Excellency the Most Reverend James Testa, Archbishop of Heraclea, and the Very Reverend Father Raes[12]—has the honor of inviting Your Holiness to send two churchmen or theologians who enjoy your confidence, with the status of observer-delegates, to the Second Vatican Council. Would you be so kind as to let us know their names before 15 September?

As soon as these names have been forwarded to us, we shall send our acceptance together with the necessary information, which we would ask you to communicate to the persons concerned.

The statute for observer-delegates, herewith enclosed, defines their rights and duties.[13] Our Secretariat will see to it that they have all the possible information in which you are likely to be interested.

It is our hope and our prayer to Our Lord that the presence and activity of the observers will contribute effectively to the growing understanding and appreciation of each other among all those who bear the name of Christians and are united spiritually in the Eucharist. May the grace of Our Lord Jesus Christ, the love of God the Father, and the fellowship of the Holy Spirit be with you.

It is in this spirit that I beg Your Holiness to accept the expression of my religious respect and my brotherly affection in the Lord.

19.   *24 July 1962*

Letter of Cardinal Bea to Patriarch Athenagoras concerning the invitation*

---

12. Archbishop Testa had been Apostolic Delegate to Turkey. Father Alphonsus Raes, S.J., was director of the Pontifical Institute for Oriental Studies in Rome, later prefect of the Vatican Library.

13. According to the *Ordo Concilii:* Delegated Observers can attend the closed assemblies where *schemata* or drafts are discussed; they are excluded from commission work meetings, unless with the chairman's permission, for special reasons; they have no right to speak or to vote at the general assemblies; the SPCU mediates between the organs of the Council and the Observers whatever information is necessary for following more closely and competently the Council work; the SPCU can invite to its meetings with the Observers competent people, including the Council Fathers, in order that the Observers are exactly informed on the conciliar themes. *AAS,* 54 (1962), 618.

Your Holiness,

While arranging for you to receive this invitation to send observers to Vatican Council II, I wanted to enclose this letter of explanation. The Reformation Churches and the World Council of Churches have already been invited, and some of these bodies have by now sent us the names of their observers. I am quite aware of the difficulties which the Ecumenical Patriarchate has to face in this delicate matter. Hence, after due reflection, our Secretariat took the view that it would be better to send an individual invitation to each of the autocephalous Churches of the Orthodox world, taking care to mention the contacts already made with the see of Constantinople. There was all the more reason for this step in that we have been directly approached by some of these Churches.[14]

Moreover, the date for the Council is drawing near, and we are under the pressure of practical requirements as we adopt this measure, for which, as we know, the way has been prepared by the introductory work undertaken by Your Holiness and your collaborators.

It is therefore with calm confidence that we have decided to send official invitations to the venerable Churches of the East, which, in spite of nine centuries of separation remain in the highest degree our brothers.

In this spirit I beg Your Holiness to be so kind as to accept the expression of my religious respect and my feelings of deep veneration in Christ the Lord.

20. *30 August 1962*

Letter of Archimandrite Symeon, Chief Secretary of the Holy Synod, to Monsignor Willebrands, thanking him on behalf of the Patriarch for his letter of 3 July**

His Holiness, our venerated father and master, the Ecumenical Patriarch Athenagoras has instructed me to inform you that he received your letter of 3 July and read it with great pleasure. He has made the contents of your letter known to their Eminences, the members of the Holy Synod.

In conclusion, at the request of the Patriarch, I send you his best wishes and convey his great affection.

I remain, with charity in Christ, . . .

---

14. The SPCU sent invitations directly to the Churches of Alexandria, Antioch, Jerusalem, Cyprus, and Greece.

21. *10 October 1962*

Letter of Cardinal Bea to Patriarch Athenagoras in reply to the message delivered orally by Bishop Emilianos Timiadis who conveyed that it was impossible to send observers to the Second Vatican Council*

I was very touched by the message which Your Holiness had delivered to me by word of mouth through His Excellency Bishop Emilianos Timiadis, and I thank you for it with deepest feeling.[15] Obviously it is a matter of sincere regret for us that the Orthodox Churches cannot be officially represented at the Council by observer-delegates. But we understand the difficulties of the situation for the Orthodox Churches, and we shall continue to do all in our power to maintain fraternal relations with them. Although our Churches are not yet ready to deal with the matter of complete union, our contacts and brotherly collaboration in things that have no direct bearing on the points at issue between them will still certainly serve significantly to create increasingly close relations. I hope that the Council itself will make an effective contribution to this cause. Furthermore, we shall remain united in prayer, asking that the unity which the Lord so ardently desired will in fact be achieved.

I should like to assure you that I am always at your bidding to do what I can in this connection.

I ask Your Holiness to accept the assurance of my prayers for your venerable self and your pastoral work, and of the charity which I bear you in Christ Our Lord.

22. *10 October 1962*

Communiqué of the Ecumenical Patriarchate on the inception of the Second Vatican Council**

Subsequent to the proposal by the Vatican that observers be sent to follow the work of the Second Vatican Council of the Roman Cath-

---

15. On 7 October, the Patriarch, because of a presumed lack of unanimity among the Orthodox Churches, asked his personal representative in Geneva to the World Council of Churches to communicate verbally the news to Pope John and Cardinal Bea. Bishop Emilianos did so in Rome on 9 October. On 11 October, the solemn opening of the Council, the SPCU received a telegram from the Patriarchate of Moscow that it was sending Observers.

olic Church, which is meeting today, the Ecumenical Patriarchate examined the matter on behalf of the Orthodox Church, and came to the conclusion, in agreement with the local holy Orthodox Churches, that the despatch of Orthodox observers to this Council was not feasible.

The Ecumenical Patriarchate, together with the individual Orthodox Churches, expresses its best wishes for the success, in the genuine spirit of Christ, of the work of this Council, which the whole Orthodox world will follow with great interest and attention.

The Orthodox Churches nourish the hope that wider horizons of Christian spirit and understanding will be opened up, and that favorable conditions will thus be created in the near future for useful contacts and fruitful exchanges of view, in the Spirit of Christ and of brotherly love, with the aim of promoting the total Christian unity for which Our Lord prayed.

23. *8 December 1962*

Letter of Cardinal Bea to Patriarch Athenagoras, introducing his emissary Fr. Pierre Duprey who will convey information about the First Session of the Second Vatican Council*

The fortunate opportunity provided by the departure from Rome for the Near East of the Reverend Father Pierre Duprey, who during these weeks of the first session of the Council has served as interpreter-theologian for our observers, enables me to send you this message in evidence of my faithful affection in the Lord.[16]

I must, in the first place, thank you for the sensitive acts of kindness which you have always shown in my regard and in particular for the gifts that you sent me by means of Archimandrite Scrima.

In my turn I am asking Father Duprey to present you with a volume which has just been published on the problems of Christian unity—problems which Your Holiness has so much at heart.[17]

And since the solemnities of the Nativity of our divine Savior Jesus Christ and the feasts of the New Year are near at hand, I wish to

---

16. Pierre Duprey, of the White Fathers, was professor at the pontifical seminary of St. Anne in Jerusalem and the editor of *Proche–Orient chrétien*. After the Council's First Session he joined the SPCU staff, became under-secretary in 1963, and secretary in 1985.

17. The book is Cardinal Bea's collection of articles and lectures, *Vers l'Unité Chrétienne* (English edition, Chapman, 1963, *The Unity of Christians*).

send you all my good wishes both for your venerated self personally and for your pastoral activity. May the year which is about to begin see the further development of the relations between our Churches, and this in an atmosphere of calm confidence and closeness.

Such will be the object of the prayer which I shall make at the commemoration of the Nativity of the Prince of Peace who comes to save the world.

It is in this spirit that I beg Your Holiness to accept this expression of my religious regard and the assurance of my brotherly affection in the Lord.

### 24.	*30 May 1963*

Telegram from Patriarch Athenagoras to Pope John XXIII, expressing his sympathy and good wishes for the recovery of the Pope's health**

Personal.

United with Your venerable and beloved Holiness in the spirit and love of Our Lord, we have been continually in heart and mind with you throughout the great moments of your sacred efforts to make the spirit of Christ prevail in this world. We are particularly united in prayer with Your Holiness in the trying illness which you, our dear brother, are now undergoing and we pray fervently to the Lord for the full restoration of your health, which is so precious in itself and valuable for the whole of Christianity.

### 25.	*1 June 1963*

Telegram from Cardinal Amleto Cicognani, Secretary of State, to Patriarch Athenagoras, thanking him on behalf of the Pope*

His Holiness John XXIII, deeply touched by the good wishes and prayers expressed by Your Holiness, enjoins on me the duty of conveying his warm gratitude and his desire to offer himself for the cause of peace in the human race and the unity of Christians.

### 26.	*4 June 1963*

Statement of Patriarch Athenagoras at a meeting of the Holy Synod on the death of Pope John XXIII (3 June)**

From the time of the election of Pope John XXIII and his enthronement in the see of ancient Rome, we have had the joyful presentiment that future relations between the Ecumenical Patriarchate and the Vatican would undergo significant developments—an augury of closer relations and of cooperation in the spirit of Christ of both East and West, more particularly on the moral and social plane—and that this would happen in the not too distant future.

For in the person of the late venerable leader of our sister Church of Rome we discerned an inspired laborer well able to meet the challenge of present circumstances, and to train his gaze on those points of the teaching of the Lord and of apostolic tradition which are common to both the Orthodox and Roman Catholic Churches.

At this solemn moment we send up our prayer to our Lord and God for the hierarchical head of the Roman Catholic Church, that his soul may find rest in that region where the light of Christ's face dominates all.

27.   *5 June 1963*

Telegram from Archimandrite Symeon, Chief Secretary of the Holy Synod, to Cardinal Cicognani, expressing the condolence of the Patriarch and the Synod on the death of Pope John XXIII**

His Holiness the Ecumenical Patriarch Athenagoras and the Holy Synod have learnt with deep grief of the decease of His Holiness Pope John, the worthy leader of the venerable Roman Catholic Church, and have instructed me to convey to Your Eminence their deep sympathy and warm feelings of condolence, as they pray for the repose of the soul of the late chief dignitary of his Church.

28.   *7 June 1963*

Telegram from Cardinal Aloisi Masella, Chamberlain, to Archimandrite Symeon, thanking the Patriarch and the Holy Synod for their sympathy and prayers*

We beg you be so good as to communicate to the revered Ecumencial Patriarch and the Holy Synod our deep-felt thanks for their sympathy and prayers. May the life of John XXIII, which was offered for peace and Christian unity, help to bring about the fulfilment of the prayer of our one Lord: *ut unum sint* ("that they may be one").

PART II

Growth and Fruits of Dialogue

Nos 29–56

**June 25, 1963–
February 10, 1964**

Pope Paul VI ... Patriarch Athenagoras I
(1)
Election of Paul VI (29, 32) ■ Invitation to Second
Session of Council (30–31) ■ First personal letter of
Pope Paul VI to Patriarch Athenagoras and latter's
reply (33, 35) ■ Preliminaries to meeting in Jerusalem
(36–38, 41, 44–46) ■ Pope and Patriarch on Mount of
Olives (47–50), and sequel (51–53)

29. *25 June 1963*

Letter of Cardinal Bea to the Patriarch Athenagoras, announcing the election of Pope Paul VI*

Your Holiness,

As the result of the election conducted by the Cardinals gathered in conclave according to the prescriptions of the Holy Roman Church, Cardinal Giovanni Battista Montini,[18] Metropolitan Archbishop of Milan, was appointed to succeed His Holiness Pope John XXIII of blessed memory. He has decided to take the name of Paul VI.

I am happy to carry out the task laid on me by the Holy Father of acquainting Your Holiness, Ecumenical Patriarch and Archbishop of Constantinople, and through you your whole Church, with this happy event in the holy Roman Church.

May the Holy Spirit in his kindness inspire the hearts and direct the endeavors of all those who work for the building up of the people of God towards the point where the prayer of our one and only Lord finds its fulfilment: *ut unum sint.*

Please accept, Your Holiness, the expression of my respectful and brotherly feelings in the Lord Jesus.

30. *8 July 1963*

Letter of Cardinal Bea to the Patriarch Athenagoras, conveying Pope Paul's invitation to send observers to the Second Session of Vatican Council II*

Your Holiness,

Pope Paul has decided that the Second Session of the Second Vatican Council will open on 29 September. In the name of the Holy Father, I have the honor, as President of the Secretariat for Christian

---

18. G. B. Montini, born in 1887 at Concesio in nothern Italy, entered Vatican service in the Secretariat of State (1932) and remained there until Pope Pius XII appointed him Archbishop of Milan in 1964. He was elected Pope on 21 June, and installed on 30 June.

Unity, to inform you of this decision, and to invite you to send two clerics or theologians who enjoy your confidence as observer-delegates of your Church at this Council. Each Autocephalous Orthodox Church has been invited in the same way to send two observer-delegates.

The First Session of the Council has shown that the real position of these observer-delegates turned out to be something very different from that of mere spectators. Actually, besides being present at all the general assemblies of the Council they were able, by means of meetings arranged each week with the members of the Secretariat and with bishops and theologians, to tell us of their reactions and their points of view on the subjects under discussion in the Council.

Furthermore, the observer-delegates were entirely free to enter into personal contact with the fathers of the Council, whether individually or in groups at meetings quite often suggested by the fathers themselves.

These arrangements provided the opportunity for opening up a genuine and brotherly exchange of views.

I should like to indicate to Your Holiness the further detail that an archbishop member of our Secretariat is ready to come, together with the Secretary, Monsignor Willebrands, to furnish you with all the explanations that you would like to have on this subject, and to confirm the above invitation. I should be grateful if you could tell me as soon as possible what would be the most convenient date for this visit, preferably in the very early part of September.

In his first public address of 22 June, Pope Paul VI expressed his intention "of continuing with all his strength the great work undertaken and set under way with so much hope and under happy auspices by Pope John XXIII, that is to say, the achievement of this *ut unum sint* (Jn 17:21), awaited so eagerly by all." By his invitation the Pope is showing that he hopes that the presence of observers will contribute effectively to a greater understanding and appreciation of one another among those who are baptized in Christ and are spiritually united in the Eucharist.

It is in this spirit that I beg Your Holiness to accept the expression of my devout respect and my brotherly affection in the Lord.

31.　*22 August 1963*

Letter of Patriarch Athenagoras to Cardinal Bea, acknowledging receipt of the invitation**

Your Eminence, Cardinal Augustin Bea, President of the Vatican Secretariat for Christian Unity, may grace and peace from God be with you.

It was under happy auspices that, having just returned by the grace of God from our journey to the Holy Mountain [Mt. Athos] and to Greece, we had the pleasure of receiving your letter of 8 July, and of reading it out at a session of our Holy Synod. In it you convey the very moving desire of the new Pope of Rome, our beloved brother in Christ Paul VI, that a Roman Catholic archbishop, accompanied by the Very Reverend John Willebrands, should visit us to discuss the question of sending observers to the Second Vatican Council for the Second Session which has yet to begin.

In this connection we should like you to know that the matter is already being examined by our Commission for Ecumenical Affairs, and that we shall very soon reply regarding the substance of your letter. We express our cordial best wishes that the endeavors made in purity of heart and in the spirit of Christ for the drawing together and the collaboration of the Christian denominations may go ahead happily. We ask on behalf of Your Eminence God's most powerful blessings. May his grace and infinite mercy be always with you.

Your Eminence's dear brother in Christ, . . .

32.   *9 September 1963*

Letter of Metropolitan Maximos to Pope Paul VI, conveying the congratulations of the Patriarch on his election to the See of Rome**

Your Holiness,

His Holiness, the Ecumenical Patriarch Athenagoras, on his felicitous return from his visit to the Holy Mountain for its millenary, and his journey through the provinces of Greece that come under the jurisdiction of Constantinople, received with joy the news then officially communicated to him by a letter dated 25 June from His Eminence Cardinal Augustin Bea, that the Cardinals gathered in conclave had chosen, in accordance with the relevant requirements of the Holy Roman Church, Your venerable and beloved Holiness as Pope of Rome, under the name of Paul VI.

Your accession to the Apostolic See of ancient Rome, in succession to the blessed Pope John XXIII of happy memory, who labored so mightily for the betterment of relations between the Churches and showed himself equal to the demands of time and circumstance, is doubtless the result and expression of the ideas not prevalent in the Holy See with regard to the promotion of the dialogue between Christians. This dialogue is the necessary presupposition for the advance of man in general, and the Christian in particular, towards peace, progress, dignity—towards all, in short, that confirms his inalienable rights and sacred mission in the world.

Acting under supreme instructions, I dutifully convey to Your Holiness [the Patriarch of Constantinople] for a long and fruitful service in the holy sister Church of Rome, for the furtherance of the spirit of unity in the Christian world, and for the glory of the name of Our Lord Jesus Christ.

In conclusion I remain, with all due respect, . . .

33.   *20 September 1963*

The first letter, in Pope Paul VI's own hand, to the Patriarch Athenagoras, expressing his desire to do all in his power to reestablish perfect harmony among Christians*

We have just had the joy of receiving the good wishes and congratulations which you sent us by His Eminence Maximos, Metropolitan of Sardis, in reply to the letter written in our name by His Eminence Cardinal Bea just after our election. We should like to tell you that the feelings expressed in this letter have found a deep echo in our heart. The task which the Lord has confided to us as successor in this see to the leader of the Apostles makes us solicitous for all that concerns the unity of Christians, and all that can help to restore perfect harmony among them.

Let us entrust the past to the mercy of God, and listen to the advice of the Apostle: "forgetting what is behind us, I am stretched forth towards that which is ahead, that I may seek to seize it even as I am seized by him." We have been seized by him through the gift of the good news of salvation, by the gift of the same Baptism, and of the same priesthood, in which the same Eucharist is celebrated—the one sacrifice of the one Lord of the Church.

May this celebration enable us to have more and more in view "the thoughts which are in Christ Jesus," and to understand deeply the meaning and the implications of his prayer to his Father, "that they may be one, I in them and you in me, so that they may be made perfect in their unity." May the Lord open our hearts to the inspirations of his Spirit, and guide us to the fulfilment of his will.

May the grace of the Lord Jesus Christ, the love of the Father, and the fellowship of the Holy Spirit be with you.

34. *25 October 1963*

Letter of Patriarch Athenagoras to Cardinal Bea, thanking him for forwarding the Pope's letter**

Your Eminence, Cardinal Augustin Bea, may the grace and peace that come from God be with you.

It was with joy that we received your letter dated 20 September last, in which you enclosed the letter of His Holiness, our very dear and esteemed brother, Pope Paul VI. We had the happiness of reading this letter aloud at a session of our Holy Synod with feelings corresponding to those contained in it.

We thank you warmly, and inform you that the letter of reply to His Holiness, which we postponed writing because of the Pan-Orthodox Conference which took place in the meantime, will be despatched quite soon.

We would ask you to be so good as to send us a copy of your highly valued study, *Toward Christian Unity.* We embrace you with a holy kiss, and remain with special appreciation and brotherly love.

Your Eminence's dear brother in Christ, . . .

35. *22 November 1963*

The first letter of Patriarch Athenagoras to Pope Paul VI, in reply to his letter of 20 September 1963**

To Paul, the very blessed and holy Pope of ancient Rome, greetings in the Lord.

We received with joy and love the valued letter of Your beloved and honored Holiness dated September of this year. We read this letter first privately, and then at a session of our Holy Synod, giving thanks on this further occasion to our common God and Savior.

At the appropriate time, and with brotherly feeling, we sent you our fraternal message of congratulation and our most cordial wishes on your election by the divine grace and good pleasure to the prestigious see of ancient Rome, and your enthronement there.

At this time we rejoice in a special way as we learn from your letter, as well as elsewhere, that the prayer of the beginner and ender of our faith, Christ our God, for the unity of those who were to believe in Him, and the exhortation of the Apostle to forget the things that are behind, are finding a deep echo in these our present times. In the same way we rejoice at your heartfelt desire for the complete fulfilment of the Lord's holy will for unity.

We on our part have learned from the Lord to look upon each other as belonging closely together, as befits members of his holy Body which is the Church, so that in accordance with what is involved in the mutual relations of members, we have one Lord and Savior, whose grace we share together in the sacraments. For these reasons we realize that there is nothing more precious which we can offer one another than fellowship in love, which according to the Apostle, "covers all things, hopes for all things, endures all things" (1 Cor 13:7). This fellowship was formerly strong in the bond of peace of our holy Churches, and is now being renewed, through the Lord's grace, "to the praise of His glory" (Eph 1:12–14).

As ministers then of Christ and dispensers of the mysteries of God in the Churches of the saints (1 Cor 4:1; 14:33), let us look once more from the high vantage point of charity, with a contrite heart and simple eye, towards the Lord's will, and place ourselves and our whole life at his service, so that we may find grace, and that the Kingdom of God may come upon the face of the earth.

With these thoughts and hopes in mind, we thank you warmly for your communication. Once again we express the hope that Your Holiness will enjoy good health and preside gloriously over the holy Church of ancient Rome for long years to come, with the blessing and grace of Our Lord, to whom be glory and power, together with the Father and the Holy Spirit, now and forever. Amen.

Your venerable and most esteemed Holiness's
dear brother in Christ, . . .

36.　*6 December 1963*

Communiqué of the Ecumenical Patriarch on the announcement of the Pope's journey to the Holy Land**

His Holiness the Ecumenical Patriarch Athenagoras, while presiding this morning, 6 December, at the liturgical celebration in the historic and holy Church of St. Nicholas of Tsibali, announced the news from the Vatican with great joy, amid a thickly thronged congregation. With warm feeling and holy enthusiasm he extolled the historic decision of His Holiness the Pope of Rome, Paul VI, to visit Jerusalem in the course of next January, and to pay homage as a pilgrim at the holy places of Christendom.

The Patriarch went on to bring out the importance of this decision, inspired by God as he felt it to be, of the venerable head of the Roman Catholic Church. He was emphatic that it would be a work of divine Providence, if, on the occasion of this sacred pilgrimage of His Holiness, all the heads of the holy Churches of Christ, of the East and West, of the three confessional groupings, were to meet one another in the holy city of Sion, so that in a common contribution of spirit and heart, and with warm prayers rendered the more seemly by propitiatory tears, they might kneel at Golgotha, which was moistened with the blood of Christ, and at the holy and life-giving Tomb, from which arose pardon and life for all peoples. And this that they might open up, in the spirit of unity, a new and blessed road, to the glory of the name of Our Lord Jesus Christ, for the good of all humankind, and which would lead further to the restoration of all things, according to his will.

37. *9 December 1963*

Letter of Cardinal Bea to Patriarch Athenagoras, introducing his emissary, Father Duprey, who will provide information about the Pope's journey to the Holy Land and the Second Session of the Vatican Council*

The announcement that the Holy Father Paul VI will be making a pilgrimage to the Holy Land must certainly have reached you, but I should like, in agreement with the Sovereign Pontiff, to let you know more in detail the reasons that have moved Pope Paul VI to take this step.

For this purpose, I am sending you my colleague, the Very Reverend Father Pierre Duprey, Under-Secretary of our Secretariat, so that he can give you all the necessary information by word of mouth.

He will then be in a position in his turn to acquaint us, should you think fit, with your wishes and desires.

He will use this occasion, too, to give you any information which you would like to have about the course of events at the Second Session of the Council and the further developments envisaged.

It is in this spirit of confident collaboration and sharing of interests that I express once more to Your Holiness my deep and religious respect, and my brotherly affection in the Lord.

38.   *11 December 1963*

Communiqué of the Ecumenical Patriarchate on the journey of the Pope to the Holy Land**

His Holiness [Patriarch Athenagoras] gave audience yesterday, Tuesday 10 December, to the Very Reverend Father Duprey, a special emissary from the Vatican. Father Duprey formally presented his letter of credence from his principal, and in accordance with his instructions provided information about the pilgrimage of His Holiness Pope Paul VI to the Holy Places.

39.   *20 December 1963*

Letter of Cardinal Bea to Patriarch Athenagoras, offering his good wishes for the feasts of Christmas and New Year*

As within a few days we shall be joyfully celebrating the festive season of the Nativity of our divine Savior Jesus Christ, I take this opportunity of offering you my best wishes for the forthcoming year. May it be rich in everything that contributes to the drawing together and mutual understanding of Christians; and may it witness a growth and deepening of brotherly exchanges between our Churches. These wishes, I know, are matched by your own deepest desires. I pray God to give you a generous measure of his grace, so that you may face your heavy task with good health, in joy and peace.

I should like, too, to thank you for the welcome which you gave the Very Reverend Father Duprey during his recent visit to the Patriarchate. I was very touched by the kindnesses which you and those near you showed him.

Please accept, Your Holiness, the expression of my deep and religious respect and my brotherly love in the Lord.

40.   *24 December 1963*

Telegram from Patriarch Athenagoras to Pope Paul VI, sending him good wishes for the feast of Christmas**

As we move towards the moment for adoration of God the Word made man, we joyfully send Your beloved and esteemed Holiness, on the occasion of this great and holy feast, our brotherly greeting, with cordial good wishes both for yourself and your holy Church.

41.   *26 December 1963*

Letter of Patriarch Athenagoras to Pope Paul VI, telling him that his representatives were on their way to expound the Patriarch's views on the desired meeting at Jerusalem**

To Paul, the very blessed and holy Pope of ancient Rome, greetings in the newborn Lord.

It is with special pleasure that we proceed herewith to inform Your beloved and highly esteemed Holiness that we have decided, in joint accord with our Holy Synod, to send you our representatives, their Eminences Bishops Meliton and Athenagoras, Metropolitans respectively of Helioupolis and Theira and of Thyateira. They are coming in answer to the message recently brought by a special envoy of your Church about your journey to the holy city of Jerusalem and the brotherly spirit which has inspired this thoughtful gesture towards us, and to implement the desire for a meeting, which we expressed as soon as the news came of your pilgrim journey—a desire which you yourself echoed in favorable terms.

Their Eminences, our envoys, bring Your venerable Holiness, together with our brotherly greetings, the ideas and wishes which we here have about the meeting. At the same time they are empowered to work out in a brotherly spirit, in conjunction with the corresponding representatives on your side, the details of the holy meeting for which by the divine good pleasure both of us long.

With fervent good wishes and buoyant hopes we commend to

your charity the eminent delegates whom we have appointed. We confide the happy outcome of their mission on behalf of the Church to the Lord, and to the good will and judgment of Your Holiness, and remain with brotherly love and special respect.

Your venerable and highly esteemed Holiness's

dear brother in Christ, . . .

42.   *27 December 1963*

Telegram from Pope Paul VI to the Patriarch Athenagoras, conveying his best wishes for the Christmas season*

We are deeply touched by the good wishes which you have so kindly sent us for this feast in which we celebrate the mystery of the Eternal Word who became man to reconcile and bring together the children of God. We thank you for this, and in our turn we send you our wholehearted and warmest wishes.

43.   *28 December 1963*

Telegram from Cardinal Bea, sending his good wishes to the Patriarch*

We were very glad to receive His beloved Eminence the Metropolitan Athenagoras. We thank you from the bottom of our heart for your wishes, and hope from the Lord a year rich in the fruits of charity and growing closeness. With respectful and fraternal feelings.

44.   *28 December 1963*

Address by the Metropolitan Athenagoras of Thyateira,[19] on the occasion of his visit to Pope Paul VI (the Metropolitan of Helioupolis and Theira was prevented from going to Rome)**

---

19. Born on the island of Patmos in 1912 (Theodoritus Kokkinakis), the Metropolitan of Canada was educated in Cyprus and at the General Theological Seminary in New York City. He served as bishop in the U.S. Western States diocese, later bishop in Boston where he was also president and professor at the Holy Cross Theological School. Shortly after this papal audience, in March 1964 he became Archbishop of Great Britain, and co-chaired with Archbishop Robert Runcie the Anglican-Orthodox Doctrinal Commission. He died in 1979.

Your Holiness,

Conscious as I am of the importance of this moment when an historic step is being taken, I am overwhelmed by deep feeling. For, after so many years of silence the Latin West and the Greek East are now intent, with mutual feelings of respect and love arising from the dictates of the Gospel and of Christian hearts, on meeting one another. They have decided further to greet one another with brotherly love, to exchange views, and if possible to join together in dialogue, for the sake of the peace of the world and the well-being of the holy Churches of God.

This is the reason, Your Holiness, why my emotion is so visible. But now, recollecting myself, I convey to your keeping this letter from the Patriarch, and with it the love in Christ, the peaceful regard, and the good will, both of the leader of the Eastern Orthodox Church, the Ecumencial Patriarch Athenagoras, and of the Holy Synod round about him.

It seems, most blessed Father, that by divine inspiration both of you are climbing the mountain of the Lord. You are making the ascent from one side and the Ecumencial Patriarch Athenagoras from the other. Christian men and women who understand the full significance of your upward journey are praying that you will both meet at the summit, where once the Lord planted his footsteps, just by the place of the Cross and the empty Tomb. Under the shadow of the Cross you will together restore solidarity among Christians, confident that this is what the Lord wills—that we may love one another, and that we may be one as he is with the Father.

Peter and Andrew were brothers. For centuries they were not on speaking terms, but now here they are both expressing a desire to meet and talk to one another. This wish moreover is the command of our common Teacher. May the Lord bring this apostolic meeting to a successful conclusion, to the glory of his Church, and for the heartening of the faithful.

Your predecessor of unforgettable memory John XXIII summoned the Second Vatican Council for the renewal of the Western Church. Perhaps Your Holiness has been destined, as the Bishop who is first among equals of the Church, to cooperate with the other Patriarchs and leaders of the East and the West in calling together a conference in which representatives of all Christians may study how to lessen the inroads of sin, how to protect the Christian fellowship, and how to defend the freedom and peace of the peoples who are now menaced by the common enemy, atheism and tyranny.

I pray together with His Holiness the Ecumenical Patriarch that the Holy Spirit may lead you to accomplish great works for the glory of Christ. I now place in your hands the Patriarchal letter.

May Your Holiness enjoy many years of health and happiness.

45.   *30 December 1963*

Telegram from Pope Paul VI to Patriarch Athenagoras, expressing joy at the prospect of their coming encounter*

It was with great joy that we welcomed your delegate, the Metropolitan Athenagoras, and we see in this visit a mark of your Christian charity, and a pledge of our meeting soon to take place. We express our very deep gratitude to you in the Lord.

46.   *30 December 1963*

Letter of Pope Paul VI to Patriarch Athenagoras, thanking him for sending the Metropolitan Athenagoras of Thyateira*

Beloved Brother in Christ,

In these days when we are more especially responsive to the divine peace and heavenly joy given to the world by Our Lord Jesus Christ, who took it on himself to be born at Bethlehem for our salvation, we felt deeply touched by the letter handed to us on your behalf by the eminent Metropolitan Athenagoras of Thyateira.

The sensitive and kindly words in which he expressed your feelings and those of the members of the Holy Synod found a deep resonance within us. In giving thanks to almighty God for this further mark of his infinite goodness, we make our own the song of the angels: "Glory to God in the highest."

We were particularly glad to find that our mutual desire to meet had done away with the hindrances which could have arisen from matters of detail and protocol, which bears out the fact that where the Spirit of God and his charity prevail all difficulties can be smoothed out.

Our pilgrimage to the land hallowed by the Word made flesh will give us a fresh opportunity to offer our humble service to the Lord of the Church, and to pray for the peace of the world and for the reign of charity that works through truth. We are happy that you have decided to associate yourself so closely with the step we are taking. We look forward to this meeting in the near future with much joy, and we assure you once more of our deepest and most sincere charity.

47.   *30 December 1963*

Procedural arrangements for the meeting of the Pope and the Patriarch, signed by Metropolitan Athenagoras of Thyateira and Archbishop Angelo dell'Acqua, Deputy Secretary of State (see Appendix I)

48.   *5 January 1964*

Address of Patriarch Athenagoras to Pope Paul VI in the Apostolic Delegation on the Mount of Olives in Jerusalem (Original in Greek; a French translation was read out by Archimandrite Symeon)

Most Holy Brother in Christ,

As through the grace of God we find ourselves on this holy earth where the undefiled feet of the Lord once stood, let us humbly give glory to the Triune God who has led us from the West and the East, and bidden us come to the same spot and share each other's company in his holy Name.

Truly this event is the cause of uttermost joy. With a premonition of this joy we have come with glad heart and moved by brotherly feelings to this encounter with Your Holiness, whom we lovingly hail with delight in this sacred place in which the voice of the Lord was heard and treasured up as it announced the good news of reconciliation and salvation, and where shortly before the sweat of agony it uttered the prayer that all who were to believe in him might be preserved in truth and unity.

We look on what is now happening to us, by the divine help and good pleasure, as events of exceptional importance and significance in the history and life of the Church, and we pray with all our heart that the good disposition and outlook which in recent times has been abundantly shown and confirmed continually on both sides, together with this blessed personal meeting, this embrace of souls, may turn out to be the beginning of a mutual exchange and a fuller conformity to the holy will of God. This would also meet the lively expectation of the centuries gone by and the demands of the present age.

The Christian world has been living for centuries through the night of division, and its eyes have been weighed down as it gazed into the darkness. May this meeting of ours be the first glimmer of dawn of a shining and holy day in which the Christian generations of the future will receive communion in the holy Body and Blood of the Lord from the same chalice, in love, peace and unity, and will praise and glorify the one Lord and Savior of all.

Most Holy Brother in Christ,

Lo, having found one another again, we meet the Lord together! Let us continue then the journey that lies ahead of us. And he, on his part will draw near and go forward with us, as he did once with the two disciples on the way to Emmaus, showing us the way on which we are to walk, and quickening our steps towards the longed for goal.

To him be glory and power and adoration for ever and ever. Amen.

49.   *6 January 1964*

Allocution of Pope Paul VI to Patriarch Athenagoras, delivered in the Patriarchal residence on the Mount of Olives in Jerusalem*   ***

Strong is our emotion and deep our joy in this truly historic hour, when after centuries of silence and waiting the Catholic Church and the Patriarchate of Constantinople find themselves once more in one another's presence in the person of their highest representatives.

Strong and deep, too, is our gratitude to you for your goodness in leaving your Patriarchal throne for the time being to come here to meet us.

But above all else it is to God, the Lord of the Church, that the voice of our humble gratitude rises.

An ancient Christian tradition has it that the "center of the world" lies at the point where the glorious cross of our Savior was raised, and where "lifted up from earth, he draws all things to himself" (Jn 12:32).

It was fitting—and Providence has allowed it—that it should be in this center for ever blessed and sacred that we, pilgrims from Rome and Constantinople, are able to meet and join in a common prayer.

This encounter is something that you have desired from the time of our memorable predecessor John XXIII, for whom you have made clear your admiration and fellow-feeling, and to whom you once applied in a flash of intuition the words of the Evangelist: "There was a man sent from God whose name was John" (Jn 1:6).

He too desired this encounter, as we both know, but his premature death did not allow him to see his heartfelt wish fulfilled. The words of Christ, "That they may be one! *Ut unum sint!,*" came back several times to the lips of the dying Pope, leaving no doubt as to one of the dearest intentions for which he offered to God his long agony and his whole life leading up to it.

Doubtless on both sides the ways that lead to union may be long and strewn with difficulties. But the two roads converge upon one another, and they reach their terminus in the sources of the Gospel. Surely it is an encouraging sign that today's meeting takes place on this ground where Christ founded his Church and poured out his blood for it. It is in any case an eloquent expression of the deep desire which, thanks be to God, is more and more inspiring all Christians worthy of the name, the desire namely to work to surmount divisions, to break down barriers, and resolutely follow the road that leads to reconciliation.

Differences on the level of doctrine, liturgy and discipline will have to be examined in due time and place, and in a spirit of fidelity to truth and charitable understanding. What can and must go forward right now is this brotherly love which is ever finding new ways of manifesting itself—a love which, learning from the past, is ready to forgive, tends to believe more willingly in good than in evil, and is above all concerned to follow the pattern of its Divine Master and to allow itself to be drawn to him and be transformed by him.

May the kiss of peace which the Lord has allowed us to exchange on this holy earth, and the prayer which Jesus Christ has taught us, and which we are soon going to recite, be the sign and symbol of this love.

It would be impossible to say how much we have been touched by this step you have taken; and not just we personally—the Roman Church and the whole Ecumenical Council will take account with deep joy of this historic event.

For our part, we raise towards God our grateful prayer, and we ask him to help us follow this course, and to pour forth on both of us, who have begun it in faith and confidence, the blessing which will ensure its happy outcome. In this spirit, it is not a good-bye which I say to you, but an *au revoir,* one based on the hope of new and fruitful encounters *in nomine Domini.*

50.   *6 January 1964*

Common communiqué of the Pope and Patriarch, published after their meeting*   **

At the conclusion of their meeting at Jerusalem the Holy Father Paul VI and the Ecumenical Patriarch Athenagoras in agreement with his Holy Synod together recognize the great significance of this event, and give thanks to Almighty God, Father, Son and Holy Spirit, who guided their steps towards the Holy Land, where our common Redeemer, Christ our Lord, lived, taught, died, rose again, and ascended into Heaven, whence he sent the Holy Spirit on the infant Church. This meeting cannot be considered as anything other than a brotherly gesture, inspired by the charity of Christ, who left his disciples the supreme commandment to love one another, to pardon offences seventy times seven, and to be united among themselves.

The two pilgrims, their eyes fixed on Christ, the exemplar and author, with the Father, of unity and peace, pray God that this meeting may be the sign and prelude of things to come for the glory of God and the enlightenment of his faithful people. After so many centuries of silence, they have now met with the desire to fulfil the Lord's will and to proclaim the ancient truth of his Gospel confided to the Church.

These common feelings have been made manifest to all the members of the respective hierarchies, and to all the faithful, so that they may share them in their own right, and send new prayers to God on high, that in the eyes of all Christians there may shine forth more and more the truth of the one Church of Christ and of his Gospel, which is the light and salvation of the world.

51.   *6 January 1964*

Words of Pope Paul VI about his meeting with the Patriarch Athenagoras, addressed to those gathered in St. Peter's Square to welcome the Pope's return****

You understand that my journey was not just an isolated religious occurrence; it turned into an event which may have great historic importance. It is a further link in a tradition that goes back over the centuries. Who knows? It may be the prelude to new events of some magnitude, which may bring in their train all sorts of benefits for the Church and the human race.

This evening, all I shall say is that I had this morning the great happiness of embracing—after a gap of many centuries—the Ecumenical Patriarch of Constantinople, of exchanging with him words of peace, of brotherhood and desire, on the subject of the union and concord, on the honor to be rendered to Christ, and on the service which we owe for the good of the whole human family. We hope that these beginnings will bear good fruit, that the seed will spring up and become fully ripe.

52. *8 January 1964*

Telegram from Pope Paul VI to Patriarch Athenagoras, conveying his profound impression of their meeting*

Back again in Rome after the unforgettable pilgrimage during which we had the joy of meeting you, we wish to tell you again of the profound impression left in our soul by the talks we had together, and to assure you that we hope and pray that God may deign to bring these to fruition for the good of the whole Christian world.

53. *10 January 1964*

Telegram from Patriarch Athenagoras to Pope Paul VI, expressing his joy over their meeting**

Having stored up in our heart the luminous figure of Your beloved and esteemed Holiness, following on our meeting with you in Jerusalem, we returned to our see last night, 9 January, full of religious satisfaction and spiritual joy. We send you and your holy Church a cordial and brotherly greeting in loving union and form the wish that the voice arising from the Holy Tomb may always prompt our hearts to good things, strengthening us and the whole Christian world and guiding us to the fulfilment of the will of its divine Founder.

54. *15 January 1964*

Telegram from Patriarch Athenagoras to Pope Paul VI, in reply to the telegram of 8 January**

The brotherly mess..ge by which Your beloved Holiness told us of your happy return to your venerated see was read out at the first session of our Holy Synod yesterday, and filled us all with great joy. We thank you from our hearts, and express once more our finest feelings in Christ. We hope that the prayer which we made together in the Holy Land will be heard by Our Lord.

55. *16 January 1964*

Letter of Pope Paul VI to Patriarch Athenagoras, thanking him for the visit of the Metropolitan Athenagoras of Thyateira*

The unforgettable memories left in our soul by our encounters at Jerusalem have been with us all the time since our return, and we were just about to write to you when, at the hands of the distinguished Metropolitan of Thyateira, there arrived a new sign of your sensitive charity.

We cannot tell you how grateful we are for this touching gesture, which symbolizes, in spite of our differences, the abiding efficacy of the one sacrifice of Christ, and our sharing in the same priesthood and the same sacraments.

This new proof of friendship, added to the splendid gifts which you made us in Jerusalem, has the effect of strengthening still further those bonds which Providence allowed us to form in such happy and unusual circumstances. May God grant that this renewed meeting between the ancient See of Rome and the venerable Patriarchate of Constantinople may result in a copious pouring forth of grace over the whole Church. This is our dearest wish: its fulfilment we entrust to the Father of lights and his beloved Son Jesus Christ. In the charity of this same Christ we send you once more an expression of our esteem and affection.

56. *10 February 1964*

Letter in reply of Patriarch Athenagoras to Pope Paul VI**

To Paul, the most blessed and holy Pope of ancient Rome, greetings in the Lord.

We received the precious letter of Your beloved Holiness of 16 January last, and had the joy of reading it privately and then before a session of our Holy Synod. This was the letter which you sent us following the visit made on our behalf by his Eminence the Metropolitan

Athenagoras of Thyateira. We received the letter at the hand of your inter-Nuntio in Ankara, His Excellency Archbishop Francesco Lardone, with whom we spoke at length about Your venerable Holiness, to our great content of soul.

We thank you from our heart for the fraternal contents of your missive in which you manifest anew your happiness over the blessed meeting in Jerusalem, and signalize it in your description as a fruit of God's grace for the Church. We on our part entrust to God the Father of lights, and to his beloved Son Christ Our Lord, the fulfilment of the good work that has been begun, and embracing Your Holiness with a holy kiss we remain with brotherly love and special respect.

Your venerable Holiness's
dear Brother in Christ, . . .

PART II

Growth and Fruits of Dialogue

Nos 57–116   March 2, 1964–
                             September 23, 1965

Pope Paul VI . . . Patriarch Athenagoras I
(2)
Restoration of head of St. Andrew (66–67) ■
Invitations to Third Session of Vatican Council (71–
75) ■ Third Pan-Orthodox Conference of Rhodes
(76–77) ■ Decision to enter into closer relations with
Catholic Church (86–89) ■ Visit to Istanbul by
Cardinal Bea: harmony between policy of Rhodes
and *Decree on Ecumenism* of Vatican II (92–94) ■
Invitation to Fourth Session of Vatican II (100–101,
111, 116)

57. *2 March 1964*

Telegram from Pope Paul VI to Patriarch Athenagoras, expressing best wishes for the latter's restoration to health*

Having heard with sorrow of your ill health, we fervently pray God to come to your aid, and express our best wishes for your speedy recovery.

58. *27 March 1964*

Telegram from Patriarch Athenagoras to Pope Paul VI conveying good wishes for the feast of Easter**

We address a warm and brotherly greeting to Your beloved and esteemed Holiness on the occasion of the light-bearing feast of the Resurrection, which is being celebrated next Sunday by the sister Church of the West, and we pray the Lord to grant rich grace to yourself and to the same sister Church, and to increase our charity, to the praise of his glory.

59. *30 March 1964*

Telegram from Pope Paul VI to Patriarch Athenagoras thanking him and conveying good wishes*

Your Holiness's telegram touches us deeply, and revives in our soul the emotion aroused by our unforgettable meeting at Jerusalem. On this holy Easter feast, we fervently pray to the Lord of the Church to grant you in abundance the joy of his Resurrection.

60. *10 April 1964*

Letter of Cardinal Bea to Patriarch Athenagoras, giving him prior notice of the arrival of a Papal delegation*

Your Holiness,

I am happy to send you the news that His Grace, Joseph Marie Martin, Archbishop of Rouen, member of the Secretariat for Unity, together with Monsignor Willebrands and the Very Reverend Father Duprey will be going to Istanbul on 20 April next to meet Your Holiness.

This visit was decided on in a recent interview with the Holy Father with a view to furthering the happy contacts begun at Jerusalem and during the visits to Rome of His Excellency the Metropolitan Athenagoras of Thyateira. I am especially glad that your health has been restored, so that you can take up once again the tasks imposed on you by your onerous office. I thank the Lord for this and pray that he will give you strength and health in good measure.

It is with these feelings that I ask Your Holiness to accept the expression of my religious respect and my brotherly affection in the Lord.

61.   *18 April 1964*

Letter of Pope Paul VI to Patriarch Athenagoras, introducing the Papal delegation*

Beloved Brother in Christ,

This letter will be brought to you by our dear brother, His Grace Archbishop Joseph Marie Martin, Archbishop of Rouen, who together with our sons Monsignor Willebrands and the Very Reverend Father Duprey, is coming to Istanbul to tell you how vividly we recall our blessed meeting in Jerusalem, and how we feel that it has marked the beginning of a new period in the relations of the Holy See and the venerable Ecumenical Patriarchate.

Through this visit we wish to renew the kiss of peace exchanged on the Mount of Olives, and to tell you once more how you yourself, your clergy and all your faithful, are present in our prayer. We should be happy, too, if this visit provided the opportunity for strengthening the bonds which we have already formed, and making them firmer still.

At this time when you are about to celebrate the bright and glorious feast of Easter, we pray our one Lord that his victory over sin and death may support within you an ever more lively hope, one that will strengthen in your heart the joy that he came to give us, and which no one can take from us, seeing that our hope cannot be deceived. May the Risen Christ, by whose death we are reconciled to the Father, inspire us in our efforts to reestablish the unity of all those who are redeemed by him and believe in his name.

It is in this spirit that we ask the Father of lights to grant Your Holiness, the members of your Holy Synod, your clergy and faithful, an overflowing measure of his grace, and that we assure you once again, beloved brother, of our deep affection for you in the Lord.

62.   *19 April 1964*

Telegram from Patriarch Athenagoras to Pope Paul VI, thanking him for his telegram of 2 March*

Having returned to the Phanar after my illness and taken up my duties again, today during the Divine Liturgy in the Patriarchal Church I praised the Most High and prayed for the health and long life of Your beloved and much esteeemd Holiness. I give thanks from my heart for your warm brotherly concern. I am happy to feel myself within close reach of your love, which I think over eagerly and constantly ever since the day of our meeting in the holy city of Jerusalem, and I hope earnestly that our *au revoir* will be fulfilled in fact.

63.   *23 April 1964*

Telegram from Patriarch Athenagoras to Cardinal Bea thanking him for the visit of the Papal delegation*

The delegation sent by His Holiness arrived on Monday. They were cordially received on our part, and brought us much joy and consolation, so that we were sorry to see them take their departure today. We express our satisfaction over this fresh evidence of the brotherly love of His Holiness.

64.   *29 April 1964*

Telegram from Cardinal Bea to Patriarch Athenagoras, thanking him for the welcome given to the Papal delegation*

As soon as His Excellency Archbishop Martin, Monsignor Wille- brands, and the Very Reverend Father Duprey returned, I wished to lose no time in thanking Your Holiness for the warm and cordial welcome given them.

The exchange of views which this visit made possible was certainly very fruitful and full of hope for the development of brotherly relations between our two Churches.

I am glad to take this opportunity to extend to Your Holiness my respectful, brotherly, and also most cordial good wishes for the feast of Easter. I entreat the Risen Lord to grant you and your entire Church his strength, joy, and blessing in generous measure.

I beg Your Holiness to be so good as to accept the expression of my brotherly feelings in the Lord.

65.   *19 May 1964*

Letter of Patriarch Athenagoras to Pope Paul VI, thanking him for the visit of the Papal representatives and for the letter brought by Archbishop Martin of Rouen**

To Paul the most blessed and holy Pope of ancient Rome, greetings in the Risen Lord.

While still under the influence of the religious feelings aroused in us by the recent visit of the representatives of Your esteemed Holiness, the Most Reverend Joseph Marie Martin, Archbishop of Rouen, and his companions, Monsignor Willebrands and the Very Reverend Father Pierre Duprey, we thank you warmly in this brotherly letter for the indication of your Christian dispositions. These afford further and clear evidence of the importance which you attach to our meeting on the Mount of Olives and in the Holy City, and to the new and blessed period in the relations of the two Churches which then began. At the same time we should like to thank you for your ready good will in strengthening and increasing the holy bond of mutual peace and love which was thus happily established.

Together with their Eminences the Metropolitans who form our Holy Synod, we gladly received the good wishes for the light-bearing feast of the Resurrection which you kindly conveyed to us in the letter which His Grace the Archbishop of Rouen presented when making the above mentioned visit. We thank you wholeheartedly for these wishes and we beseech Christ our God, who through his death on the Cross entered into his glory, to take special care of you, so that you may enjoy good health for many years to come and cast lustre on the see of ancient Rome. May he enable you and the sister Church with all its members, over which you preside, to shine forth with a share in that inexpressible light of the Resurrection, and with glad hearts experience the joy arising from it.

May he also increase love within us, so that having this as our guide in everything, we may be made worthy to celebrate and glorify his precious and magnificent name with one voice and one heart.

It is with this wish that we embrace Your venerable Holiness with a holy kiss, and remain with brotherly love and fitting marks of honor.

Your esteemed Holiness's
beloved brother in Christ, . . .

66. *20 June 1964*

Letter of Cardinal Bea to Patriarch Athenagoras, informing him of the Pope's decision to restore the relic of St. Andrew to the Church of Patras*

Your Holiness,

I hope that your recent bout of poor health, of which I heard during my last journey in America, has left no ill effects, and that you are now completely well again.

During his last visit Bishop Willebrands confided to you that the Holy Father intended to restore to the Church of Patras the precious relic which it had entrusted to Pope Pius II in 1462.[20] Since then Bishop Willebrands has paid a visit to Patras, where he was in touch with the Metropolitan Bishop Constantinos, who subsequently officially expressed his desire, which is also that of the entire body of his faithful people, to see the valuable relic return to his city. Today I have the joy of informing you that the Holy Father has decided to send back the precious object, which has found a safe shelter in Rome for five centuries. The Holy Father announced his decision publicly on 23

---

20. Pope Pius II (1458–64) gave a detailed account of the transfer of the relic of St. Andrew's head from Patras to Italy by Thomas Palaeologus, who was compelled to seek refuge in Rome before an imminent Turkish invasion of Patras. The Pope arranged spectacular ceremonies for the reception of the relic. Cf. Pii Secundi, *Commentarii Rerum Memorabilium* (Romae, 1584), 352–372; and for the fullest modern study, S. Lambros, *Neos Hellenomnemon* (Athens, 1913), X, 33–79.

A papal delegation returned the relic to Patras, 24–25 September. Later, other relics originally from the East but transferred to Italy, were returned: St. Saba, from Venice to Jerusalem (25–26 October, 1965); St. Titus, from Venice to Heraklion in Crete (12–17 May, 1966), cf. below N. 93; St. Isidore, from Venice to Chios (16 June, 1967); St. Mark, from Venice to Cairo and to Alexandria (24–28 June, 1968); St. Cyril, from the Vatican to Constantinople (30 November, 1974), cf. below N. 322; St. Spyridon, from Rome to Corfu (11–13 December, 1984).

June in the evening. The date for the ceremony in which the relic will be handed back has not yet been finally decided on. It will not be long deferred, but time must be allowed for the fashioning of a reliquary worthy of what it is to contain.

I hope that this gesture, by which the Holy Father, in all charity and sincerity and with entire lack of self-interest, is meeting the trust placed in him by the Christians of Patras, will play its part in intensifying and furthering the new spirit, brought about by the holy encounter at Jerusalem, which is entering into the relations between the Catholic Church and those of the Orthodox world.

It is with these feelings that I ask Your Holiness to accept the expression of my respectful and brotherly affection in Christ Jesus.

67. *27 June 1964*

Telegram from Patriarch Athenagoras to Pope Paul VI, thanking him for the transference of the relic of St. Andrew*

While staying at the Theological College of Halki I learnt with deep feeling and joy the good news of 23 June about the brotherly and highly significant decision of Your beloved Holiness to restore the precious relic of St. Andrew, the First-Called Apostle, to the Church of his martyrdom. The whole Orthodox world rejoices. We thank you personally in a brotherly spirit, and ask the Lord, by the intercession of his Apostles Peter and Andrew, to bless our sister Churches aspiring towards unity.

68. *27 June 1964*

Telegram from Patriarch Athenagoras to Bishop Willebrands on the occasion of his episcopal ordination**

Close to you in meditation and prayer during your fitting ordination to the episcopate at the hands of His Holiness Pope Paul VI himself, I congratulate you heartily, and pray that God in his goodness will grant plentiful grace for your work and apostolate.[21]

---

21. John Willebrands was consecrated titular bishop of Mauriana, 28 June.

69. *28 June 1964*

Telegram from Patriarch Athenagoras to Pope Paul VI for the feast of his patron saint*

We send Your beloved Holiness, on the occasion of your patronal feast-day the *aspasmon agapis* [greeting of charity]. We hope from our heart that the Lord may multiply the years of your life, and may strengthen and comfort you for your many-sided responsibility in the government of the holy Church of Rome, and for the good of the sacred work of unity among the Christian Churches.

70. *29 June 1964*

Telegram from Pope Paul VI to Patriarch Athenagoras, thanking him for the two preceding telegrams*

Your Holiness,
Doubly touched by your joy at the return of the venerable head of St. Andrew and your thoughtful good wishes, we gladly send you our warm thanks and at the same time assure you afresh of our brotherly feelings. We earnestly ask the Lord to pour forth on you his bounteous blessings.

71. *3 July 1964*

Letter of Cardinal Bea to Patriarch Athenagoras, sending him a copy of the letter addressed to the heads of the Orthodox Churches, inviting them to send observers to the Third Session of the Vatican Council*

Your Holiness,
The frequent contacts which we have had with your Church during these last months have kept you informed about the next period of the Vatican Council. For this reason there was no need for you to be told again about its opening date. I should like, however, to make available to you the text of the letter which I have sent to all the Patriarchs of the Orthodox Churches which have not yet been officially informed of this matter.

I am happy to take this opportunity to express once more to Your Holiness all my deep and very respectful brotherly affection in the Lord.

To His Beatitude . . .

Your Beatitude,

I should like to inform you that the Third Session of the Second Vatican Council will begin on 14 September 1964. It will continue until 20 November.

You are aware that the invitation extended to the Orthodox Patriarchate by His Holiness Pope Paul VI to send observer-delegates to the Council was one which included all the sessions of the Second Vatican Council, and reached forward to the day on which, as we humbly hope, in reliance on the goodness of God and the help of the Holy Spirit, it will be brought to a happy conclusion. For this reason I can assure Your Beatitude that observer-delegates from your Church will always be received with great fraternal charity, if you and your Church decide that it is possible to send them.

Allow me to take this opportunity to recommend to your charitable prayers the work of the bishops of the Catholic Church who are gathered in Council with the aim of finding the ways which best meet the needs of the service of God in our contemporary world, and of putting into practice everything that can really contribute to the strengthening of peace, love, and brotherly fellowship between people, especially among those who make claim to the title derived from the holy name of Jesus Christ.

Be so kind, Your Beatitude, as to accept the expression of my respectful and very brotherly affection in Christ Jesus.

72. *8 September 1964*

Telegram from Patriarch Athenagoras to Cardinal Bea, telling him of the decision of the Holy Synod to send three observers to the Third Session of the Council*

The Holy Synod of our Church today decided to send three observers to the Third Session of the Vatican Council. Their names will be soon sent to you.

We announce this news with joy, and express our best wishes for the success of the Council and for a plentiful gift of grace from the Lord.

73. *10 September 1964*

Telegram from Patriarch Athenagoras to Cardinal Bea, giving the names of two delegated observers to the Council*

Further to our telegram, we send the news that the Holy Synod decided to send as observers to the Third Session of the Vatican Council Archimandrite Panteleimon Rodopoulos, Rector of our Theological College at Boston, and the priest John Romanides, professor at the same College.

74. *11 September 1964*

Telegram from Cardinal Bea to Patriarch Athenagoras, thanking him for sending delegated observers*

We have received the telegrams from Your Holiness announcing the decision of the Holy Synod regarding the sending of observers for the Third Session of the Vatican Council. We thank you wholeheartedly for this brotherly gesture and your prayers for the success of the Council. We shall receive the observers with joy, being sure that their presence will contribute to an increase of fraternal love to the glory of the Lord.

75. *24 October 1964*

Telegram from Patriarch Athenagoras to Cardinal Bea, giving the name of a third observer for the Vatican Council*

We are happy to inform you that by a decision of the Synod Archimandrite Maximos Agiorgousis has been appointed as a further observer for the work of the Third Session of the Vatican Council.[22]

---

22. Maximos Agiorgousis was the parish priest of St. Andrew's church in Rome. He later became Metropolitan in Pittsburgh, USA.

76.   *29 October 1964*

Message from Pope Paul VI to the Third Pan-Orthodox Conference of Rhodes. (With the text were included translations in Greek, Arabic, and Russian, all signed by the Pope)*

Your Excellencies
and dear Brothers in Christ,

It is from the bottom of our heart that we send you our fraternal greeting. While your brothers of the Roman Catholic Church are gathered in Council and asking themselves what courses to follow to show themselves more and more faithful to God's designs for his Church—and this in a period which is so rich in opportunities but at the same time so full of temptations and trials—you too are preparing to devote yourselves to the same problems, so as on your part also to make an ever better response to the same demands of the Lord.

Thoroughly seized as we are by the importance of this venerable assembly, with fervent prayer we call down on it the light of the Holy Spirit.

Please accept our assurance that we ourselves, together with the Council gathered together at this very moment, and the whole Catholic Church, will follow with a very special interest the progress of your work, and will associate it in fervent prayer with what is taking place at the same time close to the tomb of the Apostle Peter. We are fully confident that the grace of the Lord will descend in all the more generous measure in your case as well as ours, in that a common charity has inspired and enkindled this common prayer.

Remembering the counsel of the Apostle Paul, "Carry one another's burdens, and thus you will fulfil the law of Christ," we make bold to count on the aid of your prayer, Excellencies and dear brothers in Christ, so that the Lord may give us the graces necessary for the faithful carrying out of the task to which a mysterious design of his Providence has called us. May the Holy Mother of God, who is our Mother and yours, whom we honor and to whom we pray with a like fervor, intercede in her kindness, so that we may grow continually in the love of her Son, our one Lord and Savior. May the charity nourished at the Lord's table make us more anxious day by day for "the unity of the Spirit in the bond of peace" (Eph 4:3).

77. *5 November 1964*

Telegram from Metropolitan Meliton to Pope Paul VI, thanking him for his message**[23]

We are gathered together by the grace of God in a Pan-Orthodox Conference in that island of Rhodes mentioned in the journeys of St. Paul, and there received your kind message with joy. We sincerely appreciate the expressions of love and peace in the one same Lord which you were good enough to send us on your own behalf, as well as that of the Second Vatican Council and the whole Roman Catholic Church. By a unanimous decision we send Your Holiness our heartfelt thanks. In the same spirit, and in the hope that the Lord, "who redeemed the Church in his own blood," will through the intercession of his most Holy Mother give comfort and strength both to you and to us, so that we may enjoy the blessing of brotherhood in Christ, we return the greeting of love and peace in the Lord. "Persevering in prayer" and "anticipating one another in the honor which we show each to each," we make our way along the road of the divine counsels, in expectation of the fulfilment of the will of Our Lord Jesus Christ for his Church, since "he is faithful for ever."

78. *19 November 1964*

Letter of Pope Paul VI to Patriarch Athenagoras, sending him an episcopal ring which had belonged to Pope John XXIII*

To our venerable and dear brother in Christ Athenagoras, Archbishop of Constantinople and Ecumenical Patriarch.

We gladly seize every opportunity which Providence offers us to give proof of the feelings of fraternal love which inspire us in your regard, especially since our unforgettable encounters at Jerusalem at the beginning of this year.

Realizing that an affectionate link bound you to our predecessor of holy and venerated memory, Pope John XXIII, we have chosen as

---

23. Born in Constantinople in 1913 (Saterios Hatze), Meliton became Metropolitan of Helioupolis and Theira in 1950 (later, of Chalcedon), and was President of the Second (1963) and Third (1964) Pan-Orthodox Conferences.

a present for you, from among the articles which belonged to him, a valuable episcopal ring which we send you together with this letter.

We know that this will be for you a treasured keepsake of that unforgettable Pontiff, who was responsible in such large measure for the widespread ecumenical movement which is fortunately sweeping through the Catholic Church today. It is our desire that this gift should furnish proof of the affectionate interest with which we follow everything to do with you personally and with the venerable Orthodox Churches.

It is with these feelings that we express once again to Your beloved Holiness our fraternal charity and our union in Christ, our one and only Savior.

79.   *28 November 1964*

Telegram from Patriarch Athenagoras to Pope Paul VI on the occasion of his journey to Bombay*

On the occasion of the visit of Your beloved and venerable Holiness to Bombay, I wish you most heartily a good journey with good health, and a happy return to the Eternal City.[24]

With much brotherly affection, . . .

80.   *1 December 1964*

Telegram in reply from Pope Paul VI to Patriarch Athenagoras*

I am profoundly touched by the wishes of *bon voyage* to Bombay that Your Holiness has so kindly sent us. For reasons unforeseen we are obliged to make a landing for technical purposes. We are sorry that this cannot take place at some spot where it would have been possible to meet you. We express once more our fraternal affection.

81.   *21 December 1964*

Telegram from Pope Paul VI to Patriarch Athenagoras, sending him good wishes for the feasts of Christmas and New Year*

---

24. The Pope participated in the 38th International Eucharistic Congress, in Bombay, 2–5 December.

May the Word made flesh in the womb of the Virgin grant you abundant light and strength, and may he grant us to see, during the coming year, a growth in love between all Christians, and a strengthening of the peace promised to all men of good will.

82. *23 December 1964*

Telegram from Patriarch Athenagoras to Pope Paul VI, sending his good wishes in return**

We greet Your beloved and venerable Holiness with a loving and respectful embrace, on the occasion of the imminent great feast of the birth of Christ the Savior, which we are happy to celebrate in common. May the Lord strengthen you and all men for the promotion of the blessed work of Christian unity until the union of all is achieved. May he grant you, your holy Church, and the entire world, a peaceful and favorable New Year.

83. *24 December 1964*

Telegram from Patriarch Athenagoras to Pope Paul VI, thanking him for his letter of 19 November*

I thank you cordially for your kind letter of 19 November, and in doing so wish you a good Christmas and a happy New Year.

84. *2 January 1965*

Telegram from Patriarch Athenagoras to Pope Paul VI, recalling the first anniversary of their meeting in Jerusalem*

Recalling our happy meeting in Jerusalem, of which as we stand before Divine Providence we now humbly celebrate the first anniversary, we tell you of our heartfelt feelings of thanks and joy for this historic event. We fervently pray to the Lord that the *au revoir* which we both look for may be in fact brought about. With much brotherly affection.

85.   *5 January 1965*

Telegram in reply from Pope Paul VI to Patriarch Athenagoras*

We are deeply touched by your kind message which has the effect of renewing in our soul the pure joys of our meeting of last year in the places sanctified by the Lord. We thank you, and pray God that in the course of the new year the relationship so happily begun by this first meeting may become stronger still. Very fraternally in Christ.

86.   *25 January 1965*

Letter of Patriarch Athenagoras to Pope Paul VI, announcing the coming to Rome of a Patriarchal delegation with instructions to communicate the decisions of the Third Pan-Orthodox Conference of Rhodes**

To Paul, the most blessed and holy Pope of ancient Rome,
greetings in the Lord.

Gladly and very lovingly we proceed in this further communication with Your beloved and esteemed Holiness, to assure you of the holy emotion and joy which fill our heart through the manifestations of God's mercy and superabundant grace which have taken place in these recent years and are ever occurring anew.

Indeed it is with joy that, especially since the time of our blessed encounter on the God-trodden Mount of Olives, which was greeted with relief and many hopes by the Christian world, we see clearly displayed on an ever wider scale the desire and readiness of the local Christian Churches for cooperation and for a joint progress towards the fulfilment of the Lord's will for the unity of all who believe in him.

Our holy Eastern Orthodox Church, in giving clear evidence both before and after this encounter, in successive Pan-Orthodox conferences, of this holy desire, and inclination, has proclaimed its decision, namely, that it is ready and eager to approach your venerable Church of ancient Rome, with a view to cultivating brotherly relations and promoting the spirit of unity in Christ.

We entrust the presentation to Your Holiness of this fraternal letter of recommendation to their Eminences Bishop Meliton of Helioupolis and Theira and Bishop Chrysostom of Myra, our beloved brothers.[25] They are coming to you, at our instance and that of our Holy Synod, so that, following the measures drawn up in the Third Conference held at Rhodes of the local Orthodox Churches, they may give the authorized Secretariat for Christian Unity information about the decisions reached there. We have no doubt that you will receive these brothers in Christ with kindness, and will commend them to the said Secretariat for this purpose. By their means we send you our warm greetings in the Lord, and embracing you with a holy kiss we remain with brotherly love and special regard.

Your venerable and esteemed Holiness's
dear Brother in Christ, . . .

87. *16 February 1965*

Address of Metropolitan Meliton of Helioupolis and Theira to Pope Paul VI **

Your Holiness,

On the instructions of His Holiness the Ecumenical Patriarch Athenagoras I and of his Holy Synod we make this visit to the eternal city of Rome and to your sacred see, so that we may convey to the venerable Roman Catholic Church, over which you gloriously preside, the joyful tidings of love and peace on the part of our holy Eastern Orthodox Church.

And now, in accordance with ecclesiastical order, we appear first before you, the sovereign Bishop of ancient Rome, and impart the embrace in the Lord of your brother in the East, the Bishop of Constantinople, the New Rome. We have the honor of handing to you his fraternal Patriarchal letter, in addition to which we assure you on his behalf that you are the object of his most cordial brotherly feelings and his ardent prayers to the Lord.

As we carry out this extremely pleasant and blessed commission, we go back in mind to that great moment of the encounter in Jerusalem, in which, after long centuries of division, alienation and isolation, you two venerable leaders, living out the agony of our common Lord,

---

25. Born in 1921 at Constantinople (Chrysostomos Konstantinides), Metropolitan Chrysostom was General Secretary of the Pan-Orthodox Conference. Long active in the World Council of Churches, he was elected Vice-Moderator of the WCC Central Committee at the 1983 General Assembly, as Metropolitan of Myra.

of his Church and his world, were moved by God to come together from the West and the East. Through a shared act of obedience to the divine will, or abnegation, of good counsel, as well as Christian generosity, with your own hands you both opened up the road of reconciliation, inaugurated the dialogue of charity, and brought before the eyes of the world the divine vision and the great name and reality of the undivided Church of Christ. In the hearts of those who "would fain see Jesus" (Jn 12:22), you enkindled the sacred fire of longing for that ancient and blessed state of the Church.

Our Orthodox East, aspiring towards the restoration of the ancient unity, beauty, and glory of the Church, has never ceased praying for total union, and has collaborated with other Christians for the development of the ecumenical spirit of reconciliation. In recent times it has turned towards its sister, your Roman Catholic Church, and in the First Pan-Orthodox Conference it unanimously confirmed its desire for this dialogue, and went on to lay down a programme for the furtherance of this sacred cause, noting that its successful outcome is to be striven for in stages and on a solid basis. It was settled that the first stage would be a general preparation, through the creation of suitable conditions and the study in detail of the subject matter of this dialogue from the Orthodox side. At the same time it was recognized that it would be useful to continue and increase the cultivation of relations with your Church by contacts between more specialized groups, in order to reach that point of brotherhood which we desire.

In this spirit, we form the conviction, which you yourself have strengthened in so many ways, that your venerable Church, too, is possessed by the same sacred desire, namely, that after the requisite general preparation on either side a fruitful theological dialogue should begin at an appropriate time between our churches. We propose then, by a unanimous decision of the Third Pan-Orthodox Conference in Rhodes, and by the mandate of His Holiness the Ecumenical Patriarch, who in accordance with our ordinances, gives effect to this decision, to enter with your permission into communication with your authorized Secretariat, and through it to give your venerable Roman Catholic Church all the information which will bring it up to date with the decisions reached by the assembly of the Orthodox Churches.

Your Holiness,

Please pray to the Lord for the success of this mission that it may be the blessed beginning of a regular well planned fostering of brotherly relations between our two Churches in a sincere dialogue of charity. By means of this dialogue may we labor together, removing the accumulated obstacles that stand in our way and preparing the ground on all sides, so that we may be soon brought into theological dialogue. Then, committing ourselves to the Holy Spirit, let us prepare the dawn of that bright day of the Lord, in which those of the West and those of the East, after the ancient fashion of our common martyrs, confessors and fathers, will eat the same bread and drink from the same chalice and confess the one faith "in one spirit," and again "with one mind strive side by side for the faith of the Gospel" (Phil 1:27), to the glory of Christ and his One, Holy, Catholic and Apostolic Church.

It is in this hope that we respectfully address to Your venerable Holiness our humble greeting and our warm thanks for this cordial reception.

May the Lord cause your years to be many and blessed.

88.   *16 February 1965*

Reply of Pope Paul VI on his reception of the Metropolitans Meliton of Helioupolis and Theira and Chrysostom of Myra*

Dear Brothers in Christ,

The first word which comes to our lips at this moment is the exclamation of the inspired author: *Haec dies quam fecit Dominus, exultemus et laetemur in ea!* ("This is the day which the Lord has made, let us exult and be glad in it," Ps 117:24). Yes, this day is one that the Lord has made; let all be given over to thanksgiving and joy.

With you we bless God for this day's encounter, since of and in itself it constitutes an event full of deep joy. In the future people will be able to say: here centuries of history reached their term; here a new stage in the relations between the Catholic West and the Orthodox East began. What a singularly solemn moment is this! It is under the gaze of God, in his presence and in his name, *in nomine Domini,* that we welcome you and open our arms to you.

First of all we greet you for the worthy persons that you are, good workmen in the great cause of ecumenism: you the Most Reverend Metropolitan of Helioupolis and Theira, who have presided with such mastery over two Pan-Orthodox Conferences; and you the Most Reverend Metropolitan Chrysostom of Myra, whose episcopal see recalls the memory of a saint greatly honored in the West, you who have acted diligently as the secretary of three Pan-Orthodox Conferences.

Reaching beyond yourselves personally we wish next to greet those whom you represent, and above all our very dear brother, His

Holiness the Ecumenical Patriarch Athenagoras I; our meeting with him at Jerusalem has been the source of feelings that words cannot express; it will never fade from our memory as long as we live.

We have no means of knowing what the future holds in store, or what developments the dialogue of charity which has been opened between the two Churches will undergo. But whatever comes of it, it is our wish that the first stage of this blessed meeting should be characterized by joy, by the calm of Christ's peace, and by a respectful and trustful attitude of expectancy on both sides.

We are happy about the wisdom and the realism of the main lines of the programme which you have just sketched. We must, by means of more numerous and fraternal contacts, restore step by step what the time of isolation has undone, and create anew, at all levels of the life of our Churches, an atmosphere which will allow us, when the time comes, to set about a theological discussion likely to yield good results. If you for your own part are studying the main subjects to be submitted to fraternal discussion in the future, you are aware at the same time how greatly the desire and preparation for this dialogue occupy the mind of the Vatican Council and of Catholic theologians. We are very glad about the meetings and the conversations which you propose having with our Secretariat for Unity, which will later give us an account of them. We retain for ourselves the right for reflection and consultation to decide on the best ways from our side of giving life and vigor to this dialogue of charity and to the progressive experience of a rediscovered brotherhood. God is our witness, our only desire is to be faithful to Christ.

Blessings on you then, my dear brothers, and thank you for your visit, and for coming as bearers of a message full of hope.

In your turn carry to him who sends you our warm and respectful greetings, together with our brotherly and most affectionate wishes for peace. And allow us to invite you to persevere with us in prayer to almighty God, Father, Son and Holy Spirit, and to invoke, too, together with us the protection of the Blessed Virgin Mary, Mother of God and our Mother. Let us ask the holy Apostles, Peter, Paul, Andrew, and all the saints to accompany us along the Lord's road in the unity of faith and charity, for his glory and our peace.

89.   *23 February 1965*

Letter of Cardinal Bea to Patriarch Athenagoras, thanking him for the visit of the Patriarchal delegation*

The visit to Rome of their Eminences the Metropolitans Meliton of Helioupolis and Theira and Chrysostom of Myra has marked a new stage in the strengthening of fraternal relations between the Ecumenical Patriarchate and the Roman Church. With our hearts full of joy, we must give thanks to God for this gift of his goodness which has allowed charity to flourish and ripen.

I am anxious to express to Your Holiness all my deep gratitude for the honor which you have done me in awarding me the Great Cross of the Order of St. Andrew.

I also thank you for communicating to the Secretariat for Christian Unity the decisions of the Third Pan-Orthodox Conference of Rhodes. We have to bring our desire of mending the earlier severed bonds into line with the practical possibilities for development of a vast and complex situation, and it is against this background that I view these decisions, the realism and wisdom of which are appreciated by the Holy Father. They will be carefully studied on our part, and we shall try to do everything possible to bring about a prudent progress along the new way which is thus opened.

Speaking on a personal note, I hope to visit Istanbul in the near future, and I make bold to hope that the proposals to be submitted to Your Holiness will meet with your acceptance. I have great joy in anticipation as I look forward to this forthcoming first meeting with you.

Be so good, Your Holiness, as to receive this expression of my very respectful and fraternal affection.

90.   *8 March 1965*

Letter from Patriarch Athenagoras to Cardinal Bea, thanking him for his letter of 23 February**

It was with pleasure that we received your valued letter of 23 February, and after personal perusal read it out at a session of our Holy Synod. This was the letter which you sent us subsequent to the meeting you had with our Patriarchal delegation, their Eminences Meliton Metropolitan of Helioupolis and Theira and Chrysostom Metropolitan of Myra, and in which you made it clear that you were overjoyed at the sight of the new road that is being opened up in the mutual relations of our two Churches.

We thank you warmly for your letter, and congratulate you for the great zeal which you display in the restoration of Christian unity, a work so pleasing to God. We would like you to know that we are keenly looking forward to your visit here, and we embrace you with a holy kiss, and remain with brotherly love and fitting respect.

91.   *11 March 1965*

Telegram from Patriarch Athenagoras to Pope Paul VI, thanking him for the welcome given to the Patriarchal delegation*

On the return of our representatives, the Metropolitans Meliton of Helioupolis and Theira and Chrysostom of Myra, we were informed in detail about their mission to Your beloved Holiness and your venerable Church. We were deeply moved by your brotherly message of charity, peace, and mutual support in Christ, and by the cordial reception extended to the above mentioned by you personally and by all your office bearers, and we hasten to express our heartfelt thanks to you. United in prayer and in the hope of the day which the Lord is preparing, let us glorify his Name together for all that he grants us in his grace.

92.   *31 March 1965*

Letter of Pope Paul VI to Patriarch Athenagoras telling him that a Papal delegation headed by Cardinal Bea will be coming, and emphasizing the harmony between the decisions of the Third Pan-Orthodox Conference and the Decree of the Vatican Council, "Unitatis Redintegratio"*

Beloved Brother in Christ,
    The visit to Rome of your two eminent envoys and the letter from Your Holiness which they brought me have revived the memory of our meeting in Jerusalem, a memory which we keep in the depths of our heart. Today it is our dear brother Cardinal Augustin Bea who comes to bring you our kiss of peace and brotherly love.
    The President of our Secretariat for Unity has brought us up to date with decisions of the Pan-Orthodox Conference, which were transmitted to him by your distinguished delegates. The programme there outlined seems to us to meet the requirements of the factual situation which history has bequeathed us, and by the same token those

of our common advance towards the unity willed by the Lord, the desire for which has been so marvelously enkindled by his Spirit of love in the hearts of the Christians of our time. Your Holiness remembers that it was in great part because he was anxious to contribute to the restoration of unity among all Christians that our predecessor of venerated memory felt urged to summon the Second Vatican Council. We can assure you that this concern still occupies our mind too, and that it is shared by the fathers of the Council, as they have shown by their solemn approval of the *Decree on Ecumenism.*[26] This important document which begins with the very words "Unitatis Redintegratio" is inspired throughout by a readiness to engage in dialogue, and by the conviction that favorable conditions for dialogue and an atmosphere conducive to its fruitful development must be called into being. Surely the happy harmony easily perceived between the decisions of the Conference of Rhodes and those of the Vatican Council is a fresh sign of the action of the Holy Spirit. And a sign which fills us with hope, for we believe that he who summons forth and initiates this activity is able in his own mysterious way to bring it to a happy issue, through an ever more pure and demanding fidelity to our one Master, Christ, who is our way, our truth and our life.

The object of our efforts will be to put into practice this common programme of a brotherhood and a combined action into which we feel our way again step by step on all levels of the life of our Churches and in all the fields of their activity. Neither the length of the road we must follow, nor the difficulties foreseen or unforeseen which bestrew it, can bring us to a halt, for our resolution is founded on that hope which cannot deceive.

It is in order to take a new step along this road—this dialogue of charity mutually decided on—that we send a select delegation to your venerable see as a sign of respect and a pledge of brotherhood.

This meeting finds its place in the light of Easter, whose dawn is even now mounting on the horizon. It thus gives us, my dear brother, the opportunity of sending you our heartfelt good wishes. May the Risen Lord, the ground of our common faith, fill you with his light, his strength, and his joy. May all those who call upon him share more and more in his Resurrection and his life, so that they may become one, as he and his Father are one.

---

26. At the end of the Third Session, 21 November, 1964, Pope Paul VI, "together with the Fathers of the Sacred Council," promulgated *Unitatis Redintegratio,* the decree on ecumenism. Cf. Ecumenical Documents I, *Doing the Truth in Charity,* eds. Thomas F. Stransky and John B. Sheerin (Paulist Press, 1982), 17–33.

It is in this spirit that we embrace you with a holy kiss, and that we express again all our deep affection in him who died and rose again on our behalf.

93.   *3 April 1965*

Address delivered by Cardinal Bea during his visit to Patriarch Athenagoras*

Your Holiness,

Within a short space of time after the visit made to the Holy Father last February by the very distinguished delegation sent by Your Holiness, an official delegation of the Holy See is appearing today at the venerable Ecumenical Patriarchate. The representatives whom you sent came to communicate officially the decisions reached unanimously at the Third Pan-Orthodox Conference of Rhodes. At the same time, "after centuries of silence and waiting," to use the expression of the Holy Father at Jerusalem (1/5/1964), it made a further advance in the dialogue of charity with the Church of Rome, so that at the solemn moment when he received your delegation the Holy Father was able to repeat the words of the Psalmist: "This is the day the Lord has made; let us be glad and rejoice in it" (Ps 117:24). Our visit today is meant to return that of your own delegation, and to continue the dialogue of charity already entered upon, with a view to drawing closer still the bonds which link us each to each like brothers.

What joy this must bring to heaven and earth! What joy, in the kingdom of eternity, for the blessed soul of Pope John. What joy for the whole Church of Christ both in East and West. What joy, too, all this must bring, I am sure, to Your Holiness, you who have for many years spoken and labored, have prayed and suffered, to hasten the longed for hour when we shall open our arms once more to each other like brothers, and set out on the same road towards the goal of our yearnings—the unity willed by Christ. Allow me to add that it is a great joy for all of us, and especially for me, to be able to speak to you face to face, to embrace you in the love of Christ, and to thank you for all you have done for the great cause of unity. For all this let there be praise and thanks to God our Father, through Christ, in the Spirit who is love. May the holy Mother of God and the holy Apostles Peter and his brother Andrew join their intercession to the act of thanksgiving which we make together.

However, the dialogue of charity which we want to carry further by our presence here is not restricted to an exchange of visits and the kiss of peace. Its first and most definite and practical effect is the decision we have taken together to make preparations in the midst of our respective Churches for all that unity involves, and by so doing to work strenuously together to bring about that complete unity which the Lord intended, and for which he begged in his burning prayer to the Father on the eve of his passion and death. The Holy Father was filled with joy by your decision, since it fits in perfectly with what the Second Vatican Council proclaimed at the end of its Third Session in the *Decree on Ecumenism*. In this authoritative document the Council does in fact exhort "all the Catholic faithful to recognize the signs of the times and to take an active and intelligent part in the work of ecumenism" (N. 4). Furthermore this decree states that "concern for restoring unity pertains to the whole Church, faithful and clergy alike. It extends to everyone, according to the potential of each, whether it be exercised in daily Christian living or in theological and historical studies" (N. 5). As one would expect, when this kind of concern is felt, the "higher gift" of charity should occupy the foreground, and that in all the fulness which, according to St. Paul, is proper to it—this charity which is "patient, kind . . . which rejoices in the truth, which puts no limit to its forbearance, to its trust, its hope, its power to endure" (1 Cor 13:4–7). Herein are picked out in detail all the riches which can be and are being brought to bear in our fraternal relations by the dialogue of charity on which we have entered, and which we can follow up from now onwards, in spite of the differences which still separate us. The dialogue of charity is already beginning to bring about unity, and is at the same time the best preparation for the search for unity in the matters that still divide us, particularly certain points of doctrine.

After dealing with the general preparation, the Council declares in the same decree, with reference to the relations of Catholics with the venerable Churches of the East: "Catholics are strongly urged to avail themselves more often of these spiritual riches of the Eastern Fathers, riches which lift up the whole man to the contemplation of divine mysteries."

"All should realize that it is of supreme importance to understand, venerate, preserve and foster the exceedingly rich liturgical and spiritual heritage of the Eastern Churches, in order faithfully to preserve the fullness of Christian tradition, and to bring about reconciliation between Eastern and Western Christians" (N. 15). To conclude, this decree says, a little further on: "After taking all these factors into consideration, this sacred Synod confirms what previous Councils and Roman Pontiffs have proclaimed: in order to restore communion and unity to preserve them, one 'must impose no burden beyond what is indispensable' (Acts 15:28). It is the Council's urgent desire that every effort should henceforth be made towards the gradual realization of this goal in the various organizations and living activities of the Church, especially by prayer and by fraternal dialogue on points of doctrine and the more pressing pastoral problems of our time" (N. 18).

Of course there is a lot to be done all over again. It is not going to be easy to fill in a deep ditch which has been there for nine centuries, and we have no illusions on that score. But the Lord for whom "one day is like a thousand years and a thousand years like a day" (2 Pt 4:8) can also perform miracles when we ask him with a faith capable of moving mountains (cf. Mt 17:19; 21:21; Mk 11:23). And we may add that he gives proof of this by such striking events as have occurred in these last few years: the encounter of Your Holiness with Pope Paul VI in Jerusalem, the glorious return of the head of St. Andrew to the city of Patras, not to mention the imminent return of the head of St. Titus to Crete and the relics of St. Saba to his monastery near Jerusalem. All these facts show us that the Lord has already done wonderful works, and that he is ready to do still others, if we only ask him with faith, in a spirit of humility and repentance. "All things are possible to him who believes," Jesus seems to be saying in our time to the Christians of the whole world. This is the same Jesus whose redemptive death and glorious Resurrection we are making ready to celebrate. We believe that he who has triumphed over sin and death will triumph also over the scandal of division, and that he will be the source of our perfect union with him, and in him with the Father. With this thought in mind, I am happy to offer Your Holiness here and now, in the name of the Holy Father, warm good wishes for the feast of Easter: "Christ is risen from the dead, Alleluia!" He has brought his peace and left it with us, and he says to us: "Have courage, I have overcome the world" (Jn 16:33).

94.   *3 April 1965*

Address of Patriarch Athenagoras in welcoming Cardinal Bea**

Our most holy Church of Constantinople, with its gaze fixed now as always on the Resurrection of Christ, in the unfailing light and pure joy of that event welcomes you, and in my person embraces you in the love and peace of Christ, most eminent and esteemed Cardinal Augustin, together with your dear and distinguished fellow workers—all of you honored and beloved envoys of our brother in Christ in the West, the very holy and blessed Paul VI.

Truly your visit to us is a matter of joy in the Lord on both sides, and we hail it as a new and significant stage in the period of the Christian history of East and West which is now being opened up.

Blessed then be the Lord who stands in our midst, the cause of all good things and the fulfilment of all our yearning.

Let us first of all turn our mind and heart towards him, and together thank him for leading us, as we now see, to give effect to his holy will. By this blessed meeting once again he gives his Church a new sign, and imparts to us a new and holy experience of brotherhood in him.

With deep awareness and appreciation of these gifts of Christ, and of the value of your presence here, we say to you in the words of the Prophet: "How beautiful are the feet of those who bring glad tidings of peace, who bring glad tidings of good things!" (Is 52:7; Rom 10:15). In you we see messengers of peace and of good things, both for the Church and humankind at large.

For this reason our heart is filled with emotion as we receive the glad news of the brotherly response from the West which you bring us. We gather this missive from your honored hands, and with deep love and esteem we turn our thoughts towards the one who entrusted you with it, our most holy brother Pope Paul VI, beloved partner in the exchanges on the Mount of Olives and fellow builder of Christian unity. Filled with sacred memories of that blessed meeting between us, we send him our cordial brotherly salutation and our warm thanks for the mission on which you come. You are here to manifest to our Orthodox Church, in a more concrete form and within the context of sacred historical responsibilities, the positive response of the venerable Roman Catholic Church to the recent official communication, through our Patriarchal delegation, of the decisions of the Third Pan-Orthodox Conference. These in a similar concrete fashion expressed the desire of the Orthodox to carry out the dialogue of charity without delay, and to make a careful preparation for the theological dialogue.

His Holiness, in coming forward with this positive response in the name of the venerable Roman Catholic Church, could not have communicated it to us, and through our lowly self to our entire Orthodox Church of the East, by means of a more suitable person than Your Eminence. For we know well that since the time when Pope John XXIII, that unforgettable and inspired herald and worker for Christian peace and unity, summoned you to be responsible for the promotion of Christian unity, you have been the best and most diligent interpreter of the spirit and the sincere dispositions both of that late holy Pope and of our brother gloriously exercising the chief priestly office in Rome today. You have been the faithful and tireless worker for the ideal of unity, and have contributed greatly, in cooperation with the devoted helpers who are standing here at your side, both to the cultivation of this ideal within the domain of your own Church, and to its promotion in dealings with our Church, and more generally with the whole Christian world. For this reason we thank you in a special manner for the blessed fact of your arrival here.

This moment offers Christians and the world the sacred witness of the full agreement of the Orthodox and the Roman Catholic Churches in their aim to reestablish unity. And this, with the fear of God, in loyalty to the truth and to love, with eagerness and understanding, and systematically following a set programme. But for an accurate appreciation of the significance and holy grandeur of this moment, we must take account of it both as oppressively overshadowed by the past, and as seen under the hope enkindling light of future prospects.

Why should we hide it? If we turn our gaze backwards we perceive with alarm a recent "yesterday" heavily subjected to opposing claims, alienation, and antagonistic strivings, and having as its characteristic features sundering and mutual separation, themselves deriving from and maintained by the absence of charity.

But glory be to God, maker of "today!" Today we fasten our gaze on the historic happenings we have lived through, and we discover the firm basis of our ancient brotherhood, and upon it we see the work of rebuilding going ahead. Today, both in the West and in our East decisions are being taken and gestures of love and edification made which would have seemed incredible a short time ago. At this point we take the opportunity of assuring you that every positive action of this kind taken by you is greeted with the greatest joy and satisfaction on our side. We follow with great attention and interest the work of the Second Vatican Council, and more generally every evidence of ecumenical intent proceeding from your venerable Church. We greatly appreciate all the edifying decisions and moves made by it. Of course we do not fail to recognize the number and the gravity of the problems before us. But in the restoration of charity, as we bring an end to estrangement and bridge gulfs, we judge our differences under a new light. Standing closer to one another, we seek the best road towards the future, one which promises a rectification of past wrongs and the restoration of the ancient beauty of the one and undivided Church.

Consequently how sacred and full of responsibility is the work of the present time, which by divine condescension has been placed in our hands! Towards this work Christians and the entire world gaze with hope, awaiting from us the signal for the abolition of the dividing wall of schism and for the restoration of the unity of all, so that the peace of Christ may prevail over the earth.

Let us then go forward. Let us remove the obstacles. "Let us make straight the paths of the Lord" (Is 40:3; Mt 3:3; Mk 1:3; Lk 3:4). Let us submit ourselves entirely to his holy will, "looking to each other's interest and not merely to our own" (Phil 2:4). Above all let us pray with humility. As we proceed with this spiritual and practical preparation, "forgetting what lies behind, and straining forward to what lies ahead" (Phil 3:13), and maintaining in charity our exchanges with one another in order to present the truth of Christ shining more brightly, let us make our way to the Easter which we share together, in virtue of which we are to be made worthy of proclaiming the Risen Lord to the whole world.

To him be glory in his saints for all ages. Amen.

Welcome, my brothers!

95.   *4 April 1965*

Address of welcome to Cardinal Bea at the Theological College of Halki, given by Bishop Andrew of Claudioupolis on behalf of the Rector**

This venerable and long famous sacred Theological College welcomes you, Your Eminence, with profound emotion and deep and inexpressible joy. It welcomes you as the first high and official visitor from the Church of Rome. And it is with a joy beyond words that it religiously receives your blessing, which it sees as a presage of communion between our two Churches.

It welcomes you together with the first signs of Spring, this breathtaking burst of Nature's beauty. But it welcomes you even more, at this beginning of the dialogue, as a sweet-smelling perfume of great price, to a meeting of historic importance for the whole world, a meeting on this far side of the centuries, directed towards the complete unity of the Church of Christ: unity in spirit, and unity of worship.

And this hill, this sacred Theological College, as a spiritual center, as a theological foundation, as a lofty teaching post of the divine message to man, and also as a seat of Orthodox theology,[27] looks towards a collaboration with the theological universities of Rome for the sake of Christian truth, as this is taught through the course of history. This teaching takes its rise from the great gift which was made to the human race in the divine Revelation, through which the unity of the Church is assured, and with it the one and only salvation of the whole human race.

In the midst of this whole movement of love of the two Churches, a movement directed towards better dealings with one another and the closing of the gap between us as we both meditate on the Christian spirit—at such a point then our College looks with intense interest on this visit of yours, which it sees as a golden link in the chain of relations between our Churches, and as the announcement of a new brotherhood indissoluble in love.

This visit, Your Eminence, forms the most significant event, as far as relations between our two Churches are concerned, that has occurred throughout the whole history of our College from the times of its foundation. Your visit is the dawn of a new spirit of love which binds together the two centers of our Churches, and the world will rejoice because of it. For this reason we, too, sing with all our hearts: "Hosannah, blessed is he who comes in the name of the Lord!"

96.　*4 April 1965*

Address of Cardinal Bea at the Theological College of Halki*

My dear Students,

I am very glad to be here to greet you in your fine theological school, where His Excellency the Rector and all the professors have welcomed me with so much kindness and affection. I have heard talk about Halki for a long time past, and today I see with joy that the praise I heard of it was not exaggerated, but expressed the simple truth. Your Rector has invited me to say a few words to you, and I do this very willingly to encourage you in the double work, which is not always easy, of your formation in the spiritual life and in your theological studies. I do not think I can do better than remind you of the profound words of St. Paul: "The love of Christ impels us who have

---

27. The College, on the island of Halki in the Sea of Marmora, served until recently as a training center for the clergy of the Ecumenical Patriarchate.

reached the conviction that since one died for all, all died. He died for us all so that those who live might no longer live for themselves, but for him who for their sakes died and was raised up" (2 Cor 5:14–15). It would be hard to find a thought or a rule more appropriate for anyone who in our time wants to consecrate his life to the service of the Church; hard, too, to find a principle of life more attractive and convincing for contemporary man, or more necessary for the world in which we live and work, than that expressed in this passage of the Second Letter to the Corinthians. St. Paul is speaking of the apostle whose faith in the mission and the sacrifice of Christ for human kind will not let him rest, who calls his powers into play and deploys them in all sorts of ways so that men and women—all of them—may know and accept Christ, that they may be taken hold of by him and transformed, and may receive salvation in him both in time and in eternity.

1) For every priest and servant of the Church this faith in Jesus Christ, priest and victim on behalf of all mankind, will first and foremost shape his personal life, deepening his own union with Christ, and transforming his life in accordance with the example of the life, sacrifice, and work of Christ. He knows indeed that Christ, by the power which has been conferred upon him, gives eternal life to all those whom the Father has given him (Jn 17:2), and that this takes place and must take place first of all through and in virtue of the sacrifice of Jesus, according to his word: "And for their sake I consecrate myself, that they also may be consecrated in truth" (Jn 17:19). Thus he "came not to be served by others but to serve, to give his life a ransom for many" (Mt 20:28). In the same way, in a life and activity consecrated to the service of the Kingdom of God, it is holiness and sacrifice which make action effective for the good of souls. It is a general law that only he who has life can communicate it, and that he communicates it in the degree in which he has it; and the life so communicated will be the better in so far as the life of him who communicates it is better. In the supernatural order of life in Christ this means that a man serves all the more perfectly as a means of communicating this life in so far as he is the more closely united to its source, to the Blessed Trinity, to Christ and to his Church, "Mother of all the living." Since this union is a gift of the love of God for men, of his "philanthropy," the person who wishes to cooperate in the communication of supernatural life ought himself to live in the Holy Spirit, and thus in holiness; and he will be the better able to cooperate in the measure in which his holiness is greater.

2) There is a second idea which I should like to outline for you. Men and women of our time, by a special grace which the Lord gives

them, are becoming more and more aware of the essential and indispensable part played in carrying out the work of Christ among humankind by the unity of all those who already know Christ and believe in him. It is in fact this unity which will bring the world to faith, as Christ himself tells us in his sacerdotal prayer when he entreats the Father for the unity of his followers, so that by this "the world may believe that you have sent me" (Jn 16:21). Unity is the sign by which the world is to know and recognize the divine mission of Christ, to believe in him, and to find its own salvation in him. Now the source of such a unity is once more Christ himself, it is union with him in accordance with his words: "that they may be one in us," that is to say, that they may be one in virtue of their union with the Father and the Son. This grave and urgent duty of bringing about unity leads us back once more to union with Christ and to the transformation of our life after the pattern of the life of Christ, according to the well known saying of St. Paul: "with Christ I am crucified, and it is no longer I who live, but it is Christ who lives in me." It is then first of all this union and transformation into Christ which we ought to look for on our own behalf, and it is to it that we ought also to lead the faithful committed to our priestly ministry and apostolate.

These then are some thoughts on what an authentic and elevating programme of life consecrated to Christ and his Church could be. This programme is always relevant, but how much more in our own time! What makes it especially pertinent nowadays is the powerful operation of the Holy Spirit, who is inspiring Christians with a deep feeling of regret, of repentance, of *metanoia,* with respect to divisions, and with a nostalgia for unity in Christ. This unity is insistently called for by the immense needs of mankind today. On the one hand, the human race is continually threatened by grave dangers to peace and harmony among peoples, and on the other it is in search of its own unity on every level, right up to the unity of the entire family of man. It is clear that this unity can only be found and implemented in Christ, for "there is no other name in the whole world given to men by which we are to be saved" (Acts 4:12). We are dealing then with matters of major moment for humanity, with God's plan for it, and thus with the supreme glorification of God in mankind. We must all make a serious and unremitting effort to advance the designs of God and with them the best interests of mankind. May the Lord enable you to prepare yourselves effectively, both by your studies and the cultivation of an interior life, for this eminently apostolic task. This is what I wish you from the bottom of my heart, and what I was anxious to tell you, while thanking the Lord for my being here among you.

97. *10 April 1965*

Letter of Cardinal Bea to Patriarch Athenagoras, thanking him for the welcome*

I do not want to wait any longer before expressing my deep gratitude for the very sensitive and considerate kindness which you heaped upon me. This gratitude is shared by those who accompanied me, and, while it is directed to you in the first place, it applies also to all your helpers, who made it their constant care that our stay at Istanbul should pass by profitably and well. They achieved their aim perfectly, and I must tell you that my memory of this first meeting is suffused with joy and deep feeling, and that it was for me an unforgettable experience.

I would be happy if you would transmit my warmest thanks to your eminent fellow workers.

Once more I wish Your Holiness a good and holy feast of Easter, and I ask you kindly to accept the expression of my very respectful and brotherly affection in the Lord.

98. *15 April 1965*

Telegram from Patriarch Athenagoras to Pope Paul VI, sending him Easter greetings*

As we direct our brotherly greetings in the Risen Christ to Your venerable and beloved Holiness, we wish you length of days to celebrate for a long time to come the life-giving Resurrection of the Lord, and to see the world at peace, in accordance with the desire expressed in your discourse of Palm Sunday.

99. *18 April 1965*

Telegram from Pope Paul VI to Patriarch Athenagoras sending him Easter greetings*

Your Holiness's best wishes for Easter revive in us cherished memories of the historic meeting at Jerusalem, the fruits of which we see ripening in our drawing together more and more in a brotherly spirit. May the Risen Christ bless our efforts and pour forth his peace and Easter joy into your soul.

100.   *31 May 1965*

Letter of Cardinal Bea to Patriarch Athenagoras, inviting him to send observers to the Fourth Session of the Vatican Council*

I have the honor of informing you that the Fourth Session of the Vatican Council will begin on 14 September 1965. Given the fact that His Holiness Pope Paul has announced that this next session of the Council will be the last one, we cannot yet say exactly how long it will last. However, the conclusion of the Council is expected to take place in all probability before Christmas 1965.

We give thanks to God as we remember the fraternal collaboration of the observer-delegates of the Ecumenical Patriarchate during the preceding session of the Council. We hope that this collaboration will continue during the Fourth Session, and that it will play its part in creating still closer relations between our Churches in the charity and truth of Christ.

I would ask you to be so kind as to let us know the names and addresses of the observer-delegates of your Patriarchate. This would enable us to send them more detailed information together with the documents for the next session, either directly or by the means you judge most appropriate.

The memory of the meeting which God Our Lord granted me to have with you is still very fresh in my mind. It is in a spirit of joy and gratitude that I would ask Your Holiness to accept the expression of my brotherly and respectful feelings in Christ Jesus.

101.   *10 June 1965*

Letter of Patriarch Athenagoras to Cardinal Bea, assuring him that the names of the observers will soon be forwarded**

We in our turn remain affected by the happiness brought about by the visit here of Your very dear and esteemed Eminence, and it was thus that we received with joy your letter of the 31st of last month, and read it both privately and aloud in a session of our Holy Synod. In it you inform us that the next and last session of the Second Vatican Council will begin on 14 September next, and ask us to let you know the names of the observers who will attend the Council on behalf of our Holy Ecumenical See.

We thank you warmly for the above mentioned announcement,

and we inform you that the names of the observers who will be sent to follow the work of the Council during its Fourth Session will be communicated to you very soon.

We embrace you with a holy kiss, and remain with brotherly love and appropriate respect.

102.   *13 June 1965*

Letter to Pope Paul VI from Patriarch Athenagoras, brought by Metropolitan Meliton, in reply to the Pope's letter of 31 March*

To Paul, the most blessed and holy Pope of ancient Rome, greetings in the Lord.

We were extremely anxious to convey to Your beloved and esteemed Holiness very clearly, by a special envoy, our profound interior joy and heartfelt gratitude for your sending us the distinguished delegation headed by His Eminence Cardinal Bea, in response to the visit to you of our own Patriarchal delegation, and for this reason we postponed writing to you until the present.

Now that we are able to send you on our behalf our beloved brother in Christ, His Eminence Metropolitan Meliton of Helioupolis and Theira, we forward at his hands our fraternal letter, and entrust him with the care of communicating by word of mouth our cordial brotherly greeting in the Lord.

In fact, beloved brother in Christ, the visit of your worthy delegation was the cause of much joy to our whole Church here and to me personally. It granted our two Churches a further opportunity of communion in the love of the Lord, and it marked a new and significant stage in the development and promotion of brotherly relations between them.

We welcomed His Eminence Cardinal Bea, President of the Secretariat for Christian Unity, together with his distinguished companions, with much love and befitting honour, and we received from the Cardinal's hand Your Holiness's much appreciated letter. At the same time we listened with uplifted hearts to his exposition of the views of your venerable Church. These concern the new prospects, arising by the grace of God from the Third Pan-Orthodox Conference and the Third Session of the Vatican Council, for more direct communication and contact between our Churches, and our working together with a view to the full restoration of brotherly communion.

We made a personal perusal of your letter, and then read it out with the care called for at a session of our Holy Synod. We took special joy in the information conveyed here as before that the anxiety, so pleasing to God, for Christian unity which was shown by your predecessor of holy memory, especially in his summoning of the Second Vatican Council, is also a matter of loving concern both for you and the venerable members of that Council.

From the brotherly letter of Your Holiness and the comments furnished by your distinguished representative, and indeed in a more general way the recent happy events brought about in the relations of the two Churches, together with the constructive exchange of views between them, we realize with joy that we have made our way successfully to a point of agreement. This bears on the fostering of brotherly relations through the dialogue inspired by the love of Christ, as a means of making that further progress which will enable us to face the problems which we both have concerning the capital and sacred theme of unity.

At this new God-given stage, we turn our gaze with confidence to the future, as it lies in the hands of our common Lord. It is our unshakeable purpose to bring about, in the service of God and in conjunction with Your Holiness, the prerequisite conditions for achieving the good goal: we shall conquer difficulties by practical steps and loving deeds, and set up once more the ancient unity.

Filled then with these feelings and dispositions, we again warmly thank you for this new witness which you have afforded us of the common nature of the aims, so pleasing to God, which both our Churches are pursuing. We thank you, too, for all the ways in which you have shown your brotherly love, and especially for so thoughtfully sending us the precious pectoral cross of your unforgettable predecessor, Pope John XXIII. This we shall keep as a valuable relic with the same deep affection and honor as we do the revered memory of that great hierarchical head.

And now we greet you with a holy kiss in our common Lord, and warmly entreat him to preserve you in health and length of days, in his peace and joy. We remain with brotherly love and special marks of honor.

> Your venerable Holiness's
> dear brother in Christ, . . .

103.   *18 June 165*

Telegram from Patriarch Athenagoras to Pope Paul VI on the second anniversary of his election to the See of Rome*

We cordially congratulate you on the second anniversary of your illustrious election. May the Lord grant to Your venerable Holiness physical and spiritual strength and vigor, so that for a long time to come you may honor the see of ancient Rome, and further the progress of the work so pleasing to God, the practical achievement of Christian unity.

104.   *21 June 1965*

Telegram from Pope Paul VI to Patriarch Athenagoras, thanking him for his good wishes*

The good wishes which Your Holiness sends us for the second anniversary of our election touch us deeply. We thank you wholeheartedly, and take this opportunity of assuring you that we shall continue with the help of God to pray and act for the great cause of Christian unity.

105.   *23 June 1965*

Telegram from Patriarch Athenagoras to Pope Paul VI on his patronal feast*

On the occasion of the sacred feast of St. John the Forerunner, Your venerable and beloved Holiness's heavenly patron, we are glad to be in touch with you again and send you our warm congratulations and our cordial good wishes for a long life blessed by the Lord. May you see peace reigning throughout the whole world, in accordance with your celebrated message. With much esteem and brotherly affection.

106.   *27 June 1965*

Telegram from Pope Paul VI to Patriarch Athenagoras, thanking him for his good wishes*

We were very touched by the thoughtful good wishes of Your Holiness on the occasion of the feast of our holy patron St. John. We thank you wholeheartedly and gladly assure you again that we are united in prayer on the great issues of the Church and of peace in the world.

107.   *9 July 1965*

Letter of Cardinal Bea to Patriarch Athenagoras in reply to the Patriarch's letter of 12 June*

Your Holiness,

I am very sorry that a temporary illness prevented me from meeting His Eminence Metropolitan Meliton of Helioupolis and Theira during his recent visit to Rome. I regret this all the more, as I would have been happy to tell him how grateful I am for the gift which he brought me on your behalf. This photograph which brings back to mind the time, all too short, which I spent with you and the hierarchy and faithful people of your Church, has caused me keen pleasure, and I should like to express my deep gratitude.

I thank you also for the letter in which you inform me that observers are being sent from the Ecumenical Patriarchate to the Fourth and last Session of the Vatican Council, and that their names will be shortly released. You know that they will be welcomed with a deeply sincere brotherly love, and that we shall do our utmost to enable them to follow the work of the Council as well as possible.

Would Your Holiness be so good as to accept the expression of my feelings of respectful and brotherly affection in the Lord.

108.   *10 July 1965*

Letter of Pope Paul VI to Patriarch Athenagoras, thanking him for the presence in Rome of Metropolitan Meliton, and for the gift of an icon of the two holy apostles Peter and Andrew*

Very dear brother in Christ,

It was an unexpected joy on our part to receive the visit of His Eminence the Metropolitan Meliton of Helioupolis and Theira, who handed us the letter from Your Holiness. We thank you for this pleasant surprise, but above all we wish to tell you how moved we were by the magnificent icon of the two holy brother apostles, Peter the Coryphaeus and Andrew the First-Called.[28] It expresses so beautifully the

---

28. *Coryphaeus* originally signified the leader of a dramatic chorus in ancient Greece. In Greek Christian writing, the word has long been used to designate the leading position of Peter with the band of Apostles. For Andrew as *Protokletos,* the "First-Called," cf. Jn 1:40–41. Andrew is traditionally regarded as the founder of the Church

deep meaning of our holy encounter and the fraternal embrace which we exchanged at Jerusalem with the light of Christ and the look of his face upon us. This icon sums up a whole programme, for which reason we have decided to entrust it to the keeping of our Secretariat for Christian Unity.

This programme is expressed in happy and well chosen terms by the letter which Your Holiness sent us, and we should like very much to express our gratitude to you for it. May the Spirit of the Lord cause all Christians, following the lead of their pastors, to strive to make this programme become increasingly, day by day, truth and life.

It is with these thoughts in mind that we express once more our deep and brotherly affection in Christ Jesus, our one and only Lord.

109.   *26 July 1965*

Letter of Patriarch Athenagoras to Cardinal Bea in reply to his letter of 9 July, thanking him for the visit of Bishop Willebrands**

We gladly received the letter of the 9th of this current month of July from Your very loved and esteemed Eminence, and read it privately and then before a session of our Holy Synod. In it you inform us that, owing to an upset to your health you were unable to meet His Eminence Metropolitan Meliton of Helioupolis and Theira who had just come to Rome, and you thank us for sending you our photograph.

We express our sympathy with regard to the illness of which we hear from your letter, and we wish you a speedy and complete recovery for the good of the Church of Christ.

On the occasion of the visit here a few days ago of those who accompanied you before, Bishop Willebrands of Mauriana and Father Pierre Duprey, we recalled with gladness of heart the days which Your beloved Eminence came to spend with us, the brotherly talk and good thoughts which we exchanged with one another, and the prayers which we sent up to the Lord that he might direct us all to the longed for

---

at Byzantium, later Constantinople, the New Rome. As Peter is acknowledged as the founder of the Church in the Old Rome, a symmetry is seen between the two Apostles and their sees, and this is made more significant as Peter and Andrew are brothers (Jn 1:40).

The icon which depicts the fraternal embrace of Andrew and Peter was then given by Pope Paul to the SPCU; it now hangs in the main conference room of its offices.

union of our Churches and in our working together for the glory of his name.

In conclusion we beg for Your very beloved Eminence the choicest gifts from God's hand, and remain with much love and fitting respect.

110. *19 August 1965*

Letter of Pope Paul VI to Patriarch Athenagoras, thanking him for a gift*

Very dear brother in Christ,

It was a happy surprise to receive the present which Your Holiness so kindly sent us. This gesture brings out once again with delicate sensitivity the feelings of affection which unite us. And so in expressing our gratitude to you, dear and venerable brother, for this fine gift, we thank God with deep joy for allowing this love to deepen and expand, thus fulfilling step by step this prayer of your holy liturgy: "Let us love one another, so that with one mind we may confess the Father, Son, and Holy Spirit, the consubstantial and undivided Trinity."

We should like very much also to thank Your Holiness for the interest which you are taking in the Vatican Council, and for the prayers which you devote to it, which will stand us in good stead on the eve of the opening of the Fourth and last Session. May the Lord cause this session to be rich in useful decisions not only for the renewal of the Catholic Church, but also for that of the whole Christian world.

We express once again, beloved brother, our feelings of sincere and deep affection in Christ Jesus Our Lord and Master.

111. *25 August 1965*

Letter of Patriarch Athenagoras to Cardinal Bea, communicating the names of the delegated observers to the Fourth Session of the Council**

Supplementary to the contents of our letter to you of 10 June this year, we are happy to inform you that by synodical procedure we have appointed as observers of the work of the Second Vatican Council, for its Fourth and last Session, His Excellency Metropolitan Emilianos of Calabria and the Very Reverend Archimandrite Maximos Agiorgousis.

We pray wholeheartedly for the success of the work of the Council during this next period, and embrace Your Eminence with a holy kiss, remaining with brotherly love and special regard.

112. *26 August 1965*

Letter of Patriarch Athenagoras to Cardinal Bea, congratulating him on his being nominated member of the Academy of Athens[29]**

We have learned with a quite special joy that Your dear and esteemed Eminence has been proclaimed as a member by the Academy of Athens. This distinction, accorded to you who have won such an honorable name in the intellectual world at large, could not fail to touch us and our Holy Synod very deeply, holding in high esteem as we do your many sided work and your brilliant personality.

By a synodal resolution, then, we cordially congratulate you on this well deserved distinction. We pray good health and length of days for you, and embracing you with a holy kiss, we remain with brotherly love and befitting respect.

113. *11 September 1965*

Telegram from Patriarch Athenagoras to Pope Paul VI on the opening of the Fourth Session of the Vatican Council*

As the opening of Fourth Session of the Second Vatican Council draws near, we send Your beloved and venerable Holiness our brotherly congratulations and our best wishes for a magnificent and happy conclusion of its work for the benefit of the whole Church of Our Lord Jesus Christ.

---

29. The Academy of Athens, founded in 1926, has sixty "regular members" chosen within Greece for their eminence in one of three divisions: science, literature and the fine arts; moral and political thought (including philosophy and theology); and forty "foreign associates" similarly distributed. Cardinal Bea was elected one of these.

114.   *14 September 1965*

Telegram from Pope Paul VI to Patriarch Athenagoras, thanking him for his good wishes for the Fourth Session of the Council*

The message which Your Holiness sends us, and which will be read at the opening of the Fourth Session of the Ecumenical Council, touches us deeply. We hope with you that the work of the Council will be blessed by God, and will lead to fruitful decisions for the good of the whole Church of Christ.

115.   *22 September 1965*

Letter from Cardinal Bea to Patriarch Athenagoras in reply to his letter of 26 August*

The insistent demands made by the activities of the first days of the Council prevented me from thanking you as promptly as I would have liked for the many kind and thoughtful signs of good will which you have shown me quite recently. The telegram of good wishes for the feast of St. Augustine, the letter of congratulations for my election to the Academy of Athens, the present which you arranged for the Very Reverend Archimandrite Scrima to bring me, amount in fact to so many touching indications of the extent of your obliging and unfailing affection. I recently had the opportunity of saying so to His Eminence the Metropolitan Chrysostom of Myra, who passed through here briefly.

I am very keenly aware that the congratulations on the honour done me by the Academy of Athens were offered not only in the name of Your Holiness, but also in those of their Excellencies the Metropolitans of the Holy Synod, whom I had the pleasure of meeting when I made my visit to the Ecumenical Patriarchate last April. I would be grateful if you were kind enough to transmit my thanks to the Holy Synod.

I beg Your Holiness to accept the expression of my respectful and brotherly affection in Christ Jesus.

116.   *23 September 1965*

Letter of Cardinal Bea to Patriarch Athenagoras, thanking him for the presence of the observers at the Council*

The news that His Excellency Metropolitan Emilianos of Calabria and the Very Reverend Archimandrite Maximos Agiorgousis had been appointed as observers of the Ecumenical Patriarchate at the Fourth Session of the Second Vatican Council was received with joy, and I should like to thank you very much for this.

You know how much the fathers of the Council appreciate the presence of these observers. Their being here is not only a tangible proof of the interest shown by your Church in the Vatican Council, but brings us valuable help and collaboration.

The applause of the fathers after the reading out of Your Holiness's telegram to the Holy Father for the opening of the Fourth Session clearly showed how much these feelings were shared by the bishops gathered around the tomb of the holy Apostle Peter.

Please accept, Your Holiness, my great gratitude, together with the expression of my feelings of respectful and brotherly affection in Christ Jesus.

PART II

Growth and Fruits of Dialogue

Nos 117–178   **September 29, 1965–
August 8, 1967**

Pope Paul VI . . . Patriarch Athenagoras I
(3)

Cancellation of historic anathemas between
Constantinople and Rome (119, 121–124, 126–130)
▪ Marriages between Catholics and Orthodox (146)
▪ Visit of Archbishop of Crete (147, 150, 156)
▪ Nineteenth centenary of martyrdom of Sts. Peter
and Paul, Orthodox participation (148, 155, 159–160,
162, 167, 169–170) ▪ *Ecumenical Directory* issued at
Rome and shown to Patriarch (159–161) ▪ Visit by
Pope Paul VI to the Ecumenical Patriarchate of
Constantinople (171–178)

117. *29 September 1965*

Telegram from Patriarch Athenagoras to Pope Paul VI on the occasion of his journey to the United Nations*

We follow with our prayers and affection Your beloved and venerable Holiness in your new and historic journey to the United Nations,[30] in order to bring to this institution and through it to the whole of mankind the message of peace of Our Lord Jesus Christ and of good will to men. We hope with all our heart that Almighty God will strengthen you in your sacred mission of worldwide importance, and that your call will find an echo in the hearts of the mighty ones of the earth, so that the peace and love of God will keep the whole world in its protection.

118. *2 October 1965*

Telegram from Pope Paul VI to Patriarch Athenagoras, thanking him for his good wishes on the occasion of his last journey*

Many thanks to Your Holiness for your fine message. We shall leave for the headquarters of the United Nations with the brotherly support of your prayers and good wishes, and to a world racked with anxiety we shall strive to be a witness of the love of God and a messenger of the Lord who is Prince of Peace.

119. *18 October 1965*

Letter of Cardinal Bea to Patriarch Athenagoras about the anathemas of 1054*

The Very Reverend Archimandrite Andrew Scrima, your personal representative at the Ecumenical Council, will at my request have

---

30. The Pope addressed the General Assembly of the United Nations in New York City, 4 October.

already communicated to you the essentials of what I am now going to say, but I think I ought to confirm the message which he has delivered by word of mouth.

When His Eminence Metropolitan Meliton of Helioupolis and Theira, and more recently His Eminence Metropolitan Chrysostom of Myra visited Rome, they suggested that it would perhaps be possible to make a new and combined study, going right to the heart of the matter, of a canonical question which for nine centuries has helped to complicate and poison the relations between the Roman Catholic Church and the Patriarchate of Constantinople.

On our side preliminary historical investigation of this matter has already been carried out, and it is our opinion that a commission of four members appointed by us, and an equal number appointed by the Ecumenical Patriarchate, could be set up. I am proposing to Your Holiness that this commission have as its task to study this project, and to work out a formula which could be published simultaneously at Rome and Istanbul. This commission could meet, if you agree, at Istanbul, so that these contacts could take place quite soon, perhaps at the beginning of November. I am happy to take this opportunity to express once again to Your Holiness my feelings of respectful and brotherly affection in Christ Jesus.

120. *12 November 1965*

Letter of Pope Paul VI to Patriarch Athenagoras thanking him for his prayer for the success of the Council*

Venerable and very dear brother in Christ,

At the moment when the Council is about to reach its conclusion—this Council which you have so often kindly let us know was the matter of your fervent prayers to Heaven—we feel ourselves constrained to tell Your Holiness how much we thank you for this brotherly support. As we have asked only just now of the pastors and the faithful people of the Catholic Church, so we want also to ask Your Holiness to continue this kindness, so that the Council may come to completion under the blessing of God. May the steps which have been taken there be courageously and intelligently implemented, above all with regard to the approach to full unity on the part of all Christians, in order that this Council may produce rich fruit for the peace of the world and the reign of God.

We eagerly seize this opportunity to tell you again, venerable and beloved brother, how great an affection we bear you, and how this makes us enter personally into both your joys and tribulations, and leads us to assure you that you can always count on finding in us an open heart, and one anxious in all circumstances to make clear the deep reality of its fraternal feeling.

May the Lord whose Spirit is guiding us grant you richly of his light and strength and keep us in his love.

121. *16 November 1965*

Letter of Cardinal Bea to Patriarch Athenagoras, giving him the names of the Catholic members of the Joint Commission appointed to study the anathemas of 1054*

The Archimandrite Andrew Scrima's journey to Istanbul gives me the opportunity of entrusting him with a reply to the recent telegram by which you told me that you were in agreement with the proposals contained in my letter of 18 October 1965.

I should like first of all to thank you for receiving these proposals so favorably, and to let you know definitely that we have immediately begun work, with proper circumspection, in preparation for this encounter. It seems to me indeed highly important that at this juncture great discretion should be used with regard to the meeting, to avoid furnishing a pretext for the further spread of inaccurate rumors which are already going the rounds in the world press. These are such as to make it harder for the Joint Commission to carry out the delicate task confided to it.

The special Commission which the Holy Father has decided to appoint expects to arrive at Istanbul on Sunday 21 November at 7:30 p.m. (Flight OA 266). This Commission will have as its president His Excellency Bishop Willebrands, and will comprise the following members:

Monsignor Michele Maccarrone, President of the Pontifical Committee for Historical Studies; the Very Reverend A. Raes, S.J., Prefect of the Vatican Library; the Very Reverend Don Alphonsus Stickler, Rector of the Pontifical Salesian Athenaeum; the Very Reverend C. J. Dumont, O.P., Director of the *Istina* center.

Bishop Willebrands will be accompanied by the Very Reverend Father Pierre Duprey, whose presence could prove useful to the Commission.

In the hope that God will bless these efforts which have no aim other than conformity to his mysterious designs and faithful obedience to his holy will, I beg Your Holiness to accept the expression of my deep and respectful affection in the Lord.

122.　*22 November 1965*

Address of Metropolitan Meliton of Helioupolis and Theira, Co-President of the Joint Commission, at the inception of its work**

Dear Brothers,

Welcome! Now that we have prayed together, glorifying and thanking our heavenly Father, allow me to express in my own name and that of my brothers our great joy at your arrival and presence here among us.

Personally I am especially fortunate, since I have the honour of conveying to you, distinguished and very dear representatives of the venerable Roman Catholic Church, the cordial greetings of His Holiness our Ecumenical Patriarch and of our Holy Synod, and of assuring you that the Church of Constantinople welcomes you with feelings of the deepest brotherly love and honour. We greatly appreciate the fact that you have been so willing to incur the trouble of coming here for this happy and blessed meeting, and we thank you warmly for this courteous and cordial gesture.

We come together as instructed by our Churches to make a common study of a particular subject—those events of the year 1054 which took place between the sees of Rome and Constantinople, and by cooling the charity between them contributed to the separation of our Churches. We are to explore together some way of rectifying from either side what can be rectified, with the aim of removing an obstacle to the further development of brotherly relations and the dialogue between our Churches.

Even though we here, as a study group required to submit our findings to our Churches, have only a limited mandate—the final approval and decision to act resting with our Churches themselves— still the work ahead with which we have been entrusted is sacred and important, in so far as by this means we are called upon to justify the common holy desire and hope of our Churches for the building up of charity.

The Providence and accommodating kindness of God has laid upon us, through the medium of our Churches, a responsibility which, while doing us honor, makes certain demands upon us. We are not to lose sight of two realities, one divine and the other human, which press upon us. On the one hand is the fact "what is impossible to men is possible to God" (Mt 19:26), and on the other we must ask what are the possibilities offered us by the particular positions of our Churches in the present stage of our relations.

We are to advance towards our work with the firm resolution of offering the best that is within us—what we find it possible to do in our highest moments under the controlling influence of the Holy Spirit. In the most conciliatory and constructive way we are to interpret and formulate the common desire and will of our Churches. Above all, in doing this we are to commit ourselves and one another to the mystery of God's love and ordering power.

Presupposing this, and keeping in view the general basic data of both sides up to this moment, I shall attempt a brief overall review of our subject matter as a first modest contribution to our work.

1. *Where do we come together?*

We encounter each other on the road where love is being restored between the Roman Catholic and the Orthodox Church, a road which was opened up by Pope Paul VI and Patriarch Athenagoras I through their holy meeting in Jerusalem, and then widened by exchanges and declarations of good quality, and by significant acts on both sides. This has been so on the one hand between the Roman Catholic Church and the Church of Constantinople and also the other local Autocephalous Orthodox Churches, and on the other hand between the Roman Catholic Church and the Orthodox body as a whole. Furthermore, we meet in the favorable climate of Christian ecumenism, facing a general call of the Christian and non-Christian world for reconciliation, peace, and the activity of every person in a position of responsibility who can contribute to this cause.

2. *What are we seeking?*

We are seeking through deeds which are really positive and conducive to the restoration of charity, to obliterate the grievous acts of the past which then banished charity between the two Churches, helped to break their links, and in time became symbolic of their division. In this way what we do will have the most considerable and effective results possible for an easier development of further fraternal relations between the two Churches in the contemporary context.

3. *Who are those immediately concerned?*

The sad events of the year 1054 involved the sees of Rome and Constantinople, thence taking on a further extension; and the persons who played the leading roles (which included mutual anathemas) belonged to these same Churches. Hence the two sees of Rome and Constantinople are first and most immediately concerned in restoring the former state of affairs. The task of putting right those earlier deeds falls under their jurisdiction and is their responsibility, and calls on their part now for justice and a willingness to serve others. The Church of Constantinople is convinced that, just as in former times the negative effects went on to become the possession of the Orthodox East, so now the beneficent sequel will also become a common possession in those parts. It is in this spirit that the Church of Constantinople understands its duty of service in the present situation towards its sister Orthodox Churches in various places.

4. *From what points of ecclesiastical principle do we proceed?*
   We proceed from the following matters of principle:
   a) That the desire for rectification is common to both Churches, i.e., that of Rome and that of Constantinople.
   b) That the rectification is to take place mutually, with each of the two Churches playing its part, according to the traditions and customs of each.
   c) That the declaration of the common desire, decision, and action will itself be made in common.

5. *Character of the act*
   The act of rectification which is the object of our study will be an act of love, removing an obstacle to our endeavor to cultivate brotherly relations between the two Churches. In a more general way it contributes to the promotion of the dialogue between the Roman Catholic Church and the entire Orthodox Church, aiming at the right achievement, with God's guidance, of the unity they desire.
   This act does not mean the restoration of full communion between the Roman Catholic and Orthodox Churches, seeing that it does not bring about any transformation of the present situation of the two Churches as regards dogmatic teaching, canonical order, divine worship, and Church life generally. Nor does it imply the restoration of a common sacramental life.

6. *The usefulness of the act and the outlook implied in it*
   If the act under study is to be justly appreciated, it must be seen within the wider outlook of the two Churches, which involves the fulfilment of the divine will "that they may be one." As regards this final aim, this act amounts to a new and positive step of historical impor-

tance, for the following reasons. In place of the symbol of enmity and division, it raises aloft the symbol of love and *rapprochement;* it becomes the beginning of rectification of other historical mistakes; it gives a firm basis for confidence, and creates a favorable psychological factor; it prepares suitable conditions for the examination of differences; above all it thus gives wider scope for the activity of the Holy Spirit.

From this point of view the usefulness of the act extends to the whole body of the Roman Catholic and the Orthodox Churches. Moreover it furnishes a contribution to the general cause of Christian unity, since it becomes an example of activity for other Christian Churches as well. In addition to which it meets a basic need of the contemporary world, contributing to universal peace through deeds which can serve as an example to others.

Humble servants as we are, appointed for such a great and good work, let us apply ourselves to the faithful carrying out of our task, keeping in mind the words of those who announced the good news: "charity casts out fear," and "charity builds up" (1 Jn 4:18; 1 Cor 8:2). Thus like men rendered free from fear by Christian love, let us build through that love in Christ our common Lord, to whom with the Father and the Holy Spirit, be glory for ever and ever.

123. *22 November 1965*

Address of Bishop John Willebrands, Co-President of the Joint Commission, in reply to the address of Metropolitan Meliton (a summary based on notes taken during the speech)*

The Church of ancient Rome has taken note of the feelings and desires of its sister Church of new Rome with regard to the tragic happenings of 1054, particularly the mutual excommunications which at that time created a state of conflict and enmity between the two Churches. These feelings were directly communicated to our Church by His Eminence Metropolitan Meliton when he came to Rome to deliver the icon of the holy Apostles Peter and Andrew to Pope Paul VI as a present from Patriarch Athenagoras.

The Holy Father was very moved to learn that Patriarch Athenagoras I desired that the faults of the past should be set right, and he not merely approved this desire but made it his own. To give some effect to this common policy the Pope has created a special commission to examine these regrettable events from the historical, canonical, and theological points of view, together with their subsequent bearing on the life of the Church.

I have the honor of introducing the members of the Commission: Monsignor M. Maccarone, President of the Pontifical Committee for Historical Studies, Rome; the Very Reverend Father A. Raes, S.J., Prefect of the Vatican Library, Rome; Monsignor Christophe Dumont, O.P., Director of the *Istina* Study Centre, Paris; the Reverend Father P.A. Stickler, Rector of the Pontifical Salesian Athenaeum, Rome; the Very Reverend Father P. Duprey, Under-Secretary of the Secretariat for Christian Unity.

After preparatory studies and researches the Commission worked out a plan for a common declaration, and we have sent this on to His Holiness the Patriarch as a subject matter for study in the session of the combined working group. This plan will be freely discussed and subjected to a further handling carried out in common by the group. Then, if by the Lord's grace we reach agreement on a written statement to which we can all subscribe, this will be presented to the heads of our Churches, His Holiness Pope Paul VI and His Holiness Patriarch Athenagoras I, for their approval.

While leaving the Commission fully free to discuss matters and make proposals, what His Holiness has in mind is not to try to analyse and unravel all the still obscure historical details, but to heal the situation by purging memories of the past, so as to

- attain new relations between our Churches,
- make our dialogue deeper, more open, and more inspired by the Holy Spirit,
- make the communion between our Churches more fraternal, more profoundly rooted in Christ, and more fully pervasive of Church life,
- prepare the ways of the Lord, who will lead us to the fulness of communion in him.

Before leaving Rome I spoke in confidence to the observers of the Orthodox Churches, and told them, by way of information, that we were going to Constantinople and why. Those concerned were: His Excellency Metropolitan Emilianos; Archpriest Vitaly Borovoy of the Moscow Patriarchate; Archpriests Milin and Kasič of the Serbian Orthodox Church; Archimandrite John of the Bulgarian Orthodox Church.

Furthermore, after the meeting of the Joint Working Group of the Roman Catholic Church and the World Council of Churches, which ended Saturday 20 November, I confidentially informed Dr. Visser 't Hooft.[31]

Invocation of the Lord's blessing. Conclusion.

124. *23 November 1965*

Minutes of the proceedings of the Joint Commission* **

Members of the Commission:

Representing the Roman Catholic Church:

His Excellency Bishop John Willebrands, President;
Monsignor Michele Maccarone;
Rev. Father Alphonsus Raes;
Rev. Father Alphonsus Stickler;
Rev. Father Christophe Dumont.

Representing the Orthodox Church of Constantinople:

His Eminence Metropolitan Meliton of Helioupolis, President;
His Eminence Metropolitan Chrysostom of Myra;
Rev. Father Gabriel, Chief Secretary of the Holy Synod;
Rev. Father George Anastasiadis;
Rev. Father Evangelos, Great Archdeacon.

Acting as secretaries:

Rev. Father Pierre Duprey;
Rev. Father Andrew Scrima;
Rev. Father Paul, Under-Secretary of the Holy Synod.

The Catholic delegates, having arrived at Istanbul 21 November 1965, presented themselves to His Holiness Patriarch Athenagoras.

The sessions of the Joint Commission took place in the Patriarchal Palace, and were presided over alternately by His Excellency

---

31. The WCC Central Committee, at its meeting in Enugu (Nigeria), 12–21 January, 1965, and soon afterwards Pope Paul VI, approved the establishment of a Joint Working Group which would recommend to the parent bodies both the agenda and the means of collaboration in study and action. Dr. W. A. Visser 't Hooft and Bishop John Willebrands were the co-chairmen.

Bishop Willebrands and His Eminence Metropolitan Meliton of Helioupolis.

On Monday 22 November, at the first working session, His Eminence Metropolitan Meliton welcomed the visitors and set out in exact terms the purpose and task of the Joint Commission. His Excellency Bishop Willebrands replied on behalf of the Catholic Commission, expressing his happiness at this encounter and in the new experience of working together. He emphasized the full agreement between what His Holiness Pope Paul VI desired and what Metropolitan Meliton had said about the work of the Commission in his exposition.

The Commission set about examining a proposed common statement on the events of 1054, which statement served as a basic text for a discussion of the events themselves and their effects on subsequent relations between the two Churches. This examination and discussion was carried on into the afternoon of the same day and throughout the whole following day. It led to a unanimous agreement on the nature of the events in which the Churches of Rome and Constantinople were involved, and on the possibility of a common statement on their part regretting these events and removing them from the memory and the midst of the Church, so that they could no longer serve as an obstacle towards a drawing together in charity.

The French and Greek texts of this statement were closely studied, so that each should correspond exactly to the other. These texts were formally approved during the afternoon session of Tuesday 23 November with a view to being submitted for confirmation by the two Churches, and are attached to these minutes.

The Orthodox delegation then tabled the proposal that a motion on both sides recording their common desire to express regret for all that called for regret, and to make good all that could be made good, concerning the events under study affecting both Churches, should be passed in each of these Churches, in accordance with the text of the common statement. This proposal was carefully examined and discussed. The Catholic delegation showed itself favorable to this proposal, and prepared to recommend it to the attention of Pope Paul VI. The Orthodox delegation brought forward a draft plan of possible action by the Ecumenical Patriarch.

The two delegations had the opportunity of exchanging their views on what would be the most appropriate procedure for producing such declarations on either side, and for promulgating them in conjunction with the common statement in one concerted action.

The Joint Commission had no power to make decisions, each of the delegations being obliged to refer the results of the discussions and exchanges of view to the higher ecclesiastical authority of its Church.

125. *2 December 1965*

Letter of Patriarch Athenagoras, thanking Pope Paul VI for his letter of 12 November*

To Paul, the most blessed and holy Pope of Ancient Rome, greetings in the Lord.

We received with affection and read with pleasure, both privately and at a session of our Holy Synod, the precious and brotherly letter of the twelfth of last month from Your beloved and venerable Holiness. In it you show your love for us and your keen interest in our concerns, an interest indeed which you never cease to manifest in a practical way on every occasion.

By a decision of our Synod, we send Your venerable Holiness the warm thanks of our holy Church and our own personally for this attitude of yours so full of eagerness and brotherly love. We pray wholeheartedly that our Lord and Savior may ever increase the joy that comes from brotherhood and good will, and that he may lavish on Your Holiness, whom we can never forget, a rich store of his grace and blessing, as you go about the work of applying the decisions of the Second Vatican Council now auspiciously ending, for the good of the venerable Roman Catholic Church and the whole Christian world.

We embrace Your Holiness with a holy kiss, and remain with brotherly love and fitting respect.

Your venerable Holiness's
dear brother in Christ, . . .

126. *2 December 1965*

Letter of Patriarch Athenagoras to Cardinal Bea on the work of the Joint Commission**

The letter from Your dear and esteemed Eminence brought by the Very Reverend Archimandrite Andrew Scrima and delivered to us on 16th of last month was read out in a session of our Holy Synod. In it you inform us that His Holiness Pope Paul VI, our beloved brother in

Christ, has set up a special Joint Commission under the presidency of His Excellency Bishop John Willebrands, to enter into study here with the corresponding Patriarchal Commission of our clergy on the important subject which has occupied us lately.

The findings of this common study are known to you through the report of the Commission headed by Bishop Willebrands which has now returned to Rome. We received this Commission on its arrival here with love and great joy and honour, and we understand that there is no need to supply you with further information about the conclusions reached.

We glorify then the venerable name of the all-good God who richly blesses this mutual endeavor of ours to fulfil the will of his beloved Son concerning his holy Church; and we warmly congratulate Your dear Eminence on the wise directives which you gave the Commission and your sincere Christian attitude. We embrace you with a holy kiss, and remain with brotherly love and fitting marks of honor.

127.   *7 December 1965*

A Common Declaration[32] made by Pope Paul VI and Patriarch Athenagoras, expressing their decision to remove from memory and from the midst of the Church the excommunications of 1054*   **

1. Full of gratitude towards God for the favor which in his mercy he has granted them of meeting one another in brotherly fashion in the sacred places where the mystery of our salvation was brought to fulfilment by the death and resurrection of the Lord Jesus, and where the Church received its birth by the outpouring of the Holy Spirit, Pope Paul VI and Patriarch Athenagoras I have kept in view the plan they then formed, each for his own part, to leave nothing undone in making such overtures as charity inspires and which could facilitate the development of the fraternal relations thus inaugurated between the Roman Catholic Church and the Orthodox Church of Constantinople. They

---

32. At this last solemn session of Vatican Council II in St. Peter's Basilica, Bishop Willebrands read the public declaration in French. Then the Pope exchanged the kiss of peace with Metropolitan Meliton, the Patriarch's representative. In the Cathedral of St. George at the Phanar in Constantinople, the same text was read in the presence of the Patriarch and of Cardinal Lawrence Shehan (Baltimore), the Pope's representative.

are persuaded that they are thus answering the call of divine grace, which is today leading the Roman Catholic Church and the Orthodox Church, together with all Christians, to overcome their points of difference, so as to be once more "one" as the Lord Jesus asked for them of his Father.

2. Among the obstacles along the way, as these brotherly relationships of trust and esteem are developed, there looms the memory of the decisions, actions and painful incidents which came to a head in 1054 in the sentence of excommunication passed on the Patriarch Michael Cerularios and two other persons by the legates of the Roman See, led by Cardinal Humbert, which legates were then themselves the object of a corresponding sentence on the part of the Patriarch and the Synod of Constantinople.

3. Nothing can be done to change the fact that these events were what they were in that particularly disturbed period of history. But now that a calmer and fairer judgment has been made about them, it is important to recognize the excesses by which they were marked, and which brought in their train consequences which, as far as we can judge, went beyond what was intended or foreseen by those responsible. Their censures bore on particular persons and not on the Churches, and were not meant to break the ecclesial communion between the sees of Rome and Constantinople.

4. It is for this reason that Pope Paul VI and Patriarch Athenagoras I in his Synod, being certain that they are expressing the common desire for justice and the unanimous feeling of charity of their faithful people, and remembering the Lord's command: "If you bring your gift to the altar and there recall that your brother has anything against you, leave your gift at the altar, and go first to be reconciled with your brother" (Mt 5:23–24), declare in mutual agreement:

a) that they regret the offending words, the baseless reproaches, and the blameworthy symbolic acts which on both sides marked or accompanied the sad events of this time;

b) that in the same way they regret and remove from memory and from the midst of the Church the sentences of excommunication which followed, the remembrance of which acts right up to our own times as an obstacle to our mutual approach in charity, and they condemn these to oblivion;

c) that they deplore, finally, the troublesome precedents and the further happenings which, under the influence of various factors, including misunderstanding and distrust on both sides, eventually led to a real rupture of ecclesial communion.

5. Pope Paul VI and Patriarch Athenagoras I together with his Synod are aware that this gesture, expressive of justice and mutual forgiveness, cannot be sufficient to put an end to the subjects of difference, ancient or more recent, which still exist between the Roman Catholic Church and the Orthodox Church, and which through the action of the Holy Spirit will be surmounted through the purification of hearts, through regret for the wrongs done in the course of history, and through a practical desire to reach a common understanding and expression of the apostolic faith and the demands it lays upon us.

In carrying out this symbolic action, however, they hope that it will be acceptable to God, who is quick to pardon us when we pardon one another, and that it will be appreciated by the whole Christian world, but above all by the general body both of the Roman Catholic Church and the Orthodox Church, as the expression of a sincere mutual desire for reconciliation, and as an invitation to follow up, in a spirit of trust, esteem, and mutual charity, the dialogue which will lead them with the help of God to live afresh, for the greater good of souls and the coming of God's kingdom, in the full communion of faith, of brotherly harmony, and of sacramental life, which obtained between them throughout the first thousand years of the life of the Church.

128.   *7 December 1965*

The Brief *Ambulate in Dilectione* of Pope Paul VI deleting from the memory of the Church the excommunication of 1054***   *

AD FUTURAM REI MEMORIAM[33]

(For the future memory of this matter)

"Walk in love, even as Christ loved you" (Eph 5:2). These words of exhortation of the Apostle of the Gentiles apply to us who are called Christians after the name of our Savior, and they put pressure on us, especially at this time when we are driven more strongly to widen the field of our charity. Yes, by the grace of God our souls are inflamed with the desire of making every effort to bring about the restoration of

---

33. Immediately after Bishop Willebrands had pronounced the Common Declaration, Cardinal Bea read the Pope's response.

unity among those who have been called upon to preserve it, since they have been incorporated in Christ. And we ourselves, who by a disposition of divine Providence occupy the Chair of St. Peter, taking this commandment of the Lord to heart, have already repeatedly signified our very firm resolution of seizing every occasion which proves useful and well designed to carry out this will of the Redeemer. We turn over in mind the sad events which, in the wake of serious dissensions, led in 1054 to strife between the Churches of Rome and Constantinople. It was not without reason that our predecessor, Pope St. Gregory VII, wrote after the event: "In the same measure as concord first proved a source of good, the subsequent cooling of charity on both sides proved a source of harm" (*Ep. ad Michael. Constantinop. imp.,* Reg. I, 18, ed. Caspar, p. 30). What was more, things reached such a point that the Papal legates pronounced a sentence of excommunication against Michael Cerularius, Patriarch of Constantinople, and two other churchmen, and the Patriarch, together with his Synod, adopted the same measures in reprisal. But now that times and minds have changed, we are very happy indeed to find that our venerable brother Athenagoras I, Patriarch of Constantinople, together with his Synod, are at one with us in desiring that we be joined by charity, "the pleasant and healthy bond of minds" (cf. St. Augustine, *Serm.* 350, 3; PL 39, 1534). And so, being anxious to make further progress along the road of brotherly love, by which we could be led into perfect unity, and to remove obstacles and shackles, in the presence of the bishops gathered together in the Second Ecumenical Vatican Council, we declare that we regret the words and deeds that were said and enacted at that time and cannot meet with approval now. Furthermore, we wish to cancel out from the memory of the Church and remove from its midst the sentence of excommunication then pronounced, and to have it buried in oblivion. We rejoice, too, that it has fallen to our lot to carry out this deed of fraternal charity here at Rome, near the tomb of the Apostle Peter, on the very day that in Constantinople, called the New Rome, the same thing is happening, and when both the Western and Eastern Churches are celebrating in a religious manner the memory of St. Ambrose, recognized by both as Bishop and Doctor. May the most kind God, cause and source of peace, bring this mutual good will to a happy issue; and may he turn to good account, for his own glory and the benefit of souls, this public testimony of Christian brotherhood.

Given at Rome, by the resting place of St. Peter, under the Seal of the Fisherman, 7 December 1965, in the third year of our Pontificate.

129.   *7 December 1965*

Patriarchal "Tome" by means of which Patriarch Athenagoras and his Synod remove from memory and from the midst of the Church the anathemas of 1054**

ATHENAGORAS

by the grace of God Archbishop of Constantinople, the New Rome, and Ecumenical Patriarch.[34]

In the name of the holy, consubstantial, life-giving and undivided Trinity.

"God is love" (1 Jn 4:9), and love is the God-given characteristic by which the disciples of Christ are recognized, the force which keeps his Church together, and the principle there of peace, unity of mind and heart, and of order, and by the same token a perpetual and striking manifestation of the Holy Spirit within it.

Those then who have been divinely entrusted with the administration of the Churches of God must always take care of this "bond of perfection" (Col 3:14), and bring it into use with the greatest attention, solicitude and vigilance.

If it should happen that, as of old, love should grow cold and unity in Christ be broken, we must in all urgency lay constraining hands on this evil, and provide a remedy.

It came about that in the year 1054, by decrees known only to God, it was the lot of the Church to be terribly storm tossed, so that the general relationships between the Churches of Rome and Constantinople were thrown into jeopardy, and the love that kept them together was so far injured that anathema found place in the midst of the Church of God. The legates from Rome, Cardinal Humbert and his colleagues, anathematized Patriarch Michael Cerularius and his two auxiliaries, and Patriarch Michael Cerularius with his Synod similarly anathematized the document of the Roman legates, together with those who displayed it and those involved with them. In view of all this, an obligation became incumbent on the Churches of Rome and Constantinople to imitate the divine goodness and love for humankind by jointly putting these matters right and restoring peace.

---

34. Immediately after the reading of the Common Declaration, the Patriarch gave his response to the Holy Synod.

Whence now that in these recent times the good pleasure of God has been made manifest in our regard, and has shown us the way of reconciliation and peace, by means among other things of what has been accomplished by the blessed, fruitful, and indeed mutual care both of the Old and the New Rome for the cultivation of brotherly relations with one another, it has seemed right to each of us that we should take steps to correct what happened in the past, and as far as lies with us to remove what can be removed from the serried obstacles before us, with a view to the promotion and increase, the building up and the perfection of love.

Accordingly we, that is to say our humble self, together with the very venerable and highly honoured Metropolitans, our beloved brothers and colleagues, considering the present moment a time acceptable to the Lord, have met in Synod and taken counsel together. Finding ourselves in fellowship of view and intention with ancient Rome, we have decided to remove from memory and the midst of the Church the aforesaid anathema pronounced by Michael Cerularius, Patriarch of Constantinople, and his Synod.

Whence we declare and set down in writing that the anathema pronounced in the main Chancellery of the Great Church in our part of the world, in the year of salvation 1054, in the month of July, of the seventh indiction, is henceforth removed from memory and the midst of the Church, and is to be regarded as such by all. And this by the mercy of the God of all pity: may he, through the intercession of our all-blessed Lady, Mother of God and ever-Virgin Mary, of the holy glorious Apostles, Peter the first as leader of the group and Andrew the First-Called, and of all the saints, grant peace to his Church and guard it for all ages.

In confirmation of which, and as a lasting sign and constant witness, the present Patriarchal and Synodal deed has been enacted, having been drawn up and signed in the sacred register of our holy Church, and an identical copy having been sent to the holy Church of ancient Rome, for cognizance thereof and to be deposited in its archives.

In the year of our salvation 1965, 7 December, of the fourth indiction.

Athenagoras the Patriarch of Constantinople so declares.

[Subscribed by:] Thomas of Chalcedon, Chrysostom of Neo-Caesarea, Jerome of Rodopolis, Symeon of Irinopolis, Dorotheos of the Princes' Isles, Maximos of Laodicea, Chrysostom of Myra, Cyril of Chaldia, Meliton of Helioupolis and Theira, Emilianos of Miletus.

130.   *7 December 1965*

Address by Metropolitan Meliton during his meeting with the Pope after the ceremony in St. Peter's Basilica**

Your Holiness,

"He who is and was and is to come" (Rv 1:4), the Lord of history who transcends history and redeems it, he who is to come again with glory to sum up all history in himself and give it a conclusion, honors us with the privilege of living through the present sacred and historic moment.

Glory and thanksgiving be to him, together with the Father and the Holy Spirit.

Witnesses of your good words and your act of charity, we humble ambassadors of your brother bishop of Constantinople, in fulfilment of the command laid upon us by him and his Holy Synod, bring you and this Synod gathered around you the following announcement. At this very moment your brother Athenagoras I, moved by the same spirit and interpreting the sentiment of love and peace of the whole Orthodox world as this found expression in the Third Pan-Orthodox Conference of Rhodes, is taking action from the see of our common father of the undivided Church, John Chrysostom. During the celebration of the latter's Divine Liturgy and his anaphora to our common Redeemer and Lord Jesus, offered in honor and memory of our common holy Father your predecessor in Milan St. Ambrose, he is removing from memory and the midst of the Church the anathema pronounced by the Patriarch Michael Cerularius in the year 1054.

See now how the two apostolic sees of the Old and the New Rome have, by counsels known only to the Lord, bound up the past and are now freeing the present and opening up the future! By means of a common declaration and a mutual ecclesiastical enactment, they are nullifying the anathema—this symbol of the schism—and in its place are elevating charity, symbol of their renewed coming together.

Even though differences of view remain with regard to doctrine, canonical order, and divine worship, and so far no fellowship in the use of the sacraments has been achieved, nevertheless the basic presupposition of a gradual resolution of these differences, namely brotherly charity, is today given its proper place, officially and ecclesiastically, as between the two first sees of the West and the East.

Holy Father,

Soon we shall be celebrating Christmas, the feast *par excellence* of divine love and peace.

You, the first bishop of Christendom, and the second in rank, your brother bishop of Constantinople, following on today's sacred event will be able this year for the first time after long centuries of schism to turn with one voice and one heart towards those men and women who, both inside the Church and outside it, are awaiting good will and peace. And this time, not only through prayers and good words but by deeds, you will be able to proclaim to them with the angels, in the power of the Prince of Peace, the heavenly message of Christmas: "Glory to God in high heaven, and on earth peace to those on whom his favor rests."

131.   *20 December 1965*

Letter of Pope Paul VI to Patriarch Athenagoras, commenting on the ceremony of 7 December, and offering best wishes for the Christmas season*

Very dear brother in Christ,
   The feelings which Your Holiness was so kind as to convey to us following on the step which we took at the meeting of the United Nations Organization in New York touched us deeply, and we are happy to express our whole brotherly gratitude to you.
   Already when we decided to accept the invitation to take part in the ceremony commemorating the twentieth anniversary of this international body, Your Holiness kindly and discreetly let us know that your heart was with us in this move, and that your prayer for its successful outcome was rising ardently to Heaven. This assurance encouraged us greatly in our hope.
   Since then the Lord has enabled us to take a new step along this way of reconciliation, of which we both like to see the starting point in the brief moments of our meeting on the Mount of Olives. The desire of which we spoke to you in our first letter, to leave the past in the hands of God so as to devote ourselves entirely to the preparation of a better future, has found a deep expression in our common declaration of 7 December. Together let us thank God for it, from whom "every good gift comes" (Jas 1:17), and as we draw near to the holy feasts of Christmastide, let us entrust this future to him, asking him that we may prepare for it and build it up wisely and steadfastly in his light, who is truth and love inseparably.
   These are the good wishes that we entertain for you, venerable and very dear brother, for your Holy Synod, your clergy and your people.

Hoping that circumstances will enable us to meet again one day—a desire you were kind enough to impart to us—we ask you to accept the assurance of our great esteem and warm affection in the Lord.

132. *Christmas 1965*

Christmas letter of Patriarch Athenagoras to Pope Paul VI**

To Paul, the most blessed and holy Pope of ancient Rome, greetings in the Lord.

Our heart filled with other worldly joy arising from the supernatural mystery of the birth according to the flesh of our Savior Jesus Christ and from the divine grace recently shown us, we gladly make our way, as it were, through this fraternal letter to pay a festive visit to Your very beloved, esteemed, and venerable Holiness.[35] We embrace and hail you in the newborn Christ, and entreat from God the giver of all good things the most promising favors for you and your venerable Church during this new year now taking its rise out of the goodness of the Lord.

With a truly full joy, we, together with the pastors and the devout people who take their name from Christ and fill out his Body, arrive this year at the great feast of our piety, which we celebrate after having just enriched it with a work of peace. We draw satisfaction and calm of mind from what has taken place, and we experience within our innermost being the deep meaning of the Apostle's thought when he wrote to the Corinthians: "The old order has passed away; now all is new! All this has been done by God, who has reconciled us to himself through Christ and has given us the ministry of reconciliation (2 Cor 5:17–18). May he bless and lead to further results this new period, ushered in under happy omens, in the mutual relations of the two sister Churches. May he do this through the light which has dawned upon the world through his birth, and guide his holy Church and all mankind to unity and peace.

With this wish we embrace Your Holiness again with a holy kiss, and remain with brotherly love and fitting marks of honor.

Your venerable Holiness's
dear brother in Christ, . . .

---

35. The Patriarch occasionally used this figure of speech in which the writer of the letter is imagined to be making a personal visit to the recipient. The ancient use occurs already in the letters of St. Basil (4th century).

133.   *31 March 1966*

Easter letter of Pope Paul VI to Patriarch Athenagoras*

Very dear brother in Christ,

We are making ourself ready, with a heart full of love and gratitude, to celebrate the glorious Resurrection of Our Lord Jesus Christ, who loved us so much as to become one of us and to give up his life "to gather into one all the dispersed children of God" (Jn 11:52). As we contemplate the unfathomable mystery of the love of the Father, who "in Christ is reconciling the world to himself ... and has entrusted the message of reconciliation to us" (2 Cor 5:19), we are quite naturally moved, beloved brother, to give expression to the union of charity between us. This year our joy is all the greater, since we are celebrating this great feast on the same date, thus bearing witness more clearly before the world that our faith in the central mystery of our religion is one and the same. Indeed, as St. Paul tells us, "if Christ had not been raised, our preaching is void of content, and your faith is empty too" (1 Cor 15:14).

We know that Your Holiness shares this joy, and that you, too, would like all Christians to come to agreement on the date on which Easter is to be celebrated.[36] Is it not a fact that your Church is studying this question of the date of Easter, and that it has its place in the programme of the Pan-Orthodox Pre-Council? It is being studied, too, by the non-Chalcedonian Eastern Churches, and the matter has been raised also within the World Council of Churches.

You have heard that the Catholic bishops assembled at the recently concluded Vatican Council have stated that they have no

---

36. There is evidence that the Council of Nicea (325) wished to end the "scandal" of variant local dates for Easter by ruling that the feast should be celebrated on the Sunday which follows the first full moon after the spring equinox (21 March). Historical events, including the acceptance or rejection of general calendar reforms, again led to different dates. Today in celebrating Easter, Catholics, Anglicans and Protestants, joined by the Armenian Orthodox and the Syrian Orthodox of India, follow the calculations of Pope Gregory's calendar reforms (1582) according to the Nicean formula. Following the same formula but using the old Julian calendar and lunar calculations favored about the time of the Nicean Council, are all the Churches of the Byzantine tradition, together with the Orthodox Coptic, the Ethiopian, and the Syrian Church of Antioch.

At Vatican Council II, in 1963 an appendix to the *Constitution on the Liturgy* stated that there would be no objection "if the feast of Easter were assigned to a particular Sunday of the Gregorian calendar, provided that those whom it may concern give their consent, especially the brethren who are not in communion with the Apostolic See." *AAS* 56 (1964), 133–134. Cf. Ecumenical Documents I, *Doing the Truth in Charity, op. cit.,* 171–175.

objection to stabilizing this date on a fixed Sunday. The Council however expressed the desire that nothing should be done without agreement with the other Christian Churches.

We are well aware that the question is a complex one, but we should like to let you know that we would be very willing to examine any proposal tending towards a closer collaboration on this subject. Such a collaboration meant to lead us to a solution acceptable to all would be completely in keeping with the decision of the holy Council of Nicaea, which asked that all Christians should agree in celebrating the resurrection of our great God and Savior Jesus Christ on the same date. We should like you to know, too, with what keen interest we are following the preparatory work of the Pan-Orthodox Pre-Council which will have so many problems to tackle. Here again we would examine very favorably any form of exchange of views which you might consider possible and desirable.

What we should like, in fact, is that the contacts established by the sending of observers from your Church to the Vatican Council (and for whom we wish to thank you once more) should not cease with the end of the Council, but should go on developing into an ever stronger brotherhood between our Churches.

Before finishing this letter, may we thank you once more, and tell you how much we appreciated your kindness in sending us recently a gracious gift at the hands of His Eminence Metropolitan Meliton of Helioupolis and Theira.

May Christ risen from the dead fill you personally, your clergy and your people, with his light and joy, and may he give us all to live more and more a life hidden with him in God, while we wait in hope for the manifestation of that same Christ, who is our life, and with whom we also shall be made manifest, filled with glory (cf. Col 3:3–4).

It is with these feelings that we express once again to Your Holiness our deep and brotherly affection in Christ Jesus our one and only Lord.

134. *Easter 1966*

Easter letter of Patriarch Athenagoras to Pope Paul VI**

To Paul, the most blessed and holy Pope of ancient Rome, greetings in the Lord!

Having endured the Cross and been consigned to the tomb, Christ the Son of the living God made death die and rose from the dead, causing us, now dead to sin, to rise with him. For this reason we rejoice and exult, since life has risen upon us from the tomb, and with minds and hearts irradiated by the light of the Resurrection we celebrate the feast of feasts, greeting and embracing one another with the thrilling cry: "Christ has risen!"

With this sacred salutation on our lips and in our heart, we gladly come on this elect and holy day to make a spiritual visit to Your beloved, esteemed, and venerable Holiness, in order to increase and deepen the joy we both feel, and also to confirm the truth that we are disciples of Christ who have love for one another, and that we are held in the unity of the love of the Christ who suffered and rose again.

May Christ our true God who brought about the salvation of men and bestowed on them the gift of eternal life by means of his suffering and Resurrection, keep you in good health and enable you for many years to celebrate with joy of soul the chosen and resplendent day of the life-bringing Resurrection. May he give peace to his Church which he won for himself at the cost of his own blood, and may he call all to unity in the light of his Resurrection.

We embrace Your beloved Holiness in the Risen Christ, and remain with brotherly love and special esteem.

Your venerable Holiness's
dear brother in Christ, . . .

135. *8 April 1966*

Telegram from Patriarch Athenagoras to Pope Paul VI in reply to his 31 March letter*

United in the same Christ and celebrating together his triumph over death, we embrace Your beloved and honored Holiness, and send you, your hierarchy, and your people the greeting: *Christos anesti* [Christ has risen]!

136. *23 June 1966*

Telegram from Patriarch Athenagoras to Pope Paul VI on the occasion of his patronal feast*

I deeply rejoice with Your venerable and beloved Holiness in the feast of your patron, St. John the Precursor. I cordially congratulate you and wish you firm health, a long life, and all the kind gifts of heaven, for the good of the Church and the common cause of unity.

137.   *25 June 1966*

Telegram in reply from the Pope to Patriarch Athenagoras*

The good wishes of Your Holiness for the feast of our holy patron touch us deeply, reviving cherished memories and causing us to desire with you more and more ardently the attainment of perfect unity. We ask God to hasten the hour, and offer Your Holiness deeply felt thanks for your brotherly gesture. We assure you of our deep and faithful affection in the Lord.

138.   *29 June 1966*

Telegram from Patriarch Athenagoras to Pope Paul VI for the feast of St. Paul*

As, together with Your dear and honorable Holiness, we relived the feast of Paul, the great apostle to the nations, whose name you bear and whose zeal you share, we celebrated a liturgy today in our Patriarchal Cathedral. We brought our mind to dwell on your illustrious self, and intoned a *Te Deum,* asking God in his goodness to strengthen your will in your wonderful campaign for universal peace. May your years be long and continually distinguished. With cordial affection.

139.   *2 July 1966*

Telegram from Pope Paul VI in reply to Patriarch Athenagoras*

The affectionate telegram of good wishes sent by Your Holiness for our name day touches us deeply, and is a new and valuable witness to the good will which you bear us. We thank you for it, and in our turn lift our prayers to God for your cherished self.

140. *28 July 1966*

Telegram from Pope Paul VI to Patriarch Athenagoras, thanking him for the welcome given to the Pope's brother*

The cordial welcome which Your Holiness kindly gave our brother Lodovico touches us deeply, and we are anxious to express personally our keen gratitude in return.

141. *7 December 1966*

Telegram from Patriarch Athenagoras to Pope Paul VI on the first anniversary of the mutual lifting of the anathemas*

United in the apostolic priesthood, in charity, peace, and the ministry of Christ, as well as in the communion of hearts, with Your venerable and beloved Holiness, we celebrate together with you today by prayers of thanksgiving the first anniversary of the mutual lifting of the anathemas between our two Churches. As we recall after an interval of a year that sacred moment of 7 December 1965, we take full stock of the blessed and salutary implications of this historic ecclesiastical act carried out together. We look with further hope in the Lord towards the following stages, and towards new ecclesiastical acts of the same order of importance, by which the dialogue of charity will reach fulfilment and the unity of the Church be built up. With these hopes and aspirations, we greet Your Holiness with a holy kiss on this anniversary given us by God, and we pray earnestly for the Lord's protection for you, and for the well-being of the holy Roman Catholic Church.

142. *7 December 1966*

Declaration of Patriarch Athenagoras on the first anniversary of the mutual lifting of the anathemas**

It is with deep gratitude towards Our Lord Jesus Christ, who made a gift of unity to his divided Church in the lifting of the anathemas of the year 1054, that we hail the first anniversary of this historical ecclesiastical event.

The seventh day of December 1965 forms a light which melts the gloom of the dark periods of the Church's past, and illuminates the path that her present and future must take.

Now that a year has gone by, we can discern more clearly and appreciate more fully the fact that while we asked little of the Lord he was pouring great gifts on his Church. From what followed we are able to conclude that the Holy Spirit moved our thoughts and written words, not according to the measure of human prudential considerations, but according to the measure of the gift of Christ, and led our steps far beyond our hopes and even beyond our charity, towards a new and constructive theological outlook on the viewpoints that cause ecclesiological differences between the two Churches, Roman Catholic and Orthodox.

The further we move onwards from the historical moment when the Churches of Rome and Constantinople carried out their mutual historical act, 7 December 1965, the more we become aware of its value as setting a pattern for a new way of approach, ecclesiastical and theological, to the problem of Christian unity.

Today, as we find ourselves in this new stage of the relations between the two Churches, we feel our responsibility all the greater for urging on the sacred cause of unity with unremitting energy.

For this reason we make clear the Pan-Orthodox attitude of love, peace, and obedience to the will of our Lord for the unity of his holy Church, and declare that in all humility we shall render further service to the truth of the undivided Church, and hold ourselves ready to follow up what was done on 7 December by a new series of ecclesiastical deeds of love, thus allowing scope for the power and operation of the All-Holy Spirit.

As we contemplate the rapid developments of every kind in the world of today, we obtain a clearer insight into the hidden meaning of the saying that "the kingdom of heaven suffers violence."

At the present time there confronts us the acute problem for all mankind of the abrupt change of the world and the threat of annihilation that hangs over it. Modern man and his world cannot support any further the luxury of Christian division, of calculations and reservations of a non-spiritual kind, or armchair academic discussions that never end. Mankind and the world need an answer. And this can only be the urgent manifestation of the one Christ through his one Church.

In this matter the greatest share of responsibility is borne by our two ancient Christian Churches, the Roman Catholic Church of the West and the Orthodox Church of the East: both must advance courageously through practical measures towards unity.

I count myself happy that my words have not settled into a monologue, but form part of a dialogue with a revered and beloved brother, the Pope of Rome Paul VI, apostle of unity and peace.

143. *10 December 1966*

Telegram in reply from Pope Paul VI to Patriarch Athenagoras*

We are wholeheartedly at one with Your Holiness in thanksgiving to the Lord who enabled us to celebrate last year's ceremony of reconciliation. May he who is and was and is to come cause the past to be purified by his mercy, and the present and the future to be fashioned in full fidelity to his will, which is to see us united in an ever deeper communion. In thanking Your Holiness, we express once more all our brotherly affection, and we assure you of our prayer for yourself, your clergy, and the body of your faithful.

144. *14 December 1966*

Letter of Bishop Willebrands to Patriarch Athenagoras, thanking him for the welcome given him on his recent visit to the Phanar*

I should like to express my great gratitude to you for the very fatherly welcome which you were kind enough to give the two of us, Father Duprey and myself, during our recent visit to the Ecumenical Patriarchate. We were very touched by the many marks of paternal affection which you showed us, and by the brotherly and attentive kindness which the Metropolitans and other dignitaries of the Ecumenical Patriarchate extended to us. I give thanks to the Lord who has enabled us to enjoy this charity once more, and I confide to him the prayerful wishes which arise from the bottom of my heart as the holy Christmas season draws near—wishes for your Holiness, your Synod, your clergy and faithful. I ask the Word made flesh to fill you with his light and strength, and enable you to give effect to the great designs which you carry in your heart.

Be so good, Your Holiness, as to accept the expression of my feelings and deep and respectful affection in Christ Jesus Our Lord.

145.   *20 February 1967*

Telegram from Patriarch Athenagoras to Pope Paul VI, congratulating him on his efforts for peace*

Having returned from our Theological College at Halki, where we spent some time in repose, we send Your venerable and beloved Holiness our deeply felt thanks for your gift, and express our cordial gratitude for the friendly sentiments that you have shown many times over for our Church and for me your brother. At the same time we renew our congratulations for your tireless exhortations for world peace: these will, we are sure, produce results.

146.   *22 February 1967*

Letter of Cardinal Bea to Patriarch Athenagoras I, informing him of a forthcoming decree of the Pope on marriages between Catholics and Orthodox*

One of the canonical rules in force in the holy Roman Catholic Church, and one from which only the Holy See was empowered to dispense, rendered invalid the marriage of a Catholic which was not celebrated before a Catholic priest. This law had awkward consequences in the case of a marriage between members of the Catholic and Orthodox Churches. As these cases became more numerous, the Second Vatican Council decided to change this law for an Eastern Catholic marrying a member of an Orthodox Church. Two years of experience have made it clear that this measure itself was sometimes capable of producing grave difficulties, in so far as it brought about a canonical situation which was different on this point as between Eastern and Western Catholics, and this at a time when these marriage cases are becoming more numerous in the West, where an ever increasing number of Orthodox faithful are living.

For this reason the Holy Father, taking account of the fact that both Catholics and Orthodox hold marriage to be a sacrament instituted by Christ Our Lord, has decided that henceforth when a member of the Catholic faithful marries an Orthodox faithful, the marriage is valid if it is celebrated before an ordained minister, whether he be a Catholic priest or an Orthodox one. Obviously they still have to meet the other requirements of the law, including the general rule that a Catholic must normally have his or her marriage celebrated before a

Catholic priest. However, as has just been said, the failure to observe this rule no longer renders the marriage invalid, where it is celebrated before an Orthodox priest. Furthermore the Holy Father has determined that in these cases every Catholic bishop can dispense his faithful from this general rule, and give permission, if he prudently judges this to be fitting, for the marriage to be celebrated in the Orthodox Church by an Orthodox priest. It is hoped, moreover, that by means of fraternal contacts, the Catholic and Orthodox parish priests will see to it that in these cases the marriage is entered in the registers of the respective parishes.

The Holy Father hopes that, through these new canonical measures, such marriage cases will cease to be the occasion of friction between Catholics and Orthodox, as they have so often been in the past. He hopes, too, that Catholic and Orthodox bishops will find it possible to enter into collaboration with the same spirit of understanding on either side, both with regard to the practical application of these measures and to finding a satisfactory solution to the points which still cause difficulty in this area.

We have been anxious to let you know forthwith the content and the spirit of this decree, which will be made public on Saturday 25 February, and will be effective as from 25 March next, the Feast of the Annunciation of the Virgin Mary.

A copy of the Latin text of the decree is enclosed with the present letter.[37]

I beg Your Holiness kindly to accept the expression of my feelings of respectful and fraternal charity in Christ Jesus Our Lord.

147.   *28 February 1967*

Letter of Patriarch Athenagoras to Cardinal Bea, informing him of the forthcoming visit to Rome of Archbishop Eugenios of Crete**

Your Eminence, Cardinal Augustin Bea, much loved brother in Christ our God, grace and peace from God be with you.

Having many grounds for expressing gratitude, both in the name of our Holy Synod and our own personally, to His Holiness the Pope

---

37. *Crescens Matrimoniorum,* a decree from the Congregation for the Eastern Church, 22 February, 1967. *AAS* 59 (1967), 165–166. Cf. Ecumenical Documents I, *Doing the Truth in Charity, op. cit.,* 136–137.

of Rome Paul VI, our dear and venerated brother, and desiring to convey our thanks by means of representatives as well as by letters, we have charged His Eminence, Archbishop Eugenios of Crete, to proceed to Rome with his retinue, and on obtaining an audience with His Holiness, to submit the respects of the Church and people of Crete for the restitution of the holy head of the apostle, St. Titus.

With this in mind we should like to ask you to use your kind offices with His Holiness to arrange an appointment on a suitable day and time for this visit, and to acquaint us with these details.

From Rome the Archbishop of Crete wishes to go up to Venice, to express his thanks also to the Patriarch of the city, Cardinal Giovanni Urbani.

And here we emphasize again the happiness we feel in all our dealings with you, and look forward to seeing you again on the first opportunity. We embrace you with a holy kiss, and remain with brotherly love and fitting marks of honor.

Your Eminence's beloved brother in Christ, . . .

148.   *18 March 1967*

Letter of Pope Paul VI to Patriarch Athenagoras for the feast of Easter, giving him notice of the forthcoming celebrations of the nineteenth centenary of the martyrdom of the Apostles Peter and Paul*

Very dear brother in Christ,

With this new celebration of the Easter of the Lord, as we contemplate the Father of glory and "the working of his great might which he accomplished in Christ when he raised him from the dead and made him sit at his right hand in heavenly places" (Eph 1:19–20), our heart is filled with feelings of wonder, of adoration, and of thankfulness. It is our desire to share these feelings with Your Holiness, so that the same joy may inspire us both in our common adherence to the Risen Christ, the foundation of our faith (1 Cor 15:17).

We find all the more pleasure in doing so in this particular year when we are preparing to celebrate officially the nineteenth centenary of the martyrdom of these two great witnesses to the faith, Saints Peter and Paul. In a letter recently addressed to the bishops and faithful of our Church, we notified them that this year of celebration would begin at Rome 29 June next, on the feast of the two great princes of the Apostles. We told them that our hope was that this commemoration would be expressed on the part of the whole Church mainly by a great act of faith, and we asked them to associate themselves with it, for we are convinced that what the modern world needs first and foremost is faith, perhaps more than was ever so in the past.

Beloved brother in Christ, we should like to acquaint you with this hope and desire, knowing as we do how fervent is the devotion which your Church renders to Saints Peter and Paul, and how vivid is its awareness that we are members of the household of God, built upon the foundation of the apostles and prophets, Christ Jesus himself being the cornerstone (Eph 2:20).

We should like also to take this opportunity to tell you that the tombs of the two Apostles are places of pilgrimage open to all Christians, and that we will be very happy, especially during the centenary year which is soon to begin, to welcome our brothers of the East who would like to come with members of their faithful to pray there.

We have not forgotten that you will be celebrating your birthday on 25 March, and we assure you that we will remember you more particularly before the Lord on that day.

It is with these feelings that we express again to Your Holiness our attitude of respectful and brotherly affection in the Risen Christ, Our Lord.

149. *24 March 1967*

Telegram from Patriarch Athenagoras to Pope Paul VI for the feast of Easter*

On the occasion of the glorious feast of the Resurrection of the Lord we embrace Your dear Holiness with brotherly love, and pray that Easter light and joy may be plentifully shed on you and on the whole body of your venerated Church. May the Risen Lord cause our peace and unity to grow more and more *ad gloriam nominis sui* [to the glory of his name].

150. *7 April 1967*

Letter of Cardinal Bea to Patriarch Athenagoras on the visit of the Archbishop of Crete to Rome*

Your Holiness,

I thank you for the letter which you addressed to me dated 28 February, and which reached me 31 March. This letter brought us the glad tidings of the coming visit to Rome of your representative His Eminence Archbishop Eugenios of Crete.

I immediately communicated to the Holy Father the news of this forthcoming visit, and he was very glad to hear it. Since April falls during Lent, and the beginning of the month is largely taken up with visits and various kinds of meetings, the week 21 to 28 May would be the most convenient for the visit of His Eminence the Archbishop of Crete. The meeting with the Holy Father could take place on one of the first three days of this week (Monday, Tuesday, or Wednesday), or in the following two days (Friday or Saturday).

We are extremely happy at the prospect of receiving this dear brother as our guest. I would be very grateful to him if he let us know in due course the date and time of his arrival, so that I can make the necessary arrangements.

We thank Your Holiness both for your letter and for the visit of which it gives us notice, and we ask you to accept the expression of our feelings of respectful and very deep affection in Christ our Savior.

151.   *11 April 1967*

Telegram from Patriarch Athenagoras to Pope Paul VI on the occasion of the publication of the Encyclical *Populorum Progressio**

The last famous encyclical of Your beloved Holiness, *Populorum Progressio*,[38] has produced a very deep impression here, and makes us proud to see, through this historic event, that you are inviting all people to form a world of brotherhood and friendship for the happiness of humankind. So, full of faith, we warmly congratulate you, our venerable brother, and send our best wishes for your invaluable health.

152.   *13 April 1967*

Telegram in reply from Pope Paul VI to Patriarch Athenagoras*

We are deeply touched by the kind welcome given by Your Holiness to our recent encyclical *Populorum Progressio,* and we thank you for the very cordial terms of your message. May it be God's will to

---

38. *On the Development of Peoples,* promulgated on 26 March. *AAS* 59 (1967), 357–399.

make our strivings for a more brotherly world bear fruit, and may he fill Your Holiness with his choicest blessings.

153. *29 April 1967*

Telegram from Patriarch Athenagoras in reply to Pope Paul VI's letter of 18 March*

We received the letter of 18 March from your beloved and venerable Holiness with deep feelings. We delayed thanking you until the eve of the Resurrection in order to couple the expression both of our gratitude and our need of your prayers. In a few days' time Your Holiness will have a full answer.

154. *2 May 1967*

Letter of Cardinal Bea to Patriarch Athenagoras, notifying him of the visit of Father Duprey*

The Very Reverend Father Pierre Duprey is soon to visit Istanbul to take part in the meeting of the executive committee of the Institute for Theological Research at Jerusalem.[39] I should be glad if this provided an occasion for granting him an audience in which he could give Your Holiness up to date news about various features of the recent activity of our Secretariat.

I am happy to take this opportunity to renew my best wishes to Your Holiness for the radiant feast of the Resurrection of Our Lord, and to ask you to accept the expression of my very respectful and fraternal affection in Christ Jesus.

155. *15 May 1967*

Letter of Patriarch Athenagoras to Pope Paul VI in reply to his letter of 18 March**

To Paul, the most blessed and holy Pope of ancient Rome, greetings in the Lord.

---

39. After his pilgrimage to the Holy Land, Pope Paul VI decided to make available acreage on the outskirts of Jerusalem (Tantur) which had been donated to him for theological research. An Academic Council of Catholic, Orthodox, Anglican and Protestant scholars planned the Ecumenical Institute and carried on its directions.

As we informed Your beloved and reverend Holiness with joy at the time by telegram, we gladly received your valuable and brotherly letter of 18 March this year, and read it both privately and in the first session of our Holy Synod after Easter. In it you caused us to participate, on the occasion of Easter this year, in your feelings of wonder, adoration, and gratitude towards the Father of glory, who raised the Lord from the dead and seated him at his right hand in the heavenly places; and at the same time you let us know of the preparations under way for celebrating this year the feast of the nineteenth centenary of the martyrdom of the two princes of the Apostles, Peter and Paul, beginning at Rome on 29 June, the day of their commemoration.

In reply to Your venerable Holiness we express again our warm thanks for your letter, and at the same time we have the joy of telling you that we will be duly sharing in this celebration—we and our holy Church, which in a quite special way honors the struggles and martyrdom of the two great Apostles who witnessed to the faith by their blood. We shall send a Patriarchal delegation at the opportune time to be present at the celebrations to be carried out in Rome, and of this we shall give you good notice.

May the Lord our God, through the intercession of the martyrs who were the first leaders, lend support to his Holy Church, which he won for himself at the cost of his own blood; may he give length of years to Your venerable Holiness, and may he strengthen you in the service of worldwide and historic significance, which you render as first Bishop.

We embrace Your Holiness with a holy kiss, and remain with brotherly love and fitting esteem.

Your venerable Holiness's
dear brother in Christ, . . .

156.   *23 May 1967*

Address of the Archbishop Eugenios of Crete in the course of his visit to Pope Paul VI*

Your Holiness,

It is with deep emotion that we, together with our brother bishop, His Excellency Metropolitan Philotheos of Hierapytne and Seteia, and the Very Reverend Archimandrite Photios Hatzakis, come into your presence to carry out a sacred injunction by conveying to you the cordial brotherly greetings and warm thanks of our Ecumenical Patriarch

Athenagoras. At the same time we should like to express, as we are really bound to do, our own undying gratitude and that of the clergy and people of the Church of Crete for the restoration to us by His Eminence Cardinal Giovanni Urbani, Patriarch of Venice, with the brotherly approval of Your most revered Holiness, of the precious relic of the head of St. Titus, the first bishop of Crete.[40]

For this reason we are deeply grateful, first to Your Holiness, and then to the famous city and the venerable Church of Venice, which for three centuries has guarded the precious head of the first bishop, protector and patron of our island, in the patriarchal Basilica of St. Mark, and honored it with every sign of reverence. We are grateful, too, to the worthy prelate who presides over the Church of Venice for receiving with brotherly charity the request of Church of Crete, as transmitted by our lowly self, and giving us back this treasure of our love and piety, more valuable than precious stones and more highly reputed than gold. The transference of this relic a year ago from Venice to Heraklion, the sacred see of the Church of Crete, was celebrated by the whole people with joy of soul and a deep stirring of religious feeling, and was greeted by the combined prayer of Roman Catholics and Orthodox in the hallowed Cathedral of St. Titus.

But our hearts, Holy Father, are filled with unspeakable joy also by the welcome fact that by restoring the precious head of St. Titus to the archbishopric of Crete, where he was appointed bishop by Paul the Apostle to the Gentiles, and where he sanctified the land through his teaching, work and death, the venerable Church of Old Rome did more than make an outstanding gesture of brotherly love towards the Church of the New Rome, of which the sacred archbishopric of Crete is part and member. In addition it confirmed the great effort being made by the two ancient Churches to establish and develop the dialogue of love, to relegate past grievances to oblivion, to reach a common understanding and collaboration in the face of contemporary social problems, and to foster the theological dialogue, with the objective purpose of returning, when the Lord wills it, to the time before 1054, when the two Churches lived together, sharing the one chalice of the immaculate body and precious blood of our Savior Jesus Christ.

This new period of charity, in which the two sister Churches make their way through the world, setting equal store by unity and coexis-

---

40. Cf. the Pauline epistle, Ti 1:4–5. Although Greek, Crete had been under Venetian control from 1211 until 1669 when the Turks completed their conquest. In the course of the drawn-out struggle, the relic of St. Titus was removed to St. Mark's in Venice.

tence, was opened up by the most blessed Pope John XXIII of unforgettable memory, and also by Your Holiness and your beloved brother, our venerable Ecumenical Patriarch Athenagoras I, who presides over the Eastern Church. This period is advanced by the evangelical words, by the great hearted deeds, and by the noble labors of both of these leaders, as they draw strength from the grace which is in Christ Jesus.

We, the hierarchy of the Church of Crete, our clergy and pious people, accept and duly honor this pure and highly valued service of Your Holiness [of Rome] and His Holiness [of Constantinople], and in our humble way we work together with you both, and join our prayers to yours, that the Lord may plentifully bless your labors and bring you both to see your good designs passing into fulfilment—designs for his Church and for peace, for justice and the well-being of mankind, and for the good of the world—unto his glory, which is that of the Father, Son and Holy Spirit.

We respectfully offer Your venerable Holiness our warm thanks for the honor of this holy meeting, and for your cordial welcome, and we reverently beg your prayers and blessings, acceptable as they are to God, for the Church of Crete and ourselves, and humbly pray that God may make the years of your life many and in every way blessed.

Finally we would ask you to receive this triptych, a work of Byzantine art and skill, as a gift of the archbishopric of Crete to Your Holiness, and as a sign of our deep reverence, love and gratitude.

157.   *24 May 1967*

Telegram from Patriarch Athenagoras to Pope Paul VI thanking him for the welcome given to the Archbishop of Crete*

The fatherly welcome to the delegation from Crete by Your venerable beloved Holiness touched us very much. We are happy to express our deep gratitude.

158.   *28 May 1967*

Telegram in reply from Pope Paul VI to Patriarch Athenagoras*

We are very touched by the cordial message which Your Holiness sends us in connection with the visit of the Archbishop of Crete, and are happy to tell you of our joy at this brotherly encounter.

159.   *2 June 1967*

Letter of Cardinal Bea to Patriarch Athenagoras, sending a copy of the *Ecumenical Directory**

With a view to furthering the application within the Catholic Church of the conciliar *Decree on Ecumenism,* His Holiness Pope Paul VI has approved and confirmed with his authority the present Directory, which was prepared by the bishops and other members of our Secretariat gathered in plenary sessions. The Holy Father has ordered that it should be published, and that these new directives should have right of law, abrogating any former ones that might run counter to them.[41] These directives, which are meant to guide the Catholic faithful in their contacts with their Christian brethren, are inspired by a care for truth and for respect of others, especially the venerable Orthodox Churches to whom we are so closely bound. They are meant to answer to the present situation, while at the same time being open to developments to which the Holy Spirit will lead us through experience.

As you will notice, this Directory insists several times that the new opportunities which it opens up should be used by agreement with the corresponding Orthodox authority.

Our intention in sending you this Directory at first hand is to testify to our desire to see the collaboration between our Churches become stronger and more developed at every level of their life.

160.   *7 June 1967*

Letter of Patriarch Athenagoras to Pope Paul VI, informing him that a delegation will represent him and will be in Rome at the celebration of the nineteenth centenary of the martyrdom of the Apostles Peter and Paul**

To Paul the most blessed and holy Pope of ancient Rome, greetings in the Lord.

Following upon our fraternal letter of the 15th of last month to your very beloved and esteemed Holiness, we gladly send you the news that on the 29th of the current month, the day of the commemoration of the two holy leaders of the Apostles, Peter and Paul, and the opening

---

41. *Ad totam Ecclesiam,* the *Directory Concerning Ecumenical Matters,* Part One. *AAS* 59 (1967), 574–592. Cf. Ecumenical Documents I, *Doing the Truth in Charity, op. cit.,* 41–57.

of the festal solemnities for the nineteenth centenary of their martyrdom, we and our holy Church will be represented by their Eminences
Metropolitan Chrysostom of Austria and Chrysostom of Myra, and by
the Very Reverend Archimandrite Gennadios Zervos, who will all
come to Rome on a day to be arranged with the Secretariat for Christian Unity.

Once again we warmly thank Your venerable Holiness, and
embrace you with a holy kiss, remaining with brotherly love and fitting
marks of honor.

Your venerable Holiness's
dear brother in Christ, . . .

161.   *14 June 1967*

**Letter from Patriarch Athenagoras to Cardinal Bea, thanking him
for the text of the *Ecumenical Directory*****

We received your letter of the 2nd of the current month, and read
it aloud at a session of our Holy Synod. Included with this letter you
sent us the text of the Directory drawn up under your presidency by
the Secretariat for Christian Unity with a view to furthering the application of the *Decree on Ecumenism* of the Second Vatican Council.

We thank Your Eminence both for the letter and for sending the
Directory, and we inform you that the Directory has been sent on to
our Commission for Ecumenical Affairs to be studied by it.

We embrace you with a holy kiss, and remain with brotherly love
and fitting marks of honor.

162.   *20 June 1967*

**Letter from Cardinal Bea to Patriarch Athenagoras concerning the
forthcoming arrival of the Patriarchal delegation in Rome***

Immediately after receiving your letter I handed it to the Holy
Father for whom it was intended.

The Holy Father has informed us that in this letter of reply to his
Easter message, you told him that a delegation from the Ecumenical
Patriarchate would be coming to Rome to join in the celebrations
which will mark the opening of the nineteenth centenary of the mar-

tyrdom of the holy Apostles Peter and Paul. We shall be very happy to receive this delegation, and I am taking action forthwith to see that you have a copy of these celebrations of 28, 29 and 30 June. We are waiting for your envoys to let us know the date and time of their arrival, so that we can take proper steps to welcome them.

163. *21 June 1967*

Telegram from Patriarch Athenagoras to Pope Paul VI, conveying good wishes for the anniversary of his enthronement*

On the anniversary of the enthronement of Your venerable Holiness, we have the happiness to send you cordial congratulations and to wish you continuing health for long and glorious years.

164. *22 June 1967*

Telegram from Pope Paul VI to Patriarch Athenagoras, thanking him for the delegation to the celebrations for the nineteenth centenary of the martyrdom of the Apostles Peter and Paul*

We thank Your Holiness from the bottom of our heart for sending a delegation to the solemnities inaugurating the centenary year of the martyrdom of Saints Peter and Paul, and we assure you that we will welcome your representatives with joy and brotherly love. We express once again our deep affection in the Lord.

165. *23 June 1967*

Telegram from Patriarch Athenagoras to Pope Paul VI, conveying good wishes for the feast of his patron saint*

Another occasion of happiness for me as brother of Your beloved and deeply respected Holiness: your patronal feast. With great joy then, and in union with our Holy Synod, we hope that you will celebrate this day many a long year for the happiness of the Church.

166.   *23 June 1967*

Telegram in reply from Pope Paul VI to Patriarch Athenagoras*

Very touched by the fraternal good wishes of Your Holiness, we thank you with all our heart and repeat that we are deeply united in prayer in Christ Jesus.

167.   *28 June 1967*

Telegram from Patriarch Athenagoras to Pope Paul VI, associating himself with the solemnities of the nineteenth centenary of the martyrdom of the Apostles Peter and Paul*

We share in thought in the solemnities of the nineteenth centenary of the martyrdom of the great and glorious Apostles Peter and Paul who belong to us both, and in the consecration of this year of the Lord to the strengthening of the virtue of the faith which inspires millions of souls to proclaim his name and grace. We fervently pray with you for the holy Church of Christ, for the clergy and faithful, and for the establishment of peace in the world. May the All High grant Your venerable Holiness and our Churches, by the intercession of the two leaders, Peter and Paul, that the longed for day may come when we meet one another in the common breaking of bread, and drink from the same chalice. With you we thank Your dear Holiness, and we embrace you in Christ.

168.   *29 June 1967*

Telegram in reply from Pope Paul VI to Patriarch Athenagoras*

The good wishes of Your Holiness and your Holy Synod are a precious source of strength for us. We thank you and ask the Lord to fill you with his grace.

169.   *29 June 1967*

Letter of Patriarch Athenagoras to Cardinal Bea, thanking him for the information about the celebrations of the nineteenth centenary of the Apostles Peter and Paul**

We are glad to receive from your dear Eminence the letter of the 20th of this month now ending, by which you conveyed to us the programme of celebrations for the inauguration of the ninteenth centenary of the martyrdom of the holy leaders of the Apostles, Peter and Paul.

We thank you for sending us this programme, and sincerely rejoice with you on this feast which we keep together for the martyrs of the faith whom we both honor. It is our desire to arrive at the day when we drink the chalice of Christ together. We pray that God may give you a long and healthy life, full of salutary effects. We remain with brotherly love and befitting esteem.

170.   *4 July 1967*

Telegram from Pope Paul VI to Patriarch Athenagoras, thanking him for the presence of his delegation at the celebrations of the nineteenth centenary of the Apostles Peter and Paul*

The participation by the delegation sent by Your Holiness in the celebrations for the nineteenth centenary of the martyrdom of the two leaders of the Apostles was a matter of joy for our whole Church. May the kiss of peace exchanged in the course of the liturgy be the harbinger of the concelebration which will one day be the fruit of the full unity which we so desire to see restored in complete fidelity to the Lord's will. We give renewed expression to Your Holiness of our deep brotherly charity in Christ.

171.   *13 July 1967*

Message of Pope Paul VI to Patriarch Athenagoras, conveying his intention to visit the Phanar*

PAUL VI

intends to go to Istanbul to make a fraternal and official visit to Patriarch Athenagoras;

to strengthen the bonds of faith, charity, and friendship which unite the Pope to him;

in memory of the meeting at Jerusalem, and in gratitude to the same Patriarch for sending his representatives again and again to Rome;

to ask him to be so good as to unite himself spiritually to the celebration of the centenary of the holy Apostles Peter and Paul.

desires also to express the wish that study for the restoration of perfect communion between the Orthodox and the Catholic Churches, under the guidance of the Holy Spirit and with the intention of carrying out Christ's precept concerning charity in union and truth, may be undertaken in a spirit of serenity and may make progress for the glory of God and for the good of his whole Church.

He begs Patriarch Athenagoras then kindly to indicate which in his opinion are the best ways for sincerely attaining this difficult but holy aim.

This visit does not involve any decision, but is meant simply as a sign of the respect and affection which the Bishop of Rome and the head of the Catholic Church feels for the great and venerated Patriarch.

It is meant to give added firmness to the commonly felt hope for Christian brotherhood between the Churches and for peace in the world.

It is intended that the visit should be made on the afternoon of 25 July, feast of the holy Apostle and martyr James. The necessary agreement of the authorities concerned has been obtained.

If a visit of this kind is acceptable, it would be best not to announce the news until midday Saturday 15 July 1967.

In nomine Domini.

172.   *25 July 1967*

Address by Pope Paul VI in the Cathedral of the Phanar on his visit to Patriarch Athenagoras*

A little more than three years ago, God in his infinite kindness enabled us to meet one another on that holy soil where Christ founded his Church and poured out his blood for it. We had both come as pilgrims to that spot where the glorious cross of our Savior was raised on high, and whence "lifted up from the earth he draws all things to himself" (Jn 12:32).

Today it is the same love of Christ and his Church that brings us once more as pilgrims to this noble land where the successors of the Apostles gathered together of old in the Holy Spirit to witness to the faith of the Church. Here we summon up the memory of the four great Ecumenical Councils of Nicaea, Constantinople, Ephesus and Chalcedon, which the Fathers went so far as to compare to the four Gospels. Coming as they did from the whole Christian world of that period, they met on these occasions for the first time. Inspired by the same fraternal charity, they gave our faith an expression so rich and concentrated that it still nourishes the loving contemplation of all Christians in our own day.

Is there not a sign of the workings of divine Providence in the fact that this pilgrimage enables us to fulfill the desire expressed in the *au revoir* which we exchanged at Jerusalem, after Your Holiness said: "Having each sought to come together, together we found the Lord"?

Is not the hidden cause of our meeting, and of the continuing rediscoveries by our Churches of one another, this unceasing search for Christ, and for fidelity to Christ—this search which makes our paths converge upon him? At the beginning of this year when we celebrate the nineteenth centenary of the supreme witness to the faith of the Apostles Peter and Paul, we find each other again, to exchange once more the kiss of fraternal charity, in the place where our fathers in the faith met one another to confess with one heart the holy, indivisible and consubstantial Trinity.

In the light of our love for Christ and of our brotherly love for one another, we are making further discovery of the profound identity of our faith; and the points on which we still differ ought not to hinder us from seeing this deep unity. Here, too, moreover, our charity ought to help us as it helped Hilary and Athanasius to recognize the identity of the faith beyond variations of vocabulary, at a time when serious differences were dividing the Christian episcopate. Was it not the practice of St. Basil himself, in his pastoral charity, to defend authentic faith in the Holy Spirit while avoiding the use of certain words which, for all their accuracy, could have acted as a stumbling block for one part of the Christian people? And did not St. Cyril of Alexandria consent to leave in abeyance his magnificent theology in order to make peace with John of Antioch, once he became certain that beyond differences in expression their faith was one and the same?

Surely there is here a domain in which the dialogue of charity can be profitably carried further by putting to one side quite a number of obstacles, and by opening up ways leading to full communion of faith, and doing this in the truth. To find ourselves again one in a combination of fidelity and diversity can only be the work of the spirit of love. If unity of faith is required for full communion, a diversity of customs is no obstacle—rather the reverse. We know that St. Irenaeus "who lived up to his name, since he was a peacemaker in both name and conduct" (Eusebius, *Hist. Eccles.*, v.24, 18), said that difference of customs "confirms agreement in the faith" (*ibid.* 13). As for the great doctor of the Church of Africa, Augustine, he saw in the diversity of customs one of the reasons for the beauty of the Church of Christ (14 *Ep.* 32).

Charity allows us to become more aware of the very depth of our unity, while at the same time making us feel greater pain at the fact that this unity cannot yet reach fulfillment in concelebration, and it urges us to try all possible means to hasten the day of the Lord's coming. Thus we see more clearly that it is on the heads of the Churches and their hierarchy that the obligation rests to guide the Churches along the way that leads to finding full communion again. They ought to do this out of recognition and respect for the fact that they are pastors of the part of the flock of Christ entrusted to them, and out of concern for the cohesion and growth of the people of God, and should avoid everything that could scatter it or cause confusion in its ranks. Thus here and now, through this very effort, we could bear a more effective witness to the name of Christ, whose will it is that we should be one so that the world may believe.

Charity is that living context necessary for the ripening of the faith, and communion in the faith is the condition for the full manifestation of charity expressing itself in concelebration.

May the Lord, who for the second time has enabled us to exchange the kiss of his love, enlighten and guide our steps and efforts towards this day which we deeply desire. May he give us the grace to be more and more inspired solely by concern for the faithful accomplishment of his will for the Church, and may he grant us an acute feeling for the one thing necessary, to which everything else must be subordinated or sacrificed. It is in this hope that with "unfeigned charity" (Rom 12:9), we embrace you with a holy kiss (Rom 16:16).

173. *25 July 1967*

Address of welcome in reply by Patriarch Athenagoras**

Most holy and very beloved brother in Christ,

Thanks be to God, the author of marvelous things, who has today deemed us worthy—ourself, together with our hierarchy, clergy and people, and associated with us in prayer our holy brothers who preside over the Orthodox Churches in various places, and the reverend brethren of the other Christian Churches—to receive with boundless love and the highest regard Your very beloved and most revered Holiness, as you come to bring the kiss of ancient Rome to her younger sister.

Welcome then, holy brother and successor of Peter, one with Paul in name and manner, messenger of love, unity and peace!

Peter and Andrew, brothers by blood and Apostles, rejoice with us, and their exultation is shared by the choirs of the holy Fathers from West and East, North and South, who were made perfect in their witness to the common faith of the undivided Church and in the hallowing action of their united liturgical practice. And it is shared with them by all the generations that have yearned to see this day.

We thank you for this great manifestation of your feeling for our beloved country and our Church.

Most Holy Brother,

When you and I descended in peace from the Mount of Olives, as from the first step on the stairway of reconciliation, we took the road to Emmaus, walking with the Risen Lord and looking forward to the breaking of bread: thus we pursued our way up to the present time, holding exchanges with one another in charity. And our hearts were burning within us; nor did the Lord leave us.

In accordance with his never failing word, "Behold I am with you" (Mt 28:20), he has led us from stage to stage and brought us face to face with the painful points of our common history. He has ordered us to remove from our midst and from the midst of the Church, and indeed from memory, the veil of division. And this we have done, within the measure of our weakness. But our one and common Lord, who provides for us with exceeding abundance beyond what we can do or conceive, blessed us and increased the measure of his gifts to his Church and to us. And behold we have in our midst, despite all human expectation, the Bishop of Rome, the first in honor among us, "the one who presides over charity"[42] (Ignatius of Antioch, *Letter to the Romans, ad init,* P.G. 5, 801).

And behold us both, face to face with our common and holy responsibility towards the Church and the world.

Where and how shall we proceed from this point onwards?

It is true that the goal and the ways leading to it are in the hands

---

42. The closest *literal* translation of St. Ignatius of Antioch's famous phrase, practically identical with the French "qui préside à la charité." Cf. P. Camelot in *Sources Chrétiennes* 10 (ed. 4), Paris 1969, p. 107; *prokathêmai* (3) in G. W. H. Lampe, *Patristic Greek Lexicon,* Oxford 1961.

of God. But it is not I, it is the Lord who says: "that they all may be one" (Jn 17:21).

Submissive to his words and will, we look towards the union of all, to the full communion of charity and faith expressed in concelebration with the common chalice of Christ, in a common expectation of and hope for One who will come again to bring time and history to fulfilment and to judge the living and the dead.

How shall we proceed? As far as lies with us, by a preparation of the whole Catholic and Orthodox worlds in conscience and will, reaching outward expression in statements by the hierarchies on both sides, by the clergy and by the faithful, whose voice is a valuable guide and consolation in these present times. If we make our way in this fashion, we humbly believe that we will be answering the demands laid upon us by the inescapable realities of the present juncture in history, which itself comes under the controlling supervision of God.

Since we are called upon to be servants of the Lord, of his Church, and of his whole world, let us work together in carrying out the design of God who leaves the ninety-nine sheep in order to save the one which was lost (Mt 18:11), for whose sake we are held to a common concern and witness.

But let us begin with ourselves. Let us make every possible sacrifice, and with full self-abnegation do away with everything on either side which in the past had the appearance of contributing to the integrity of the Church, but in fact only helped to produce an almost unbridgeable division.

Let us build up the Body of Christ, joining together what was divided and gathering what was scattered *(Liturgy of St. Basil).* Let us join together what was divided, wherever this is possible, by deeds in which both Churches are involved, giving added strength to the matters of faith and canonical discipline which we have in common. Let us conduct the theological dialogue according to the principle: full community in the fundamentals of the faith, liberty both in theological thought, where this is pious and edifying and inspired by the main body of the Fathers, and in the variety of local customs, as was favoured by the Church from the beginning.

As we go about this, let us keep in view not merely the unity of our own two holy Churches, but also our role of service on a wider scale, offering ourselves singly and together to all other beloved brothers of the Christian world as examples and agents in the full carrying out of the Lord's will for the unity of all, so that the world may believe that Christ was sent by God.

But let us extend our vision yet further, and look towards all who believe in one God, creator of humankind and the universe. In collaboration with them let us serve all, without distinction of race, religious faith, or other persuasions, acting constructively to bring about the emergence of goodness and peace in the world, and the dominance of the Kingdom of God on earth.

Filled with such thoughts and feelings, we hail Your Holiness's advent to us here in the East as a new and outstanding day of the Lord in the history of our two Churches of Rome and Constantinople, in that of the Roman Catholic and Orthodox world, of all Christendom and humankind in general.

Blessed are you, brother, as you come in the name of the Lord.

174. *25 July 1967*

Order of the service of prayer which took place in the Patriarchal Cathedral in the course of the visit by Pope Paul VI to Patriarch Athenagoras (see Appendix II)

175. *25 July 1967*

Note handed by Pope Paul VI to Patriarch Athenagoras in view of the latter's impending visit to the Orthodox Patriarchs*

Pope Paul VI kindly requests Patriarch Athenagoras to convey to the Orthodox Patriarchs, on the occasion of his forthcoming visit to them, the expression of the Pope's deep and brotherly charity, and to assure them of his eagerness to do all in his power to hasten the day when all Christians will find themselves once more united in charity and truth.

176. *25 July 1967*

The Brief *Anno Ineunte* handed by Pope Paul VI to Patriarch Athenagoras after Bishop Willebrands had read it out in the Latin Cathedral of the Holy Spirit, at the end of a joint prayer service* ***

At the beginning of the "Year of Faith," which is being celebrated in honor of the nineteenth centenary of the martyrdom of the holy

Apostles Peter and Paul, we Paul, Bishop of Rome and head of the Catholic Church, convinced that it is our duty to undertake any action that may serve the universal and holy Church of Christ, meet once more our beloved brother Athenagoras, Orthodox Archbishop of Constantinople and Ecumenical Patriarch. We are inspired in this by a burning desire to see the prayer of the Lord pass into effect: "That they may be one as we are one: I in them and you in me, so that they may be made perfectly one, and that the world may know that you have sent me" (Jn 17:22–23).

This desire inspires us with a resolution to do everything in our power to hasten the day when full communion will be reestablished between the Church of the West and that of the East. And this with a view to setting up anew an order of unity among all Christians which will allow the Church to bear more effective witness to the fact that the Father has sent his Son into the world so that in him all may become sons and daughters of God and live as brothers and sisters in charity and peace. Being convinced that "there is no other name given to men under heaven by which we may be saved" (Acts 4:12), and which can give them true brotherhood and peace, we harken to the message which John the beloved disciple sent from Ephesus to the Churches of Asia: "What we have seen and heard we declare to you, so that you and we together may share in a common life, that life which we share with the Father, and with his Son, Jesus Christ" (1 Jn 1:3).

God has granted us to receive in faith what the Apostles saw, understood, and proclaimed to us. By Baptism "we are one in Christ Jesus" (Gal 3:28). In virtue of the apostolic succession, we are united more closely by the priesthood and the Eucharist. By participating in the gifts of God to his Church we are brought into communion with the Father through the Son in the Holy Spirit. Having become sons in the Son in very fact (cf. 1 Jn 3:1–2), we have become mysteriously but really brothers among ourselves. In each local Church this mystery of divine love is enacted, and surely this is the ground of the traditional and very beautiful expression "sister Churches," which local Churches were fond of applying to one another. (Cf. Decree, *Unitatis Redintegratio,* 14.)

For centuries we lived this life of "sister Churches," and together held the Ecumenical Councils which guarded the deposit of faith against all corruption. And now, after a long period of division and mutual misunderstanding, the Lord in enabling us to discover ourselves as "sister Churches" once more, in spite of the obstacles which were once raised between us. In the light of Christ we see how urgent is the need of surmounting these obstacles in order to succeed in bringing to its fulness and perfection the already very rich communion which exists between us.

On both sides we profess "the fundamental dogmas of the Christian faith on the Trinity, on the Word of God who took flesh of the Virgin Mary," as these "were defined in the Ecumenical Councils held in the East" (cf. *U.R.,* 14), and we have true sacraments and a hierarchical priesthood in common. In view of these facts it behooves us in the first place to work together in a fraternal spirit in the service of our faith, to find the appropriate ways which will lead us further on as we try to develop and make real in the life of our Churches the communion which, although imperfect, exists already.

Next we must on either side, by making the most of our dealings with one another, deepen and adapt the formation of the clergy, and the education and the life of the Christian laity. What we are concerned with is, by means of a sincere theological dialogue, itself made possible by the reestablishment of fraternal charity, to come to know and respect one another amidst the legitimate variety of liturgical, spiritual, disciplinary, and theological traditions (cf. *U.R.,* 14–17), in order to reach agreement in a sincere profession of every revealed truth. To restore and maintain communion and unity we must indeed be careful "not to impose anything which is not necessary" (cf. Acts 15:18; *U.R.,* 18).

We must continue our journey with greater urgency *in nomine Domini,* in hope and charity, relying on continual prayer, inspired only by a desire for the one thing necessary (Lk 10:42), and resolved to make everything subordinate to that.

177.   *25 July 1967*

Order of the service of prayer in the Cathedral of the Holy Spirit in the presence of Pope Paul VI and Patriarch Athenagoras I (see Appendix III)

178.   *8 August 1967*

Letter of Bishop Willebrands to Patriarch Athenagoras after Pope Paul VI's visit*

Your Holiness,

After returning to Rome I feel a need to tell you of the feelings of joy and gratitude which filled my heart when the Holy Father made his visit to Constantinople. The shortness and crowded nature of the visit left no time for saying by word of mouth the things that arose in one's mind, so that all one could do was to live to the full these moments that came from the Lord. For the Lord was with us—as the Pope said in his speech at the audience of Wednesday 2 August at Castelgandolfo, the first to rejoice over this meeting was the heavenly Christ. Before all else, we must send up thanks to him, because in his mercy he has made us witnesses of the miracles which he works in the Church.

I wish also to tell Your Holiness how utterly thankful I am for all that you have done for the unity of the Church, and more especially for the reconstitution in full and perfect unity of our two Churches— these Churches which His Holiness the Pope, in the message which I had the joy of reading in his name in the Church of the Holy Spirit, was pleased to call sister Churches, because of the communion which exists between us in the Lord. Was it not in fact this communion in the Lord that we celebrated, and which, as it was shown forth in the heads of the two Churches, filled the hearts of Christian people with joy and gratitude?

I beg of the Lord that we may advance together, in the Holy Spirit who is light and strength, along the road of unity, towards the day which we shall be *teteleiōmenoi eis hen* [made perfect in one].

In asking your blessing I beg Your Holiness to accept the expression of my deep and devoted religious feelings.

PART II

Growth and Fruits of Dialogue

Nos 179–258   August 14, 1967–
                                               July 8, 1968

Pope Paul VI . . . Patriarch Athenagoras I
(4)

Visit by Patriarch Athenagoras to Rome (186, 188–197) ▪ "Day of Peace" (202, 204–207) ▪ Towards a common date for Easter (218–219, and cf. 133) ▪ Death of Cardinal Bea (233–234, 239) ▪ Visit by Pope Paul VI to World Council of Churches, Geneva (254–255)

179. *14 August 1967*

Letter of Cardinal Bea to Patriarch Athenagoras, notifying him of a visit to the Phanar by delegates from the Secretariat*

Your Holiness,

Following on the events which the Lord allowed us to experience, I am anxious to tell you how full of joy I am, and to say how much I felt present among you in spirit on 25 July. I give thanks to God who in a wonderful way makes the work which he began amongst us go forward and will bring it to fulfilment.

After the meeting of the Central Committee of the World Council of Churches in Crete, Very Reverend Father Jérome Hamer, assistant secretary of our Secretariat, will go to Istanbul to pay you his respects. He will arrive 28 August (Flight OA 266), and will be accompanied by the Very Reverend Father Pierre Duprey. I hope that you will be able to receive them about this time.

I ask Your Holiness to accept the expression of my feelings of respectful and fraternal affection in Christ Jesus.

180. *23 August 1967*

Letter of Patriarch Athenagoras to Bishop Willebrands, thanking him for his letter of 8 August**

His Excellence the most Reverend John Willebrands, Bishop of Mauriana, beloved brother in Christ, grace and peace from God be with Your Excellency.

We still remain under the pleasant influence and the fond impressive memories of the great event, of historic importance for the world, of the official visit to these parts of His Holiness, our greatly beloved and revered brother Pope Paul VI of Rome, and of his esteemed entourage. In the latter you were rightly included as one who helped to bring the message of the love of Christ and of peace and blessed reconciliation in his name. We gladly then received your letter of the 8th of this month, in which you express your joy over the happy occurrence.

We read your letter privately and before our Holy Synod in session, and by a synodal decision we now thank you for thus expressing your delight and setting this great event in high relief. We devoutly hope that it will be the blessed beginning of a journey in which all of us will find our steps guided toward final unity, to the glory of the name of Christ, the Founder of our Church.

We hope that the Lord will enable us to repay this visit soon, and that we will come to Rome, as is our intention, in the near future, and see you again. We pray that God may bestow his best blessings on you, and that he may make the years of your life many, healthy and effective for good.

181.   *6 September 1967*

Telegram from Patriarch Athenagoras to Pope Paul VI, expressing good wishes for the recovery of the Pope's health*

Since the health of Your unforgettable and venerable Holiness is extremely precious for the whole Church, for humanity, and for me personally, I extend you my entire sympathy in this recent illness, and send my best wishes for a speedy and complete recovery.

182.   *13 September 1967*

Telegram in reply from Pope Paul VI to Patriarch Athenagoras*

We are deeply touched by your thoughtful sympathy over our recent illness, and are anxious to convey our feelings of keen gratitude, and to assure you of our faithful and affectionate remembrance in the Lord.

183.   *25 September 1967*

Telegram from Patriarach Athenagoras to Pope Paul VI on the latter's 70th birthday*

Full of joy at the improvement in the precious health of Your venerable and loved Holiness, we cordially wish you for your seventieth birthday a long life blessed by God for the greatest good of the whole Church and the entire world. With all our affection in Jesus Christ.

184. *27 September 1967*

Telegram in reply from Pope Paul VI to Patriarch Athenagoras*

Keenly touched by the fresh mark of affection which comes from Your Holiness on the occasion of our birthday, we thank you for your kind message and assure you of our faithful remembrance in prayer.

185. *29 September 1967*

Telegram from Patriarch Athenagoras to Pope Paul VI on the Bishops' Synod**

Feeling ourselves with deep love and esteem very close in heart and spirit to Your Holiness, we send you and your Synod of Bishops a cordial message of brotherly love, as the Synod happily sets about its work.[43] With our whole heart we wish full success to the Synod in its labours for the good of the holy Roman Catholic Church, which we greatly love, and for the whole of Christianity. We keep for the future, when we come to Rome, our personal expression of appreciation towards the Synod, and embrace Your dear Holiness with a holy greeting.

186. *6 October 1967*

Letter of Patriarch Athenagoras to Pope Paul VI, concerning his forthcoming visit to Rome**

Most Holy Brother in Christ,
    You know that we have always had the desire to come to Rome and visit you in your venerable see as a further sign of our deep brotherly love and of the honor in which we hold you, and also to strengthen those fraternal relations between the holy Roman Catholic Church and our holy Orthodox Church which through the Lord's bounteous blessing have been freshly restored and are growing day by day.

---

43. Before the opening of the Fourth and final session of Vatican II, the Pope instituted the Synod of Bishops. Cf. *Motu proprio, Apostolica Sollicitudo,* 15 September, 1965. *AAS* 57 (1965), 775–780. The Fourth Session declared such synods "will bear testimony that all bishops in hierarchical communion share in the care of the universal Church (sollicitudinis universae Ecclesiae)." *Christus Dominus,* on the pastoral office of bishops in the Church, 5.

But the love and goodness of your brotherly heart anticipated us and enabled us to receive you three months ago in our humble abode in the sacred land of the Ecumenical Synods of the early Church, and to enjoy sharing the time with you in the love of Christ.

Not only this. The historical event of your visit to our Church of Constantinople brings closer the fulfilment of that desire which we have long nurtured.

And now that the moment appointed by God has come, we hasten with joyful heart to let you know that we intend to come to Rome on 26 October, feast of the holy great martyr Demetrius Myrobletes—to that venerable Rome dignified by the blood of the holy Apostles and the common martyrs of our Christian faith—to visit you, its great and worthy Bishop, Pope and Patriarch of the Holy Roman Catholic Church of the West.

We look to this visit and the meeting with you as a new opportunity for confirming what has so far been achieved in the name of the Lord in vindication of our charity, and for opening up a further stretch of the road along which our two Churches can make steady progress towards Christian unity and the service of peace in the world. In expectation of seeing Your venerable Holiness face to face and of embracing you in your see of ancient fame in Rome, we remain with deep and brotherly love.

187.   *9 October 1967*

Telegram from Pope Paul VI to Patriarch Athenagoras, thanking him personally and in the name of the Synod for his telegram of good wishes*

The message from Your Holiness was received with joy by ourself and by the Synod of Bishops. We thank Your Holiness for your prayer, and hope that the Lord will enable the Synod to contribute by its work to our continued progress in a rediscovered brotherhood. While awaiting the joy of receiving Your Holiness, we assure you again of all our fraternal charity.

188.   *17 October 1967*

Telegram from Pope Paul VI to Patriarch Athenagoras then at Bucharest, in reply to the Patriarch's letter of 6 October*

We thank Your Holiness with all our heart for your letter and the sentiments expressed in it. We are looking forward with joy to receiving you and being able once more to make plain, in the midst of the Synod of Bishops now assembled, our feelings of deep and brotherly affection in Christ Jesus.

189.   *26 October 1967*

Address of Patriarch Athenagoras in the Basilica of St. Peter at Rome during his visit to Pope Paul VI**

Most holy brother in Christ,[44]

Great indeed is the God and Father of Our Lord Jesus Christ, who alone does wonderful works in the Holy Spirit. May his name be always glorified, now and forever in the ages to come.

"According to the good pleasure of His will" (Eph 1:6), we were given the honor, on that historical day 25 July of the present year of salvation, of seeing Your Holiness become a traveller like Paul, conveying glad tidings of peace and good things, and coming from this ancient city, the old Rome, which is venerable to the whole Christian world, to the new Rome, and bringing from the West to the East the kiss of love and peace, and giving an outstanding example of brotherly love by being present among us. For this holy initiative we bring Your Holiness today our personal acknowledgement, appreciation, and thanks, together with those of our Church, and indeed of people all over the world.

See how the same God of wonderful things is blessing us once more. What for a long time was growing and flowering in our heart and that of our Church as an ardent desire and lovely hope is today being experienced as a sacred reality leading us once again into the "mystery of His will" (Eph 1:9).

Most holy brother in Christ,

In the course of carrying out our service of charity, unity and peace, we have just a short time ago embraced venerable and honored brothers in our Eastern part of the world, and have arrived today in the eternal city of the Romans, the dwelling place of the leaders of the Apostles Peter and Paul, and glory of the Christian world, to meet

---

44. In the presence of the Synod of Bishops, presided over by the Pope.

Your Holiness as brother to brother. With such dispositions we render you the kiss of the charity and peace of the Lord Jesus and bring you the tribute of our high regard.

We are especially happy to do this, not simply towards the venerable Bishop of Rome, who bears the apostolic grace, and is the successor of a great constellation of wise and holy men who bestowed luster on this see (the first in honor and rank in the ordered whole of Christian Churches throughout the world)—men whose holiness and wisdom and whose struggles for the common faith in the undivided Church are a permanent possession and a treasure of the whole Christian world. Not simply this, but we so act towards a Pope of outstanding spiritual outlook and Christian inspiration, who has reached the highest honors with humility, and whose feelings of responsibility towards the Lord, towards the fragmented Church, towards the manifold tragedies of this world, lead him day by day from the practice of charity to constructive action for the vital service of God, the Church, and of humankind.

We stand in this holy place, at the side of Your Holiness, near the altar of sacrifice, preparing ourselves in heart and spirit for the future advance to a common Eucharist, and as we carry out in our souls the service of the washing of the feet, we hear at this extraordinarily holy moment the blood of the Apostles Peter and Paul crying out, we hear the voice of the Church of the catacombs and of the martyrs of the Colosseum, and the voice of our common Fathers and teachers, calling on us to leave no ways and means untried to complete the holy work that has been begun—that of the perfect recomposition of the divided Church of Christ—so that the will of the Lord may be fulfilled, and the world may see the first mark of the Church according to our Creed, namely that she is "One," shining forth brilliantly.

The Ecumenical Movement, the Second Vatican Council, the Pan-Orthodox Conferences, the Lambeth Conferences, the world congresses of other Christian Churches and denominations, the meetings and communications between Your Holiness and other Christian leaders, have exposed to universal gaze the grave sin of division in the Church, in such a way that today no local Church, no responsible Christian pastor and teacher, can fail to recognize the more than urgent necessity of remedying this wrong.

On the other hand, the fact that we have all issued forth from our isolation and self-sufficiency to seek the solid ground on which the undivided Church was founded, has revealed to us the truth that the things which unite us are well in excess of those that divide.

These two realities fill our hearts with the firm hope that the whole

Catholic Church and the whole Orthodox Church, by a common agreement of all their members, and with a sense of responsibility, will make the forward journey towards union with each other.

In the course of this common advance—which will be an advance towards the truth, an advance towards "what was believed always, everywhere, and by all"[45]—we are called upon to continue and intensify the dialogue of charity, so as to make this a reality antecedent to theological discussion. As for the theological dialogue properly so called, let us by common consent conduct this with a view, on the one hand, to the interpretation of what we both already live out in common in our Church life, and on the other, to the exploration of the truth in a spirit of charity and edification, and its formulation in a spirit of service.

Thus we hope to be brought to an exact appreciation of those principal matters of faith which it is absolutely necessary that we profess in common, and to distinguish these from the other elements of the life of the Church, which, since they do not affect the faith, can find free expression in the usages and characteristics proper to each Church according to its tradition—and these things should be respected on both sides.

Obviously we cannot determine in advance the length of the journey. This is a matter of faith in the ultimate issue, of many prayers, of holy patience, of diligent work, but above all it is a matter of charity. Because only by charity will we be able to sift out the negative elements from the heritage of the past, to remove the obstacles piled up before us, and fully restore brotherly confidence in one another, creating with mutual respect a new mentality—awareness of our closeness—and safely and solidly building our unity in Christ Jesus, who is the Head of the Church.

Holy Brother,

May this meeting of ours be well pleasing to the Lord, and form a new stage in the movement of the Churches towards him and towards one another.

With this ardent wish we hail Your Holiness, together with this venerable Synod gathered about you, the entire hierarchy throughout

---

45. That is, the decennial conference of all of the bishops of the Anglican Communion, "bound together not by central legislative and executive authority, but by mutual loyalty sustained through the common counsel of the Bishops in conference" (Lambeth Conference, 1968).

the world, the devout clergy, the religious orders, and the entire people, who are dear also to us, of the holy Roman Catholic Church.

"So may God, the source of hope, fill you with all joy and peace in believing, so that through the Holy Spirit you may hope in abundance" (Rom 15:13).

190.   *26 October 1967*

Address by Pope Paul VI in the Basilica of St. Peter as he welcomed Patriarch Athenagoras***   *

Beloved Brother in Christ,

We come "all with one heart" (Acts 1:14) to offer thanks to God for the wonderful things which he is accomplishing these days in his Church. Is it not in fact to his all-powerful kindness that we owe the deep joy of being here together to exchange once again the kiss of peace and reconciliation, in the midst of our brothers in the episcopate, on the tomb of the first among the Apostles and glory of this Church of Rome, whose fervent people stand round about us, sharing in our spiritual gladness and our prayer?

Before letting our hearts speak it was right to begin by acknowledging publicly that it is from the God of lights that every good gift descends (Jas 1:17), and in giving him glory to open ourselves to the light of his Spirit, who alone can be our guide in the understanding of his mysterious designs.

For a long time past, beloved and venerated brothers, you made no secret of your desire to visit us in our Roman Church, and lo, today the Lord has given us to have you in our midst! You represent the tradition of those Churches of "Pontus, Galatia, Cappodocia, Asia and Bithynia," to which "Peter, apostle of Jesus Christ" (1 Pt 1:1) sent that letter which so well reflects the life of the early Church with its faith and hope. This letter carried, together with its teaching and exhortations, the greetings of the Church of Rome (cf. 1 Pt 5:13). It is then as it were a first witness to those relations which developed so fruitfully during the following centuries—though we must recognize that misunderstandings and collisions took place also. Even after the unhappy time of the rupture, there were ceaseless efforts to put things right, especially in the thirteenth and fifteenth centuries. These attempts, unfortunately, had no positive effects of any lasting kind. On the other hand, such efforts have never been freed as much as they are today from every political consideration, from every aim other than the pure and simple desire to give practical effect on earth to Christ's will for his Church. We are indeed moved on both sides by the simple desire to purify our souls in obedience to the truth, so as to love one another like brothers, holding one another dear with unfeigned hearts, and without giving up (cf. 1 Pt 1:22). Are not the straightforwardness of our intentions and the genuineness of our decision in themselves a sign of the action of the Holy Spirit, this powerful action making for renewal and deepening, which we experience with wonder both in the Church as a whole and in each of the Christian faithful?

We take pleasure in saying this over again and meditating it with you afresh during this year of faith, at the beginning of which we made a point of visiting you in that noble country of yours. As we called at Smyrna and Ephesus we heard echoing in our hearts the message which the Spirit addressed to the Churches of Asia by means of John: "He who has ears to hear, let him hear what the Spirit says to the Churches" (Rv 2:7,11,29; 3:6,13,22). The Spirit, who causes us to know Christ (cf. 1 Cor 12:2), who enables us to guard the deposit entrusted to the Church (2 Tm 1:14), who causes us to penetrate into the mystery of God (1 Cor 2:11) and his truth (Jn 16:13), since he is life (Gal 5:25) and interior transformation (Rom 8:9,13)—this same Spirit asks of us, more urgently than ever before, that we should be one so that the world may believe (Jn 17:21). This call to us by the Holy Spirit we see manifested first in the renewal which he evokes everywhere in the Church. This renewal, this attitude of the will seeking a greater degree of attentiveness and willingness to learn, is really the most fundamental condition for drawing close to one another (cf. *Unitatis Redintegratio,* 6). The Second Vatican Council in the Catholic Church is one of the stages of this process. Its decisions are being put into practice step by step with prudence and determination on all levels of Church life. The Synod of Bishops here present is a sign of this, in so far as it provides, in a time like ours when problems arise on a world scale, a better cooperation under new forms between the local Churches and the Church of Rome which presides over charity (cf. Ignatius of Antioch, *To the Romans, ad init.*). We have also undertaken a revision of our canonical legislation, and without waiting for the completion of this, we have already taken action, by issuing new directives, to eliminate certain obstacles to the full development in the daily life of the Church of the sense of brotherhood that has been recovered step by step between the Orthodox and the Catholic Churches.

We know that an effort of renewal of this same kind is being made in the Orthodox Church, and we are following the forms of its development with all the attention which charity could urge. You too feel the need which we have just mentioned of providing a better cooperation between the local Churches. The First Pan-Orthodox Conference of Rhodes, which was largely the result of the patient and sustained efforts of Your Holiness, was an important step in this direction, and it is significant that the programme which it drew up, although fixed on independently of that of Vatican Council II, and in essentials before it, yet runs strangely parallel to it. Surely this is a further sign of the action of the Spirit, inviting our Churches to take active steps on their own part so as to make possible the restoration of full communion between them.

We must courageously follow up and develop this effort on both sides, being as far as possible in contact with each other as we do so, and cooperating in ways that should be discovered by joint effort. We shall manage to surmount the things that still separate us, not so much by arguing about the past as by working together in a positive sense, and thus responding to the Spirit in what he seeks of the Church today.

If we see in the efforts for renewal a sign of the Spirit's action, as he incites us to restore full communion between ourselves and prepares us for it, does not the modern world, too, invaded by unbelief in many different forms as it is, remind us in a pressing manner of the need for unity between us? If the unity of the disciples of Christ was given as the great sign which was to call forth the world's faith, is not the unbelief of many of our contemporaries itself also a way by which the Spirit speaks to the Churches, and makes them newly aware of the urgent need to fulfil the command of Christ, who died "to gather into one all the dispersed children of God" (Jn 11:52)? This common testimony, one and varied, definite and persuasive, to a faith humbly sure of itself, breaking forth in love, and casting rays of hope round about—is it not this that the Spirit is asking first and foremost of the Churches today?

This is the reason why we decided to consecrate to the faith—to its renewal and deepening—this nineteenth centenary year of the martyrdom of Peter and Paul, such martyrdom being the supreme testimony to their faith, charity (Jn 15:13) and hope. What kind of a renewal would it be that did not issue in a strengthening of the faith, in a greater warmth of charity, and a greater certainty of hope? What kind of a renewal would it be that did not revive our faith in this deep and mysterious communion, established between us by a same obedience to the Gospel of Christ, by the same sacraments, and above all by the same Baptism and the same priesthood which offers the same Eucharist—the unique sacrifice of Christ—by a same episcopacy received from the Apostles to guide the people of God towards the Lord and to preach his word to it (cf. *U.R.,* 15–17)? There are so many ways used by the Holy Spirit to make us tend with our whole being towards the fulness of that communion, already very rich but still incomplete, which unites us in the mystery of the Church.

With that other aspect of the Spirit's activity which we touched on at the beginning—his activity in each of the Christian faithful, and the effects of holiness and generosity thus produced—we come to another condition fundamental to the progressive closing of our ranks. This is conversion of the heart (cf. *U.R.,* 7), which makes us listen to the Holy Spirit in our personal lives and follow out with ever increasing sensitivity and openness whatever he demands of us. Without this continually renewed effort to be faithful to the Holy Spirit, who transforms us into the image of the Son (2 Cor 3:18), there can be no true and lasting brotherhood. Indeed it is only when we have become sons in the Son in very fact (1 Jn 3:1–2) that we become in a real and mysterious way brothers between ourselves. "For they can achieve depth and ease in strengthening mutual brotherhood to the degree that they enjoy profound communion with the Father, the Word, and the Spirit" (*U.R.,* 7).

This striving towards sanctity, on the other hand, brings into play the whole of that spiritual patrimony which we mentioned a little while ago, and which the Second Vatican Council took pleasure in recalling at some length (cf. *U.R.,* 13–18). How helpful it is for us, and how it creates bonds of brotherhood, to know by faith that in this race we run to lay hold of Christ (Phil 3:12), "we are surrounded by such a great cloud of witnesses" (Heb 12:1), and that among them in the first place are all the martyrs of our common faith, who, as you recalled with kind discernment in the letter announcing your visit, are the finest ornament of the Church of Rome. All these saints of the East and West are here with us; they rejoice, and beg him who has begun this wonderful work to bring it to fulfilment. In addition, all those saints who stood firm in the midst of innumerable difficulties, sufferings and temptations, as if looking on the invisible God (Heb 12:27), teach us by their very example to proceed straight ahead, stretching out with our whole being (Phil 3:13), "keeping our eyes fixed on Jesus, who inspires and perfects our faith" (Heb 12:2).

Is not all this brought to mind and symbolically expressed by the fact that your visit takes place at the time when the Western Church is preparing to celebrate the Feast of All Saints, "a huge crowd which no one could count from every nation and race, people and tongue" (Rv. 7:9)? With the eyes of our faith fixed on this people of the elect gathered round about the Risen Christ as he is seated in glory at the Father's right hand, united among ourselves in a fraternal charity that nothing must dim, and moved by the simple desire to obey the Spirit in what he asks of the Church, with a hope that is stronger than all obstacles, we shall go forward *in nomine Domini.*

191.　*26 October 1967*

Liturgical celebration in the Patriarchal Basilica of St. Peter for the visit of Patriarch Athenagoras to Pope Paul VI (see Appendix IV)

192.　*26 October 1967*

Speech by Cardinal Bea at the welcome offered to Patriarch Athenagoras in the presence of members of the Synod and members of the Roman Curia*

Your Holiness,

Now it is the turn of the Synod of Bishops, of distinguished members of the Roman Curia, and of the Rectors of the universities and teaching bodies of this city to have the honor of welcoming you. In their name, and with all my heart, I say to Your Holiness: Welcome to this Church of Rome that for a long time past you desired to visit.

This reception seems to me to take on a symbolic significance. You have before you, Your Holiness, those who here in Rome and throughout the whole Catholic world are the most closely involved in implementing the decisions of the Vatican Council, that is to say, in the updating of the Church. Now, as the Holy Father was saying again this very morning, this renewal is the fundamental condition for progress in our advance towards unity.

These dignitaries are here gathered to welcome Your Holiness, you who are one of the most resolute protagonists of this renewal in the Orthodox Church.

As we look at what has been accomplished in these recent years to bring all baptized people togehter, we are forced to cry out with St. Paul: "How deep are the riches and the knowledge of God! How inscrutable his judgments, how unsearchable his ways!" (Rom 11:33). May the Lord give to the one Church as to the other something of his spirit of counsel and of strength to guide them in this effort, and enable them to overcome all obstacles.

We thank Your Holiness for your presence among us this evening, and say to you once again from the bottom of our hearts: *Ad multos annos! Eis polla ta eti!* ["May your years be many!" in Latin and Greek respectively].

193.   *26 October 1967*

Address in reply by Patriarch Athenagoras to the Cardinals and members of the Synod of Bishops**

We thank Your beloved Eminence with all our heart for the greetings you have given us on behalf of the venerable assembly here present, and for the sincere feelings you have expressed, which we much appreciate.

We thank each one of you, eminent members of the hierarchy and highly esteemed members of the clergy of the holy Roman see, for your presence here, which gives me the much desired opportunity of meeting you, making your acquaintance, and showing you my affection and esteem.

We greet each one of you with brotherly feelings, and through you we extend our greeting to the whole venerable Roman Catholic hierarchy throughout the world. As we find ourselves in your midst, we have a strong feeling of brotherhood. This is not due to chance or to the sentimental impulse of the moment, but is based on truth in the Holy Spirit. Both you and we, Bishops of the holy Roman Catholic Church and our holy Orthodox Church, are bearers of the Holy Spirit as it were in earthenware vessels: we hold the priceless pearl of the apostolic succession, which has been handed on to us without interruption by the imposition of hands.

Since we are bearers of such an incalculable treasure, we are called upon to work with apostolic responsibility, so that the apostolicity of the holy Church of Christ may shine forth in sanctity and unity, and her witness be thus rendered richer in results throughout the whole world. Thus, too, is the bringing of the good news to all creation to be achieved in practice, and God's grace and his Kingdom to come upon all.

It is for this reason that we are here today, so that together with the chief pastor of the Roman Catholic Church, whom we greatly love and honor, and with all of you, we may give common witness to the holy desire which has laid hold of us all, to go forward in the direction we have taken, in love and patience, setting right on both sides the mistakes of the past and whatever helped to divide us, and making straight the way of the Lord.

We look to that great and holy moment, when the bishops of the West and the East concelebrate around the same altar, and in a common Eucharist lift on high the chalice of the Lord. Perhaps that hour may be tardy in coming. But the hour of love is already present.

Let us love one another, brothers, so that we may profess our faith with one mind.

194.   *28 October 1967*

Address by Pope Paul VI at the conclusion of the visit by Patriarch Athenagoras *

Very loved Brother in Christ,

How are we to tell you the feelings that take hold of our heart at the final moment of the fraternal visit of Your Holiness, which has enabled you to venerate the tomb of the holy Apostles Peter and Paul in this nineteenth centenary year of their martyrdom?

We wish first of all to thank you for taking this step, and to thank also the Metropolitans and other persons who came with you. We feel deep joy over this further meeting, which has strengthened the bonds of brotherly love between us, united as we are in the same prayer to the Lord.

With all our heart we give thanks to the Lord who has enabled us to experience these rich full hours passed in a common prayer with our brothers in the episcopate and with the Christian people, as well as in a more intimate talk between ourselves which drew our thoughts and hearts closely together.

We shall now go ahead with greater confidence along the ways where the Gospel leads us, to give joyful testimony to our faith in Christ before a world which awaits our witness.

And we ask Almighty God to guide your steps and ours, so that the Roman Catholic Church and the Orthodox Churches, in fidelity to the Spirit of truth and charity, may take the road that leads to full communion.

195.   *28 October 1967*

Common declaration by Pope Paul VI and Patriarch Athenagoras at the end of the Patriarch's visit to Rome*   **

Pope Paul VI and the Ecumenical Patriarch Athenagoras I give thanks in the Holy Spirit to God, the author and finisher of every good work, for allowing them to meet one another once again in the holy city of Rome, in order to pray together with the Bishops of the Synod of the Roman Catholic Church and with the faithful people of this city, to greet one another with a kiss of peace, and to talk together in a spirit of charity and fraternal openness.

While recognizing that in the journey towards the unity of all Christians there is still a long way to go, and that between the Roman Catholic and Orthodox Churches there still exist points to be clarified and obstacles to be overcome before arriving at the unity in the profession of faith which is necessary for reestablishment of full communion, they rejoice at the fact that their meeting has played a part in helping their Churches to make a further discovery of themselves as sister Churches.

In the prayers which they offered, in their public declarations, and in their private discussion, the Pope and the Patriarch wished to emphasize their conviction that an essential contribution for the restoration of full communion between the Roman Catholic Church and the Orthodox Churches is to be found within the framework of a renewal of the Church and of Christians, in fidelity to the traditions of the Fathers and to the inspirations of the Holy Spirit, who remains always with his Church.

They recognize that the true dialogue of charity which must underlie all the relations between themselves and between their Churches, must be rooted in a complete fidelity to the one Lord Jesus Christ, and in a mutual respect for their own traditions. Every factor which can strengthen the bonds of charity, of communion, and of common activity, is a cause of spiritual joy, and is to be encouraged; whatever can damage this charity, communion, and common activity, is to be abolished with the grace of God and the creative power of the Holy Spirit.

Pope Paul VI and the Ecumenical Patriarch Athenagoras I are convinced that the dialogue of charity between their Churches should bring forth fruit in an unselfish collaboration and common action upon the pastoral, social, and intellectual levels, with a mutual respect for the fidelity of members on either side to their own Church. It is their wish that regular contacts may be made in depth between Catholic and Orthodox pastors for the good of their faithful. The Roman Catholic Church and the Ecumenical Patriarchate are ready to study practical measures for solving pastoral problems, particularly as regards marriages between Catholics and Orthodox. They would hope for a better collaboration in works of charity, to help refugees and those who suffer, and to promote justice and peace in the world.

By way of preparation for fruitful contacts between the Roman Catholic Church and the Orthodox Church, the Pope and the Patriarch give their blessing and pastoral support to every effort of collaboration between Catholic and Orthodox professors in the study of history, of the traditions of the Churches, of patristic and liturgical matters, and in a presentation of the Gospel which would correspond at one and the same time to the authentic message of the Lord and the needs and hopes of today's world. The spirit which should inspire these efforts is a spirit of loyalty to the truth and of mutual comprehension, with a real desire to avoid the rancors of the past and every kind of spiritual or intellectual domination.

Pope Paul VI and Athenagoras I remind the authorities of the nations and all the peoples of the world of the thirst for peace and justice present in the heart of individual men and women. In the name of the Lord they beseech them to look for every means of promoting this peace and this justice in all the countries of the world.

196.   *30 October 1967*

Telegram from Patriarch Athenagoras to Pope Paul VI, thanking him for the warm welcome in Rome*

While still under the strong influence of the deep and holy feelings which were uppermost during the whole time of our visit to you—a visit which we look on as a gracious gift bestowed by God on his Church and on ourself—we hasten to express once more our cordial thanks for the warm welcome and the brotherly attentions which we and the honorable members of our party enjoyed at your hands and those of your venerable hierarchy. May Our Lord accompany us always along the road of peace and unity. May we press ahead firmly, increasing the love within us; and may he bless our efforts. May he grant Your Holiness a long life with good health.

197.   *30 October 1977*

Telegram in reply from Pope Paul VI to Patriarch Athenagoras*

We thank Your Holiness from the bottom of our hearts for the very cordial feelings you have so kindly conveyed. The faithful people of Rome, the Roman Catholic hierarchy, and we ourself in a special way remain still affected by the deep emotions which we felt during the visit paid by Your Holiness to us in person and to the holy Church of Rome. We renew the expression of our dedication to the Lord and the service of his Church, and we ask him in his goodness to shed on us all his spirit of peace, of spiritual joy, and brotherly union. May he bless you, my dear brother, in a very special manner, and also the hierarchy, clergy, and all the faithful members of your holy Church.

198.   *20 November 1967*

Telegram from Patriarch Athenagoras to Pope Paul VI, expressing good wishes for the recovery of the Pope's health*

I am following each day with deep spiritual recollection your improvement in health. Yesterday, Sunday, I sang a *Te Deum* full of joy in the Patriarchal Church, thanking God for your happy and speedy restoration to health. I embrace you with great love in Jesus Christ.

199.   *24 November 1967*

Telegram in reply from Pope Paul VI to Patriarch Athenagoras*

We are much touched by this new mark of brotherly affection on the part of Your Holiness. We thank you wholeheartedly for your prayer, and give renewed expression to our deep union of heart in the charity of Christ.

200.   *7 December 1967*

Telegram from Patriarch Athenagoras to Pope Paul VI on the second anniversary of the lifting of the anathemas*

Today, the anniversary of the lifting of the anathemas, after thanking the Lord for this great blessing, we congratulate you and thank you all the more as we pray to the Lord of peace. We hope one day for the desired union in the same chalice, to the glory of Christ.

201.   *9 December 1967*

Telegram in reply from Pope Paul VI to Patriarch Athenagoras*

Deeply touched by the feelings expressed by Your Holiness, we thank the Lord with you for his great mercy, awaiting from him the gift of light and strength to go forward on the way which the Holy Spirit has caused us to take, and to arrive at the point where we communicate together in his precious and redeeming Blood.

202.   *9 December 1967*

Letter of Cardinal Bea to Patriarch Athenagoras on the forthcoming publication of a message from Pope Paul VI asking that 1 January be consecrated as "the Day of Peace"*

On 15 December next there will be made public a message from His Holiness Pope Paul VI asking that the first day of January be consecrated to peace. The Holy Father wished that this message, which he is sending to the heads of state and to all his brothers in the episcopate, should be sent to Your Holiness before that date, so that you may be directly and personally informed.

The Pope hopes that you will be willing to associate himself with this appeal, and to recommend prayers for this intention to your clergy and faithful people on this first day of the new year, together with any other course of action which you judge suitable to promote the idea and desire of peace.

203.   *Christmas 1967*

Christmas letter of Patriarch Athenagoras to Pope Paul VI**

With our heart full of sacred memories of the blessed visit of two months ago and the meeting with Your beloved Holiness in the Eternal City, we are deeply moved as we hear today the heavenly angels singing the sweet hymn of peace at the manifestation in the flesh in this world of our Lord and Savior Christ—singing, we may add, of that peace of which Your beloved Holiness is the dignified champion.

Having reverently made our way in spirit to Bethlehem and there adored the new born Child who is God before all ages, we joyfully journey by means of this brotherly letter to congratulate Your venerable Holiness and to celebrate with you and your most holy Church the present great feast of the divine gratuitous self-giving and love of humankind, the feast of peace and hope.

May Christ our God who was born in a cave and laid in a manger grant Your venerable Holiness for many years to respond afresh to his birth according to the flesh, and to keep this feast with exultation of soul. May he grant that the new year of his grace on whose threshold we stand be to you, to all those who love his coming, and to the whole world, health giving, joyful, peaceful, and constructive in what regards Christian unity and the fullest ecclesial communion.

With this wish we embrace Your beloved Holiness, greeting you in the newborn Christ, and remain with brotherly love and special esteem.

204. *28 December 1967*

Letter of Patriarch Athenagoras to Cardinal Bea in reply to his letter of 9 December**

We received with joy the letter of the 9th of the present month from Your very dear and esteemed Eminence, together with the enclosed copy of the message of His Holiness Pope Paul VI which was to be made public on the 15th, and in which he asks that the first day of January be consecrated to peace.

We thank Your Eminence for sending us this message before its publication, and inform you that we too will be publishing a message dealing with the subject of peace.

We embrace you in the newborn Christ, and remain with brotherly love and befitting esteem.

205. *30 December 1967*

Telegram from Patriarch Athenagoras to Pope Paul VI on the Day of Peace*

We entirely share the anxious concern of Your dear and venerable Holiness for the establishment of a true peace in the world, and give fraternal support to your excellent move. We shall dedicate the first day of the new year to peace, and we shall unite ourself with you on that day in prayer and in exhortation for the triumph of peace. We have already issued a message to this effect. May the God of peace grant our prayers, and the world harken to our words; and may the peace of Christ reward the good-heartedness of Your dear Holiness.

206.   *1 January 1968*

Letter of Patriarch Athenagoras to Pope Paul VI on the Day of Peace**

We were very glad to receive the splendid message sent us from Your venerable and dearly loved Holiness, in which you formulate the idea that the first day of the new year, 1 January 1968, should be consecrated to peace.

We appreciate very highly indeed both the existing need of working in every way possible for world peace, a cause of capital importance, and the agonized concern which you feel on this account. But seeing also that the common action of the Christian Churches is required in order that the holy efforts on behalf of peace should have the greatest possible outcome, we deliberated with our Synod and forthwith reached agreement with your brotherly proposal.

We have already sent you notice of this by telegram, and now proceed to let you know that today, the first day of the new year, both in our Cathedral Church, as we presided in choir with the beloved members of our Holy Synod, and in the churches of our archdiocese and the other dioceses where the respective bishops were celebrating, our announcement on the subject was released and read out in the course of the Divine Liturgy, and prayers were offered for the peace of the whole world.

Considering as we do every opportunity of common prayer, spiritual fellowship, and collaboration with Your Holiness for the good of the Church of Christ and the world a matter of special joy, we felt very happy that at the threshold of the New Year, we were both there before the all-good God, of like mind with one another concerning peace for all mankind.

We warmly thank you, then, for making us a sharer in your proposal. This furnishes new evidence that you neglect no opportunity and spare no pains in devoting yourself to the service of this sublime good which is the peace of the world. With joy we send you under the same cover a copy of our message corresponding to your own on this matter, and we ask that the Lord our God may hear the prayers of all of us, and that the world may take to heart the ideal of peace and make this a reality over the earth.

In conclusion we embrace you in the new born Christ, and remain with brotherly love and special esteem.

207.   *5 January 1968*

Telegram in reply from Pope Paul to Patriarch Athenagoras*

We thank Your Holiness with all our heart for your valuable help in promoting the prayer for peace, and keenly appreciate this brotherly collaboration. The prayer of his children united in charity is of powerful avail with their Father. With deep love in Christ.

208.   *12 January 1968*

Letter of Pope Paul VI to Patriarch Athenagoras, thanking him for his Christmas letter*

Very dear brother in Christ,

The feast of Christmas brings us back each year to a more intense contemplation of the mystery of the infinite love of our God and Father who so loved the world that he sent his Son into that world that it might be saved by him. The joy and thanksgiving which fill our heart at the thought of this infinite condescension of our Father bids us quite naturally exchange our feelings with our brothers, and very particularly with Your Holiness, whose recent visit has left such indelible memories in our soul.

United as we are with you in a common adoration of the Word made flesh, we confide to the Lord our desires and plans, and our determination that in so far as it lies with us the year now beginning will see fresh progress in our advance towards the restoration of full communion and the complete manifestation of our unity in Christ. We know that this desire is yours, too, dearly loved brother, and you have said so again in expressive terms in the letter which you kindly sent us, and for which we thank you. The Lord who wills this unity, and has put into our hearts this eagerness to overcome all the obstacles that still stand in the way of its full achievement, cannot fail to bless our efforts and make them rich in results.

Moved by these feelings, and in this hope, we assure Your Holiness once more of our feelings of respectful and deep brotherly love in Christ Jesus our Lord.

209.   *16 January 1968*

Telegram from Patriarch Athenagoras to Pope Paul VI on the occasion of the earthquake in Sicily*

We were greatly saddened by the earthquake catastrophe in Sicily. By a decision of the Synod we express our great sympathy to Your much loved Holiness, and pray consolation from on high for the distressed, and help in rebuilding from the ruins. With all our affection.

210.   *21 January 1968*

Telegram in reply from Pope Paul VI to Patriarch Athenagoras*

We warmly thank Your Holiness and your Synod for the feelings of keen sympathy expressed on the occasion of the heavy catastrophe which has fallen on Sicily. We give renewed expression to our brotherly affection.

211.   *23 January 1968*

Letter of Patriarch Athenagoras to Pope Paul VI on the Patriarch's recent visit to the Pope**

Since our happy return by God's grace to our see, we have been recollectedly and prayerfully thinking over the significance of the God-given event of our journey to Rome and our visit to Your beloved and esteemed Holiness in that most ancient episcopal see. In doing so we find our hearts grateful to God, and we mount in contemplation of the mystery of his all-wise and all-good ordering of things.

In very fact we consider that our new meeting in the Lord, our prayer together, the dialogue and the common witness of love and peace which we funished to the Church and the world, represented God's favor descending on us from high, and was at the same time the service and fulfilment of his holy will. The building up of charity among the brethren and of unity in the Church is God's work, and we are his fellow workers.

Having been dignified by the great gift of cooperating with God and of conducting under the new commandment of charity the new journey of either Church towards the other and towards their union, we do well to give glory again and again to God, the author of wonderful things.

But what am I to say personally of the special goodness of God towards me, in that he bestowed upon me an elder brother in the ancient venerable Church of Rome, a good and holy fellow bishop, Your beloved and revered Holiness, foremost figure of charity, peace, and Christian unity?

From the beginning of the new history of the Church, in the chapter concerning the communion between our Churches, you have followed in the steps of Paul, and have continually offered yourself through prayer and love, through holy humility and generous minded action, to bring together those who stand divided. Not for a moment have you failed to give from the overflowing goodness of your heart and spirit unsparing proofs of your brotherly attitude towards us.

When however the moment decided on by the Lord came for our embrace in Rome, you, while clad in all the brightness of a pure evangelical brotherhood, and mounting above all things other than this before God, the Church, and the world, gave us, our times, and eternity, the greater sign—that of charity. For this reason our heart remains filled with boundless gratitude to you.

We call to mind those genuinely sacred moments of our visit to you: the embrace in the porch of St. Peter's, the pious homage which we paid together to the objects of reverence in the Basilica, our approaching the altar together, and our praying there together in repentance and reconciliation, and in the hope that we might drink of the Lord's chalice together, and also the good words and the public declaration on either side of our determination to build up the Body of Christ. Moreover we recall our pilgrimage to the most honored sanctuaries of Rome, made illustrious by the blood of the Apostles and Martyrs Peter and Paul, and the blood, too, of other Christian generations whose piety stretches through the centuries. This pilgrimage took place in the loving company of venerable members of the hierarchy, our brothers, cardinals and bishops, and of the clergy, the monks, and the pious people of Rome. We recall in addition our private brotherly conversations, our friendly dealings in the Lord with the venerable hierarchy, and all the signs of love and honor paid both to our lowly person and our honorable company by you, by your holy Church, and the pious body of the faithful. All this was brought to pass in the spirit of Christ, and in the unique climate of your hospitality, which from the beginning of our stay to the end gave us the true feeling that we were really in our brother's house.

We took with us all that was accomplished in Rome, and this not just as a memory, but as an ever living experience, and we have consigned them as an invaluable element in the treasury of Christian things to the conscience, life, and history of our Eastern Church. And now from there we revisit Your Holiness in our minds, and we proffer you and your holy Church our own deep personal thanks, those of our Church, and those of the honorable colleagues who kept us company.

May the Bridegroom of the Church who led us to the great and holy period of time that we lived through in Rome direct our steps to the fulfilment of his will.

Having said this, we embrace Your beloved Holiness in the Lord, and remain with brotherly love and special esteem.

212.   *13 March 1968*

Letter of Pope Paul to Patriarch Athenagoras in reply to the Patriarch's 23 January letter*

Your Holiness, beloved brother in the Lord,

At this time of the year when the Lord is calling us to meditate more deeply on the great stages of salvation, and to live them afresh within ourselves with greater fidelity and love, it is with a real spiritual joy that we let our thoughts go back to the meetings that God in his goodness allowed us to have with you, both in your see of Constantinople and here in the holy city of ancient Rome. The letter which you kindly sent us on 23 January prompts us to give thanks to the Lord of the Church who permits us to be the humble instruments of his saving work in the world to which he was sent by his Father (Jn 17:18).

It is for us a cause of great consolation to note how many pastors and faithful members of our Churches have derived from the events of these last months new inspiration to enter into the dialogue of charity which should lead us to find full communion again in the love of Christ and the service of our neighbor. And it is above all the Christian people, guided by its shepherds, who ardently desire to see the dawning of that day when the Lord grants us the grace of celebrating together the holy Eucharist, by means of which this communion is fully signified and given to all.

So our heart is full of hope. God who began this work will bring it to completion (Phil 1:6). With confidence in him who has promised to be always with us (Mt 28:20), and in his Spirit, who by the power of the Gospel continually creates and renews the youth of the Church, setting it on the way to perfect union with its Bridegroom, we declare to you, dear brother in Christ, our firm intention of continuing and strengthening our efforts in league with yourself and all the venerable heads of the Orthodox Churches, so that in and by us God's mysterious designs for the world, which is his work and which he loves with an eternal love, may find fulfilment.

We take advantage of the visit by your dear fellow worker, His Eminence Metropolitan Meliton of Chalcedon, to give renewed expression to the feelings which come from the very bottom of our heart. Remembering the kiss of peace which the Lord has allowed us to exchange several times, we once more convey to Your Holiness all our affectionate and brotherly esteem in Christ Jesus.

213. *19 March 1968*

Telegram from Patriarch Athenagoras to Pope Paul VI, thanking him for the visit to the Phanar by Cardinal Maximilian of Fürstenberg*

We are full of gratitude towards you as we send our warm thanks for the new joy brought us by the visit of His Eminence Archbishop Maximilian of Fürstenberg. You are continually refreshing our life by kind thoughts, by sending delegates, letters, telegrams, presents, and expressions of affection. We keep on praying for your precious health and for a new opportunity of seeing one another.

214. *25 March 1968*

Telegram from Pope Paul VI to Patriarch Athenagoras, sending his good wishes for the Patriarch's birthday*

On this Feast of the Annunciation, which is also the date of your birthday, we entrust you once more to the protection of the most holy

Virgin, and send you our best wishes, while assuring you again of our brotherly affection in the Lord.

215.   *8 April 1968*

Easter letter of Pope Paul VI to Patriarch Athenagoras*

Your Holiness,

"Praised be the God and Father of our Lord Jesus Christ, he who in his great mercy gave us new birth . . . through the resurrection of Jesus Christ from the dead" (1 Pt 1:3). With our heart full of thanksgiving and joy, we send you our brotherly greetings in the Lord and our best wishes for the feast of the Resurrection of our great God and Savior Jesus Christ.

On this day all men and women, but especially those who have been baptized into the death and resurrection of Christ, rightly send up fervent thanksgiving to the Father of light, who in Christ has reconciled all beings with himself and brought us to peace by the blood of his Cross (Col 1:20). By the death and resurrection of Christ we have access to the Father, and thus we are the fellow citizens of the saints and members of the household of God; we form a building which rises on the foundation of the apostles and prophets, with Jesus Christ himself as the cornerstone (Eph 2:18–20). By setting us at peace with God, the Risen Christ brings us peace between ourselves. Having become sons and daughters in him, we become in a real sense brothers and sisters of one another.

Is not this annual celebration of the death and resurrection of Our Lord the great source of our hope, of our hope for a world which needs him so much, and of our hope for ourselves—we who try hard to renew ourselves by a spiritual transformation of our judgment and by putting on the new man who was created according to God in justice and the holiness of the truth (Eph 4:23–24)? This hope is our strength; it supports us as we try to serve him and to serve his Church. It is also the pledge of our victory over the forces which tend to weaken and divide us, and to dim the radiance of the Church before the world, thus slackening the growth of the kingdom of God.

This hope which springs out of our living faith in the Resurrection of Christ ought to urge us to strive ever to carry forward and give increased depth within the Church to the renewal of which we speak, which is directed in its entirety to the flowering of faith, hope and charity in each and all. This hope ought to prompt us to purify and enliven our determined desire for a fidelity which is more attuned and open to what the Spirit is asking today of the Church (Rv 2:7,11,17,29; 3:6,13,33). Such fidelity would have in view an active preparation of ourselves to make possible the restoration of our full communion, of that unity which could fully render the witness which is meant to call forth the faith of the world.

May the celebration of the holy Feast of Easter bring the full joy of the Lord to you, to all your clergy, and to all the faithful of your Church. May he who is our hope cause us to become more intimately brothers of each other in him, at this time when we exchange the kiss of peace with Your Holiness and give renewed expression to our fraternal affection.

216. *Easter 1968*

Easter letter of Patriarch Athenagoras to Pope Paul VI**

To Paul, the most blessed and holy Pope of ancient Rome, greetings in the Lord.

Once more we offer up hymns of thanksgiving to the all-merciful God and Father at the annual commemoration of the holy Passion and the Resurrection of Our Lord. With songs of victory we glorify and proclaim the greatness of him who arose gloriously from the tomb, and with exceeding great joy of soul and spirit we praise and applaud the eternal Easter: "For behold, through the Cross joy has come into the whole world."

Today, with the stainless light of the Resurrection casting its radiance round about us, we experience within ourselves the great truth that through his death on the Cross the Lord entered into his glory, and is with us who have been baptized in his name all days until the end of the world, as he truly promised, and that he is calling his holy Church and its worthy members to resurrection and glory.

And just as he is not only the Lord of life and death, but also the first fruits of those who have fallen into the sleep of death, becoming one in his Resurrection and glory with the Father, so he wills that those whom he drew to the Father through his Cross and Resurrection should be for ever children of the resurrection and glory.

The resurrection to which he calls us is the rising and making firm in our hearts of those sacred feelings of faith in him, of love for one another, of our own spiritual renewal, and through us that of the Church and the whole world. In doing this we are announcing his death and proclaiming his Resurrection.

The glory for which the Lord who has risen in glory predestines us is that with which his Church from the beginning until now, and from now until the consummation of the ages, must be clad, as it preserves its own unity, its concord and peace, and displays them as a message to the world. As the Church lives out these things in its own experience, and teaches its own children thoroughly about them, it exhibits in itself an anticipatory likeness of the glory of the Lord and sets it before the eyes of the outside world.

As we fix our gaze with courage on the Risen Lord, the hope is enkindled within us that in the not distant future as shall behold the holy Church in the course of renewal, and shall have part in the joy of its unity in the glory of the Lord.

In this hope, for the fulfilment of which we are always most willing to contribute the modest offering and service that lies at our disposal, we joyfully greet Your very dear and venerable Holiness through this brotherly Easter letter on the great and holy feast which is again near at hand. We wish you, your venerable Church, the clergy, and the whole body of your faithful, the rich blessing and grace of our Risen Savior Christ. We embrace you in that same Risen Christ, and remain with brotherly love and special esteem.

Your venerable Holiness's
dear brother in Christ, . . .

217. *13 April 1968*

Telegram from Patriarch Athenagoras to Pope Paul VI, thanking him for his 8 April letter*

On this great day we wish Your venerable Holiness all the joy and the happiness that comes from the triumph of the Resurrection of Our Lord. With much affection.

218. *30 May 1968*

Letter of Cardinal Bea to Patriarch Athenagoras on the date of Easter*

In the Easter letter of 1966 the Holy Father spoke to you about the desire expressed by the Second Vatican Council for a uniform date for Easter. We are very much aware of the difficulties raised by this kind of question. I thought it might be useful for Your Holiness and your Church, as a contribution to the study of this problem, to have at hand the work by Professor Peri which has just been published, and which I shall be sending you soon under separate cover.[46]

I note once more that we should like to reach the point of celebrating the feast of the Resurrection of the Lord together, and this by way of fraternal collaboration. In this spirit, I beg Your Holiness kindly to accept the expression of my respectful and fraternal feelings in the Risen Christ.

219.   *12 June 1968*

Letter of Patriarch Athenagoras to Cardinal Bea on the date of Easter**

We have been happy to receive your letter of 30 May last. We perused it in private with the care which it called for, and then read it aloud before a session of our Holy Synod. In it you refer to what His Holiness Pope Paul VI had to say in his Easter letter, in which he expresses the wish for a uniform date for celebrating Easter, and you renew this same hope and desire that through a general collaboration between the Christian Churches it may become possible to keep this great Christian feast on the same day.

By a decision of the Holy Synod we thank you for your letter with this proposal, and would like you to know that an authorized commission here is already studying the question.

We ask Christ's most powerful blessings for you, and call down upon you his grace and infinite mercy.

220.   *23 June 1968*

Telegram from Patriarch Athenagoras to Pope Paul VI, congratulating him on the anniversary of his enthronement*

We have celebrated the historic anniversary of the election and enthronement of Your beloved and deeply respected Holiness. With all our heart we wish you strong health and many years ahead for the well-being of the Church and the glory of its Founder, Jesus Christ.

---

46. Vittorio Peri, *The Date of Easter: Notes on the Origin and Development of the Easter Question among Christians* (Vatican Polyglot Press, 1968).

221.   *24 June 1968*

Telegram from Patriarch Athenagoras to Pope Paul VI for the feast of his patron saint*

Another occasion for thanking God for Your venerable and beloved Holiness: your patronal feast-day. We take pride and joy in your glorious Papal reign, and wish you all heavenly favors. With much affection and respect.

222.   *30 June 1968*

Telegram in reply from Pope Paul VI to Patriarch Athenagoras*

We are very touched by the repeated marks of affectionate fellow feeling which Your Holiness has kindly shown us in recent days on the anniversary of our election to the see of St. Peter and on our patronal feast. In union of prayer and hope, we assure your Holiness again of our renewed feelings of brotherly affection in the Lord.

223.   *25 July 1968*

Telegram from Pope Paul VI to Patriarch Athenagoras on the anniversary of his visit to the Phanar*

On this anniversary of the day when we had the great joy of meeting Your Holiness and of making a visit to Turkey, with the memory of that unforgettable hour strong within us, we should like to send you our warmest good wishes, and to exchange with you that holy embrace, which is an expression of the charity which unites us, a pledge of the unity for which we hope, and a symbol of the peace which we pray the Lord may grant His Church.

224.   *25 July 1968*

Telegram from Patriarch Athenagoras to Pope Paul VI on the anniversary of the Pope's visit*

This day, 25 July, was wrought by the magnanimity, the richness of heart, and the initiative, which calls for imitation, of Your dear and venerable Holiness, blessed of God. We greet this day as its first anniversary arrives, and celebrate it as a new era of the Church, having just sung a *Te Deum* in our cathedral, where we keep your blessing for ever. With our Holy Synod then and our faithful people we express our deep gratitude to Your Holiness for this historic event. We wish you length of days in full health for the good of the Church and humanity, and hope for a time when we see one another again in Rome. With much affection and esteem.

225.   *9 August 1968*

Telegram from Patriarch Athenagoras to Pope Paul VI, expressing the Patriarch's agreement with the encyclical *Humanae Vitae**

We, together with the members of our Holy Synod at its last session, read with deep feeling the telegram from Your beloved and venerable Holiness on the anniversary of the great historic event constituted by your visit and blessing, 25 July 1967. We thank you wholeheartedly, dearly esteemed brother, for the telegram, and all the more for the visit. We assure you that we remain close to you, above all in these recent days when you have taken the good step of publishing the encyclical *Humanae Vitae*.[47] We are in total agreement with you, and wish you all God's help to continue your mission in the world. With much brotherly affection.

226.   *21 August 1968*

Telegram in reply from Pope Paul VI to Patriarch Athenagoras*

We were very touched by the agreement which Your Holiness was kind enough to express on the subject of the encyclical *Humanae Vitae*. We thank you with all our heart for standing at our side in defence of this doctrine, and we assure you again of all our deep affection.

---

47. On the regulation of births, 25 July, 1968. *AAS* 60 (1968), 481–503.

227. *21 August 1968*

Telegram from Patriarch Athenagoras to Pope Paul VI on the Pope's journey to Bogotá*

All our best wishes and prayers accompany Your venerable and beloved Holiness in your pilgrimage to Bogotá. May God protect you and give you heart in this great new mission. With much brotherly affection.

228. *24 August 1968*

Telegram in reply from Pope Paul VI to Patriarch Athenagoras*

We were deeply touched by the warm message from Your Holiness telling us that you were united with us in prayer during our journey. We thank you and assure you of our faithful and constant affection in Our Lord.

229. *24 September 1968*

Telegram from Patriarch Athenagoras to Pope Paul VI offering his good wishes for the Pope's birthday*

The birthday of Your beloved and venerable Holiness gives us a happy occasion of getting in touch with you again and congratulating you. May God in his kindess give you many years of firm health, together with the power to confront the great problems of our age. With much affection.

230. *3 October 1968*

Telegram in reply from Pope Paul VI, thanking Patriarch Athenagoras*

We were keenly touched by the new mark of affection from Your Holiness for our birthday. We thank you for the kind thought of your message, and assure you of our faithful prayers.

231.   *25 October 1968*

Telegram from Patriarch Athenagoras to Pope Paul VI on the first anniversary of the Patriarch's visit to Rome*

In praying to our common Lord we renew our thanks to Your beloved and venerable Holiness. We remember the great day of the visit which we paid you, exactly a year ago, in your venerable see of Rome, and also our prayer together in the sacred Basilica of St. Peter, the loving embrace in Jesus Christ, and all the abundant goodness and nobility of your rich heart. Our mind goes back with great charity towards you, towards the respected hierarchy of the Roman Catholic Church, and the clergy and the pious people of the eternal city. Together with warm thanks for the more than brotherly welcome extended to us and those with us, our heart sends up ardent prayers to the Lord that his will may prevail, and that the dawn of his glorious day may come when we glorify his name in a common liturgy and in sacramental intercommunion.

232.   *27 October 1968*

Telegram from Pope Paul VI to Patriarch Athenagoras on the anniversary of the Pope's visit to Rome*

In these days that mark the anniversary of the unforgettable visit of Your Holiness, our heart is close to you in prayer to thank God for having given this joy to his Church, and to ask him to guide and strengthen our steps in our advance towards full unity in him.

With the whole of our brotherly love in Jesus Christ.

233.   *16 November 1968*

Telegram from Patriarch Athenagoras to Pope Paul VI, offering condolences for the death of Cardinal Bea (14 November)*

With deep regret we have learnt of the death of Cardinal Augustin Bea, our well loved brother, an inspired worker for Christian unity, to which he gave so much of his strength. We share wholeheartedly in the mourning of the holy Church of Rome for this great loss, and beg the

Lord who is master of life and death to grant his soul eternal reward among the saints.

234.   *16 November 1968*

Telegram in reply from Pope Paul VI to Patriarch Athenagoras*

We thank you for sympathy in the loss of dear Cardinal Bea, and our prayer mounts towards God with yours for the repose of the soul of this great servant of the cause of Christian unity, and for the successful continuation of the work to which he devoted himself with so much zeal.

235.   *26 November 1968*

Letter of Bishop Willebrands to Patriarch Athenagoras to give advance notice of the Bishop's visit to the Phanar*

Your Holiness,

I should like first of all to thank you most deeply for the letter which you kindly sent me on the first anniversary of your visit to Rome. This letter reached me at a time when dear Cardinal Bea was already ill, but when we were hoping that he would recover from this attack, and I was anxious that his reply should be in advance of my own. The Lord has decided otherwise, and you will understand that if it is only today that I manage to tell you how intensely I have relived, over this anniversary period, the deep spiritual joys occasioned by your visit of last year, I have nevertheless been profoundly united with you in thanksgiving and gratitude.

With a view to informing Your Holiness and your Holy Synod of the active measures undertaken by our Secretariat since that encounter, and submitting to you some suggestions which were made during the plenary meeting which took place in Rome from 4 to 14 of this month of November, our Holy Father Pope Paul VI wished me to visit you, accompanied by the Very Reverend Father Pierre Duprey. If these dates suit you, I thought that we might arrive at Istanbul on Sunday, the 8th, in the evening (6:15 p.m., by Company BEA), and leave again for Rome on the morning of Wednesday the 11th (by Alitalia at 9:50). It will be part of our mission to receive any suggestions that you might like to make us, to ensure that the progress on the way of unity is continued—a way marked out by the three holy and radiant meetings between Your Holiness and Pope Paul VI. Hoping with joy to meet you soon, I beg you kindly to accept the expression of my very respectful affection in Christ Jesus Our Lord.

236. *6 December 1968*

Telegram from Patriarch Athenagoras to Pope Paul VI on the third anniversary of the lifting of the anathemas*

On the historic anniversary of 7 December 1965, with deep feeling we glorify God who has granted this grace to the Church to which we belong in common. We are grateful to Your highly regarded and beloved Holiness, and hope that you will be able to rejoice over this as we come to share in the same holy chalice.

237. *10 December 1968*

Telegram in reply from Pope Paul VI to Patriarch Athenagoras*

We thank Your Holiness for your friendly message, and assure you that we have commemorated in thanksgiving with you the historic anniversary of 7 December 1965. With all our heart we assure you again of our good wishes, our prayers, and our affection in the Lord.

238. *14 December 1968*

Letter of Bishop Willebrands to Patriarch Athenagoras, thanking him for the welcome given him at the Phanar*

Your Holiness,

Now that I have come back to Rome, I should like to thank you earnestly, both on my own behalf and that of Father Duprey, for the welcome, so full of charity and kind attentions, which you extended to us on our recent visit to the Ecumenical Patriarchate. I should be very grateful to you if you would kindly let their Eminences the Metropolitans know how thankful we are for the frank, fraternal, and fruitful conversations which we were able to have with them.

We should like to thank you in a special way for the valuable souvenir which was presented to us on your behalf: this is a further sign of the good will which you bear us.

As the feast of Christmas draws near, I beg you to accept my most sincere good wishes and the assurance of my prayers for your intentions. May the God who was before time began, and who became a tiny infant for our sake, give you a long and healthy life and fill you with his blessing and strength during the year soon beginning.

I ask Your Holiness kindly to accept the expression of my respectful affection in Christ Jesus Our Lord.

239.   *16 December 1968*

Letter of Bishop Willebrands to Patriarch Athenagoras, thanking him for condolences on the death of Cardinal Bea*

We were deeply touched by the feelings of esteem and affection for Cardinal Bea which you have shown, and are particularly grateful for the prayers offered on behalf of our lamented President.

I take the liberty of enclosing with this letter souvenir photographs of the late Cardinal, meant for yourself, the members of the Holy Synod, and those who knew him personally at the Patriarchate.

240.   *23 December 1968*

Telegram of good wishes from Patriarch Athenagoras to Pope Paul VI for Christmas**

In singing the praises of the Redeemer who came to us in a manger within a cave, and feeling more deeply in him the love we have for one another, we are gladly united on this great feast with your very dear and venerable Holiness in a warm prayer for the peace of the world and the union of all. May the newly born Saviour grant you to celebrate this world saving birth for a very long time to come, and out of his goodness bestow upon you, the Church, and the whole world an auspicious new year, filled with heavenly gifts.

241. *24 December 1968*

Telegram from Pope Paul VI to Patriarch Athenagoras for Christmas*

We received with deep feeling the good wishes of Your beloved Holiness for the holy and radiant feast of the Nativity of our one and only Lord and Savior. May he deign to hear and grant the prayers we make together for peace in the world and the union of all. With love in Christ, and the desire that the Lord may fill Your Holiness, the Holy Synod, your clergy, and all your faithful with his blessings.

242. *Christmas 1968*

Christmas letter of Patriarch Athenagoras to Pope Paul VI**

To Paul, the most blessed and holy Pope of ancient Rome, greetings in the Lord.

As we take the road towards Bethlehem to contemplate once more the supernatural mystery of the divine Incarnation and to worship the God-Man who is our Savior and Lord, we also contemplate anew the divine-human mystery of the Church which derives from this source. As we do so we hear more clearly the divine will and calling, and we see from the actual condition of things round about us that in no other way than unity can the glory of the Body of Christ reach its perfection.

It is in this frame of mind that we hasten to meet Your most blessed and venerable Holiness in spirit once again in the holy communion of peace and love, and to pray with you to the Lord of all for the Church and the world.

We send the brotherly salutation of the festive time to Your much loved Holiness and so doing we look over the stretch of road thus far covered with you which leads towards the unity of our Churches. We praise the name that is to be most highly hymned, that of our common Lord, for allowing us to serve his holy will, for allowing us to join together in no small measure what before was separated, to establish charity in our midst, to set up as a vital experience shared by both what was lived out by our common ancestors and fathers in the faith, that is to say, a spiritual communion strong and secure in the Lord.

We would have desired to have this communion brought to its completion in the concelebration of the divine Eucharist, so that the

Lord might be glorified, the Church shine forth, and the world believe, but in accordance with the unsearchable counsels of God, this has not yet been granted us—it will be, however.

Possessed by this faith and gladdened by the hope arising from it, we thank the Lord for the meeting points recently provided by the mission to you of our dear and eminent Metropolitan Meliton of Chalcedon, and the mission from you of His Excellency Bishop Willebrands of Mauriana and the Very Reverend Father Duprey, both of them held here in affectionate regard. We are confident that these communications between us and the discussions that were then entered into will prove to have a constructive effect in the further development of our brotherhood.

Already we stand on the threshold of the coming year, and take note of how everything round about us has evolved in such a short time, and of how time has become more precious than before, both in itself, and as the occasion for bringing out the importance of eternal values. In view of this we assured you that we are at your side in spirit at every moment, in all your good designs, sometimes suffering with you, at other times rejoicing with you, going forward in unbroken union with you in the charity of Christ in the endeavor to make the Kingdom of God prevail upon the earth. In this you will have throughout the new year in the person of my humble self a brother who walks with you and is ready in conjunction with you to open up new paths leading to the perfect fulfilment of the Lord's will.

In confirmation of this deliberate and wholehearted choice, we should like you to know that now, as we prepare to celebrate the holy birth in the flesh of Our Lord Jesus Christ, and persevere in prayer and petition, maintaining a deep recollection so that we may worthily approach the holy altar on which we are about to offer the spotless Lamb, we feel ourselves nearer to you more than ever before in the holy fellowship of the love of Christ.

In this fellowship, as we officiate at the sacred rites with the choir of their worthy Eminences the Metropolitans, we shall remember from out the diptychs of our heart your honored name, holy brother and Bishop of ancient Rome, at the offering of this same precious Body and Blood in the Divine Liturgy of our holy predecessor, St. John Chrysostom, whom we both look on as a Father.

And we shall say on the holy day of Christmas before the altar, as we say to you now: "May the Lord God remember your chief-priesthood now and forever through the ages to come."

Having said this, we embrace Your deeply loved Holiness with a greeting in Christ Our Lord, who was born from the all-holy Virgin in Bethlehem, and remain with brotherly charity and special esteem.

243.   *7 January 1969*

Letter in reply of Pope Paul VI to Patriarch Athenagoras*

We have received with joy and deep feeling the good wishes which Your beloved Holiness so kindly sent us for the holy and radiant feast of the Nativity of our one Lord and Savior.

May he deign to give ear to the prayers which we both make for the peace of the world and the union of all. We assure you again of our love in Christ, and say that we hope that the Lord will fill Your dear Holiness, your Holy Synod, your clergy, and all your faithful people with his blessings in the course of the New Year.

244.   *10 January 1969*

Letter of Pope Paul VI to Patriarch Athenagoras on the development of relations between the Churches of Rome and Constantinople*

Beloved brother in Christ,

At the very time when we were celebrating the birth in the flesh of "our great God and saviour Jesus Christ" (Ti 2:13), the letter from Your Holiness arrived to increase the joy that was filling our heart. This letter, overflowing in its entirety as it was with love of the Lord and of your brothers, fitted in so well with our own thoughts and our own eager hope, that from the bottom of our heart we say to you as to a beloved brother: thank you! Thanks for this perceptive affection and this unfailing and fervent prayer which we value so highly. Thanks for the greetings so filled with high regard and charity contained in your Christmas message. Thanks for that remembrance during the celebration of the Divine Liturgy where we find ourselves so closely and mysteriously united in Christ. We should like to tell you how much we too desire to concelebrate this Divine Liturgy with Your Holiness. We beg the Lord again and again to grant this shining gift to his Church.

Is it not, when one comes to think of it, a painful duty involved in the pastoral charge which the Lord has entrusted to us, to have sometimes to delay the fulfilment of our desires because of the solicitous care which we must have for all those in our charge, and also because we must honor visibly, in the clear light, every expression of the Lord's will? We make a point of repeating to you that we should very much like to explore, together with Your Holiness, the ways that could lead us to that great day which would mean the combined celebration of our Churches within the context of a fully recovered communion.

The specific proposals for this purpose which we recently made through our representatives are now being studied by your Holy Synod. Rest assured that we are moved purely and simply by the desire to go forward in fulfilling the Lord's will as far as is practically possible, given the complex conditions produced by a centuries old history. We are therefore quite ready to examine any modifications or suggestions that you might care to indicate, so that we may both make a surer and by the same token more rapid progress towards this much hoped for goal.

In the course of this striving, an increasingly deep communion in the charity of Christ provides not only a powerful source of strength for both of us, but also and above all else opens us in our inmost being to the gift for which we hope, and serves to implore that gift from God by our whole manner of life.

It is with such feelings that we renew our most cordial good wishes at the beginning of this new year. May these desires, which we share alike, become in increasing measure those of all the bishops, priests, and faithful people of the Churches. May increasing testimony be given everywhere to that true charity which always has been and will be the sign by which people recognize the disciples of him who has loved us so much.

We assure Your Holiness that we faithfully remember you at the altar of the Lord, and we express once more our brotherly affection and high regard in Christ Jesus Our Savior.

245. *19 January 1969*

Letter of Bishop Willebrands on the discussions during his recent visit*

Your Holiness,

I am glad to be able to tell you that the Holy Father fully agrees with the suggestion made by the Synodal Commission with which we held talks at Istanbul, to make preparations for publishing the various speeches and letters exchanged between the Church of Rome and the Orthodox Churches in these recent years. In order to put this plan into practice within the general guidelines drawn up during the talks at Istanbul in December, Father Pierre Duprey and Father Christophe Dumont have been designated as our representatives in the joint commission of four persons which is to carry out this work. We should be happy to know the names of two members appointed by Your Holiness. The persons concerned on both sides could settle down to work, prepare the plan of the publication, and start gathering the material. It seems right that the commission should meet without undue delay to reach agreement on the general idea of the work and the way of going about it. The first meeting could well take place at Istanbul, if that is convenient for you, while the date could be decided by agreement between the members appointed. It seems likely that once the work is sufficiently advanced and the material assembled and arranged, a second meeting of the commission will be required to settle practical details of the production. This second meeting might perhaps be held in Rome.

As for the other proposals which we made to the Synodal Commission, we wait on a reply from Your Holiness. The Holy Father made a point of telling me this morning that he was very inclined to the view that a working group should study the theological reasons which either hinder or allow a practical expression in worship and sacramental participation of the profound communion which, although not yet complete, exists here and now between the two sister Churches. This is in line with the desire expressed in your recent letter—a desire which is identical with that of His Holiness, as he clearly said in his reply to you. He quite favored, too, the idea that this same working group or another should examine the obstacles which the first examination might bring to light in exact detail, and that they should do this with a view to surmounting them. In saying this the Holy Father makes it clear, as he wrote recently to Your Holiness, that he is prepared to examine with the greatest good will any modification, suggestion, or other method of proceeding which you might propose, and which you might judge to be more in line with the policy laid down in the Fourth Pan-Orthodox Conference. The important thing is that we should together discover the most effective means of advancing towards the longed for day when our celebration of the Eucharist can reach its full development in concelebration.

In the keen hope that the Lord will enable us soon to take important new steps along this road, I beg Your Holiness kindly to accept the expression of my affection and high regard in Christ the Savior.

246.   *24 January 1969*

Telegram from Pope Paul VI to Patriarch Athenagoras on the twentieth anniversary of the Patriarch's enthronement*

On the occasion of the twentieth anniversary of your enthronement, we should like to be united with you in your thanksgiving for the things that the Lord has been pleased to do through you, and to offer our best wishes. *Ad multos annos!* With all our deep and brotherly love in Christ Jesus.

247.   *13 February 1969*

Letter of Patriarch Athenagoras to Bishop Willebrands, thanking him for the souvenir of Cardinal Bea**

We received with joy and read aloud in a session of our Holy Synod your letter of 16 December last year, in which you sent us a souvenir photograph of Cardinal Augustin Bea of blessed memory. He was a man who worked tirelessly for the furtherance of the holy cause of Christian unity, and for this reason is specially honoured by us.

We thank you warmly for this communication, and embrace you with a holy greeting, while remaining with brotherly love and befitting esteem.

248.   *1 April 1969*

Easter letter of Pope Paul VI to Patriarch Athenagoras*

Beloved brother in Christ,

In his goodness God has enabled us to celebrate once again the glorious feast of the Resurrection of Our Lord and Savior Jesus Christ, and thus commemorate the central event in his divine design for the redemption and sanctification of the world (Acts 2:23–24). Our heart is filled with thanksgiving and joy, so that at the urging of fraternal charity we are anxious to share these feelings with Your Holiness and tell you of our hope, which is supported by prayer, that "this day which the Lord has made" will be for you, and for the hierarchy, clergy, and people of your Church, a day of spiritual consolation and deep inward joy.

As we contemplate the power of God made manifest in the Resurrection of Christ (Eph 1:19–21), we remember that it is this Christ whom we all preach; that it is he who through the Holy Spirit "has called and gathered into the unity of faith, hope and charity the people of the new covenant which is the Church" (*U.R.* 2), and that his work must be carried on right up till its perfect conclusion, when he comes again. If this Spirit has spoken to the Churches over the course of two thousand years, he does not cease to do so today. Fidelity to Our Lord and Savior requires of us that we should remain resolved to maintain and deepen our understanding of all that the Spirit has said to the Church in the past to guide and animate it; but the same fidelity also demands of us that we should be constantly on the alert to hear his voice today, just as we must be tomorrow.

This openness to the influence of the Holy Spirit will enable us, who are already united by such intimate bonds of faith and sacramental life, to deepen further the meaning and the requirements of this unity which we now possess, and to turn it to greater account. We express this unity already in the common celebration of the mysteries of our redemption: God grant that we may also be soon able to do this by celebrating the glorious Resurrection of the Lord on the same day!

With all our heart we ask the Risen Lord to pour forth his bounteous Easter grace on Your Holiness and on your Church and we assure you again of all our brotherly affection in him who is the Alpha and the Omega, the beginning and the end (Rv 21:6) of all our striving.

249. *4 April 1969*

Telegram from Patriarch Athenagoras to Pope Paul VI for Easter*

Jesus is risen! As we experience in our lives in these days the miracle of the Resurrection of Our Lord Jesus Christ, we fraternally embrace Your beloved and venerable Holiness, wishing you all the joy of Easter, and a glorious life, rich in achievement for your historic apostolate.

250.   *22 April 1969*

Telegram from Patriarch Athenagoras to Cardinal Willebrands to congratulate him on his appointment*

The appointment of Your beloved Eminence as President of the Secretariat for Christian Unity makes us very glad indeed. Cordial congratulations and best wishes, in the certainty that you will bring what has been begun to its glorious end. With much affection.

251.   *26 April 1969*

Telegram in reply from Cardinal Willebrands to Patriarch Athenagoras*

I wish to say how entirely thankful I am to Your Holiness for your cordial wishes, and I share in your hope that the Lord will bring to fulfilment the work that has been begun. With respectful affection.

252.   *6 May 1969*

Telegram from Patriarch Athenagoras to Pope Paul VI on the occasion of the appointment of thirty-five new Cardinals*

Sharing in the joy imparted by the appointment of thirty-five new Cardinals, and of Cardinal Willebrands as President of the Secretariat for Christian Unity, we thank Your venerable and beloved Holiness for the new brilliance, strength and happiness given to the Church. May you be able to enrich it from day to day.

253.   *12 May 1969*

Telegram in reply from Pope Paul VI to Patriarch Athenagoras*

We thank Your Holiness wholeheartedly and are grateful to God that we find in you, whatever the occasion may be, a brother so kind and perceptive and so close in the charity of Christ.

254.   *12 June 1969*

Telegram from Patriarch Athenagoras to Pope Paul VI on the Pope's journey to Geneva*

The Christian world has greatly profited by the very significant journey of Your venerable and beloved Holiness to Geneva. On the one hand you have borne your witness of Christian appreciation of the work and toil of all those of good will (2 Cor 11:27). On the other, by the very fact of paying a visit to the World Council of Churches, you have emphasized the great Christian truth that, going side by side with every other kind of human work, there is the spiritual work which has as its aim understanding, correspondence of feeling and outlook, and Christian unity. United with you in spirit and in prayer, we followed your journey and set store on what you said. We congratulate you, and give renewed expression to our hope and certainty that the great day of the Lord will come when we shall all, pastors and faithful people, find ourselves united in the same Body and Blood of Christ.

255.   *21 June 1969*

Telegram in reply from Pope Paul VI to Patriarch Athenagoras*

The support and prayers of Your Holiness are a source of strength to us and a precious encouragement. We thank you then wholeheartedly for your telegram about our recent visit to Geneva, and we assure you once more of our brotherly charity and of our union with you in the hope of soon seeing the day when we can communicate in the Blood of Christ from the same chalice.

256.   *20 June 1969*

Telegram from Patriarch Athenagoras, congratulating Pope Paul VI on the anniversary of his election to the See of Rome*

We heartily congratulate Your loved and venerable Holiness on the great event of your enthronement, and we pray the Lord to grant you long years in full health for the benefit of his whole Church.

257.   *24 June 1969*

Telegram from Patriarch Athenagoras to Pope Paul VI on the feast-day of his patron saint*

We congratulate Your Holiness wholeheartedly on your patronal feast-day, and wish you all good things from heaven.

258.   *8 July 1969*

Telegram in reply from Pope Paul VI to Patriarch Athenagoras*

We thank Your Holiness with keen feeling for the good wishes which you sent us for our feast-day and the anniversary of our election to the see of Rome. We express our deep gratitude for the valued help of your constant prayers, and we assure you again of our brotherly affection in Christ.

PART II

Growth and Fruits of Dialogue

Nos 259–300   **July 8, 1969–**
                                             July 16, 1972

Pope Paul VI ... Patriarch Athenagoras I
(5)
Plans for publication of communications between
Rome and Constantinople (259, cf. 245) ▪ Visit by
Cardinal Willebrands to Constantinople for feast of
St. Andrew (268, 271, 273–276, 278) ▪ Presentation
of the *Tomos Agapis,* Cardinal Willebrands at
Constantinople (289), Metropolitan Meliton at Rome
(290ff.), on sixth anniversary of lifting of the
anathemas ▪ Death of Patriarch Athenagoras I (298–
300)

259.　*8 July 1969*

Letter of Patriarch Athenagoras to Cardinal Willebrands on a joint commission for the publication of the communications between the Churches of Rome and Constantinople**

Your Eminence Cardinal John Willebrands, President of the Vatican Secretariat for Christian Unity, very dear brother in Christ, grace and peace from God be with you.

This follows upon what our representative, His Eminence and dear brother in Christ Metropolitan Meliton of Chalcedon conveyed to you by word of mouth during his last visit to Rome about something that had been discussed here in due course. This was the question of setting up a joint commission from both Churches for the publication in an official volume [*Tomos*] of the texts of the correspondence, the speeches on various occasions, the addresses and messages, which were exchanged during these recent times when relations and contacts between the Churches have been restored. We now hereby inform you that the members of the commission from the side of our Orthodox Church have been appointed by a Synodal decision. They are the Very Reverend Archimandrite Damaskinos Papandreou, Director of the Orthodox Centre at Chambésy near Geneva, and the Reverend Deacon Bartholomew Archondonis from the staff of the Sacred Theological College of Halki. We communicate this news to you for use in Rome.

Wishing you strength from God in all things, we call down upon you his grace and infinite mercy, and so remain with brotherly love and befitting esteem.

260.　*12 July 1969*

Letter of Cardinal Willebrands to Patriarch Athenagoras accompanying the despatch of the new Roman liturgical calendar with commentary*

Your Holiness,

The liturgical reforms decided on by the Second Vatican Council are now at the very last stage. The revised "Roman Calendar" was published 21 March last. It occurred to me that Your Holiness might like to have a copy. I have had a short document drawn up which brings out the main lines of these reforms, and I enclose a copy with this letter. As soon as the translation into modern languages of this volume have been made, I shall send you a copy of this too.

I am happy to take this opportunity of asking your Holiness to accept the expression of my respectful and brotherly feelings in Christ Jesus.

261.   *19 July 1969*

Letter of Cardinal Willebrands to Patriarch Athenagoras in reply to the Patriarch's 8 July letter*

I thank your Holiness very much indeed for the letter in which you tell me that Archimandrite Damaskinos Papandreou and Deacon Bartholomew Archondonis have been appointed members of the commission which is to arrange for the publication of the written communications exchanged between the Ecumenical Patriarchate and the Church of Rome. I hope that this commission will be able to proceed actively with the work and bring it happily to term. On our side a first inventory of the texts has already been drawn up, and the work will be taken up again as soon as the holiday season is over.

262.   *23 July 1969*

Letter of Patriarch Athenagoras to Cardinal Willebrands in reply to the Cardinal's 12 July letter**

With much joy we have received your letter and read it both privately and before a session of our Holy Synod. Attached to the letter you sent us a copy of the "Roman Calendar," remodelled and published on the basis of the liturgical reforms in the Roman Catholic Church as decided on by the Second Vatican Council, and you let us know that you intend to send us a copy of the volume in which the Calendar is translated into modern languages.

By a synodal decision we thank Your dear Eminence in this reply for the despatch in question, and as we beg the choicest gifts from God on your behalf, we remain with brotherly love and much esteem.

263.   *29 July 1969*

Telegram from Patriarch Athenagoras to Pope Paul VI on his journey to Africa**

Our brotherly thought and heart accompany you in prayer in your pilgrim journey of love and hope to Africa.[48] We hope with all our heart that your presence on African soil will be like a visit of the Risen Lord whom we have in common, and will be a great opportunity for an out-pouring of peace and love on all our African brothers and sisters. May God be with Your Holiness.

264.   *12 August 1969*

Telegram in reply from Pope Paul VI to Patriarch Athenagoras*

We are deeply touched by this fresh testimony of affection and brotherly concern which you kindly showed us in connection with our apostolic pilgrimage to Africa, and would like to say how grateful we are and how we remain joined with you in thought and prayer.

265.   *26 September 1969*

Telegram from Patriarch Athenagoras to Pope Paul VI for the Pope's birthday*

Every day brings me to the side of Your beloved Holiness, but your birthday presents me with a special occasion for wishing you length of days for the well-being of the Christian Churches, and a journey for both of us along the road to Emmaus towards a new meeting with Jesus Christ in his holy chalice.

266.   *1 October 1969*

Telegram in reply from Pope Paul VI to Patriarch Athenagoras*

---

48. The Pope visited Uganda, 31 July–2 August.

We keenly appreciated the kind and thoughtful wishes expressed by Your Holiness for our birthday. We send you our lively thanks, and assure you again of our brotherly affection.

267.   *13 October 1969*

Telegram from Patriarch Athenagoras to Pope Paul VI on the beginning of the Synod of Bishops**

Always close in heart and spirit to Your venerable Holiness, we remembered you and your Holy Roman Catholic Church (since the sacred Episcopal Synod was assembling in your presence) in our prayer yesterday during the Sunday celebration of the Divine Liturgy in our holy Patriarchal Cathedral.

We send our cordial greetings and those of our Church to Your highly beloved Holiness and through you to the reverend members of the Synod. We pray the Paraclete to strengthen you in your great and holy responsibility, and to give success to the work of the Synod under your enlightened guidance, for the good of the Roman Catholic Church, our beloved sister.

268.   *15 October 1969*

Letter from Cardinal Willebrands to Patriarch Athenagoras on the Cardinal's intention of going to the Phanar for the feast of St. Andrew*

Ever since the time when the Holy Father called me to take over the Presidency of the Secretariat for Christian Unity, I have wanted to make a visit to Your Holiness and the Ecumenical Patriarchate. It seems to me that the Feast of St. Andrew could be a favorable occasion for fulfilling this wish.

Accordingly I thought of arriving at Istanbul in the afternoon of Saturday 29 November and leaving in the late morning of Wednesday 3 December, if you find these dates convenient. Before making any preparations to carry out this plan (which will allow us, I hope, to see exactly where we are in the relations between the two Churches, and to give new impulse to our joint effort), I am anxious to submit the project to Your Holiness to see if these dates suit you.

They occur immediately after the plenary session of our Secretariat, and would enable me, among other things, to tell you what took place.

Looking forward with hope and joy to this new meeting, I beg Your Holiness to accept the expression of my respectful affection in Christ Jesus.

269. *17 October 1969*

Telegram from Pope Paul VI to Patriarch Athenagoras, thanking him on behalf of the Pope and the Synod for his good wishes*

We personally and all the members of the Synod are very grateful for the feelings expressed by Your Holiness and the venerable Church of which you are the worthy Pastor. We thank you very sincerely for what you said, and we pray the Spirit of the Lord that this Synod may be a new step towards the restoration to full communion of the two sister Churches. In our own name and that of the members of the Synod, we convey to Your Holiness, your clergy and faithful people, our deep affection in Christ the Lord.

270. *25 October 1969*

Telegram from Patriarch Athenagoras to Pope Paul VI on the second anniversary of the Patriarch's visit to Rome*

Two years have gone by since our happy meeting in the holy basilica of the Apostle Peter in the eternal city. As we gaze in thought at this lapse of time, we gratefully glorify the most holy Name of the Lord, who has blessed and rewarded the intention and the toil in which we stand together. The cause of the unity of the Christian world is continually going ahead. Hearts are being warmed, minds enlightened, and consciences purified, to welcome the great and holy day when our sacred rites, which we have begun to share since then but have not yet carried to completion, will be celebrated in full together.

As this happy anniversary comes round, we greet Your very venerable and highly regarded Holiness in brotherly fashion, and we thank you from the bottom of our heart for all the marks of friendship which you showed towards us and those with us during the days of our unforgettable stay at the Vatican. We hope that the holy day will soon come when we shall be united, and will take part together before the altar in the Eucharistic offering, for the good of Christians over the whole world and for those who have gone before us in faith and hope.

271.   *31 October 1969*

Letter of Father Jérome Hamer, O. P., Secretary of the Secretariat for Christian Unity, to Patriarch Athenagoras, on the forthcoming visit of Cardinal Willebrands to the Phanar**

Your Holiness,

As soon as we received your telegram we set about the preparations for the visit which Cardinal Willebrands will soon make to you for the feast of St. Andrew. I shall accompany His Eminence, as will Father Duprey, the Under-Secretary, and Father Fortino of the staff of our Secretariat.

We shall arrive on Saturday 29 by Pan-American, Flight 114, at 4:25 p.m., and will leave again on Wednesday 3 December by Pan-American, Flight 119, at 12:00 noon. Father Duprey will not be leaving until 5:00 p.m. on 4 December, on his way to Athens, since he has to take part, at 4:00 a.m. in Istanbul, in the meeting of the commission for the publication of the documents exchanged between the Ecumenical Patriarch and the Holy See.

I should be grateful to Your Holiness if you could arrange a time for a visit to the Governor of Istanbul and one to the Armenian Patriarch, as part of our program. On our side we are writing to the Apostolic Nuncio to ask him to provide for the celebration of the liturgy at the Catholic Cathedral on Sunday afternoon, and then for a meeting with the various Catholic communities. A brief time also should be left during our stay for a visit to Bishop Tcholakian. We have written about this visit, too, to the Apostolic Nuncio.

As I wait with joy to meet Your Holiness, I beg you be so good as to receive the expression of my very respectful affection in the Lord.

272.   *2 November 1969*

Telegram from Pope Paul to Patriarch Athenagoras on the second anniversary of the Patriarch's visit to Rome*

As we relive in spirit the blessed days when we had the joy of receiving a well loved brother into our house, we give thanks to the Lord for what he has enabled us to do together for the much desired restoration of unity between Christians. We join in the prayer of Your Holiness, hoping from the Holy Spirit the light and strength which will enable us to intensify this effort and hasten the day when concelebration will seal and manifest the reestablishment of full communion between the Catholic and Orthodox Churches. Rest assured of our deep fraternal charity in the Lord.

273.   *21 November 1969*

Letter of Pope Paul to Patriarch Athenagoras on the feast of St. Andrew and the visit of Cardinal Willebrands to the Phanar*

Beloved Brother in Christ,

We should like to take the opportunity provided by the visit of our brother, Cardinal John Willebrands, to the Ecumenical Patriarchate, to entrust him with this message for you, which will renew the expression of our esteem and our very real and brotherly affection. This visit fits in with our desire to see the contacts between our Churches become more numerous, and in conjunction with Your Holiness to have an examination made from time to time of any measures that can further our progress towards the reestablishment of full communion.

We are happy that this visit is taking place on the feast of St. Andrew, the patron of your Church, and we cannot help calling to mind on this occasion the beautiful icon, representing the two brothers Peter and Andrew embracing one another, of which you made us a gift after our meeting in Jerusalem. That representation involves a whole programme for ourselves and our Churches, which must act more and more together, with one heart and spirit, to serve their Lord and fulfil his will today.

May Andrew, the First-Called of the Apostles, make this visit an occasion for adding to our common will as we exchange information and decide on the objectives to which we must next direct our efforts.

We thank Your Holiness in anticipation for the kind welcome which you have in store for our delegates, and we assure you that we remain deeply united with you in the charity of Christ.

274.   *30 November 1969*

Address by Patriarch Athenagoras in welcome of Cardinal Willebrands (at the end of the Divine Liturgy in the Patriarchal Cathedral)**

The fact that the holy and glorious Apostle Andrew the First-Called should today, the very day on which we keep his sacred memory, be receiving the embrace of his own brother Peter, the leading figure among the Apostles, in the midst of a Church given over to festive rejoicing, is something pleasing to God and calls on us to give him glory.

Hence with deep joy we greet Your Eminence, my dear Cardinal, and your worthy companions, and honor your presence in our midst, bringing as you do from the angel of the Church of the Romans, and successor of Peter, the salutation of love and hope in Christ to the holy Church of Constantinople, and also to my humble self, by the infinite mercy of God successor of St. Andrew.

We look upon this visit as a new sign and testimony of the brotherhood of our two Churches, of the wonderful progress that by the grace of God has been reached in their dealings with one another, and of their firm decision to press on further. This would entail that, being made perfect in the love of Christ and through that love removing all remaining obstacles, they would, with a common profession and testimony of the truth and the faith, bring to its consummation the mystery of the unity of the Church on earth.

From this latter point of view we appreciate this new contact made through you of the Old Rome with the New as a valuable contribution to the building up of unity, and a sacred occasion for drawing down on the Church new gifts from the inexhaustible mercy of God. We have an unshakeable belief in this, because we seek nothing other than to fulfil Our Lord's holy will, and because from this source the grace of God has already poured out rich mercies on us.

At this opportune juncture we go back in mind with deep feeling and gratitude towards God to the recent past, and fix our gaze on all the wonderful things that have been achieved: the three meetings between ourself and the Pope of Rome Paul VI, in Jerusalem, in Rome, and here itself in this holy place, where the memory of the sacred figure of our venerable brother praying with us is and will remain vividly present; the lifting on either side by common consent of the anathemas; and all the other various exchanges of deeds of charity, and of good thoughts and feelings towards one another. In a special way we remember today the visit paid us by the unforgettable Cardinal Augustin Bea, the honored predecessor of Your Eminence in the Presidency of the Secretariat for Christian Unity, whose faith and Christian courage contributed so greatly to the growth in the relations between the two Churches up to the present very happy point.

But this recent and blessed past, apart from the hope and certainty it gives us for the future, brings home to us the measure of our responsibilities for the steady continuation, with all zeal and care, of the sacred work that has been undertaken, that of making a forward march, stage by stage, to final unity.

We rejoice greatly as we see clear signs of the concern for unity growing day by day in both our Churches. In the matter of taking this progress further we base great expectations on the zeal and wisdom of Pope Paul VI, whose sincere attitude and kind brotherly overtures we value very highly. We regard as a further mark of this attitude the fact that he has placed the important charge of the Presidency of the Secretariat for Christian Unity on the shoulders of Your Eminence, in whose person we see a worthy successor to Cardinal Augustin Bea of happy memory and an energetic and wise worker who will continue the latter's extremely valuable ecumenical activity. It is our hope and desire that your period of office as President will, with the help of your worthy fellow workers, mark a new time of progress, not only as regards the unity of our two churches, but also that of all Christians.

Blessed be God in that already both in the West and the East we are living through the great season of a return to the ancient unity. Neither of us is calling the other to himself any more, but like Peter and Andrew we betake ourselves, and take each other, too, to Jesus, our one common Lord, who brings about unity. We wish to remain with Jesus, to remain together, united, and to remain the whole day, the day that belongs to the last things and has no ending.

In this desire and hope we with the whole Church exchange the embrace of love, brotherhood, and peace with the most holy Pope of Rome, our much loved and venerated brother, Paul VI, and we cordially greet you, Eminent Cardinal and dear Fathers.

Welcome, close and beloved friends!

275. *30 November 1969*

Address in reply by Cardinal Willebrands*

Your Holiness,

Allow me to begin by telling you of the joy which I feel at this moment. Quite spontaneously there come to my lips the words of the kingly prophet David: "Behold, how good it is, and how pleasant, where brethren dwell at one!" (Ps 133). In this Psalm the prophet was singing about the brotherly life which was led by the priests and levites gathered together in the temple and the holy city of Jerusalem for the service of their Lord. And it is this same joy of which the prophet sang, this joy in the Lord, that we ourselves or the bishops of our Church feel every time that we find ourselves here in the house of Your Holiness. It is this same joy in the Lord that the bishops of this holy see feel, I believe, when they come to visit us at Rome.

I feel this joy today more keenly than on other occasions because we have the favour of celebrating with you the feast of the holy patron of this Church, the great Apostle Andrew, the First-Called. Are not the bonds which united Peter and Andrew—those two Apostles who followed the Lord together, who died for him, and like him died on the cross—rich in symbolic meaning and instruction? The crosses of both St. Peter and St. Andrew receive all their glory from the Cross of the Lord. Brotherhood in the common service of the Lord unites us in affliction as in joy; today it is in joy that we meet one another again.

As I am paying a visit to this venerable Patriarchate for the first time as President of the Secretariat for Christian Unity, I should like to recall the memory of my lamented predecessor, Cardinal Augustin Bea. When Pope John XXIII announced to the world his great plan of summoning a universal council of the Catholic Church, he had a keen desire to reestablish brotherly contacts with the other Christian Churches, and to enter upon a way which would allow of progress towards unity, by showing as a living reality the communion which already existed between these Churches. It was thus that he sent for the priest Augustin Bea and asked for his help in implementing this holy design. Cardinal Bea was a man who had been matured by a long priestly life in prayer and study in the service of the Kingdom of God. He accepted this task as a new vocation, and before, during, and after the Council, gave himself completely to this mission. Without interruption he sought to serve this cause, for which he felt himself responsible. At the Council he often rose to his feet to draw the attention of the fathers to the ecumenical implications of decisions which they were preparing to take, and to the consequences which they would have for the future on relations between the Christian Churches. He not merely helped to establish contacts, but acted in the wisdom of the Lord and the charity of the Spirit to help strengthen once more the friendly ties between all those who belong to the family of God.

How great was his joy on the day when he went as a Cardinal of the Roman Church to Istanbul to have an official meeting there with the Ecumenical Patriarch, and to be received as a loved brother by him, in his house, at his table, and to seek with him the most suitable ways to deepen and develop the communion between the two

Churches, to pray with him in his cathedral and be present there at the Divine Liturgy.

What a joy it was for Cardinal Bea to read before the Council of all the Catholic Bishops the Brief *Ambulate in Dilectione,* which together with the Patriarchal *Tome* removed from memory and the midst of the Church the ancient anathemas, and consigned them to oblivion. What a joy it was for him to be able, in the presence of His Holiness Pope Paul VI, to exchange a brotherly embrace with Your Holiness before the altar of the Lord in the Basilica of St. Peter in Rome.

Since I have worked under his leadership at the Secretariat for Christian Unity from the beginning, I am more conscious than anyone else of the difficulty of succeeding him and continuing what he began. It is because I feel myself supported by the sacerdotal prayer of Christ the eternal High-Priest, who never ceases to intercede for us with his Father, and never ceases to send forth his Spirit, that in faith and hope I have accepted the responsible post to which Pope Paul VI has called me, lowly person that I am, thereby testifying to a confidence in me for which I am deeply grateful. I know that I am supported also by the prayers of all Christians, and in a special way by those of this holy Church of the New Rome, by those of its venerable Patriarch, its Metropolitans, bishops, priests, deacons, and its people, who all pray to the Lord for the unity of all who belong to him, and work to ensure that his final desire should be fulfilled without meeting obstacles of human origin.

It is with deep feeling that I remember the first visit I made to Your Holiness and to this venerable Church, and the moment when for the first time I saw the Bosphorus and the Golden Horn, the banks of which were chosen by the Emperor Constantine for the building of a city, the New Rome, which would radiate such a spiritual influence, and do so much in the service of the Lord's Gospel. I gained then an insight of some depth into the spiritual riches, the wisdom, and tradition amassed by history in this unique site.

Since then there has been a great increase in these exchanges of view, these visits made and returned, these courses of action agreed on together, which have led us, under the guidance of the Holy Spirit—a guidance which was sought with faith and followed with docility—to recognize one another as sister Churches, and to proclaim the fact officially. When we did these things, was it not the awareness of the mystery of the Church, of its unity and catholicity, which was being deepened within us? Did not the saying of Christ, "Where two or three are gathered in my name, there am I in the midst of them," become a living reality for us? When we were making progress along this way, was not the heart of each one of us burning like that of the disciples of Emmaus when they walked with the Lord and recognized him in the breaking of bread? We hope that the Lord's light and the strength of his Spirit will bring us to see the dawn of that day, when we shall be, like the disciples at Emmaus, gathered round his table for the breaking of the bread.

We may be sure that the visit of His Holiness Pope Paul VI to Your Holiness and his Church, and the visit which Your Holiness made to the Holy Father and the Church of Rome, are the expression of a brotherhood which has been rediscovered and professed before the whole Church of God and his people, and the first fruits of unity in a perfect communion with the same Lord, in the same faith and the one Eucharistic celebration. These visits have also been an occasion for the solemn affirmation of certain principles of fundamental importance for the future: those concerning the legitimate diversity in unity which the ancient Church lived out in its experience, and of which St. Irenaeus, St. Basil, St. Augustine, and St. Cyril have given testimony, and which point the way to a restored unity between sister Churches. The Holy Father and Your Holiness have stated with clarity and decision in a joint declaration their desire to see their Churches begin "unselfish collaboration and common action on the pastoral, social, and intellectual levels, with a mutual respect for the fidelity of members on either side to their own Church."

These are acts which are quite rare, if not unique, in the history of the Church, and which have expressed with clarity and depth the desire for unity of the heads of two Churches, whose Cathedrals are dedicated to the same Lord, venerated in the one case as the manifestation of the Divine Wisdom, and in the other as Savior.[49] In the title of these two Cathedrals there is surely a further expression of that unity in diversity which our churches have known as a matter of living experience, and which they must discover afresh.

The desire for unity impels us to search out all the ways and means which may lead us thither. The unity which we look for is that which reigned within the Apostolic band. It is not a question of a uniformity which would reduce all to itself, but of the unity of a body

---

49. The two cathedrals are the Church of Hagia Sophia (Holy Wisdom) which was the center of Byzantine religious life before the Turkish conquest of 1453 and later preserved as a state museum, and the Basilica of San Salvatore, the Bishop of Rome's cathedral, otherwise known as St. John Lateran.

where the harmony consists in the complementarity of the members. It is not a question of suppressing another's voice, but of singing in harmonious polyphony of the great deeds of God, "so that with one heart and voice we may glorify God, the Father of Our Lord Jesus Christ" (Rom 15:6). We believe that in this band of the Apostles Peter was the first leader, and that he was so not only in Jerusalem but that he continued this ministry at Rome, and that he has handed it on to his successors. This service of authority for the sake of unity should be studied again in the light of the Gospel and of the authentic Apostolic tradition in a dialogue of charity and truth between our Churches, as well as between all the Churches and ecclesial communities of the Christian world. Christ himself who was, is, and always will be the cornerstone (Eph 2:30), the shepherd and guardian of our souls (1 Pt 2:25), will help us clear up gradually the misunderstandings which still exist on this subject between our Churches.

To hasten this day we must patiently and continually combine our efforts to find and apply the means which enable us to communicate to our Churches in their entirety, right down to the smallest parishes, the rediscovery made by their heads, and to draw out the practical consequences of this in all aspects and on all levels of their life and interrelations. One of the principal objects of my visit to Istanbul is precisely to let Your Holiness and your Church know what has been recently going on in the Catholic Church, particularly with regard to the meeting of the Synod in Rome and the plenary session of the Secretariat for Christian Unity. By exchanging this information with that which we hope to receive from you, we shall probably be the better able to see what we can do to continue our progress with prudence and boldness towards the unity which the Lord wills for us.

To conclude, I must convey to the Church of New Rome the greetings in Christ of the Church of Old Rome, and transmit to Your Holiness the brotherly salutation of His Holiness Pope Paul VI.

276. *1 December 1969*

Telegram from Patriarch Athenagoras to Pope Paul VI, thanking him for the visit by Cardinal Willebrands*

It was with great joy that we received His Eminence Cardinal John Willebrands and his fellow workers to our Cathedral during the feast of St. Andrew. At the end of the Mass the letter from Your Holiness was read and the choirs sang your "polychronion" ["may he live many years"], after which the people applauded you with enthusiasm and signs of high regard. With many thanks and much affection.

277.   *7 December 1969*

Telegram from Patriarch Athenagoras to Pope Paul VI on the fourth anniversary of the lifting of the anathemas**

The further we move in time from the historic week of December 1965, when the infinite mercy of God allowed Your very dear Holiness and us to lift the anathemas between East and West, to minister to the Lord's will, and to give a first positive reply to the anxious yearning of divided Christians, the closer we feel to one another.

Today, on this anniversary we embrace Your venerable Holiness with a holy greeting. And now we are called to go further ahead. This is the hour for Christian courage. Let us, while loving one another, profess the ancient faith that we held in common, and let us go forward together to stand before the glory of the same altar, so that we may fulfil the Lord's will, and the Church shine forth, that the world may believe, and the peace of God come upon all.

278.   *11 December 1969*

Letter of Cardinal Willebrands to Patriarch Athenagoras, thanking him for the welcome received at the Phanar*

Your Holiness,

Now that I am back in Rome, I should like to tell you, in my own name and that of those who work with me, how grateful we are for the kind welcome which you gave us. We were extremely happy to be able to celebrate the feast of St. Andrew with you, and to have had fruitful meetings with the Metropolitans of the Holy Synod, as well as with others of your fellow workers.

This visit enabled us to relive so many rich and happy memories, and has also given us a better idea of how to continue our progress along the way decisively entered upon by Your Holiness and Pope Paul VI. I was particularly grateful, and I thank you warmly for the innumerable kindly and thoughtful attentions which were shown us on every side during those days.

With the Christmas season drawing near, I should like to offer Your Holiness my best wishes, and to assure you that I shall pray in a special way to the Word of God who became a small child for our sake, for your intentions and the fulfilment of your great design.

Please accept, Your Holiness, the expression of my respectful affection in Christ Our Lord.

279. *22 December 1969*

Telegram from Pope Paul VI to Patriarch Athenagoras on the anniversary of the lifting of the anathemas*

We share the feelings of thankfulness expressed by Your Holiness to the Lord, who has enabled us to wipe away the bad memories of the past. We too are resolved to go forward with a prudent boldness and to do our utmost to bring about the day when we are able to go up to the altar of the Lord together. With the feast of the Nativity of Our Lord soon about to dawn, we tender you, beloved brother, our best wishes, and assure you again of our very real affection.

280. *24 December 1969*

Telegram from Patriarch Athenagoras to Pope Paul VI, presenting his Christmas wishes*

As the feast of the Nativity of Our Lord occurs, we embrace Your well loved Holiness in him, with our heart full of prayers and the most fraternal good wishes, and remain your devoted brother.

281. *Christmas 1969*

Christmas letter from Patriarch Athenagoras to Pope Paul VI**

Bearing in our soul and heart the great joy which the angels announced to the shepherds, which the heavens recounted to the Magi, and which the Spirit of prophecy proclaimed through many mouths, we reverently bend our knees, and in a small Child, wrapped in swaddling clothes, we adore our great and eternal God.

On this day of good will and hope on which we celebrate the salvation of the world, we are united with Your most venerable and beloved Holiness in earnest supplication for the peace of the world and the unity of the human race. We ask in prayer of the Redeemer who came to us in a manger within a cave, that he may cause the light which rose upon the world through his birth to prevail over the darkness hovering over mankind, and to appear shining forth, guiding all into the way of peace and justice—for peace and justice raise nations on high and bring happiness to peoples.

With all our heart we greet Your most blessed Holiness on this holy and great feast of the Birth of Christ, and we beg from God, the giver of good things, the finest favors, on your own behalf and that of your venerable hierarchy, and of the whole pious body of the faithful of your Church, for the dawning new year of the Lord's kindness. We embrace Your Holiness in the newborn Christ, remaining with brotherly love and special esteem.

282.   *13 January 1970*

Letter in reply from Pope Paul VI to Patriarch Athenagoras*

Very dear Brother in Christ,

The warm good wishes that Your Holiness sent us by letter and telegram were a source of great joy to us.

Our heart filled with confidence, we turn towards the year whose course has just begun, feeling ourselves still deeply affected by the words of joy and the message of peace brought us by the feast of Our Lord's Nativity.

We ardently unite ourselves with your prayers: may justice and respect for one another raise men and women to a greater dignity both within themselves and in their material conditions. May the Holy Spirit guide us along the way of reconciliation, so that the union of our Churches may become more and more a sign shining with hope and consolation in the midst of all humankind. Supported by your brotherly and warm affection, our prayer and supplication united with yours mount towards the Father of lights, from whom every perfect gift descends.

We send our warmest best wishes once more to Your Holiness, and we ask you to receive the expression of our brotherly affection and high regard in Christ the Lord.

283. *Easter 1970*

Easter letter of Pope Paul VI to Patriarch Athenagoras*

Christ has risen! He is truly risen!

We greet Your Holiness with these emphatic and joyful words of the Roman Liturgy as we celebrate the central mystery of our Christian faith in the feast of the Resurrection of "our great God and Savior Jesus Christ" (Ti 2:13).

At this time of Easter which brings to mind the radiant and joyful victory of Christ over death and the divisions which death brings with it, we renew our faith in the Lord who is continually causing his Church to rise with him with added life and unity, so that it may serve as a more faithful and effective witness before the men and women of today. May they believe that Christ is the one and only Savior who continues his work of salvation in strength and glory by means of his Church until he comes again.

It is with these feelings of faith and hope, venerable Brother, that we express our brotherly love and respect for you. Through you we wish the bishops, clergy, and faithful of your Church the peace and joy of the Lord, who by his Resurrection from the dead has made it possible for us "to put on the new man who is created in God's image, justified and sanctified through the truth" (Eph 4:24).

284. *28 March 1970*

Telegram from Patriarch Athenagoras to Pope Paul VI on the feast of Easter*

As the great day of the Resurrection of Christ comes round, we congratulate Your beloved and venerable Holiness, and wish you all the joy and happiness of Christ. At the same time we express our desire and best wishes for the celebration one day of this feast in common. With much affection.

285. *8 February 1971*

Letter of Pope Paul VI to Patriarch Athenagoras on the development of relations between the two Churches*

The visit which the Metropolitan of Chalcedon, Bishop Meliton, is making to us in your name, is the cause of a very real joy for which we should like to thank you. In addition, this visit gives us the opportunity of confiding to his care a fraternal message, in which we should like to tell you once more how we thank the Lord for what he has enabled us to achieve during these last few years by way of reestablishing ever closer ties between our Churches.

We thank the Lord, too, for giving to his Church, in the person of Your Holiness, one of the most generous protagonists of the sacred cause of unity. During the Week of Unity we kept on reminding the faithful assembled in the Basilica of St. Peter that between our Church and the venerable Orthodox Churches there already exists a communion which is almost complete—though still short of perfection— deriving from our common participation in the mystery of Christ and his Church.

The Spirit has enabled us in these recent years to become vividly aware once more of this fact, and to perform deeds which brought out the implications of this communion in the life of our Churches and their relations with one another. At the same time, the Spirit has put into our hearts a firm intention of doing everything possible to hasten the day we so much desire, when at the conclusion of a liturgy celebrated together we shall be able to drink together from the same chalice of the Lord.

It is with this hope that we must from here on do our best to create anew between the Catholic and Orthodox clergy and faithful everywhere an attitude that is really fraternal. May the situations inherited from the past and the barriers that were formerly raised between us no longer act as a hindrance to this last step towards full communion. Are we not disciples of him who is continually making all things new?

In this spirit, and desiring a still closer collaboration in order to discover with one another the ways most conducive to reaching this goal, we assure you again, most dear brother, of our deep charity in Christ.

286.   *21 March 1971*

Letter in reply of Patriarch Athenagoras to Pope Paul VI**

To Paul, the most blessed and holy Pope of ancient Rome, greetings in the Lord.

It was a matter of great joy to us to receive the much appreciated letter of 8 February last which Your very loved and esteemed Holiness sent us by the hands of our dear brother in Christ, His Eminence Metropolitan Meliton of Chalcedon. We read your letter with close attention first privately and then aloud in Synod.

Having glorified the Word of God, who orders the affairs of his holy Church with all wisdom and goodness, for this new and holy opportunity for brotherly communion in him, we next thank you affectionately in written form. In Your much loved Holiness the Church Militant has an outstanding spokesman and worker for peace, for charity, for the unity of Christians and of the human race created in the image of God.

Coming to this fraternal reply, we hasten to assure you, our senior brother, that, submissive to the holy will of the Lord, who wants his Church to be one and visible to all, so that the whole world may find its way to it, we commit ourselves constantly and undeviatingly to the guidance of the Holy Spirit. This we do having in mind the steady pursuit and accomplishment of the sacred work which was begun and developed with you, by a holy desire on both our parts—the work of making visible and displaying to the world the One, Holy, Catholic, and Apostolic Church of Christ.

With you we join in thanking the Lord for his great gifts to us in making us aware, in the name of his precious Blood which unites all things, and which was shed for the life and salvation of the world, of the grave sin of division, and also in restoring our clarity of vision and in prompting us to return, both from the West and the East, to the blessed and ancient unity which was that of the Apostles and the Fathers.

In reality, even if the Churches of the East and the West became alienated from one another, by faults known only to the Lord, they were not alienated in the fact of their communion in the mystery of the God-Man Jesus and of his Church, in which the union of the divine and human is prolonged.

We became alienated from mutual love, and there was taken from us the good and happy gift of a unanimous profession of the faith of Christ. There was taken from us, too, the blessing of ascending together to the one altar established by the Lord shortly before his Passion, and of a perfect communion, with one mind and heart and in a common assembly, in the same precious Eucharistic Body and Blood, even though we did not cease to recognize the validity of the apostolic priesthood and the mystery of the Divine Eucharist on either side.

But see how in our days among the faithful of both East and West there is an anxiety passing previous bounds to have, through charity and likemindedness, fellowship in the truth of the faith and its profession, and to see this fellowship ritually celebrated and perfected in a sharing of the holy chalice. Thus grace has been given us in surpassing measure.

Enlightened by this grace, we see clearly that the holy cause of the visible unity of the Church and the perfect communion in it of the faithful is not a work to be left for human considerations and deliberations, given that the designs of men are unsure (Wis 9:14), but something to be experienced in the life of Christ, which finds continued existence in his Body, the Church.

Just as it was a matter of experience that we proceeded in a negative way towards division, so we are called to proceed as a matter of experience in a positive way towards perfect union in concelebration and in a common sharing of the Precious Blood of Christ from the same holy chalice. For this reason we agree with you that we must make the community of Church life as between East and West grow stronger, by working for true and firm brotherhood both among the clergy and the people of the Roman Catholic and Orthodox Churches.

We write to you from the East shortly before the Passion of the Lord. The table has been prepared in the upper room, and Our Lord desires to eat the Paschal meal with us. Are we going to refuse?

In sheer fact the impediments that derive from the heritage of history and other sources are still there, and the enemy of the Kingdom of God mounts guard over them. But we, have we not pledged our faith to him who said that what is impossible for men is possible for God, and that all things are possible to the one who believes?

With faith and hope and patience let us follow the Apostles, from whom we have grace, brotherhood, and communion.

In making this reply, with love, esteem, and the most brotherly feelings, we embrace Your venerable and very dear Holiness with a holy greeting.

287.   *2 April 1971*

Easter letter of Pope Paul VI to Patriarch Athenagoras*

Your Holiness,

Christ has risen! This exclamation gives expression to all the joy felt by Christians as their minds dwell on the glorified Christ, who in his victory over death reveals himself as "the true light which enlightens every man" (Jn 1:9). The Risen Christ is the ground of our faith, the one light which shines in all our lives, as the Easter liturgy expresses it in those rich symbols which have been passed on from generation to generation from the first centuries of the Church. The Roman Church sings this truth aloud when, at the beginning of the vigil celebration of the Resurrection, each of the faithful comes to light his or her candle from the Paschal flame: "This flame, although divided into many parts, suffers no loss from the sharing out of its light." Just as the single flame is communicated to many different candles, so we all live by the same faith in the Lord who "has risen for our justification" (Rom 4:25). In the rich variety of our traditions, it is his single light that we reflect and show forth to the world, so that all those whose deeds are done in the truth may come to the light (cf. Jn 3:21).

"The Lord of glory" (1 Cor 2:8) expects of us that we should reflect this glory with ever greater clarity, so that all may be transformed into his image (2 Cor 3:18). This continual striving after fidelity is a charge laid on all of us. And when we speak about fidelity to God's designs for his Church, how can we avoid thinking in the first place of this call to unity, which it is all the more urgent to establish between us since the bonds which unite us are of such deep reaching consequence. In touching on the matter of these bonds, we are thinking of the priesthood which on both sides we have received from the Apostles.

We should like to take this opportunity, dear brother, to tell you that the exercise of this priestly ministry today, together with justice in the world, will be the subject for reflection by the regular Synod of Catholic Bishops which will meet in Rome next autumn. We hope that we will be helped in this event by your brotherly prayers.

May the light of Easter shine with its full brilliance in the Church of which Your Holiness is the shepherd.

It is thus, my dear brother, that we give renewed expression to our fraternal charity in the Risen Christ.

288.   *8 April 1971*

Telegram from Patriarch Athenagoras to Pope Paul VI for Easter**

Christ is risen! In making a spiritual visit to Your dear and venerable Holiness for the feast of joy, hope, and peace, we impart a brotherly embrace of charity and communion, desiring that the Lord may make all things new, irradiated by the eternal light of his Resurrection.

289.   *7 December 1971*

Address by Cardinal Willebrands at the Phanar for the sixth anniversary of the lifting of the anathemas, and for the presentation of the *Tomos Agapis* to Patriarch Athenagoras*

Your Holiness,

It is now six years since by common agreement Your Holiness and Pope Paul VI, inspired by charity and the will to obey the Lord, banished from the memory and the midst of the Church the remembrance of the excommunications of 1054. On that memorable day, December 7, 1965, in your Cathedral and in the Basilica of Saint Peter, great was the emotion and keen the realization that this act of Christian reconciliation was being accomplished before "a great cloud of witnesses" (Heb 12:1)—those who in the course of the centuries have been "well attested by their faith" (Heb 11:39). They received mercy because they truly believed, with that faith which bears fruit in love for God and for our brethren. They are in the glory of God and "they follow the Lamb wherever he goes" (Rv 14:4). In this light (cf. Rv 21:23) they understand, they see that the final and definitive reality is love (cf. 1 Cor 13:13). The more our life, the life of the Churches and the life of the Church is ruled by love, the more this life is in the image and likeness of God who is love. This is the great witness that is demanded of our Churches; it is thus that God can be recognized in them. How great therefore must have been the joy in heaven on that day of December 7, 1965.

That joy in heaven has been reechoed on earth. This act of generous reconciliation has had a much wider echo than could have been humanly foreseen. The Spirit of God was at work in and through the openness to guidance of the two venerable pastors of the old and the new Rome. This act created a new situation, with openings and opportunities which we are gradually discovering.

The *Tomos Agapis,* which I have the honor to present to Your Holiness today on behalf of the Holy Father, and which includes some two hundred and eighty-four documents exchanged between the Church of Rome and the Ecumenical Patriarchate between the years 1958 and 1970, gives some idea of the distance covered. The idea of this publication was born here, in the course of the meetings in which we take our bearings and see what are the next possible stages for our journey forward—a journey which is cautious, because it must be certain—towards the restoration of full communion. This book is meant to be such a stage. It would be a good thing if our theologians could make a joint study of the implications of these texts and elucidate the theology of the Church and the idea of relations between the two Churches which inspire them. These theologians would have to make explicit this theology, which springs not only from the speeches and letters exchanged between the pastors of these two Churches, but also from the deeds which they have accomplished and which are often rich in symbolism. This volume is meant to be an occasion for discovering further, both on the speculative and on the practical level, the dimensions, the presuppositions and the implications of this theology. The theologians must evaluate its consequences upon the relations between our Churches and upon the growth of the almost total communion which already exists between them. They should do this with lucidity and with an imagination ready to divine possible new paths; let them carry out this task with an eye to the future that we must build, and with a realization of the demands of our times and the aspirations of the younger generation.

Your Holiness, I come to bring you the brotherly embrace of your loving brother, the Pope of Rome, Paul VI. He sends me to you to tell you of the events that the Church of Rome has experienced in recent months, in order that we may study our present position with you and with your Synod, and that we may concert our efforts to ensure and orient our common journey towards our one common Lord, "Jesus, who leads us in our faith and brings it to perfection" (Heb 12:2).

290. *24 January 1972*

Address by Metropolitan Meliton on the occasion of his presentation of the *Tomos Agapis* to Pope Paul VI**

Holy Father,

I give glory to God for the fact that this is now the third time I have come at a significant stage from the Church of Constantinople, to represent that Church and the venerable occupant of its see, my holy Patriarch Athenagoras, and to address Your Holiness in audience.

The first time I had the privilege of speaking before Your Holiness was in this very hall, 16 February 1965, when by mandate of the whole Orthodox body, I conveyed to you and the holy Roman Church the decisions of the Third Pan-Orthodox Conference.

The second was on 7 December of the same year, in the "Sala dei Paramenti" [Vestment Hall], immediately after the memorable ceremony in St. Peter's Basilica of the lifting of the anathemas between the Churches of Rome and Constantinople.

And now, as I carry out the instructions of the Ecumenical Patriarch and his Holy Synod, with my worthy colleagues gathered about me, I have the signal honor of placing in your sacred hands the combined work *Tomos Agapis,* sent from the hands of your brother the Patriarch of Constantinople.

The title *Tomos Agapis* given by the joint publication committee to this book is an appropriate one, since the work tells the story, stage by stage and in official documents, of a love found again in Christ between the sees of Rome and Constantinople. But, as the Greek word *tomos* indicates, the story recorded here represents only a summary section of the inexhaustible love of Christ, and on the other hand testifies to the fact that it was by incision, by sacrifices and pains, that the love between yourself and us was quickened into life.

But who is there to tell the story of what lies behind the words and phrasing of the texts of this "tome"? All the details, all the thoughts, reflections, meditations, all the religious feelings, the prayers and nights with little sleep, all the anxious longings of the faithful and of the Church, with a share thereby in the agony of Christ, for the emergence into visible fact of the divine word and will, "that they may be one"? Further still, what book could ever describe the divine design and method by which the God of Love, the God of our common fathers, moved the hearts and minds, the lips and the pens of West and East to work out this new theology of unity by dint of spiritual experience and churchly life and action, a new theology which was yet as ancient as the undivided Church? Or this new and at the same time utterly ancient confrontation on ecclesial grounds of the great scandal of division? It would be impossible.

All these things are experiences arising from God's impulse, lived out in the mystery of the divine providential design, and are treasured up as organic elements in the life of the Church. One day they will find their expression in the brilliant beauty of a perfect Eucharistic fellowship, of a single witness in unity to the world, and of the consummation and perfection of all things in Christ Jesus that bears the marks of the end time.

Just as the whole Christian mystery and fact is at once divine and human [Gr. *theandrikon*], and as the character of the Church is divine and human, so this book too contains an expression of divine and human elements. In it, as we follow the gradual path traced by the documents, we realize that divine power coexists with human weakness. With what human caution and reservations, not to say apprehensiveness, the written exchanges between our two churches began! Both parties felt themselves constrained by the heavy weight of inherited history and psychology. We were afraid. But suddenly the Spirit breathed, and love cast out fear. In this book there is the momentary appeal: "Let this chalice pass from me." But finally it is God who carries all before him: "May thy will be done."

Your Holiness,

Both after this volume and beyond what belongs to "now," may the Lord's will be done, and done in love.

291. *24 January 1972*

Dedication of the copy of the *Tomos Agapis* presented by Patriarch Athenagoras to Pope Paul VI**

To Paul VI, his loved and venerated elder brother, Athenagoras of Constantinople dedicates this volume, which contains the account of the origin and growth of charity between the Churches of Rome and Constantinople, with hope in the Lord and the devout wish that he may grant us to write the epilogue with his Precious Blood on the holy altar shared by us both.

292. *24 January 1972*

Dedication inscribed inside the casket containing the precious cross presented by Patriarch Athenagoras to Pope Paul VI**

To Paul VI from Athenagoras I, the precious Cross which has brought together again what was sundered, and on it the Divine Love crucified, on the occasion of this presentation of the *Tomos Agapis.*

293. *24 January 1972*

Address in reply by Pope Paul VI to Metropolitan Meliton*

My dear Brothers,

The occasion of our meeting today is the publication of a collection of documents exchanged between the Ecumenical Patriarchate and the Holy See during these last twelve years. This volume very appropriately appears under the title of charity. In fact, is it not charity which has urged us on both sides to resume communications which had been too long broken? The Holy Spirit who first placed this love in our hearts has brought it about that what was unhoped for when we took those first steps has become the joyful reality of today. This book shows the road which we have travelled and the way we followed by common agreement, under the guidance of the Holy Spirit.

First then, gratitude is the dominant feeling in our hearts at the end of this first stage, and we give glory to "the Father of Lights from whom comes every good endowment and every perfect gift" (Jas 1:17), for what he has kindly willed to work in us and through us. But our gratitude and thanksgiving can only please God completely when they are accompanied by petition, availability, and determination. Petition, because we know that he alone can bring to completion what he has so wonderfully begun. The hope which sustains our prayer makes us docile to what the Spirit is saying today to the Churches, and attentive not to miss the opportunities which he opens up to us. We must be resolute in going forward, convinced that prudence requires and at the same time directs the courage which is founded on faith. Our forward march together has created a new situation between us, a situation which could give rise to further progress and help us to glimpse new solutions. We must not hesitate to press onwards in complete fidelity to our whole common tradition. The faithful people turn their eyes towards their pastors, who certainly do not wish to betray their hopes but to take cognizance of them and lead them forward in the light of the Spirit who "fills and rules the whole Church" (Preface of the Mass for Christian Unity), directing it towards its true fulfilment. We are quite certain that this spirit will inspire the conversations which will be taking place at this time between our Secretariat for Unity and yourselves, eminent representatives of our dearest brother, Patriarch Athenagoras.

Your visit, our meeting, these conversations, are taking place during the Week of Prayer for Unity. There could hardly be a more favorable atmosphere for these exchanges. The new Roman Missal contains three formularies for celebration of the Eucharist for the intention of Christian unity. The proper preface which introduces the anaphora offers a thought full of theological depth concerning ecclesial unity:

> Through Christ you bring us to the knowledge of your truth,
> that we may be united by one faith and one baptism
> to become his body.
> Through Christ you have given the Holy Spirit to all peoples.
>
> How wonderful are the works of the Spirit,
> revealed in so many gifts!

Yet how marvelous is the unity
the Spirit creates from their diversity,
as he dwells in the hearts of your children,
filling the whole Church with his presence
and guiding it with his wisdom!

This liturgical prayer expresses the same thought which inspired Vatican Council II when, going back to the supreme source of unity, it declared: "This is the sacred mystery of the unity of the Church, in Christ and through Christ, with the Holy Spirit energizing a variety of functions. The highest exemplar and source of this mystery is the unity, in the Trinity of Persons, of one God, the Father and the Son in the Holy Spirit" (*Unitatis Redintegratio,* 2).

These lofty thoughts recall the greatness of the gift of unity and make us understand the intensity of the Lord's prayer for unity, a prayer to which Christian tradition has given the name of the "priestly prayer."

During this week the Christian world joins in this prayer of the Lord in a special way, meditating on the new commandment which he has given us, and which should expand and manifest itself in unity. In this evening's celebration in our cathedral, a celebration at which we thank you for your kind participation, we will all be united in prayer. We ask for the light and strength necessary to direct our forward march at a time when we are invited by God's grace to take decisive steps, not only amongst ourselves but within the whole Christian family, in a future which with all our heart we would hope is close at hand.

May this common resolve be symbolized by the sign of peace which we should now like to exchange with you.

294.   *24 January 1972*

Address by Pope Paul VI at the prayer service in the Lateran Basilica, held on the arrival of the delegation from the Ecumenical Patriarch*

We break off our exchanges with God for a moment so that they may become an exchange with the "Ecclesia," that gathering in which we are joined with you, my brothers here present. It is almost as if we sought an assurance on your side as well as ours that we are fulfilling the well known gospel saying about being gathered together in the name of Christ and as a result having him, Christ Our Lord himself, in our midst (cf. Mt 18:20). Christ is here—let us honor his presence. Let us celebrate this mystery which derives from the very fact that the reason for our meeting is that we may confess his name, and this not as external to ourselves—a name which we acknowledge and call upon—but as something that we feel in its application to our inner being. We are all Christians, we were all brought by Baptism into the Mystical Body of Christ which is the Church (cf. *Sacros. Conc.,* 6–7; *Lumen Gentium,* 15; *Unitatis Redintegratio,* 2–3), we have all become sons of God, our heavenly Father whom words cannot compass; we all have faith in Christ the Lord, and we all expect of him to be forgiven, redeemed and saved, in the one life-giving and sanctifying Spirit. Here we have already what forms the basis of that ecumenical unity which we are so eagerly seeking.

For the intention of this ceremony is ecumenical. It has been arranged to greet and welcome among us an eminent representative of the venerable Orthodox Church, the Metropolitan Meliton of Chalcedon, sent to us by His Holiness Patriarch Athenagoras of Constantinople, a man of great piety and very dear to us. The Metropolitan comes as you know to bring us the *Tomos Agapis,* the "volume of charity." This volume brings together the documentation and correspondence about the relations between the Patriarchate of Constantinople and the Church of Rome over the last twelve years. These Churches rejoice at having rediscovered that they are branches of the same tree, born of the same root, but [as Churches] are now suffering at their inability as yet to drink at the same mystical chalice, and thus together consummate that perfect communion which would allow the organic and canonical union between the two communities, a union characteristic of the one Church of Christ.

With deep joy and sincere devotion we greet this illustrious and venerated guest with the honorable persons with him among us here today. He is the bearer of a book which history will make its own. He is a guest moreover, who is no stranger to the Apostolic See and one who, by his very presence, becomes a sign, an expression of desire, a promise of the coming happy celebration of the complete communion in faith and in charity of those who have declared they are brothers hundreds and hundreds of times already, as the book demonstrates. And it seems to us that the very title that qualifies the illustrious Metropolitan of the Orthodox Church, the title of Chalcedon, makes this visit of his particularly dear and significant for the Church of Rome. It takes our mind back to our immortal predecessor, St. Leo the Great (cf. Denz. Sch. 300–302), who by means of his letter to Flavian authoritatively upheld the Christological definition of the famous Council of

Chalcedon, which made Rome and Constantinople brothers in the same definitive and felicitous faith, regarding the one divine Person and the double nature, divine and human, of Christ.

Who better than you, therefore, eminent Metropolitan Meliton, can take to Patriarch Athenagoras our thanks for the mission of devotion, courtesy and peace entrusted to you? Kindly tell that venerable man that his mission had its solemn and sacred climax here, in the sacrosanct Lateran Basilica, in the presence of cardinals, bishops, prelates and clergy of the Curia and the Diocese of Rome, and of the faithful people of the Roman Church. Be so kind as to tell him how we carried out together with intensely religious feeling a pious and conscious act of that "spiritual ecumenism," to which the recent Vatican Council exhorted us (*U.R.*, 8), because not only have we prayed *for* the brothers with whom we desire to be in perfect communion, but we have all prayed *with* them, with great joy in the Holy Spirit.

And, venerated Metropolitan Meliton, kindly tell that saintly Patriarch and the venerated brothers and faithful gathered around him that this happy celebration has made us profoundly aware of the onerous privilege we bear. It took place indeed in the basilica that in the historic and theological tradition of the Western Church is called *omnium urbis et orbis ecclesiarum mater et caput* ["mother and head of all the churches of the city and the world"], because it is the cathedral of the Bishop of Rome, successor to the blessed Apostle Peter. But it did anything but flatter our human ambition for the pastoral charge entrusted by Christ to the one who presides in this see—the charge of acting as "the perpetual and visible principle and foundation of the unity of the bishops and of the multitude of the faithful" (*Lumen Gentium,* 23). Here more than anywhere else we think of ourselves as "the servant of the servants of God." Here we see ourself as a brother with our brothers in the episcopate, and those who are in collegial solidarity with them. Here we think of the observation of another great predecessor, Gregory the Great, who, while asserting his apostolic function (cf. *Reg.* 13, 50), wished to consider the honor of the whole Church and the effective activity of the individual local bishops his own honor (cf. *Reg.* 8, 30: P. L. 77, 933). Here we remember St. Cyprian's conception of the unity of the Church: *una Ecclesia per totum mundum in multa membra divisa* (*Ep.* 36, 4), that is, like a composite and articulated body, in which parts and groups can be modelled in particular typical forms, and functions can be distinct, if they are fraternal and work to the same end. Here, in the heart of unity and at the center of catholicity, we dream of the living beauty of the Bride of Christ, the Church, wrapped in her many colored garment (Ps 44:15), clothed, that is to say, in a legitimate pluralism of traditional expressions. Here we seem to hear the limpid echo of a distant voice of yours: "Oh Peter, you foundation stone of faith!" (cf. *Menaion,* June 29).

So it remains for us to invoke that divine assistance which strengthens our weakness in the practice of the virtues necessary for ecumenism to reach its happy conclusion. We will say with St. Paul that we are "sure that he who began a good work in you will bring it to completion at the day of Jesus Christ" (Phil 1:6), convinced that at the completion of the great enterprise of setting up again the unity of Christians, one condition will necessarily be requested of all of us, a widening of charity: *dilatentur spatia caritatis,* "may the frontiers of love be expanded," we will say, to use an expression of St. Augustine dear to us (*Serm* 69; P. L. 38, 440–441). A widening of charity which will make it possible for us all to find ourselves once more united in the same Church, members of the same body of Christ. Then we will add to the *Tomos Agapis* a new, last and splendid page: the page of unity.

295.   *25 January 1972*

Press conference by Metropolitan Damaskinos of Tranoupolis and Father Pierre Duprey at the presentation of the *Tomos Agapis* [The first part of this conference, under the heading "General Presentation," contains almost verbatim, matter which makes up the Preface and Introduction to the original edition of the *Tomos Agapis*. (Cf. above, p. 24) Here are the "Particular Indications" which follow.]

PARTICULAR INDICATIONS

1. The subject in question is relations between Churches. The efforts made to repair the break between the two Churches have never before been so free of any political element and any purpose foreign to the sole desire of accomplishing the will of Christ for his Church. (Speech of the Pope, 26 October 1967, Document N. 190.)

2. On September 20, 1963 the Pope sent his first autograph letter to the Patriarch Athenagoras (N. 33). This was the first letter from a Pope to a Patriarch of Constantinople since 1584. On November 22 1963 the Patriarch replied with his first letter to the Holy Father (N. 35).

3. On the occasion of the third Pan-Orthodox Conference in

Rhodes, in October 1964, the Pope sent a message to the Conference (N. 76) and received a reply (N. 77). In February 1965 an official delegation, let by the Metropolitan Meliton, came in the name of the Pan-Orthodox Conference to inform the Holy Father of the Conference's decisions (N. 87). In the speech given on that occasion by Pope Paul VI (N. 88), the programme laid down for the development of relations between the Church of Rome and the Churches of the East is presented in summary form: "We are happy about the wisdom and the realism of the main lines of the programme which you have just sketched. We must, by means of more numerous and fraternal contacts, progressively restore what the time of isolation has undone, and create anew, at all levels of the life of our Churches, an atmosphere which will allow us, when the time comes, to set about a theological discussion likely to yield good results. If you for your own part are studying the main subjects to be submitted to fraternal discussion in the future, you are aware at the same time how greatly the desire and preparation for this dialogue occupy the mind of the Vatican Council and of Catholic theologians. We are very glad about the meetings and the conversations which you propose having with our Secretariat for Unity, which will later give us an account of them. We retain for ourselves the right for reflection and consultation to decide on the best ways from our side of giving life and vigor to this dialogue of charity and to the progressive experience of a rediscovered brotherhood. God is our witness, our only desire is to be faithful to Christ."

4. The lifting of the excommunications.

In July 1965, during a visit to Rome (N. 108), the Metropolitan Meliton raised in a more precise manner the question of the possibility of studying together the lifting of the excommunications of 1054, a question which had already been touched upon during his previous visit. A series of documents will enable the reader to follow the development of this idea to its realization (NN. 119, 121–124, 126–130).

5. The autograph message which the Pope sent to the Patriarch on July 13, 1967 to inform him of his intention of visiting him at Phanar and to give him the reasons for his visit (N. 171), and the letters which the Patriarch Athenagoras addressed to the Pope to announce his coming to Rome (N. 186), and after this visit (N. 211), indicate very clearly the spirit of these meetings and the aim pursued.

6. In the address given yesterday at the Lateran, the Pope spoke of the pluralism possible within unity. He was very explicit on this subject in the speech which he gave at Phanar on 25 July 1967 (N. 172); he spoke, among other things, of "recognizing the identity of faith beyond variety of vocabulary."

7. On July 25, 1967, in the Cathedral of the Holy Spirit at Istan-

bul, the Pope presented to the Patriarch Athenagoras the Brief *Anno Ineunte* (N. 176). This text explains why the Catholic and Orthodox Churches are "sister Churches." This official document of the Pope integrates an essential aspect of the traditional ecclesiology of the East.

8. The common declaration of the Pope and the Patriarch on October 28, 1967 (N. 195) gives very clearly the bases for dialogue between Catholics and Orthodox and affirms that the time has come to see the development of "an unselfish collaboration in common action on the pastoral, social and intellectual levels, with a mutual respect for the fidelity of members on either side to their own Church." In his speech at Istanbul (N. 172) the Pope had said: "It is upon the heads of the Churches and their hierarchies that the task lies of leading the Churches along the road which leads to finding full communion again. They must do this by recognizing and respecting one another as pastors of the portion of the flock of Christ which has been entrusted to them, by taking care for the cohesion and growth of the people of God and by avoiding anything that could scatter it or cause confusion in its ranks." This document shows very clearly the desire to put an end to every form of proselytism and "to avoid the rancor of the past and every form of spiritual or intellectual domination."

9. The last two documents (NN. 283, 284) express the desire of both sides to hasten the day when concelebration between the Pope and the Patriarch will be possible and when "that almost total communion," to quote an expression in the Pope's letter, will reach completion.

296. *24 March 1972*

Easter letter from Pope Paul VI to Patriarch Athenagoras*

Your Holiness,

"Blessed be God, the Father of Our Lord Jesus Christ: in his great mercy he has begotten us anew by the Resurrection of Jesus Christ from the dead for a living hope" (1 Pt 1:3).

As we keep the feast of the Resurrection of the Lord, it is also our own rebirth in him that we celebrate. We proclaim our certainty that the restoration of all things has already begun in Christ, and that through the Holy Spirit it goes on apace in the Church. Hence we are brought face to face once more with the real meaning of our life in this world, while in expectation of the good things to come we strive to serve the world in a spirit of justice and truth.

Because of the resurrection which we profess together, these celebrations become a time full of joy and hope for us. It is this joy that we invoke in desire for you as we send you our warm best wishes for the holy feast of Easter.

We beseech him by whom we have been begotten anew for a living hope to fill Your Holiness with his blessings, and together with you your clergy and the faithful members of your Church.

297. *30 March 1972*

Telegram from Patriarch Athenagoras to Pope Paul VI for Easter**

Christ has risen! I embrace Your venerable Holiness, whom I hold so dear, in the Risen Christ, hoping that the Lord who is risen from the dead may grant you to celebrate the light-bearing feast for many years to come. May he bless your works and days for the joy and good of the Church.

298. *7 July 1972*

Telegram from Pope Paul VI to the Holy Synod of the Ecumenical Patriarchate, upon the death of Patriarch Athenagoras (7 July)*

We have heard with great emotion of the death of our brother and dear friend in Christ, his Holiness Patriarch Athenagoras. We send you our most sorrowful condolence on the loss which has struck the entire Orthodox Church, and we pray the Lord to receive into his heavenly Kingdom one who was the great protagonist of reconciliation between all Christians and between our two Churches in particular.

We recall the encounters we had with the venerable deceased Patriarch at Jerusalem, Istanbul and Rome; and we render thanks to the Lord in the hope that the work begun by Athenagoras I will be continued, for the greater glory of God and the good of his Church.

We unite ourselves with you in prayer on this day of sorrow and we commend your Church to the favor of the Lord.

299. *9 July 1972*

Tribute by Pope Paul VI to Patriarch Athenagoras in his speech before the recitation of the Angelus, Sunday 9 July****

We wish to call your attention to two subjects on which we feel we must speak. Although they are not connected, each makes claims on our spiritual attention.

The first is the death of the venerable Greek Orthodox Patriarch of Constantinople, Athenagoras. Everybody has been speaking about him with the admiration and respect due to those commanding figures who personify an idea which powerfully influences the course of history and goes far towards interpreting the thought of God. His stately hieratic bearing was an expression of his inner dignity; his grave and simple words bore the accents of the pure goodness of the Gospel. He inspired high regard and feelings corresponding to his own. We are among those who most admired and loved him. The friendship and trust he showed us never failed to move us. As his memory comes back to mind, our sense of loss grows greater, but so does our hope of having him still close to us in the Communion of Saints.

You are aware why we are asking you to call to mind and pray for this great man of a Church which is worthy of veneration but is not yet fully united to our Catholic Church: it is because he was an unremitting laborer and apostle for the reunion of the Greek Orthodox Church with that of Rome, as well as with the other Churches and Christian communities which are not yet fully reintegrated into that single communion of the Mystical Body of Christ.

Three times we had the good fortune to meet him personally; a hundred times we had that of exchanging in writing our best wishes and our promises to do everything we could to reestablish between ourselves a perfect unity in the faith and in the love of Christ. Always he used to sum up his feelings in one supreme hope, that of being able to "drink from the same chalice" with us, in other words to celebrate together with us the Eucharistic sacrifice, which would be a unified expression and consummation of our common ecclesial identification with Christ. That is something which we, too, have greatly longed for.

As things stand, this desire, as yet unfulfilled, must remain both a legacy and the matter of our full commitment. Let us devoutly keep alive the memory of Patriarch Athenagoras and pray that, through the intercession of Mary, Mother of Christ and his Church, this desire may find fulfilment.

300.   *16 July 1972*

Telegram from Metropolitan Meliton, President of the Holy Synod, to Pope Paul VI**

We were deeply moved by the great concern shown by Your Holiness over the illness of our most revered and blessed father and Patriarch and your heartfelt sharing in our grief at his departure to the Lord.

By the decision of the Permanent Holy Synod we convey our warm thankfulness to Your Holiness in general, and we beseech Our Lord to grant you length of days and unfailing health.

PART III

The Dialogue Reaffirmed

301.   *17 July 1972*

Telegram from Pope Paul VI to Patriarch Dimitrios I[50] on his election to the See of Constantinople*

At the moment when you assume a heavy charge in the service of the Church of Christ we are anxious to convey to Your Holiness our best wishes accompanied by our fervent prayer and we assure you that you will always find in the Bishop of Rome a loving brother eager to continue working towards the day so much desired by your great predecessor when our unity will be fully refound and sealed.

302.   *17 July 1972*

Telegram from Patriarch Dimitrios I to Pope Paul VI**

Having been called by the mercy and good pleasure of God the all-good to govern the holy Ecumenical See, on assuming our Patriarchal office we send Your much revered Holiness a heartfelt greeting of love and respect. May the name of the Lord be blessed.

303.   *17 July 1972*

Telegram from Cardinal John Willebrands to Patriarch Dimitrios I*

On the happy occasion of your enthronement in the see of the Ecumenical Patriarchate, the Secretariat for Christian Unity warmly congratulates Your Holiness, and prays that the Lord may grant you plentiful blessings and the light required to guide your holy Church

---

50. Born in 1914 at Constantinople, Dimitrios Papadopoulos had been a parish pastor in Iran and Turkey, then a member of the Patriarchate's Central Ecclesiastical Commission, until his election as Metropolitan of Imbros and Tenedos in February 1972. Five months later he was elected the successor to Athenagoras on 16 July, and on the 18th, was invested with the thirteenth century title, "Archbishop of Constantinople, New Rome, and Ecumenical Patriarch, by the Grace of God."

along the ways of God. I hope that we shall maintain a close collaboration between our Churches, and make continual progress towards the fulness of a refound communion.

304.   *21 August 1972*

Letter in reply from Patriarch Dimitrios I to Cardinal Willebrands**

Your Eminence Cardinal John Willebrands, much loved and esteemed brother in Christ our God, may the grace and peace of God be with you.

With much love we received the kind and brotherly greetings and good wishes which Your Eminence sent us when we were elected to the most holy Apostolic and Patriarchal Ecumenical See and took our place there.

The manifestations of love that have come from brothers in Christ everywhere affect us deeply, swayed as we are by similar feelings towards them. We consider the development of the ties of friendship, honor and respect towards them and their Churches as one of the leading concerns in the service we render as Patriarch.

We warmly thank Your Eminence for your good wishes, and we in return wish you length of days in firm and unfailing health. We embrace you in the Lord, and remain with brotherly love and fitting esteem.

Your Eminence's dear brother in Christ, . . .

305.   *12 April 1973*

Easter letter of Pope Paul VI to Patriarch Dimitrios I*

Your Holiness,

In our prayers we are preparing to celebrate with great joy the glorious Resurrection of Our Lord Jesus Christ, an event which is central to the whole plan of salvation and forms the foundation of our faith. It is by the Resurrection of Christ that sin is forgiven, that death is conquered, and that in our reconciliation with God life and joy clearly shine forth. We give thanks to the Father that it was his good pleasure through and for Jesus Christ to reconcile all things on earth and in heaven (Col 1:20), and that by his Spirit he gives life and vigor to the

Church, so that she may announce to all people in all times the good news of salvation.

Let us listen in silence and adoration to the Word of God. As we meditate the great mystery of the work accomplished by Christ, we wish to let you, too, beloved brother, know of the joy which we feel when we celebrate the Passover of the Lord. We do this because we know that you share in the same gift by means of the same faith in Christ who died and rose again, and because you, too, are anxious to proclaim the Resurrection to the men and women of our time, such proclamation being central to the Church's mission.

"We believe and so we speak, knowing that he who raised up the Lord Jesus will raise us up along with Jesus and place both us and you in his presence" (2 Cor 4:13–14). The Apostle's faith was the very reason of his preaching. It was from that faith that there sprang his certainty that he would rise with the Lord, and it was from that faith that he drew the strength to speak to others. Today, too, this faith which is the source of the same certainty in us, keeps urging us to proclaim the Resurrection, "so that all may confess that Jesus Christ is Lord" (Phil 2:11), and that in him alone can we be saved (Acts 4:12).

But alas, a large number of our brothers in the human family do not profess this faith. They do not believe in the Risen Christ. Does not this painful realization demand of us a deepening of the faith we share together, so that we may succeed in reestablishing between our Churches that full unity which would allow us to give better testimony to the work carried out by Christ and which would give full credibility to our preaching (Jn 17:21)? In our time, more than ever before, the Spirit of God calls our Churches to profess the same faith together, so that we can say to all mankind: "What we have seen and heard we proclaim in turn to you, so that you may share your life with us. This fellowship of ours is with the Father and with his Son, Jesus Christ" (1 Jn 1:3).

Inspired with this hope, we assure you again, Your Holiness, of our very brotherly love in the Risen Christ.

306. *22 April 1973*

Telegram from Patriarch Dimitrios I to Pope Paul VI for Easter**

We rejoice in mind and heart as we celebrate the glorious Resurrection of Christ our Lord and God from the dead. With brotherly affection we send cordial greetings to Your dear and venerable Holiness in connection with this outstanding and holy day. May the Risen One grant you to glorify for many years his victory over death. May he bless your designs and deeds for the good of his holy Church. Christ is risen!

307. *25 June 1973*

Telegram from Patriarch Dimitrios I to Pope Paul VI for the tenth anniversary of the Pope's election to the See of Rome*

In a close fellowship of charity we celebrate, together with the Church of Rome, the tenth anniversary of your election, by the grace of God, to the sacred see of the successors of the Apostle Peter, and your enthronement there. We honor this anniversary in recollection and prayer for you, holy elder brother, for the holy Roman Church, and for Christian unity, of which, ever since your election, you have shown yourself the bold and prudent champion.

On this holy occasion we recall the thoughts which you have expressed about Christianity and the whole human race, we recall your deeds and eloquent signs—all of them holy, truly Christian, and worthy of the Bishop of Rome—in favor of these causes. Moreover, we recognize with full honor the fraternal debt of the East towards Your Holiness.

We visit you in spirit and exchange a holy embrace, hoping from the bottom of our heart that God will give you a long life for the good of the whole Church on earth and for that of the entire world.

308. *13 July 1973*

Telegram in reply from Pope Paul VI to Patriarch Dimitrios I*

The message which Your Holiness so kindly sent us for the tenth anniversary of our election to the see of St. Peter touches us deeply. We thank you with all our heart for this expression of charity and fraternal communion, as well as for your prayers to God, who alone gives light and strength for a ministry acceptable to him. We beseech God with confidence to grant his grace to our two sister Churches to carry out the work begun for the restoration of full unity. In a spirit then of gratitude, joy, and of prayer, we express once more our brotherly affection towards Your Holiness.

309. *20 November 1973*

Letter from Pope Paul VI to Patriarch Dimitrios I*

With great spiritual joy we unite ourself, in profound communion of faith and charity, with the prayer of your Church as it celebrates the feast of the Apostle Andrew, the First-Called, holy Patron of the Church of Constantinople. This year our spiritual participation will be made more visible by the presence of our brother Archbishop Cardinal John Willebrands, President of our Secretariat for Christian Unity. He will bring our warm fraternal greeting to you, very dear brother in Christ, to the Holy Synod, to the clergy and to all the faithful people.

Our envoy will also bring you, venerable brother, the expression of our firm hope that the Lord will grant us the light and strength necessary for reaching the end of the road leading to the full communion of our Churches. We began to walk along this road with your predecessor Athenagoras I, whom we had the joy of meeting several times and whom we esteemed and loved very deeply. We should like to assure you not only that we pray continually for this intention, but that in order to accomplish this work we are ready to collaborate in every new step thought feasible at the present time, in the spheres of both study and action.

Inspired by these sentiments of faith, hope and joy, and united with you in prayer before the Apostle Andrew, we convey once more to Your Holiness our good wishes for a fruitful pastoral ministry and assure you again of our fraternal and respectful affection in the Lord.

310. *30 November 1973*

Address by Cardinal Willebrands in the Patriarchal Cathedral*

"Blessed be the name of the Lord" who has allowed us to experience together this time when the feast of the Apostle St. Andrew was being celebrated. Andrew was the "First-Called": he is the patron of the Church of Constantinople and was brother of Peter, the leading Apostle, whose Church is at Rome. May God be thanked that he has enabled me once again, at this solemn liturgical time, to bring Your Holiness and the Church of Constantinople the greetings of His Holiness Pope Paul VI and the Church of Rome, and to assure you that he is praying that by the grace of God the two sister Churches may be fully reconciled, and that perfect communion may be reestablished between them. The Holy Father does indeed desire and is quite resolved to do everything possible to give effect to this project, thereby making his own the desire expressed by the Lord himself in his priestly prayer.

We are gathered here today to do honor to St. Andrew, the First-Called to follow in the wake of Jesus. We commemorate his holy life which found its consummation in martyrdom, the noblest sign of his profession of faith in Jesus, the Christ, the Son of the living God—a fact full of meaning.

It is indeed the profession of the true faith in the living God, Father, Son, and Holy Spirit, a profession of faith finding expression in holiness of life, which will gather us together into the unity of a single sheepfold under a single Shepherd (Jn 10:16), who is Jesus Christ, our one and only Lord.

Unity, truth, and holiness are closely bound together in the prayer which Jesus addressed to his Father, before he was glorified on the Cross, and in so doing reconciled all with God (Col 1:20): "I consecrate myself for their sakes now, that they may be consecrated in truth. I do not pray for them alone. I pray also for those who will believe in me through their word, that all may be one as you, Father, are in me, and I in you; I pray that they may be one in us" (Jn 17:19–21). The teaching which most perfectly fits our case as we search for unity is here given: holiness in the truth finds its expression in unity.

God alone is holy. But St. Peter, Andrew's brother, reminds us: "Become holy in every aspect of your conduct, after the likeness of the holy One who called you; remember, Scripture says, 'Be holy, for I am holy'" (1 Pt 1:15–16). And what is sanctity, if it is not incorporation in Christ in the mystery of the Church? What is sanctity other than participation in the divine life (2 Pt 1:4), which means the deification of man, and unity between man and God? Surely this is the fundamental unity which Christ asked of his Father for those who believe in him.

Our Churches, as means of salvation, continue their work of sanctification, by preaching the Lord's word transmitted to them in the teaching of the Apostles, by incorporating new disciples in Christ, and by celebrating the mystery of salvation in the Eucharist.

Founded as they are on the cornerstone which is Christ, nourished by the faith of the Apostles, filled with life by the continual presence of the Holy Spirit, our Churches have expressed their ineffaceable witness in the legions of holy pastors and simple faithful, in hermits and monks, martyrs and confessors, in saints of ancient times and those of our own day.

The Churches of East and West, today as well as yesterday, put forward as a pattern for living this multitude of those "who have been consecrated in Christ Jesus and called to be a holy people" (1 Cor 1:2). They are always interceding with God, and with one voice and one heart repeat the very same prayer uttered by Jesus for all who believe in God's word: "Sanctify them in truth" (Jn 17:17), and: "May they be made perfect in one" (Jn 17:23).

We were united with them during this celebration of the Eucharist, which is the sacrament of perfect unity. I have myself offered my humble prayer to the almighty and merciful God for his Church scattered throughout the entire world, for this Church of Constantinople which is the first among the Orthodox Churches, for the hierarchy and all the faithful, asking the Lord that he enable us to bear a witness of holiness in our days through truth in unity, and to bear this witness to the glory of his name now and forever. Amen.

311. *30 November 1973*

Address by Patriarch Dimitrios I in the Patriarchal Cathedral**

Your Eminence, Cardinal Willebrands, and honored companions of the Cardinal,

It is with the love, honor, and the sense of brotherhood towards the holy Church of Rome that has always existed in this holy Church of Constantinople, that we welcome you today here in our see as bearers of like sentiments on the part of ancient Rome, and especially on the part of the Pontiff who exercises his illustrious office there, our much esteemed and respected elder brother, His Holiness Pope Paul VI.

Welcome to our midst! You have come to your own, not as strangers among strangers, but as brothers among brothers. It is thus that we look upon and honor your visit—a fraternal one.

This then is first and foremost. In Christian love and brotherhood, everything can be easily understood, everything evenly ordered, everything abides in a state of fidelity, in our common Lord Jesus Christ, to the idea of the one and only Church founded by him—founded in the events that go from his Cross and through his Resurrection to the day of Pentecost. And this Church is his Body.

When we speak about "our Churches" we have no thought of abandoning that concept of the Church according to which it is One, Holy, Catholic and Apostolic; what we have in mind is the local Churches, each having its own jurisdiction, and this being held in respect. It is with this outlook that we welcome Your Eminence as a representative of the first Bishop and Patriarch of the West, His Holiness and our very dear elder brother, Pope Paul VI.

But to be clear, sincere, and honest with ourselves and with one another, and indeed with the whole world, we must repeat with emphasis that no bishop in Christendom possesses the privilege, either divine or human, of universality over the One, Holy, Catholic and Apostolic Church of Christ. We are all, whether in Rome or in this city of Constantinople, or any other city whatsoever, regardless from the Church's point of view of its hierarchical or political position, purely and simply fellow bishops under the one supreme High-Priest and Head of the Church, who is Jesus Christ, in a holy system of rank and order that has been always received by the Church since the earliest days.

In saying this we fully adhere to what Your Eminence proclaimed in the course of your address in the sacred Patriarchal Cathedral in today's solemn commemoration of Andrew, the First-Called of the Apostles. Andrew was the brother of Peter, the leading figure among the Apostles, and Andrew brought Peter to Jesus. But here it is not a question of who brought whom to Jesus. By divine decree and providential design we have all been brought to Jesus. We all stand in his presence, and we are all called upon to show our faithfulness to him.

We welcome all of you today as such fellow witnesses to fidelity to Jesus, and we desire to render this common witness with you before the whole Christian and non-Christian world.

We are well aware that the way leading to the point where we can give this combined testimony is a difficult one, since it presupposes an identity of theological, and more particularly ecclesiological points of view between Rome and this see, which are the two hearths and homes of the Christianity handed down by Apostolic tradition, from which sources all others await guidance.

We say today, speaking in a church assembly, before you, honorable representatives of the venerable Roman Catholic Church, before the whole Christian world, and the whole world itself, whether religiously practising or not, whether believing in something or nothing, that we will spare no effort in bringing all men and women to Jesus. In this we shall faithfully follow out what the Apostle of the Gentiles said: we shall be all things to all men, so that in some way or other we may save some (1 Cor 9:22).

Your Eminence,

The message which we utter today is not in the nature of a formal address in reply to the contents of your own discourse.

It is a message that springs immediately to our lips, and is free and independent, as coming from this holy Church of Constantinople and directed to the holy Church of Rome and the revered dignitary who presides over it.

It is a message of love, honor, and respect. In it we want, as Ecumenical Patriarch, to emphasize that henceforth all our Pan-Catholic and Pan-Orthodox meetings, dialogues, and deliberations, will be held on the following essential bases.

First, the supreme authority of the One, Holy, Catholic, and Apostolic Church lies with an Ecumenical Council of the universal Church.

Secondly, none of us who are bishops in the universal Church holds authority, power, or canonically sanctioned right over any other area of ecclesiastical jurisdiction whatsoever, without the canonical will and consent of the other bishop to whom such jurisdiction properly belongs.

Thirdly, from now on all our joint enterprises and deliberations directed towards unity, even though they may be worked out, in accordance with the decisions of the third Pan-Orthodox Conference, on a basis simply involving two parties, will have no definitive result, except as decided on a Pan-Catholic and Pan-Orthodox level.

In saying these things, we desire nothing other than to set the matters for discussion in a correct perspective, out of the range of misunderstandings and misinterpretations.

Yes, indeed! Holiness in truth and truth in holiness, and these as an expression of holy and true unity in Christ. This unity will be one day, when the Lord so pleases, the fulness of union in truth and holiness, in the holiness of the truth, in the truth and the holiness of the one unifying Savior, common to us both, Jesus Christ, to whom be glory for all ages.

312. *30 November 1973*

Address by Cardinal Willebrands in his audience with Patriarch Dimitrios I*

Your Holiness,

My heart is full of true and deep joy today as I make my first visit to Your Holiness since you were called to succeed the venerated Athenagoras as Ecumenical Patriarch. I must express forthwith the feelings of respect and esteem on the part of ancient Rome and the fraternal greetings of His Holiness Pope Paul VI—both people and Pope follow closely and affectionately the life of the Church of new Rome.

In the course of the year just gone by we have maintained regular fraternal relations between the Churches of Rome and Constantinople. At the same time I am very happy to be able to take up personal relations again with Your Holiness and your Church. I should like to tell you of the more important events that have occurred in the Catholic Church during the year. I should like to have some conversation about future developments in the way our two Churches feel and act towards one another, and to look ahead with you to the form and frequency of our communications. Moreover, I should like to listen to any suggestions and requests that might be made to me.

I can assure Your Holiness that on the part of the Roman Church there is a deep desire to continue the advance (counting on the Lord's grace and taking account of what is humanly possible) towards full communion. It is in obedience to the Holy Spirit that we feel obliged to continue a course of action which goes beyond our thoughts and powers. We know with a certainty instinct with hope that the Lord of the Church, Jesus Christ, will give us light and strength, and will send his Spirit to inspire our forward journey.

I am happy to communicate to Your Holiness the good wishes and expressions of high regard of all the episcopal members of the Secretariat for Christian Unity who met in Rome at the beginning of this month for the plenary session. It is also my honor to hand you the message with which His Holiness Pope Paul VI entrusted me on the occasion of this visit.

313.   *30 November 1973*

Address in reply by Patriarch Dimitrios I to Cardinal Willebrands*

We take a special pleasure in receiving, for the first time since our election, an official delegation of the holy Roman Catholic Church bringing us the very welcome greetings of Pope Paul VI, whose personality is so intimately involved with the Church of Constantinople and with the great cause of Christian unity. Furthermore we are extremely glad that it is Your Eminence who is leading this mission, for you are very dear to the Ecumenical Patriarchate and to us personally, and the whole Church of these parts honors you highly. We are glad, too, that you are accompanied by Father Pierre Duprey, who has endeared himself to all of us here, and whose part in the cultivation of relations between Rome and Constantinople is well known to us and deeply appreciated. We are glad, too, of the presence of your second companion, Father Fortino,[51] who will, we hope, walk in the footsteps of yourself and Father Duprey.

In this first group meeting with you, we are anxious to express our deep love and great esteem for the person of His Holiness the Pope, not only as our elder brother and a sincere worker for the *rapprochement* of our two Churches and an architect of Christian unity, but also as a great spiritual leader. His beneficent activity extends to all sectors of mankind's present day concerns and problems, and to matters of highest advantage for the world, and this in view of establishing a new condition of peace and brotherhood, and one that comes as close as possible to the aims of the Lord's Church and his Kingdom.

We take the opportunity provided by this meeting to assure you that the work initiated with such sincerity and zeal by our great predecessor of happy memory, Patriarch Athenagoras, will be carried on with the same consistency for the whole length of time during which God allows us to serve him in this post.

It is clear that we have entered into a new period in the relations between our Churches, a period, that is to say, in which we must grow in depth, when we need to go ahead firmly, but also with circumspection and understanding, so that the building may be solid, and not merely one for outward show—and in this we think we are of one mind with His Holiness the Pope.

During your stay you will have the opportunity of holding conversations with those here, and of exchanging ideas and information with the competent Synodal Commission. The findings of these discussions will be assessed both here and in Rome.

We want you to feel during the length of your stay as if you were at home. We do not look on you as strangers, but as brothers, sent by a great and venerable brother, to whom we would like you on your return to convey our feelings of boundless charity, honor, and brotherhood.

We are especially happy to receive at your hands a personal message from His Holiness Pope Paul VI. This furnishes a further sign of the cordiality in the relations of the two Churches, and also of the good will of His Holiness, a disposition which is matched by a like one on our side.

---

51. Eleuterio F. Fortino, then a staff member of the SPCU section on relations with the Eastern Churches, presently head of that section.

314.   *6 December 1973*

Letter of Patriarch Dimitrios I to Pope Paul VI**

We affectionately welcomed the very venerable and dear Archbishop, Cardinal John Willebrands, President of the Secretariat of Christian Unity, on his happy arrival here together with his worthy companions. He came at the bidding of Your Holiness, bringing with him your brotherly greetings for the feast of St. Andrew, the First-Called of the Apostles, founder and patron of our holy Church of Constantinople. You thus showed in a perceptible and tangible way that you were sharing in our joy, as you said in the letter which the Cardinal handed to us.

Together with the venerable Metropolitans at our side, we were deeply moved by this sign of brotherhood on the part of Your Holiness—you who are the object of our great esteem. With pleasure we saw that your message expressed the hope that the Lord will give us the necessary light and strength to reach the end of the way which leads to the full communion of our Churches. We noted also your assurance that you are ready to collaborate in every new venture directed to the progress and final accomplishment of this undertaking.

You will see from this fraternal letter of reply that there is a holy desire also on our part that our journey towards unity, entered upon in these recent years by the will and good pleasure of God, should not end simply in a renewed experience of fellowship in brotherly love. By widening the scope of our encounters and our collaboration, we should go further, sharing the same thoughts, attitudes, and activities, entering into the whole wide domain of the Churches of East and West. We should do this with holiness, with fidelity to and veneration for the truth handed down by the Apostles, and our awareness of the structure of the Church, right up to the point where we reach a full and perfect unity. This will be a unity in the faith and truth of our common Lord and Savior Jesus Christ, in a common profession of faith, to his glory and that of the One, Holy, Catholic, and Apostolic Church.

We thank Your dear Holiness with all our heart for sending us the venerable Archbishop Cardinal John Willebrands, with his worthy companions, and also for the brotherly good wishes which you expressed towards us. For our part, we assure you of our feelings of special affection in the Lord, and of honor and veneration. And we ask the Lord to grant you for many years the physical and spiritual strength necessary for a pastoral and episcopal ministry which we would wish as long and glorious as possible.

It is with brotherly affection and every mark of esteem that we have the pleasure of calling ourselves your brother in Christ.

315.   *7 December 1973*

Telegram from Patriarch Dimitrios I to Pope Paul VI for the eighth anniversary of the lifting of the anathemas**

Today, December 7, the Church and history unite in showing their gratitude to God on the eighth anniversary of the event of the abolition of the anathemas between the Churches of the Apostles Peter and Andrew. This important anniversary finds us in recollection and prayer for the One, Holy, Catholic and Apostolic Church, that is, for the Body of Christ, our one Lord; for the holy Church of Rome, for him who is its glorious Supreme Pontiff, our elder brother, Your revered Holiness. Accept, blessed and holy brother, in return for the work of which you and our blessed predecessor were the instruments of the divine will, our cordial fraternal greeting and our sincere assurance that we shall do everything in our power for the removal of every obstacle to the unity of the Church, in its Lord who knows no obstacles.

316.   *8 December 1973*

Telegram in reply by Pope Paul VI to Patriarch Dimitrios I*

With Your Holiness we give thanks to the Lord who has permitted us to cancel memories of the past which hindered our common journey towards full communion. In obedience to the Holy Spirit we have also decided to continue through prayer, study, and action our efforts to hasten the day when we shall be able to concelebrate the Divine Liturgy, which will set a seal on the full reconciliation of our Churches. On the eve of the feast of the Nativity of Our Lord we offer you, dearly beloved brother, our best wishes and renew the expression of our fraternal charity.

317.   *3 April 1974*

Easter letter of Pope Paul VI to Patriarch Dimitrios I*

"So that, just as Christ was raised from the dead by the glory of the Father, we too might live a new life" (Rom 6:4).

We address this joyful greeting to you at a time when, together with Christians spread throughout the world, we are celebrating the glorious Resurrection of Jesus, the Christ, our one and only Lord.

Today we celebrate in this common feast the reality by which we live each day, whether we are in joy or in sorrow. Today namely we are celebrating Christ's entry into the glory of the Father, who is continually calling us out of the darkness into his marvelous light (1 Pt 2:9).

Today we celebrate the God of Abraham, of Isaac, of Jacob, our God, who goes before us in a column of fire to shed his light on us (cf. Ex 13:21).

Today we celebrate the true light, the beloved Son Jesus Christ, the Risen Lord, our High-Priest, "in whom we have full assurance of our entry into the sanctuary by his blood. We have there a new and living way which he has opened up for us through the veil, that is to say through his flesh" (cf. Heb 10:19–20).

May the joy of this celebration fill our hearts as we set about proclaiming with words and acts the Resurrection of the Lord.

This year, dear brother in Christ, we are celebrating Easter on the same day, and for us this is a fresh cause of joy. Surely this is a fitting juncture for striving with increased vigor to make such a common celebration possible every year. We should work without pause until we reach the point where all Christians can honor the mighty deeds of their God on the same day, with one voice and heart, thus testifying in common, in a world which has dire need of redemption and salvation, that God's glory and his love for humankind have broken through in visible form (cf. Ti 3:4). If we could always render such testimony together, the world would certainly see therein a particularly expressive sign enabling it to recognize better the God who so loved us that he sent his only Son to give us eternal life (cf. Jn 3:16).

Such, beloved brother, are the thoughts that come to our mind as this joint celebration occurs. We very much want you to know that we are ready to collaborate in every effort made to reach this goal.

In this spirit we ask the Risen Lord to fill Your Holiness and also your clergy, and your faithful people with his joy and light. We assure you once again of our deep fraternal charity.

318. *13 April 1974*

Telegram from Patriarch Dimitrios I to Pope Paul VI for Easter**

We take special joy in the simultaneous feast of the holy Resurrection this year. We greet Your venerable Holiness thereupon, and send a warm wish that the Risen Lord may grant you to celebrate the light-bearing feast and to announce his Resurrection for as many years as possible in unfailing health. For the sister Church of your parts and its people we wish his bountiful grace, peace and blessing. Christ is risen!

319. *18 April 1974*

Letter of Cardinal Willebrands to Patriarch Dimitrios I concerning the Ecumenical Commission for the Preparation of the Holy Year*

As you know, Pope Paul VI has decided that 1975 will be a Holy Year for the Catholic Church. What is envisaged here is an important pastoral event, of which we have great hopes.

It seems likely, too, that this year could offer opportunities for meetings between Christians. Indeed the Holy Year is to be concentrated on conversion of the heart, Church renewal, and reconciliation, in other words on the three fundamental components of the ecumenical endeavor.

For this reason the Central Committee for the Holy Year, in collaboration with the Secretariat for Christian Unity, has taken the step of setting up an Ecumenical Commission whose business it would be to deal with the practical effects which the Holy Year in the Catholic Church could have on our relations with other Christians, according to the way in which it is presented and carried out.

The President of the Commission is Monsignor Charles Moeller, Secretary of this Secretariat.[52]

On the occasion of my visit to Your Holiness, I spoke to the Synodal Commission for Inter-Church Relations about the possibility of inviting the Archimandrite Basil Tsiopanas, Rector of the Orthodox Church in Rome, to take part as an observer at the Commission. We

---

52. Replacing the SPCU secretary, Jérome Hamer, O.P., in 1973.

should like to take advantage of his reactions and suggestions for the better organization of the Holy Year at Rome. Our proposal met with a favorable reception by the Commission, and was to be referred to Your Holiness.

I should like then to ask you kindly to authorize the Archimandrite Basil to take part in the meetings of the Ecumenical Commission for the Holy Year, and let us seek the benefit of his advice. I thank Your Holiness and renew my best wishes for Easter, and I beg you to accept the expression of my respectful and brotherly feelings in the Lord.

320.   *26 April 1974*

Letter in reply of Patriarch Dimitrios I to Cardinal Willebrands on the Ecumenical Commission for the Holy Year**

We received your letter of the 18th of the present month and read it at a session of our Holy Synod. In it you inform us that a special Ecumenical Commission has been set up to deal with the practical effects which the coming year 1975, destined as a Holy Year for your Church, could have on the relations of that Church with other Christians, according to the manner in which it is presented and carried out. You also tell us that you would like the Very Reverend Archimandrite Basil Tsiopanas, President of the Greek Orthodox Community in Rome, to take part in the meetings of the Commission.

In view of your request, and of the recommendation made in this matter by our Commission for Patriarchal Affairs, we approve and bless participation by our above mentioned cleric in the meetings of the Ecumenical Commission in question. We are writing to him on this matter.

We thank Your Eminence for writing to us, and we beg of God that your life may be long and healthy.

321.   *22 June 1974*

Covering letter of Cardinal Willebrands to Patriarch Dimitrios I with the Bull declaring 1975 a Holy Year*

On the Feast of the Ascension of Our Lord Jesus Christ, His Holiness Pope Paul VI announced by the Bull *Apostolorum Limina* that the year 1975 would be a Holy Year in the Catholic Church.

As Your Holiness knows, the celebration of a Holy Year is a pastoral endeavor on the part of the Catholic Church. It takes its inspiration from the Biblical Jubilee (cf. Lev 25:8–22, and Lk 4:14–21), and first became a matter of public and solemn practice during the great penitential movement which reached wide proportions among the people in 1300.

The event which is due to take place next year in the Catholic Church is meant to represent, ten years after the end of the Second Vatican Council, "a time devoted to reflection and reform of life," and also to "inaugurate a new constructive phase made possible by preceding theological, spiritual, and pastoral work. What now takes place must find its support in the bases that have been firmly and laboriously laid down in the course of recent years, and must be in conformity with the new life in Christ, and the communion of all in him who has reconciled us to the Father in his blood" (*Apostolorum Limina,* 1).

Spiritual renewal and reconciliation with God and between men are the principal aims of the Holy Year. In this context the Holy Father wished also to announce that one of the central aims of the Holy Year is reconciliation between Christians. The Bull reminds us that this year "is an opportune time for special repentance for the divisions between Christians, an occasion for renewal in so far as this is a deeper experience of the life of sanctity, which is life in Christ, and a step towards reconciliation through a more earnest dialogue and a stronger practical collaboration between Christians for the sake of the world's salvation" (*A.L.,* 7).

Acting in the spirit of communion and brotherhood between our Churches, I send you the text of the Bull, so that you may be acquainted with the aims and pastoral concerns which have inspired the declaration of a Holy Year in the Catholic Church.

I take leave also to ask you to pray that the Lord may bless our Church's pastoral effort during the year ahead.

I would ask Your Holiness to accept the expression of my respectful and fraternal affection in the Lord.

322. *30 November 1974*

Address by Father Pierre Duprey in the Patriarchal Cathedral in the Phanar**

I glorify and thank God for giving me the privilege and honor of representing today my deeply venerated master and principal, His Holiness Pope Paul VI, in this center of the holy Church of Constantinople, in the presence of the one who presides over it, and of the hierarchy gathered around him, together with the clergy and people, and also of praying with you at this unifying Eucharistic celebration, and further of signifying the spiritual presence here today of the Holy Father.

Indeed, Your Holiness, it has been the good pleasure of God that I, although unworthy of this position, should not merely be the person who bears the holy kiss of Rome to Constantinople, but that I should also be the one who brings in these corruptible hands an incorruptible relic of a saint of the One, Holy, Catholic, and Apostolic Church, namely St. Cyril, monk, evangelist and missionary.

The fact that this relic is here in our midst, in an atmosphere of brotherly love between the holy Roman Catholic Church and that of Constantinople, and more generally of the whole Orthodox Church, reminds us of the sacred responsibility and obligation which rests on us right now providing a common Christian testimony and of evangelizing the world together.

Your Holiness,

Your predecessor of blessed memory, Patriarch Athenagoras I, in the fulness of his brotherly love, together with Popes John XXIII and Paul VI, opened up a new epoch in the history of Christianity, the epoch of reconciliation.

The Holy Year which begins with the coming feast of Christmas has been proclaimed for the Catholic Church as a year of reconciliation. Standing on the threshold of this Holy Year, I, humble priest that I am, bring from the Roman Church and from him who presides over it, nothing more and nothing less than a readiness and wish for reconciliation. Because "all this has been done by God, who has reconciled us to himself through Christ and has given us the ministry of reconciliation" (2 Cor 5:18).

Such a ministry was carried out by St. Methodius and St. Cyril, a relic of this latter being here amongst us today. We are called upon, both in the East and the West, to exercise this ministry today, in union with and continuing the work of Peter, Andrew, and Cyril. We are called upon to exercise it in the midst of a world which awaits it and is thirsty for it, and to do this for the glory of our common Lord, "He who was, who is, and who is to come."

And now, Your Holiness, I have the honor of reading out before you the venerable letter which your dear brother in Christ at Rome, Pope Paul VI, sends you.

323. *30 November 1974*

Letter of Pope Paul VI to Patriarch Dimitrios I concerning the transfer of a relic of St. Cyril to Thessalonica[53]*

As in preceding years, we find ourselves spiritually united with you on this day when the Church of Constantinople celebrates its holy patron, Andrew, who was the "First-Called" and the brother of Peter, leader of the group of Apostles. This spiritual communion will be signified by the presence of our envoy. It will also be the responsibility of this latter to consign to your charge, together with this letter, a relic of the illustrious St. Cyril, who, after a life consecrated to preaching the Gospel, ended his days in Rome.

In point of fact, it came to our notice that a church to be dedicated to this saint was under construction in his native city and was on the verge of completion. We have grounds for thinking that we are acting in harmony with your own desire when we send you a relic of St. Cyril, to be passed on by you to the Church of Thessalonica. This relic has been preserved in a chapel in our residence; its transfer will bear witness to the fact that we are at one in the veneration of the saints, and will also provide a new personal bond between Your Holiness and us.

In this spirit we assure you once more of our fraternal charity in Christ.

324. *30 November 1974*

Address in reply by Patriarch Dimitrios I to Father Duprey**

Very Reverend and esteemed representative of His Holiness, the Pope of Rome Paul VI, our dear elder brother in Christ.

---

53. Cyril and his brother Methodius were Greeks from Thessalonica, well versed in the tongue of the neighboring Slav population. At the request of Prince Rastislav of Greater Moravia for missionaries who could instruct his people in their own language, the Byzantine Emperor Michael II sent the brothers into central Europe in 863. Cyril composed a special alphabet and translated the Byzantine liturgy, probably also the Latin one, and parts of Scriptures, in Slavonic forms to which today eastern and southern Slav peoples are heirs. In defense of their "vernacular mission" against Frankish (German) adversaries, Cyril and Methodius went to Rome. Pope Hadrian II upheld their cause. Here Cyril died in 869, and Methodius was consecrated a bishop. The two saints are a significant link between Byzantium, Rome and the Slav peoples. They were declared "Co-Patrons of Europe" by Pope John Paul I, 1 January, 1981.

In the communion of the saints of the Church Triumphant, we, the Church Militant, welcome and greet you in this holy center of Orthodoxy, on this sacred feast-day, as a worthy representative of His Holiness Pope Paul VI.

Today we honor the glorious Apostle Andrew, who was crucified as Christ was, who was the brother by blood of Peter, the leader of the Apostolic group, and who brought the Gospel here, and founded this holy Church of Constantinople. This festivity finds its culmination in the sacred salutation of our own brother in Rome, Peter. Who can break up brotherhood? No one and nothing. Brotherhood survives the passage of centuries, and survives even the temporary separation of brother from brother.

In the spirit of this brotherhood Andrew receives Peter's embrace.

But together with the Apostles Peter and Andrew one who was a traveller like them takes his place among us today, the missionary who brought the light of faith to many peoples and races, St. Cyril, brother of St. Methodius.

With all due honor and piety we receive from your hands the holy relic of this great saint of the Eastern Church. From the bottom of our heart we thank His Holiness for his important and religious symbolic act in giving this relic to the birthplace of St. Cyril as a permanent testimony to the fact that it was from the Church of Thessalonica, beloved of St. Paul, that the light of Christ shone forth to the north and the preaching of the Apostle of the Nations was continued.

Esteemed representative of His Holiness, this sacred relic which is handed over to us today will be conveyed to the eparchy of this see in Thessalonica, where it will be the object of homage of Christ's faithful.

But on this great and holy day we have a further word to say to the West which is our sister:

Now is the time of the judgment of the world—and also of the judgment of the Church. Above theology there is God, above Christology Christ, above ecclesiology the Church.

This is not the time for words, but time for the Word. In the Word of God, whose appearance on earth we are soon to celebrate, we hail this new encounter of the Churches of Rome and Constantinople, and we remember their common origin, for we all come from Christ and look towards Christ, who is the beginner and perfecter of our faith. To him be glory and power for all ages!

325.   *24 December 1974*

Telegram from Patriarch Dimitrios I to Pope Paul VI for the opening of the Holy Year**

At the moment when Your venerable Holiness blesses the oncoming year as a Holy one, and consecrates it to Christian reconciliation, we visit you spiritually with deep brotherly affection, expressing our hopes and desires that this year may be made manifest by God as a real step towards reconciliation in the life of the Church and of the whole world.

326.   *26 March 1975*

Easter letter of Pope Paul VI to Patriarch Dimitrios I*

"I am risen, I am with you again" (opening antiphon of the Roman Easter Liturgy).

Now that we are celebrating the liturgy of the Paschal night, that "night which God lit up with the splendor of the Risen Christ" (opening prayer of the Easter Vigil), we think of you, dear brother in Christ, and we would like to share with you the joy brought us by contemplation of the great mystery of our salvation, which is that of Christ raised from the dead through the glory of the Father, so that we too may lead a new life (cf. Rom 6:4).

At the same time, however, our joy is mingled with sadness because we are not yet in a position to keep this feast together. Not only have we not reached the moment when we can express our common faith and joy by a common celebration of the Eucharist, the "memorial of the death and Resurrection of Jesus," but this year we are separated by five weeks as we celebrate "the day which the Lord has made."

Such divergence in our practice weakens the testimony which we, as Christians, should be giving to the world together. Moreover, it makes it impossible for us to fulfill the intentions of the First Ecumenical Council of Nicaea, which would have all Christians united in the celebration of this great mystery of Christ and the Church (cf. the letter by St. Athanasius in 359, P.G. 26, 688 B-C).

Can we not find a solution to this situation? Should not the faith which we both have in the Spirit of God who guides his Church lead us to some agreement? In the past your Church has already been seriously concerned with this question. In the Second Vatican Council the Catholic Church, too, has expressed its desire that through an agreement with the other Churches we should manage to find a common date for Easter for all Christians. The World Council of Churches has been persevering in its attempts to reach this goal which we all desire.

The Catholic Church will study with great interest any proposals that may be submitted to it, especially those that come from the Orthodox Churches. It would be keen, even, to meet representatives of Christian Churches and to discuss with them the suggestions that might arise about possible practical measures.

The world in which we live has perhaps a greater need than ever that we should testify, through the power of the Spirit, to our faith in the Resurrection of Jesus Christ, Our Lord. Moreover, his Resurrection is the foundation of our faith—this faith that is called in question by many. Did not St. Paul write that if Christ be not risen our faith is vain (1 Cor 15:14)? Moved by this conviction, and trusting in the power of the Risen Christ and his Spirit, we express our hope that by celebrating the mystery of mysteries with a single heart and voice, we may be able to render glory to God, the Father of Our Lord Jesus Christ, who raised him from the dead (Rom 16:6; Col 2:12).

May the peace and joy of the Risen Christ be bestowed abundantly on Your Holiness, your clergy, and your people. In this spirit we assure you anew of our deep and brotherly charity.

327.   *27 March 1975*

Easter letter of Patriarch Dimitrios I to Pope Paul VI*

Even though we are not celebrating Easter together this year, still the Resurrection itself is one, and the Risen Jesus Christ is the one Lord of all of us. With the prayer and hope that we Christians may all be granted to keep the Feast of the Resurrection together on the same day, we make a visit in mind to Your venerable Holiness, and in your revered person to the holy Roman Catholic Church throughout the world. We direct our brotherly salutation for this feast to you, and we express the wish from our heart that the light and joy of the Ressurection may shine abroad, and may gladden your kind heart and the hearts of all brother Christians of the West. In conclusion we say: "Arise O God, and judge the earth."

328. *18 May 1975*

Letter of Cardinal Willebrands to Patriarch Dimitrios I on the possibility of arriving at a fixed date for Easter*

The Church has had the conviction from earliest times that it was important that Christians should celebrate the Lord's Resurrection on the same date, so as to give visible testimony that they stood together in the same faith in this central mystery of the Gospel announcement. The need for a common testimony seems greater than ever in today's world where rapid means of communication have, so to speak, cancelled out distance. Recently His Holiness Pope Paul VI wrote to you saying that he would like to collaborate with your Church to find a common solution which would put an end to these differences of date which the faithful people of our Churches find it so trying to maintain. You have yourself, Your Holiness, said several times, and indeed quite lately, that you hoped to see all Christians keeping Easter on the same day.

This matter has been subjected to repeated examination in your own, as well as other Christian Churches, and also by the World Council of Churches. Is not the time ripe for us all to enter on a course which would yield a decision? The Holy Father, wishing to follow up his letter to you, has commissioned me, as President of the Secretariat for Christian Unity, to work closely with your Church, together with the other Christian Churches and the World Council, to see whether there is a practical possibility of reaching a solution which would not amount to the assertion of prior claims by one tradition over another, but would be rather the outcome of an agreement reached under the guidance of the Holy Spirit. This would enable us to comply with the intention of the Fathers of the First Ecumenical Council, who wished in the first place to see us all united in celebrating the Resurrection of the Lord.

In 1977 all Christians, following their different systems of calculation, will coincide in keeping Easter on 10 April, which is the Sunday after the second Saturday of that month. Now it is precisely this date which seems in most cases to be regarded as the one best indicated for the celebration of Easter, according to the statements made by various heads of Churches and the conclusions reached by different Christian groups authorized to study this question. We are aware that a solution along these lines was already envisaged by the Ecumenical Patriarchate in 1923.

In the name of His Holiness, Pope Paul VI, we should like to propose that from 1977 onwards Easter should always be celebrated on the Sunday following the second Saturday of April. We should be very grateful if Your Holiness would let us know what you think of this suggestion.

We are submitting this proposal simultaneously to Your Holiness and all the other Christian Churches. Through contacts which we have already had on this matter with the World Council of Churches, we know that this body intends to submit a similar proposal for examination by its member Churches and to ask for their reactions.

We are very much aware that such a decision could only be taken by total agreement among all the Orthodox Churches who, at the instigation of the Ecumenical Patriarchate, have examined or are examining this delicate problem at the present time. For this reason we hope that some procedure enabling us to see whether such an agreement is possible could be instituted, with a view to our coming to some decision.

If it should so happen that your Church felt that it could not accept this proposal to stabilize the celebration of Easter on the Sunday following the second Saturday of April, we should be grateful if Your Holiness would let us know if your Church would be opposed to the Catholic Church's doing so, supposing that the other Western Churches were in favor of it. We should not want, after all, to take such a decision, if this involved the risk of creating an obstacle to the drawing together of our Churches.

I thank Your Holiness in anticipation for the care which you may choose to devote to this letter, and I ask you to accept the expression of my feelings of charity and high regard in the Risen Christ.

329.   *19 June 1975*

Letter in reply of Patriarch Dimitrios I to Cardinal Willebrands**

We received your letter of 18 May this year dealing with the question now under study of a common celebration by all Christians on the same day of the holy Resurrection. We read this letter out with due care and attention at a session of our Holy Synod.

We thank Your Eminence for the solution proffered in your letter for the problem under the form in which it presents itself today. In doing so we should like you to know that by a Synodal decision your letter was referred to our Commission for Inter-Orthodox Affairs for further study. When this has been done, we shall reply to your proposals.

We embrace you in the Lord, and remain with brotherly love and fitting esteem.

330. *14 December 1975*

Address by Metropolitan Meliton in the Sistine Chapel at the end of the liturgy celebrated by Pope Paul VI on the tenth anniversary of the lifting of the anathemas*

History is woven out of what we remember and what we forget, but its real movement is directed and brought to a head by a providential design and a divine ordering of events.

I well remember how, on 7 December 1965, after the memorable ceremony of the lifting of the anathemas between Rome and Constantinople, in the Basilica of St. Peter, and in the course of the official audience which Your Holiness granted the delegation of the Ecumenical Patriarchate in the "Sala dei Paramenti," in answering my address you recalled this story: "A certain man approached a sage of Greek antiquity and offered him a large reward to teach him the art of remembering. The sage replied that he was willing to pay him twice as much to learn the art of forgetting." And you went on to say: "A few minutes ago, we celebrated, in St. Peter's Basilica, the act of forgetting a distressing event of the past."

Today, Your Holiness, we come back to celebrate an act of remembering—remembering that we buried the past in oblivion. Not all the past, but a particular part of the past which must remain the past and only the past.

As we celebrate today the tenth anniversary of the lifting of the anathemas, the Churches of Rome and Constantinople are called on the one hand to recall and repeat everything in the past that they have in common, everything that is common to the One Holy Church of Christ, and, on the other hand, to reject everything that divides, and by judging the past in this way to build up the present so as to make the future one of complete unity.

That is why today's celebration assumes for our two Churches and, beyond and through them, for the whole Church of Christ on earth, the sense of a new ecumenical movement, founded this time on an ecclesiological basis. This movement derives, in fact, from the past, along the way of Tradition, which is one in itself and makes things one; it is formed in the present, and it is moving towards the "tomorrow of Christ," towards the Church, One, Holy, Catholic, Apostolic, visible on earth.

And coming today from the East to the West, this is the holy vision we have, this is the obedience we manifest to the Divine Will, this is how we sum up the real state of Christian society around us, and also the real state of the whole world.

We have, therefore, the sacred privilege, we humble envoys of the Church of Constantinople, to transmit to Your venerable Holiness, the embrace of our venerated Ecumenical Patriarch Dimitrios I, and to put in your hands his brotherly letter, in which two practical events are announced: the constitution, in accordance with a Pan-Orthodox decision, of a special Inter-Orthodox Theological Commission, the purpose of which will be to prepare, on the Orthodox side, the theological dialogue with the holy Roman Catholic Church; and the constitution, within the Ecumenical Patriarchate, of a Special Synodal Commission for the Theological Dialogue with Rome. We are happy because, by a positive step forward, a decade after the lifting of the anathemas and at the moment when we are celebrating this historic event, we are the spokesmen of the desire of the Christian East to give to the world, together with the Christian West, the joint testimony of one Lord, one Faith, one Baptism, one Church, and in it a single world belonging to God.

Your Holiness, allow me to conclude with nearly the same words that I addressed to you ten years ago: Now all Christians on earth are about to celebrate Christmas. Let us measure the greatness of the love for men of God who became man so that his Church may exist on earth. Let us measure our responsibility so that the angelic Christmas hymn may no longer be an idyllic flight far from reality, but rather reality itself, in other words, that glory may really be rendered to God, from the earth to the highest heavens; that peace may really be firmly established on earth; that God's will for our good may really be manifested among all in the one Church, his kingdom on earth, and that his kingdom may come. Amen.

And now allow me, Your Holiness, to present to you the brotherly letter of the Ecumenical Patriarch.

331.   *14 December 1975*

Letter of Patriarch Dimitrios I to Pope Paul VI on the tenth anniversary of the lifting of the anathemas**

To Paul, the blessed and holy Pope of ancient Rome, greetings in the Lord.

We have been ruled by the God of love, and, in serving him and him alone, and walking in the way of his love, we have been looking always to what is most perfect in the perspective of the end-time. This is unity in love, profession of the one faith in Our Lord Jesus Christ, and through this profession the culmination of our communion with one another in the Holy Eucharist. It is thus that we have been brought by divine help to the point where a full decade has passed since the lifting of the thousand-year old anathema which, by judgments known only to God, fell upon the life of our Churches.

With deep love towards the holy Church of Rome, we offer up to the Word-God of love both this sacred historical event and its tenth anniversary.

We who in the East live out in our experience the mystery of the Body of the Lord, and who are by the grace of God a bishop (albeit the least), look out, as is our duty, over Holy Church and the world which it contains. It is thus that we perceive with conviction that within the Church the time for words has now passed by. In the world words still prevail, and they lead it astray. But we, although we are in the world, are not of it. As our gaze takes in the affairs of the Church and the world with such an overview appropriate to a bishop, we are minded to say that now is the judgment of the world.

But where, most blessed brother, is the Church itself? Does it come within the very center of this judgment, or is it external to its scope? We do not ask this question of Your venerable and dear Holiness, but of ourselves, and through ourselves of the whole Church Militant of Christ.

As we make an appreciation of the Church from our position here, we make bold to say to Your Holiness that up to the present we have not run our race in vain, that we have borne aloft the witnessing sign of the Cross of Christ in the sacred land of the East, and that now the hour has come for the Word of God which stands above our words.

In this Word of God the holy Church of Constantinople embraces the Bishop of Rome and the holy Church there in a sweet-smelling offering pleasing to God that arises from the Pentarchy of the One,

Holy, Catholic, and Apostolic Church. Within that system of Churches the Bishop of Rome is marked out as the one who has the presidency of charity and honor, and we pay Your Holiness the full tribute of esteem that corresponds to that position.

In making this statement, following a deliberation and resolution of our Synod, the Holy Apostolic and Patriarchal Ecumenical See is convinced that it is expressing the mind of the early Church.

Very Holy Brother,

As we write in these terms to Your Holiness, we should like to add a further declaration. We Orthodox of the East, in all humility, but also with strict regard for the ancient tradition of the one Church, are prepared at all times to further the cause of Christian unity within the framework of principles that have always been embodied in the life of the One, Holy, Catholic, and Apostolic Church.

In this spirit we have made a Synodal resolution to promote the holy cause of the sacred ties with Rome, and to move it onwards from the stage of the dialogue of charity to that of preparation for the theological dialogue. With this in mind, after deliberations among the Orthodox Churches, we have reached the point where a Pan-Orthodox decision has been taken to set up a special Inter-Orthodox Technical Theological Commission to prepare the way from our side for this discussion.

We make this announcement with joy to Your Holiness, and at the same time would like to let you know that the list of the persons making up this Technical Commission will be given by our representatives to your Secretariat for Christian Unity, within whose competency this matter comes.

Moreover, the Church of Constantinople, which attaches very great importance to this theological dialogue, has taken a decision in Synod to appoint a special Synodal Commission of the Patriarchate, consisting of the holy Metropolitans, Meliton of Chalcedon (President), Chrysostom of Myra, Bartholomew of Philadelphia, and the Chief Protonotary and Professor of Theology, Emmanuel Photiadis.

While communicating this news to Your blessed Holiness by this brotherly letter of ours, following a Synodal decision we entrust the formal presentation of the letter to our special envoys, the holy Metropolitans, Meliton of Chalcedon, Damaskinos of Tranoupolis, Paul of Sweden, and the Very Reverend Archimandrite Basil Tsiopanas. These will come to Rome and represent us and the Church of Constantinople to Your Holiness and the Church of Rome on the tenth anniversary of the lifting of the anathemas.

As we communicate these tidings of a constructive nature with brotherly feelings to Your Holiness, who is first in rank and honor in the whole Body of the Lord, we embrace you with a holy kiss, and remain with fraternal love and special esteem.

332.   *14 December 1975*

Address by Pope Paul VI in the Sistine Chapel after the reading of the letter from Patriarch Dimitrios I*

We have just listened with deep emotion to the message directed to us today by His Holiness Dimitrios I, Patriarch of Constantinople. Yes, these words arouse in us much joy and hope, and we beg Your Eminence, who had the honor of bringing us this message, to convey to our beloved brother, the Patriarch of Constantinople, all our gratitude and special affection in the Lord. May today's meeting mark a new stage on the way to unity.

"Mighty and wonderful are your works, Lord God Almighty! Righteous and true are your ways, O King of the nations! Who would dare refuse you honor, or the glory due to your name, O Lord? Since you alone are holy, all nations shall come and worship in your presence. Your mighty deeds are clearly seen" (Rv 15:3–4). That is the song of the lamb sung on divine harps by those who have overcome evil.

Welcome among us, very dear brothers, sent by the venerable Church of Constantinople in order to render honor, glory and thanks to Almighty God for the great and wonderful actions he has carried out in modern times for his Church. Welcome among us, very dear brothers, who have come to join us in prayer and to prostrate yourselves with us before the all-holy God who had made known to us his judgments and indicated to us his just and true ways.

That is why our heart is full of joy today. And we are also happy that a delegation sent by us is praying with the Ecumenical Patriarch today in the Church of St. George of the Phanar.

Yes, we can still see vividly before our eyes the magnificent spectacle of the celebration in St. Peter's Basilica ten years ago, corresponding to what was happening in the Church of St. George of the Phanar, when we carried out the solemn and sacred ecclesial act of lifting the ancient anathemas, an act by which we wanted to remove the memory of these events for ever from the memory and the heart of the Church.

The enthusiasm and piety with which this action was received by the praying congregation in St. Peter's Basilica showed us clearly that this event was really willed by the Lord. In fact the Council fathers, who were finishing their conciliar work with God's blessing, were present on that occasion, as were the religious orders and an immense multitude of lay people from various parts of the world.

The conscience of the faithful of the Church saw in this act a sign of atonement for regrettable intentions and deeds on both sides and the manifestation of a determination to bring about together, in obedience to the Lord, a new era of brotherhood, meant to lead the Catholic Church and the Orthodox Church "with the help of God, to live once more, for the greater good of souls and the coming of the kingdom of God, in the full communion of faith, brotherly concord and sacramental life which existed between them in the course of the first millennium of the Church's life" (Joint Declaration of 7 December, 1965 [above, N. 127]).

Ten years after this event, we renew our fervent and humble gratitude to the Lord, a gratitude now grown greater as it is based on new and more momentous grounds. This act has, in fact, set free so many hearts which, up till then, had been prisoners of their bitterness, locked in reciprocal distrust. Mutual charity has become strong and active again. We all at the same moment heard the voice of the Lord, asking each of us: "Where is your brother?" (Gn 4:9). Then we began to look for one another and we ourselves had two further fraternal meetings with the venerated Patriarch Athenagoras of holy memory, whom we esteemed and loved greatly, and on various other occasions met many worthy pastors of the Eastern and Western Churches. These new attitudes of mind have spread more and more through the action of the Holy Spirit within the Christian people.

Thus, a deep purification of memory opens up an ever wider way ahead. It was in this perspective that the Second Vatican Council had clearly declared: "It is from newness of attitudes, from self-denial and unstinted love, that yearnings for unity take their rise and grow toward maturity" (*Unitatis Redintegratio, 7*).

The Holy Spirit has enlightened our intelligences and has brought us to see with increased lucidity that the Catholic Church and the Orthodox Church are united by such a deep communion that very little is lacking to reach the fulness authorizing a common celebration of the Lord's Eucharist "by which the unity of the Church is both signified and brought about" (*U.R.,* 2). In this way more stess is laid on the fact that we have in common the same sacraments, efficacious signs of our communion with God, and particularly the same priesthood, which celebrates the same Eucharist of the Lord, as well as the same episcopate received in the same apostolic succession to guide the people of God; and also that "for centuries, celebrating together the Ecumenical Councils that have defended the deposit of the faith against all corruption," we have lived "this life of sister Churches" (Brief *Anno Ineunte* [above, N. 176]).

It is charity that has enabled us to become aware of the depth of our unity. In the course of recent years, we have also seen the development of sense of joint responsibility as regards the preaching of the Gospel to every creature, which is seriously harmed by the persisting division among Christians (*U.R.,* 1).

Today the relations between our Churches are entering a new stage with the creation of new organs of dialogue, which, drawing on the great acquisitions of the last ten years, are called to increase the communion between our two Churches until it reaches fulness.

Beloved brothers, we bring you the good news that the Orthodox Churches, on the initiative of the Ecumenical Patriarchate, have decided to set up a Pan-Orthodox commission to prepare the theological dialogue with the Catholic Church, and also that this same Patriarchate of Constantinople has set up its own special commission to hold dealings with the Church of Rome. We deeply appreciate this initiative and we declare to you that we are quite ready to do the same on our side so that we may approach full communion by advancing together along the "way that is better than any other" (1 Cor 12:31), the way of mutual charity.

We hope that these new organs of dialogue will transmit Christian brotherhood and ecclesial communion, and be animated by a sincere love for the whole truth. There comes to our mind what we wrote to our beloved brother Athenagoras of venerable memory: "it behoves us in the first place to work together in a fraternal spirit in the service of our faith, to find the appropriate ways which will lead us further on as we try to develop and make real in the life of our Churches the communion which, although imperfect, exists already" (cf. Brief *Anno Ineunte*).

In this way, our hearts being "rooted in love, founded on love" (Eph 3:17), professing "the basic dogmas of the Christian faith" such as they "were defined in Ecumenical Councils held in the East" (Cf. *U.R.,* 14), living by the life of the sacraments which we have in common, and in the spirit of the communion of faith and charity that springs from these divine gifts and is strengthened in them, armed with power by his Spirit in order that the inner man may be strengthened (cf. Eph 3:16)—in this way, then, we hope that it will be possible to go ahead together, isolating the divergences and difficulties that still sep-

arate our Churches, and finally overcoming them by reflection in faith
and by docility to the impulses of the Spirit.

Thus, while we preserve respect for a legitimate liturgical, spiritual, disciplinary, and theological diversity (cf. *U.R.,* 14–17), may God
grant us to construct full unity between our Churches in a stable,
secure way.

This dialogue, long before achieving its final purpose, must aim at
influencing the life of our Churches, giving fresh life to the faith we
hold in common, increasing mutual charity, drawing closer the bonds
of communion, bearing joint witness that Jesus Christ is the Lord and
that "this alone of all the names under heaven has been appointed to
men as the one by which we must needs be saved" (Acts 4:12).

It is the divine Spirit himself who asks us to carry out this task.
And does not the unbelief that seems to be spreading in the world and
to tempt even the faithful of our Churches, does it too not call for a
better testimony of faith and unity on our part? Should not this situation drive us to do our utmost to reach as soon as possible this unity
that Christ asked of his Father for those who believe in him so that the
world might believe (cf. Jn 17:21)?

We are thus called to communicate to others the hope that is in
us and to give an account of it (cf. 1 Pt 3:1).

Once more, beloved brothers, we welcome you to this combined
prayer service, and again we thank you heartily for the good news
brought in the Lord's name.

Now as the Holy Year celebrations, in the course of which the
Catholic Church daily asked the Lord for renewal and reconciliation,
are drawing to a close, we thank the Lord for this new act of brotherhood between our Churches and for the fact that we are now committed to continue together the joint search for total unity.

May the Lord "be glorified in the Church, and in Christ Jesus, to
the last generation of eternity. Amen" (Cf. Eph 3:21).

333.   *14 December 1975*

**Address by Cardinal Corrado Ursi, head of the papal delegation,
given in the Patriarchal Cathedral at the end of the liturgy celebrating the tenth anniversary of the lifting of the anathemas***

Ten years have passed since the day of the cancelling of the
excommunications fulminated in 1054 by Cardinal Humbert against

the Patriarch of Constantinople Michael Cerularius and by the latter and his Synod against the Roman legate.

As excommunications they were directed only against individuals, not against the Churches. But that did not prevent the escalation from then onwards of a state of tension between the Churches of Old and New Rome which gravely damaged the visible communion which had united them over the centuries.

On 7 December 1965 the joint declaration of His Holiness Pope Paul VI and His Holiness the Ecumenical Patriarch Athenagoras was read, proclaiming that the excommunications were cancelled and that by the same action the sorry memory of them was erased. It was as though at that moment a ray of sunlight lit up the thick clouds which darkened the horizon of the Church of Christ, and the sun of God's charity began to cast the brightness of truth and the warmth of love over West and East.

The Roman Catholic Church, which had been opening its ears to the voice of the Holy Spirit during the Second Vatican Council, had responded with brotherly promptness to the Church of Constantinople's suggestion.

It was a victory for Christ who died and rose "to gather into one the children of God who are scattered abroad" (Jn 11:52).

As we recall that happy day in the course of the present ceremony, we have an excellent opportunity both for praising and thanking the Lord, and for reflecting calmly and with a sense of our own responsibilities. For we have now entered on the road leading towards the unity not only of the holy Churches of Rome and Constantinople, but also of the sister Churches of West and East, and, in broader perspective, of all Christian denominations. And we have done so in obedience to the Lord's command: "By this all men will know that you are my disciples, if you have love for one another" (Jn 13:35); "even as I have loved you, you also must love one another" (Jn 13:34); "that they may all be one; . . . so that the world may believe that you have sent me" (Jn 17:21).

It is on this appropriate occasion that I have been given the honor and joy of presenting to Your Holiness the greetings of His Holiness Pope Paul VI; of expressing in the name of the whole Catholic community heartfelt sentiments of veneration, respect and affection towards the person of Your Holiness, towards the whole Church of Constantinople and towards the whole of Orthodoxy, of which Your Holiness is the supreme representative; and of expressing the ardent desire of all our faithful that relations between our Churches should grow closer and closer until very soon we can celebrate the Eucharist together in unity and await together in joy the return of the Lord.

It is our conviction that perfect unity between the Churches cannot fail to contribute enormously to the achievement of peace and to good relations between peoples. If the Spirit of the Risen Lord, divine Charity in person, finds all Christians ready to be led into full ecclesial communion, there will be a rich development of communication between them, as well as of solidarity and cooperation between different social groups and different nations, even in things of the temporal order.

It is therefore our desire to labor to the utmost to open up the way of the Lord in the desert of our incomprehension and weakness; for he is ceaselessly leading us back from the dispersion in Babylon to the reconquest of the promised land of perfect communion with God and in God.

Let us bring about what the prophet Isaiah called for: "Every valley shall be lifted up, and every mountain and hill made low; the uneven ground shall become level, and the rough places plain. And the glory of the Lord shall be revealed, and all flesh shall see it together. . . . He will feed his flock like a shepherd, he will gather the lambs in his arms" (Is 40:3–5,11).

And that is why we are applying ourselves before all else to listening to the Word of God. The essence of all our endeavors to regain full communion consists in placing ourselves in Christ's presence and seeking to know his will in definite detail, so as to give effect to his original plan for the Church—the Church which belongs to him and to no other.

The unforgettable meetings between His Holiness Pope Paul VI and His Holiness and Patriarch Athenagoras of holy memory were meetings in prayer and brotherly and ecclesial charity. They prepared the way and rendered possible the new stage of theological dialogue which we are now about to arrange.

Following the path that was opened up at that time, let us persevere in oneness of mind together with Mary, the Mother of Jesus, after the manner of the Apostles and disciples in the upper room as they waited for Pentecost. Let us also continue to move forward in the way that in our time the Holy Spirit is making ever richer in results, through doctrinal dialogue and collaboration in the mission of truth and charity and the call to the spiritual order and to peace, a mission which it is the task of the Church of Christ to carry forward and expand.

Happily, considerable steps have already been taken. We are much more clearly aware that there does exist between the Catholic Church and the Orthodox Church a communion which, although still not perfect, is almost total, as the Holy Father Pope Paul VI has so aptly expressed it. This communion has its origin in one single Christian vocation, is nourished by the same sacraments, in particular by the same priesthood celebrating the same Eucharist, the single sacrifice of the Lord, and by the same episcopate received by the Apostles so that they might proclaim the good news to every creature. Since the Second Vatican Council we have rediscovered with purified hearts and in a calmer spirit that for a millennium the Eastern and Western Churches lived as sister Churches "bound together by a fraternal communion of faith and sacramental life." Although both "for many centuries . . . went their own ways" (*Unitatis Redintegratio,* 14), there was a brotherly communion in spiritual life, in ecclesiastical discipline, in liturgy and in theological pronouncements (*U.R.,* 14–17). It is this living symphony that we wish to establish anew and develop within a full communion.

Today we are happy to stress that a new era is opening up in which more organized relations will certainly enable us to set about really surmounting the differences and difficulties which still stop us from reaching full communion between our Churches. The proposal to create new means of dialogue is welcomed gladly by the Catholic Church, which in turn is ready to take corresponding measures. In short, we are firmly convinced that sincere brotherly dialogue will lead us to build up full unity between our Churches on sure and solid foundations.

When we celebrate the Nativity of the Lord concluding the Holy Year, which has been a year of conversion and reconciliation through an expansion of love, it will be the beginning of a new era of meeting between men and God, and of Christians with one another, and also of the Churches with the world.

This year as we wait for the holy feast of Christmas our hope becomes more eager than before.

It is in this spirit that I ask Your Holiness, the Holy Synod, the Bishops, clergy and faithful of this holy Church of Constantinople, to accept the Christmas greetings which I bring in the name of His Holiness the Pope of Rome Paul VI and of the whole Catholic Church. I bring the same greeting in my own name and in the name of my Church of Naples. Naples was a Greek city in origin, rich in its tally of saints, a city which for many centuries kept up a living relationship with the East and is witnessing today close brotherly collaboration between the Catholic and the Greek Orthodox communities.

I have the honor of delivering to Your Holiness this message entrusted to me by the Holy Father.

334. *14 December 1975*

Letter of Pope Paul VI to Patriarch Dimitrios I*

Now that the Holy Year celebrations, during which the Roman Catholic Church has implored Divine Providence for renewal and reconciliation, are drawing to a close here in Rome, it is with deep feeling that we thank God who "has blessed us with every spiritual blessing" (Eph 1:3). It was the Lord who ten years ago bestowed on us the grace of a great ecclesial act of reconciliation, an act that has made amends for ancient and regrettable deeds on both sides. This act is also rich with implications leading to a rediscovery and restoration between our Churches of this "full communion in faith, brotherly concord, and sacramental life, which existed between them during the first thousand years of the Church's life" (Joint Declaration of 7 December 1965; *Tomos Agapis,* N. 127). We have opted to remove for ever from the memory and midst of the Church the painful recollection of the anathemas which imprisoned hearts in bitterness and mutual distrust. It was the Spirit of God who enlightened our minds, and the love of Christ that gave new life to fraternal charity between our Churches.

Today "the love of Christ constrains us" (2 Cor 5:14) to seek out every avenue, and to be more and more attentive to the inspirations of the Holy Spirit, so as to follow up the dialogue of truth in charity: "*Veritatem facientes in caritate*" [carrying out the truth in love] (Eph 4:15). We must see to it that this dialogue proceeds in the direction leading to the perfect unity for which Christ prayed, died, and rose again. For this reason we take the greatest joy in the fact that it is possible to create new channels of theological dialogue. In this way, with charity, mutual trust and respect, and with both of us being inspired by the sole desire of serving the One Holy Church of Christ, all those elements of experience which we share together in our Churches will stand forth in clearer light. Moreover, we will be able to discuss in a brotherly spirit the difficulties which still prevent us from celebrating the Lord's Eucharist together, and to act wisely in overcoming them.

May God grant us to resolve all points of difference, and to find ourselves close together within the bounds of the total truth (Jn 1:18), so that we may praise his name who is blessed for all ages, and to do this with a single heart and in a chorus of different voices blending together. Thus, "speaking the truth in love, we are to grow up in every way into him who is the head, into Christ, from whom the whole body takes bodily growth and upbuilds itself in love" (Eph 4:15–16).

It is with these feelings of keen joy and ardent hope, just as we are preparing to celebrate the saving Incarnation of Our Lord Jesus Christ, that we assure your venerable Church, and you yourself, dearly beloved brother, of our affection in the Lord.

335.   *14 December 1975*

Address in reply by Patriarch Dimitrios I**

Your Eminence Cardinal Conrad Ursi, Archbishop of Naples, Italy, representative of His Holiness Pope Paul VI, and other dear members of the delegation of the ancient Church of Rome.

We give glory to God who has caused our Churches of the elder and the new Rome worthy to celebrate together, in corresponding ceremonies in our respective cities, the sacred and happy tenth anniversary of the lifting of the anathemas. These, as is well known, had cast a shadow over the past for both of us, from the middle of the eleventh century right up till that blessed day of 7 December 1965.

Brothers, we hail your presence among us with feelings of respect and joy. We recognize in your persons the worthy and accredited representatives of Rome rejoicing on this great anniversary, just as our representatives will be the interpreters to our elder brother of Rome and the Church there of our own joy and that of our Church here. We look upon you at this moment as a living and eloquent sign of the ever further reaching spirit of that great historic act which is bound to live on through the centuries.

We thank you, brothers, for all the kind and consoling words which you have brought us from Rome, and which come from the depths of your own hearts also. We answer you in like terms with a return of brotherly regard and love, speaking from this place and at this official moment.

May the name of the Lord be blessed!

Now that ten years have now passed since that great act of our Churches, we are clearly called upon to assess its importance and value in all its many different aspects.

Our two Churches, although setting out from ecclesiological principles which had diverged under the baneful influence of historical events, were in spite of all led steadily on by the Paraclete. Fully aware of their responsibility in the face of blunders of the remote and recent past of which no one can approve, they found themselves in agreement on the helpful attitude to be adopted on either side. This meant that they should proceed in the name of the Lord, *in nomine Domini,* to specific measures destined to rectify by ecclesiastical action the wrongs which, through judgments known only to the Lord, took place at their hands in the past.

The striking events of ten years ago are fresh in memory. We know how the two principal champions of reconciliation, our elder and dear brother of ancient Rome, Pope Paul VI, and our blessed predecessor Patriarch Athenagoras I, kept urging considerations upon their respective theologians. We know how they finally took steps themselves to "remove from the memory and midst of the Church" the anathemas extant on either side, and how in doing this they proceeded to an ecclesiastical act which serves as a model for a new kind of approach, ecclesiastical and theological at the same time, to the subject of Church unity.

So much then for those events.

But now, "straining forward to what lies ahead" (Phil 3:13), we realize with pleasure that the deed of ten years ago and the subsequent genuine manifestations of charity and growth in good relations have generated an impetus towards new and more positive developments— and this in the quite specific field of theological dialogue between the two Churches. Both of us firmly intend to take up this dialogue, and to do so moreover systematically, and in the light of the lessons of history and tradition. Thus works follow hard on the words and clear signs of charity. This is something which the two interested parties have come to realize by force of experience.

For our part, from the moment when by the grace of God we assumed the pastoral charge of this Ecumenical See, we have never for an instant ceased to be seized with a reverential awe of our responsibility as the Bishop of the leading see of the Orthodox East. We feel the same way at following our unforgettable predecessor, who had an acute and far reaching sensitivity for all that had to do with reconciliation, and was a man of ecumenical disposition and hope. A year after the lifting of the anathemas he declared officially that the Church of Constantinople was ready "to continue the work begun by the act of 7 December 1976 with a series of new ecclesiastical acts of charity," and that "scope would be given for the power and activity of the Holy Spirit" (*Tomos Agapis,* N. 142).

And now we find ourselves in the happy position of being able to inform our sister Church of Rome and her venerable head that the Orthodox Churches have reached a decision among themselves to set up a special Inter-Orthodox Technical Commission of Theologians which will be invested with the responsibility of studying and preparing everything concerning the theological dialogue with Rome, and this on a Pan-Orthodox scale.

We are sure that our brother of ancient Rome will announce a similar decision at an appropriate time, so that through the corresponding activities of the two commissions the dialogue can begin its course.

As far as we personally are concerned, we have already, of our own initiative and by the help of the Holy Spirit, been moving in this direction for quite some time past. Acting under our responsibility as occupant of the first see in the Orthodox Church, we have set in motion the recognized procedural machinery for reaching an agreed statement on the part of all the sister Orthodox Churches. We rejoice sincerely at the unanimous decision which the Orthodox world has in fact reached. We rejoice still further that God has been pleased to bear out what we said on a similar occasion two years ago, namely that whatever was to be done regarding relations and the dialogue with Rome would be done through a Pan-Orthodox decision, for this is a real requirement of our Orthodox ecclesiology in relation to the collegial co-responsibility of the Bishops in each and every part of the Church.

What will be the sequel to this theological dialogue? The answer rests in the hands of God. In any case, a right attitude, systematic theological study and research, a confrontation of the matters under discussion with charity, sincerity, and objectivity will certainly not be lacking on either side. We know that the lifting of the anathemas did not mean a simultaneous removal of our differences, or of the schism in the Body of the Church. Differences concerning dogma, doctrine, canonical order, and divine worship still remain. Historical and canonical obstacles still block the way to union. Variant versions of the nature of the Church exist on either side. Sacramental communion between each other, which is to crown the final union, has still not been achieved. It follows that the theological dialogue must go over all this ground.

On the other hand, we do not think that the dialogue can avoid facing the major problems of contemporary man. More than ever before these call for the combined strong testimony and service of our two sister Churches, whose task it is to witness to and serve the one Lord.

The union of our Churches is clearly something that has to be reached by passing through special theological, canonical, and other differences. These must be kept under control in favor of Revealed Truth. The dialogue must be at the service of this truth. When we serve truth, we serve unity—this is an indispensable principle. But as we place ourselves at the service of truth and unity, it is quite impossible to overlook man himself, as though we could divide the two realities—the Church and the members who constitute it. Nor can we see how it will be possible to enter into discussion about the unity of our Churches while keeping our faithful people ignorant of it and as it were absent from it. It is they who are tormented by the anguish of division and dissension, as well as by the danger of the shrinkage and disappearance of the Church in the midst of a world which is becoming convulsively de-Christianized and secularized, and is veering towards ideologies subversive and destructive of humanity.

What we have just said does not mean that we are preempting the main lines of the Theological Dialogue or determining its subject matter in advance. We are simply expressing our own thoughts and trying to keep in view not merely the theological texture of the dialogue, but also those implications that concern man in himself.

Now that we are about to enter into dialogue with one another as Churches, we must keep in mind one thing above all, which is this: our faithful people long more acutely than ever before to see and recognize the One True Lord in his One Undivided Church which they believe in and confess. Consequently, either Christ will be in our midst, in which case we shall take every means to ensure and protect our union in him; or he will be far from us, and then we will already have become like "branches that do not bear fruit, which are gathered, thrown into the fire and burned" (cf. Jn 15:6).

But it shall not be so among us (Mk 10:43). We shall remain in Christ. We shall have dialogue with each other in him and in his Name. And through him there will come to our Churches grace and reconciliation, peace and unity that will last through the centuries.

These, worthy representatives, are our thoughts and feelings on this auspicious day.

Convey these with great love to our very blessed brother of ancient Rome.

These are meant also for you, dear and reverend brothers, with our kiss of peace.

"May the Lord of peace himself give you peace at all times in all ways" (2 Thes 3:16).

336.   *15 December 1975*

Address by Pope Paul VI during the audience given to the delegation from the Ecumenical Patriarch*

A hearty welcome be yours, you who have brought this great good news which has stirred our feelings and filled us with a keen spiritual joy. We see more clearly outlined on the horizon that blessed and longed for day when we shall be able to seal the recovery of our full unity by celebrating the Eucharistic Liturgy together. We are now entering into a new and what we both firmly want to be a decisive phase of our reconciliation, and we do this in the deeply rooted belief that the Spirit of the Lord who began this work in and among us has it within his power to bring it to fulfilment.

We thank you from the bottom of our heart for this visit, and for the news you brought, which we had been waiting and praying for. We would ask you to express our profound gratitude to His Holiness the Ecumenical Patriarch, Dimitrios I, our very dear brother, to whom we now bear all the affection and trust which we had for his great predecessor. We beg you to tell him that we are hoping for the day when we are able to meet him and to exchange the brotherly kiss of peace with him.

As we give thanks, let us go forward with courage and decision, in the Lord's name.

337. *16 December 1975*

Article by Father Pierre Duprey in the *Osservatore Romano*, explaining the significance of Pope Paul VI's action in kissing the feet of Metropolitan Meliton in the Sistine Chapel, 14 December 1975*

"The time for words is past . . . Now is the time of the Word, the time of the Word of God . . . "

Those present in the Sistine Chapel on Sunday 14 December 1975 had the truth of these words in the Ecumenical Patriarch's message to the Holy Father brought home to them in an unexpected and startling way.

It was certainly the time of the Holy Spirit, of the Holy Spirit inspiring an action in imitation of Christ's own action.

Ten years after the "solemn ecclesial act of the lifting of the anathemas" a delegation from the Ecumenical Patriarchate had come to deliver to the Holy Father a message from the Patriarch Dimitrios which will go down in the annals of relations between the two Churches. The message and the text of the address made by the president of the Orthodox delegation, Metropolitan Meliton, announced officially that a Pan-Orthodox Commission had been set up to prepare for theological dialogue between the Orthodox Church and the Catholic Church. It was also announced that within the Ecumenical Patriarchate a special synodal commission had been established for theological dialogue with the Church of Rome. This second decision indicates the importance the Patriarchate attaches to the first decision and the degree of priority it is giving it.

The Ecumenical Patriarch stated that the announcement of these decisions at so deeply fraternal a meeting between the two Churches was an act "which is like a perfume of praise rising towards God from the pentarchy of the One, Holy, Catholic and Apostolic Church, in which the Bishop of Rome is designated to preside in love and honor." He added: "Expressing ourself in this way, after consulting our Holy Synod, our most holy Apostolic, Patriarchal and Ecumenical see is convinced that it expresses the thought of the early Church." The Patriarch ended by giving renewed assurance of his fraternal feelings towards his "beloved brother, first in rank and honor in the whole body of the Lord."

In reply the Holy Father spoke of the emotion he felt and of his joy at witnessing the entry into a decisive phase of the process of reconciliation between the Catholic and Orthodox Churches which were already "united by such a deep communion that very little is lacking to reach the fulness authorizing a common celebration of the Lord's Eucharist by which the unity of the Church is both signified and brought about . . . Today the relations between our Churches are entering a new stage with the creation of new organs of dialogue, which, drawing on the great acquisitions of the last ten years are called to increase the communion between our two Churches until it reaches fulness."

After his speech the Holy Father moved towards the Metropolitan and, to the complete astonishment of the bystanders, went down on his knees in front of him and kissed his feet.

We were now in a region on the far side of words. We were within what St. Athanasius calls "logic," that is to say within a mode of action that imitates the Logos, the Word of God. To express his deep emotion and intense joy, the Holy Father had performed an act whose deep significance needs to be pondered at length.

To those who stress the greatness of his role in the Church of Christ, the reply of Pope Paul was to state symbolically that in the Kingdom of God he who is the first must make himself the least of all and become the servant of all. This symbolic action said more than any speech could have done and demonstrated that the only authority in the Church is that which is destined for the humble service of brotherly communion in love and truth. "Servant of the servants of God." This title of the Bishop of Rome had found its full expression in this action. We know that in its original meaning this semitic type phrase meant "the most humble of God's servants."

An Athenian journalist who was deeply moved by the event was saying, "Only a very great man could humble himself like that," when Metropolitan Meliton, still reeling under the impact of what he called this "dreadful" action [= in Latin, *res tremenda*], supplied the correction: "Only a saint could."

Because he was the humblest of the servants, the Holy Father could be the servant of the servants of God, imitating the Servant whose work on earth he continues. His action is an example to all those in the Church who are called to service, to ministry.

The action will certainly have enormous repercussions since it presents the ministry of unity in the Church, the ministry of the Pope and of all the bishops, in its true light—the light of the mystery of the Word Incarnate.

The ceremony took place ten days before the end of a Holy Year dedicated to reconciliation, and represents its crown and consummation. It was a gift of the Lord to his Church in response to the immense prayer which had gone up to him all over the world and especially in Rome. As well as being a consummation, it was also a new beginning. The ceremony might have been no more than a memorial of the past, but it turned into a creative act for the future. It is the preface to the preparation of the Theological Dialogue between our two Churches. May God grant that the dialogue develop under his influence and that it be marked by his Spirit.

338. *17 December 1975*

Declaration of Patriarch Dimitrios I on the Pope's meeting with Metropolitan Meliton*

The Ecumenical Patriarch Dimitrios, referring to Pope Paul VI's act of kissing the feet of his representative, the venerable Metropolitan of Chalcedon Meliton, in Rome, issued the following statement:

‚No one, whether a Christian or not, far less we as Ecumenical Patriarch, can fail to appreciate deeply the spontaneous symbolic act of His Holiness the Pope of Rome, Paul VI—an act without precedent in the history of the Church—when, at the end of the celebration of

Holy Mass, he bent down and kissed the feet of our representative, the Metropolitan of Chalcedon Meliton, who at that moment represented the whole of Orthodoxy.

We see this great act of His Holiness as in line with the tradition of the Bishop Fathers of the undivided Church, who raised lofty things on the basis of this humility.

By this expressive sign our beloved brother the most venerable Pope of Rome, Paul VI, has excelled himself and has shown to the Church and the world what a bishop, and above all the first Bishop of Christendom, can be, namely a force for reconciliation and for the unification of the Church and the world.

339. *20 December 1975*   340.

MEMBERS OF THE TWO PREPARATORY COMMISSIONS* **

Catholic Preparatory Commission for the Theological Dialogue with the Orthodox Churches

1. Rev. Pierre Duprey, Under-Secretary of the Secretariat for Christian Unity.

2. Rev. Miguel Arranz, S.J., Professor of Liturgy, Pontifical Oriental Institute (Rome).

3. Rev. Carmelo Capizzi, S.J., Professor of Byzantine History, Pontifical Oriental Institute (Rome).

4. Rev. Christophe Dumont, O.P., Consultor of the Secretariat for Christian Unity.

Inter-Orthodox Theological Commission for the Preparation by the Orthodox Church of the Theological Dialogue with the Catholic Church

1. *Church of Constantinople:* The Metropolitan of Tyana, Panteleimon; Prof. John Zizioulas.

2. *Church of Alexandria:* Prof. Stylianos Papadopoulos; Prof. Emmanuel Constantinidis.

3. *Church of Antioch:* The Metropolitan of Laodicea, Ignatios; The Metropolitan of Biblos and Votrion, Giorgios.

4. *Church of Jerusalem:* Prof. Georges Galitis; Prof. Vlassios Feidas.

Catholic Preparatory Commission for the Theological Dialogue with the Orthodox Churches

Inter-Orthodox Theological Commission for the Preparation by the Orthodox Church of the Theological Dialogue with the Catholic Church

5. Rev. Emmanuel Lanne, O.S.B., Monk of Chevetogne, Consultor of the Secretariat for Christian Unity.

6. Rev. John Long, S.J., staff member, Secretariat for Christian Unity.

7. Rev. Pierre Mouallem, Superior General, Paulist Fathers (Melkite Church) (Lebanon).

8. Rev.J. Peter Sheehan, Assistant Director, U.S.A., Bishops' Committee for Ecumenical and Inter-religious Affairs.

9. Rev. Mgr. Eleuterio F.Fortino, Secretariat for Christian Unity, Secretary of the Commission.

5. *Church of Russia:* The Bishop of Vyborg, Cyril; Mr. G. Skobeï.

6. *Church of Serbia:* The Bishop of Marcha, Dr. Daniel (Kristich); Dr. Athanase (Jevtich), Hieromonk.

7. *Church of Romania:* Rev. Prof. Dumitru Staniloae; Rev. Prof. Dumitru Popescu.

8. *Church of Bulgaria:* The Bishop of Dragovitsa, Joann.

9. *Church of Cyprus:* The Metropolitan of Paphos, Chrysostomos; Dr. Andreas Mitsidis.

10. *Church of Greece:* Rev. Prof. Joannis Romanidis; Prof. Joannis Karmiris.

11. *Church of Poland:* Archimandrite Savvas Chrikuniak; Higumen Simon Romanchduk.

12. *Church of Finland:* Rev. Prof. John Seppala; Prof. Matthew Siidoroff.

341.　*12 April 1976*

Easter letter of Pope Paul VI to Patriarch Dimitrios I*

In these days when the Liturgy is opening our hearts Sunday after Sunday towards a deeper understanding of the central mystery of our faith, the Resurrection of the Lord, we find our thoughts turning towards Your Holiness. Given our conviction that the Lord is inviting us today to testify together to the Resurrection, this exchange of letters has come to form part of our preparation for Easter, and will continue to do so.

Indeed we believe "in him who raised from the dead Jesus our Lord, who was put to death for our trespasses and raised for our justification. Therefore, since we are justified by faith, we have peace with God through our Lord Jesus Christ" (Rom 4:24–25;5:1). Here we have the interior meaning of the greeting of the Risen Christ to his disciples, while they were still fearful and hesitant: "Peace be with you" (Lk 24:36).

We as disciples of the Risen One must be witnesses of these things (cf. Lk 24:48), witnesses of this triumph of life and love, of this victory over death and division.

But surely our testimony is made less effective by the fact that Easter is celebrated by Christians who are not fully united among themselves. May we not ask whether this lack of unity is not to some degree responsible for the discord and war which in many parts of the world claim victims and ruin?

We ought then to strive might and main towards the day when with full unity we are able to proclaim together: "It is quite true! The Lord has arisen and appeared to Simon" (Lk 24:34). This unity is something willed by God, so that everyone can believe, overcoming all fear and doubt, and fully share in the glory given by all mankind to the Lord of peace.

With these feelings of hope and joy, which are all the greater because we know that they are also those of Your Holiness, we assure you anew of our brotherly love in the Risen Christ.

342.　*17 April 1976*

Telegram from Patriarch Dimitrios I to Pope Paul VI for Easter**

We rejoice in sending Your venerable Holiness a cordial brotherly embrace, and pray that the Risen Lord may grant you to celebrate the joyful feast for a long time to come. May he increase our love to the glory of his Name.

343. *21 November 1976*

Message from Pope Paul VI to the first Conference held in preparation for the Great and Holy Council of the Orthodox Churches*

His Eminence Meliton,
Metropolitan of Chalcedon,
President of the first preparatory Pan-Orthodox Conference,
Geneva

At the moment when the first Pan-Orthodox Conference in preparation for the Great Holy Council of the Orthodox Churches is beginning its work, we send it our brotherly wishes for complete success. We join our fervent prayers with those that arise these days from all the Churches which you represent, that the Holy Spirit may enlighten and guide your assembly, equipping it for the best service of the venerable Orthodox Church. We ask the Lord that this conference may also contribute to preparing the re-establishment of full communion among our Churches and that it will hasten the day when all obstacles are overcome, and we will at last be able to celebrate his one Eucharist together.

With the expression of our brotherly affection in Christ Jesus.

344. *23 November 1976*

Telegram in reply by Metropolitan Meliton to Pope Paul VI*

The first Pre-Conciliar Pan-Orthodox Conference which is in session here at this moment has received the cordial message filled with brotherly sentiments from Your Holiness, and heard it in the love of Christ with great joy and honor. We thank you warmly for the sentiments of close interest expressed with regard to our work and above all for the assurance of your prayers. We, too, pray all together that our present Pre-Conciliar Pan-Orthodox Conference will be, with the assistance of the Holy Spirit, not only a positive contribution to the preparation of the Holy and Great Council of our Pan-Orthodox Church, but also a stage towards the promotion of Christian unity and the approach of the day when we shall all thank the Lord in full communion and give the world a combined witness of our faith in Jesus Christ. I send this message in conformity with the unanimous decision of the *plenum* of the first Pre-Conciliar Pan-Orthodox Conference, and with affection in Christ.

345.   *30 November 1976*

Address by Bishop Ramon Torella i Cascante, Vice-President of the Secretariat for Christian Unity,[54] delivered in the Patriarchal Cathedral*

Your Holiness,

It is a great joy and honor for me to take part in the celebration of the holy Apostle who is patron of your Church, and to be a sign in your midst of the relations of greater brotherhood and trust which are in continual course of development between the Churches of Old and New Rome.

I came in the first place to associate myself with your prayers, to praise God with you, and to acknowledge with adoration how great he is in his saints. But this celebration will also afford an opportunity for exchanging information about the life of our Churches—what they are trying to do now and what plans they have for the future.

Having just recently become Vice-President of the Secretariat for Christian Unity, I find I am making my first visit to Your Holiness and the Ecumenical Patriarchate. Please let me tell you how deeply moved I am to be here in these sites so full of history and redolent of Christian life. Inevitably our thoughts go out to those who went before us, and upon whom with the eyes of faith we now gaze as they gather round the throne of the Lamb. They are asking the Lord of history to hasten the day when his universal design of salvation will reach

---

54. Cardinal Willebrands became Archbishop of Utrecht and Primate of the Netherlands in December 1973, while retaining the position of SPCU president. To cover the SPCU offices full-time in the Vatican, Pope Paul appointed as vice-president Bishop Torella, December 1975.

fulfilment, when all will be united in Christ so that God may be all in all.

As humble servants of the coming Kingdom we are trying afresh to give full testimony together that all we have is from him, and that our only purpose is to proclaim by our words and deeds that he has so loved the world that he sent his Son into it so that it might be saved by him. Our brotherhood should be so close as to make it clear to the world that we are saved by the Son. I am here as the messenger of fraternal charity, sent by your brother the Bishop of Rome, His Holiness Pope Paul VI, who has asked me to hand you this letter.

346. *30 November 1976*

Letter of Pope Paul VI to Patriarch Dimitrios I*

Once more we have the joy of being present among you by means of our delegates, and of thus associating ourselves with the celebration in honor of St. Andrew the First-Called, brother of Peter who was first among the Apostles. We wholeheartedly join our prayers with yours, dear brother, with those of the Holy Synod, and of all the faithful people who gather on this day in the Patriarchal Church—that same Church in which we remember being received with so much honor and fraternal charity, and where we prayed with deep feeling.

We send you our greeting and our cordial best wishes for the feast of your Church's patron: may the peace and grace of Our Lord Jesus Christ be with you all.

When we celebrate an Apostle together, we awaken in our mind the memory of the early Church, of the time when the members of the community "devoted themselves to the Apostles' teaching and fellowship, to the breaking of the bread and the prayers" (Acts 2:42).

Our communion in prayer, and our common acceptance of the teaching of the Apostles, which we have received in order to pass it on to the whole world, move us to do everything we can to see that the difficulties which still remain between us are overcome in due order, and to make it possible to reestablish the full communion which will enable us to celebrate the Lord's Eucharist together.

May the Apostle Andrew intercede with the Father, that our common striving for full unity may meet with acceptance and blessing.

With these feelings we assure you once again, beloved brother, of our deep charity in Christ, our one and only Lord.

347.   *30 November 1976*

Address in reply by Patriarch Dimitrios I to Bishop Torrella and Father Duprey**

The joy and gladness of heart felt by the Great and Holy Church of Christ in these parts on the feast-day of this see is increased today by the presence and joint prayers of the select delegation which our beloved elder brother Pope Paul VI so kindly sent us. Your Excellency, dear brother in Christ, Pope Paul has placed upon your shoulders the very responsible duties of the Vice-Presidency of the Secretariat for Unity: we congratulate you on this, and pray that God will give you all the strength required for the discharge of this office. And you, Very Reverend Father Pierre, are well known, loved, and respected in the Ecumenical Patriarchate. The fact that you are both here for the present feast of this see furnishes a further proof that the bonds between our sister Churches are growing stronger every day.

Welcome, brothers!

We thank you for the words with which you addressed us, and especially for the brotherly message of His Holiness the Pope of ancient Rome, which we receive with deep feeling and joy.

We are acquainted with the difficulties which our brother confronts as he guides the ship of his venerable Church, and we keep on praying that the Chief Shepherd Christ may give him strength for the fulfillment of his holy will "that all may be one."

We who represent the first see of the Orthodox East are continually and earnestly praying and working with the same end in view.

In our aforesaid capacity we are indeed glad to inform you that the Pre-Conciliar Pan-Orthodox Conference, which happily concluded its work only the day before yesterday, showed special interest in promoting the relations of Orthodoxy with the Roman Catholic Church, our sister. It decided to recommend to the local Orthodox Churches that they take active steps with regard to the Inter-Orthodox Technical Commission for the Preparation of the Theological Dialogue between our two Churches, which was constituted at my instance.

We are convinced that with the assistance of the Paraclete, we will be made worthy to go forward in the pursuit and final attainment of our goal, which is full unity in the faith. In this we count on the intercession of the holy Apostle Andrew the First-Called, whose feast we are celebrating today, of his brother by blood the holy Apostle and leader, Peter, and of Our most Blessed Lady, the Mother of God and ever-virgin Mary, and of all the saints, to the glory of God.

It is in this spirit and with these feelings that we welcome you here today. We hope that your stay in Constantinople will be a pleasant one, and that your discussions with the competent Synodal Commission here will be fruitful.

Welcome indeed, beloved brothers.

348. *26 December 1976*

Letter of Patriarch Dimitrios I to Pope Paul VI **

To Paul, the most Blessed and Holy Pope of Ancient Rome, greetings in the Lord.

We gave a loving welcome to the worthy delegates sent by Your venerable and esteemed Holiness for the feast of St. Andrew, the First-Called Apostle, which is the feast proper to our see in this part of the Holy Church. Your emissaries, His Excellency Bishop Ramon Torrella, Vice-President of the Secretariat for the Unity of Christians, and the Very Reverend Father Pierre Duprey, Under-Secretary of this same body, handed to us the brotherly message from Your Holiness for the feast-day, and assisted at the Divine Liturgy celebrated in the Patriarchal Church by ourself and the Metropolitans who make up our Holy Synod.

The fact that your delegates were present in our midst as we were carrying out the solemn ceremony brought us very deep joy, since it was a sign and visible testimony of the blessed period through which we are moving in the relations between our two Churches. This is a time of communion in prayer and charity, and one that calls for a closer approach on our part to each other, and for a full communion in the Eucharist—a blessing which the Lord has in store for us, and for which we long.

The presence here of the delegates from Your Holiness, both of them distinguished members of your Secretariat for Christian Unity, provided an excellent occasion for their conferring with our Commission for the Dialogue with your venerable Church, and exchanging views of the preparation for it. Moreover, following on the special display of interest on this subject by the Pre-Conciliar Pan-Orthodox Conference which recently met at Chambésy, near Geneva, and the decision to begin an active preparation from the Orthodox side, your delegates were in a position to provide information about the activities during the past year of the Secretariat for Christian Unity and what was being done by the Technical Commission of Theologians in Preparation for the Dialogue on the Roman Catholic side. In conjunction with all this it was possible to review certain matters relative to the various exchanges being conducted by the Christian Churches and denominations in general, not to mention other subjects which are significant and important for the present time.

Hence we cordially thank Your Holiness for your friendly festive greetings, for sending us the above mentioned ranking clerics, and for the opportunity thus provided for closer communication and consultation on affairs of special importance for the two Churches. We would wish and hope, through the assistance of the Paraclete who dwells in the Church and leads it into all truth, that we may be made worthy in the course of the coming year to see further progress in the common present endeavor to correspond to the Lord's will, so that his Holy Church may be one and united.

With this wish, we embrace Your Holiness in the newborn Christ, and remain with brotherly love and fitting esteem.

349. *16 May 1977*

Letter of Cardinal Willebrands to Patriarch Dimitrios I on the date of Easter*

Your Holiness,

In my letter of 18 May 1975 I wrote at some length to tell you that the Holy Father had commissioned me to ask you what your Church thought about the possibility of reaching a common date for the celebration of the Feast of Easter by all Christians as from 1977. The proposal was thereby made that Easter should always be celebrated on the Sunday after the second Saturday of April.

I thank Your Holiness for letting me know the position of your Church on this matter. We are aware that the subject is being examined at the present time among the Orthodox Churches.

As far as the Catholic Church is concerned—and this applies also to the great majority of the Churches consulted—a change of this kind could only be introduced, whatever be the pastoral needs for adopting it, on the condition that all Christians were in agreement with the proposal, and that a common date for keeping Easter was thus obtained.

For this reason His Holiness Pope Paul VI has judged that the time is not yet ripe for the Catholic Church to change its present method of calculating the date of Easter, and thus carry out its plan to stabilize this date on a Sunday of April from 1978 onwards.

However, this year all Christians will celebrate the Resurrection of the same Lord together, on the same day. Although it will not be possible in the near future to maintain this feast on the same date, we are convinced, after the reactions received to our proposal of 1975, that the whole Christian world is determined to reach a solution to this problem as soon as possible.

I send you here and now my best wishes for a holy and joyful Easter, and pray the Risen One to shed his blessings on you personally, on your Synod, and your faithful people. I would ask you to accept the expression of my respectful and brotherly feelings.

350. *22 March 1977*

Easter letter of Pope Paul VI to Patriarch Dimitrios I*

"God raised from the dead . . . the Author of life: to this we are all witnesses" (Acts 3:15). This announcement by Peter to the people of Jerusalem comes spontaneously to mind, my dear brother, as we turn to you, filled with the deep and ever fresh joy put into our hearts by Christ during these days when we celebrate the most glorious feast of Easter, as we all do this year at the one time.

We turn to you to repeat this fundamental affirmation of our Christian faith, and also so that we may together testify before the world: "It is indeed true. Christ has risen!" (Lk 24:34). We must unceasingly proclaim to the innumerable throngs of people who are trying today to free themselves from all sorts of oppression and to find some sense in a life which seems meaningless to them: "There is salvation in no one else" (Acts 4:12).

Since we are servants of the Author of life, we have the duty of "speaking to the people all the words of this life" (Acts 5:20). We believe in fact that, if Christ is risen, he is the first of a multitude of brethren (cf. Acts 26:23). Through his Spirit he forms for himself a holy people (1 Pt 2:9), a people made up by those who believe that in following him and carrying his Cross they will have eternal life; a people of reconciled brothers and sisters who must be a leaven in the world helping it to reach the only true civilization, which is that of love.

May the Risen Christ enable us to find this true fraternity again, so that we can witness to it together, "that the world may believe" (Jn 17:21).

With these dispositions, we assure you again, dear brother, of the entire charity we bear to you in Christ.

351.   *Easter 1977*

Easter letter of Patriarch Dimitrios I to Pope Paul VI**

To Paul, the most blessed and holy Pope of ancient Rome, greetings in the Lord.

Today Christians all over the world, in a fellowship of love and piety, worship Christ arisen from the dead; they hymn his Resurrection in songs of praise, and they carry deep in their souls and hearts the joy that derived to the whole world from his Cross.

We performed this worship in the early dawn, with our venerable hierarchy round about us, and with our clergy and pious people, and in our churches we praised and glorified the life-bringing Resurrection with spiritual songs. Now we come gladly on this holy and chosen day to make a spiritual visit to Your venerable Holiness and to hold fellowship with you. We greet you with all possible friendliness, and we express our very best wishes to you, to your venerable Church and the whole body of your faithful, in the spirit of this feast.

By the Resurrection God's providential design for man was vindicated, the power of sin and death was destroyed, and mankind is called to the attainment of salvation and eternal life.

Encouraged by this truth, we wish and hope with all our heart that the light, joy, and truth of the Resurrection may accompany you all the days of your life, so that you may be strengthened and find relief amid the responsibilities of your service as first Bishop. We embrace you with an Easter greeting and remain with brotherly love and special esteem.

352.   *20 May 1977*

Reply of Patriarch Dimitrios I to Cardinal Willebrands on a fixed date for Easter**

Your Eminence's letter of 16 March of this year was received in due course, and was read out at a meeting of our Holy Synod. In this letter, following on that of 18 May 1975, you acquainted us with the more recent view of the Roman Catholic Church, as well as that of the great majority of the Churches whose opinion was sought. This view is that no change should be introduced in the present way of keeping Easter, whatever be the pastoral needs that press for such a change, until all Christians are in agreement on the matter and accept a common date for the celebration of the feast.

We thank Your Eminence for informing us about this, and would like you to know that our Orthodox Church takes the same view on this subject as the Roman Catholic Church. In accordance with a decision reached by the First Pre-Conciliar Pan-Orthodox Conference in its meeting of November last year, we intend to submit the question to study, especially by a meeting of pastoral leaders, canonists, sociologists, historians, and astronomers, which is being called together by the Secretariat for the Preparation of the Holy and Great Council of the Orthodox Church.

We embrace you in the Lord, and remain with brotherly love and special esteem.

353.   *29 June 1977*

Letter of Patriarch Dimitrios I to Pope Paul VI, introducing his delegates to the feast of Saints Peter and Paul at Rome**

Our thoughts go out to Your venerable Holiness with love and esteem on the occasion of today's feast of the illustrious leaders of the Apostles, Peter and Paul, whose life and mission are so closely bound up with the Church of ancient Rome. Feeling as we do a keen desire to take part in a more tangible way in the Roman celebration of their sacred memory, we send you as our delegate extraordinary our dear brother in Christ, His Eminence Bishop Meliton of Chalcedon, accompanied by His Eminence Bishop Basil of Aristi, and the Archon, Great Protonotary of our Holy and Great Church of Christ, Professor Emmanuel Photiadis.

On the occasion of this auspicious feast, which celebrates at the same time Your Holiness's name-day and the anniversary of your enthronement, we have commissioned Bishop Meliton to convey our brotherly greetings to you and our heartfelt good wishes for you, your venerable Church, and the body of its faithful. We have asked him then to enter into communication with the Secretariat for Christian Unity with regard to the activities of the two respective Technical

Theological Commissions which have assumed the task of dealing with questions of method and are carrying out this and other preparations for the official Theological Dialogue between our Churches.

Since this year marks the completion of a decade since the visit of Your venerable Holiness to our see in the Phanar, we have asked His Eminence Bishop Meliton to take with him a small commemorative plaque and present it to you, both as a way of emphasizing the significance of that great historic event, and as a sign of the mutual love and deep respect that exists between your people and ours and by the grace of the Paraclete is proceeding from strength to strength.

Having said this, we devoutly hope that Christ our true God, who in his unspeakable love for humankind has lavished upon us the strength and joy that comes from reconciliation, will bless our further endeavors until we come to full communion by sharing in the Lord's chalice. May he grant you many long years of sound and undisturbed health. We embrace Your Holiness with a holy kiss, and remain with brotherly love and fitting esteem.

354.   *27 June 1977*

Address by Metropolitan Meliton of Chalcedon during the papal audience with the delegation from the Ecumenical Patriarchate*

As a Church, we live in continual communion with the saints. It is within this mystical "coming-to-be" that we endeavor to live out our fellowship with one another while aspiring towards the restoration of complete communion between East and West, which was broken for a while for reasons known only to the Lord. In doing this we seek with love, humility, patience and prayer, and with complete good will, the most promising ways and sacred means consistent with truth that may lead to the holy end in view.

It is in this spirit that we, the humble representatives of the Bishop of Constantinople, visit today the Bishop of Rome.

By an injunction of our Church we come to unite our prayers with those made by Your Holiness and the Church in Rome to the leaders of the Apostles, Peter and Paul, on this their feast-day. And we bring the embrace of Andrew to his own brother Peter, and the embrace of Andrew's successor to you, the successor of Peter.

Judged as the world judges, our presence here today might be considered as a visit of courtesy, returning that of your delegates to Constantinople for the festivities in honor of St. Andrew. But if we look at this meeting against that sacred background which I mentioned at the outset, we realize that it finds its place at the very heart of that "lived theology" which expresses itself in specific churchly deeds, in spirituality and piety, and in a sharing of the Eucharistic experience that belongs to the whole undivided Church.

In making our way with love towards the Theological Dialogue between the Roman Catholic and Orthodox Churches, we are not simply complying with the demands of technical method, or of some cold theory or speculation; we are serving the Lord and his will; we are placing ourselves at the service of the Way, the Truth, and the Life. And so, Your Holiness, our humble presence today is in the last analysis an outward expression of the inner life of the Church.

In any case, it is precisely ecclesial life and *praxis* which give content to theology, since for us in the East there is no distinction between lived or practical theology and speculative theology; rather, in our capacity as Church we do theology by living out the experience of its total mystery.

In these terms our presence at Rome needs no further justification. Over and above its primary purpose, which is to offer pious honor to the two leading Apostles, Peter and Paul, our visit marks two other anniversaries. Until recently these were internal affairs of the Roman Church; today, given the new organization of our churchly life as led in common, they have become a matter affecting the pious outlook of the Orthodox Church as well. I refer to the patronal feast of Your Holiness and your coronation in the see of Rome under the name of Paul VI—an indication that you have taken the Apostle Paul as your model.

To this we must add another fact: in a few days' time a whole decade will haved passed since Your Holiness's historic visit to the Ecumenical Patriarchate. That visit, which God inspired Your Holiness to make, was a very important step on the way to unity. How can we fail to mention such an important event when we are almost on the eve of its anniversary? How can we fail to emphasize the apostolic boldness and determination which Your Holiness demonstrated? May I add that this visit, when its real value is seen, was no ordinary visit, but one that should be understood in the biblical sense of visitation. Hence we are not concerned with simply recalling an historical fact, or giving it its just value as something that happened in the past, but rather with bringing out the theological and ecclesial contribution made by this visit to the sacred cause of unity. It is an event then which continues to be present in our journeying to that unity.

Your Holiness,

To complete what I have earlier said, allow me to impart some news about another important happening, one which stamps today's meeting with a new significance for the progress of relations between our two Churches. I come today bearing good news for Your Holiness and the Church of Rome. A few days ago the Inter-Orthodox Technical Theological Commission for the Preparation of the Theological Dialogue with the Church of Rome (a commission of which I have the honor, at its own request, to be President), had its first meeting.

I am happy to be able to tell Your Holiness that the results of this meeting were constructive and unanimously approved, and that they open the way to collaboration with the corresponding Roman Catholic Commission, with a view to seeking out the best road for the restoration of perfect Eucharistic communion between our two Churches.

Builders must not claim the right, at all costs, to see the roof put on their construction, since in the Lord's words "it is one who sows and another who reaps" (Jn 4:37). Let us pray that others may live to see the day. In the holy moment through which we are now living, it is enough to glorify God that Your Holiness has been one of the chief architects of this work. The glory belongs, and can only belong to the Lord, together with the Father and the Holy Spirit.

355.   *27 June 1977*

Address in reply by Pope Paul VI to the delegation from the Ecumenical Patriarchate*

Dear Brothers in Christ,

Be welcome among us during these days when the Church of Rome celebrates the Apostles who were its founders. We are honored by your visit, which shows how real and active is our search for full unity, and at the same time gives us an opportunity of realizing how much progress the Lord has enabled us to make. We earnestly thank you, dear brothers, for consenting to share in our prayers during these days.

Thirteen years ago we were given the grace of making a pilgrimage to the holy places where the first Ecumenical Councils were held. Then, ten years ago, we visited your holy Church, and for the second time met our venerable brother, Patriarch Athenagoras. How the memories return!

Over these last years the happy understanding between our

Churches has become deeper and more frequently expressed, with the result that now we have twice a year an exchange of delegations which enables us to impart useful information to one another, something which is quite necessary if we are to harmonize our endeavors while advancing towards renewed communion. We give thanks to the Lord who is directing his Church along this way.

We are happy to hear that the Inter-Orthodox Commission appointed to prepare for the Theological Dialogue with the Catholic Church has held its first working meeting. May the Lord give us strength and life and make us artisans of peace and unity, so that with joint forces we can proclaim his Gospel of reconciliation and salvation, of which today's world, with all its tensions and anxieties, stands in such dire need.

We thank you, dear brothers, for your presence here, which is a sign of fellowship and hope. We would ask you to carry our message of fraternal charity to the venerable Patriarch Dimitrios and his Church.

356.   *29 June 1977*

Letter of Pope Paul VI to Patriarch Dimitrios I*

It was with joy and deep feeling that we received your envoy, His Eminence Bishop Meliton, the very dear Metropolitan of Chalcedon, together with Bishop Basil of Aristi, and the Archon Great Protonotary, Professor Emmanuel Photiadis.

In these festive days which are filled with the gladness that the Holy Spirit puts into our hearts as he awakens them to thanksgiving, the presence of your representatives among us is rich with meaning. It shows clearly that the bonds of brotherhood which are being woven anew, ever more closely, between the Old and the New Rome are from now on such that whatever touches the life of one of the two sister Churches enters also into the experience of the other, through communion in the same Spirit.

As we thank Your Holiness for this new gesture of fraternal charity, we repeat our unalterable decision to go ahead, in full harmony with you, along the road which is bound to lead to our celebration of the Eucharist together. May God make this blessed hour close at hand.

It is our opinion that we ought to remain in close contact with one another in our advance to the recovery of unity, so that the various measures we take on either side may be brought into a smooth and harmonious relationship. We rejoice then at the information which our eminent envoy has passed on to us about the recent meeting of the Inter-Orthodox Commission which is preparing for the Theological Dialogue with the Catholic Church. Our Secretariat for Christian Unity will do its utmost to reply in kind to the opportunities opened up by these first encouraging results.

We should like also to tell Your Holiness how thankful we are for the handsome present which you sent us for the tenth anniversary of our visit to the Ecumenical Patriarchate. That day of July 1967 has left in our heart an ineffaceable memory which is the source of constant hope. We in our turn entrust the Doyen of your Holy Synod with a gift for Your Holiness—one which is a symbol of the deep charity which inspires us in your regard. We are happy to assure you that we are one with you in prayer and the service of our one Lord.

357.   *30 November 1977*

Address by Cardinal John Willebrands in the Patriarchal Cathedral*

In communion of faith, in union of charity, and enlivened by keen hope, we were joined today in prayer with Your Holiness, with the venerable brothers of the Holy Synod, and with all the clergy and the faithful, in honor of Saint Andrew, protector of this Patriarchal and Ecumenical see.

The Lord has given us fresh experience today of the great spiritual joy which we have known on previous occasions.

The presence, here, of this Catholic delegation sent by His Holiness Pope Paul VI, as also the presence in Rome for the feast of the Apostles Peter and Paul of the delegation sent there by Your Holiness, is a sign of the mutual fraternal ties which, year by year, become closer and more demanding for our two Churches. These are signs of ecclesial communion.

These last few years, the Spirit of Truth has led us to become freshly aware that this communion is founded on the common patrimony which comes to us from Holy Scripture, a patrimony that was lived and transmitted through the tradition of the Church, illuminated through the reflection of the Fathers, and defended and proclaimed in seven Councils which we, Catholics and Orthodox alike, consider to be ecumenical, and which were all held in these regions that are renowned among Christians everywhere.

Is it not the sacramental reality which makes this communion solid and substantially incorruptible? We Catholics and Orthodox believe, when all is said and done, that the Church is the great sacrament of salvation, the pillar and foundation of truth. This profound conviction is the fundamental reality on which the relations between our two Churches—relations between sister Churches—are based.

In the course of its journey through history, the Church has encountered and lived through many difficulties, both interior and exterior. Among these, the ones from which it has suffered most are the divergences and divisions which have torn the seamless robe of Christ. In patience and charity it is trying to overcome these through the power of the Spirit given to it by the Risen Christ. It needs to overcome them in order to be able to proclaim its own mystery to the world. It is in the Church and through it that the Kingdom of God is built up; and the Spirit, the ultimate reality of the end-time, is thus communicated to men. The community of the faithful redeemed by the blood of Christ and incorporated in him is progressively led by means of the sacraments towards transfiguration and divinization. Herein lies the profound life and reality of our Churches. It is here that there is effected the mysterious communion that unites them, a communion mysterious yet real and operative like every work of God.

In both East and West, the application in practice of these gifts, the development of the sacramental life of the Church, and the forms taken by this common faith, have been diverse, and rich and complementary in their variety.

This sacramental reality which gives us life is the basis of the firm relations which exist between our Churches. It gives consistency to the dialogue, so full of hope, that is now opening up. This dialogue should make it possible for us to tackle with Christian realism, and to clarify once and for all every point which is still a source of difficulty and keeps us from celebrating the Holy Eucharist together. It must find its place in the very heart of this mystery, at the central point where the multiplicity and variety that are visible on the surface are taken up in unity. It is there, in this light, that we shall discover and recognize one another as true brothers; that we shall recognize and discover that our Churches are truly sister Churches.

In view of this, we consider the work being done in both our Churches by the Technical Commissions responsible for preparing the Theological Dialogue as most important. And since the proximate preparation of the dialogue must necessarily be conducted in coordination, we are glad that it has already proved possible to appoint two subcommissions which will meet to see that this is done. It is urgent that we put an end once and for all to these differences inherited from the past.

For all these reasons, Your Holiness, we are profoundly glad to be here and to pray together to the Lord, certain that our common prayer is an echo in us of the prayer that Christ addressed to the Father for the Church: "That they may be one, that the world may believe" (Jn 17:21). That the world may believe! This world full of tensions and of weariness, of enmity and irresponsibility, of violence and inertia, of injustice and also of hope—this world of ours is waiting for someone to come to free it and change it, to make of it a single family living in peace and love. The Church must bear witness by its unity and the quality of its fraternal life that it is the work of the Lord. May he be with us.

I have the honor, Your Holiness, of conveying a personal message from the Holy Father, Pope Paul VI.

358.   *30 November 1977*

Letter of Pope Paul VI to Patriarch Dimitrios I*

In celebrating by the tomb of Peter the feast of his brother Andrew, our thoughts turn to you, dear brother, and our fraternal charity is expressed in a fervent prayer for your intentions and for the faithful of your Church. This spiritual encounter in prayer between the Churches of Rome and Constantinople is manifested by the presence among you of our brother Cardinal John Willebrands and those who accompany him. He brings you our kiss of peace, a sign of the fraternity which must exist and grow deeper between our two Churches.

During these last few weeks which have marked the tenth anniversary of the visit your great predecessor made to us, one could not fail to recall the beautiful icon that he sent us as a souvenir of our meeting on the Mount of Olives: Peter and Andrew embracing with the blessing of Christ the Lord. This gesture betokens the programme to be carried out through an ever greater sharing in the truth, until the greatly longed for day comes when the Bishop of Rome and the Bishop of Constantinople will be able to exchange this kiss of peace at the concelebration of the most Holy Eucharist. For this it is necessary that the obstacles that still exist between us be surmounted. We hope that the commissions we have established will be able, without delay, but with prudence, to coordinate their efforts so that the Theological Dialogue, which should allow us to resolve our last remaining differences, may begin.

During these days, we ask the Holy Spirit with special fervor to help us go forward together, with prudent courage, along this path, guided by his light and animated by his strength.

On this unity depends the credibility of the witness we have to give to Christ in the world today. This witness is our constant preoccupation. In this spirit the Synod of Bishops which has just ended has attempted to set out the means apt to ensure the Christian formation of the young, with a view to helping them become witnesses to Christ among their fellow men. We therefore declare to you once again our firm resolve to do everything possible to achieve this unity, that "the world may believe" (Jn 17:21).

We assure you, dear and venerable brother, of our deep fraternal charity.

359. *30 November 1977*

Address in reply by Patriarch Dimitrios I**

It has been the good pleasure of God that the patronal feasts of the sees of our two Churches should acquire each year the additional feature of these valuable exchange visits. The idea was mooted here a year ago, and it was agreed between us that such annual events should take place, each balancing the other.

And now, after the visit of our representatives to Old Rome for the commemoration of the two chief Apostles, Peter and Paul, today we are receiving in our see in this city, the New Rome, a visit by a group of representatives of His Holiness the Pope of Rome, for the feast of Peter's own brother, Andrew the First-Called.

We rejoice at this mutual giving and taking. We hail your presence among us as a special grace from God, as a source of joy for our Church, and a fresh infusion of strength for our devout people.

But, apart from all else, this visit of yours, brothers, emphasizes the outstanding fact of the present year. A full decade has now elapsed since the Lord guided hither the steps of our elder brother, the first Bishop of Christendom, in an historic visit to our predecessor of blessed memory, Athenagoras I, just as he led, too, the Patriarch's steps to ancient Rome, the see that "presides over charity." The history of the Church has inscribed in indelible pages, as was right, this event which sealed off a cycle of a thousand years of alienation between East and West.

Glory be to God for his providential arrangement of such important things in our regard!

We shall take a twofold course of action in return.

On the other hand, as an expression of esteem and gratitude, we shall soon send our representatives to Rome with a fraternal reply to the much appreciated letter which we have just received through Your Eminence. We are convinced that both these regular "face to face" discussions and our exchanges through "pen and ink" (3 Jn 13–14), over and above the reaching out of our hearts in fellowship of feeling, form as it were so many stones in the construction of the edifice of reconciliation and union in Christ of our Churches.

On the other hand, we should like to take advantage of the presence among us of you, who are the busy pioneers of Christian unity and men committed to its attainment, to express our thoughts about the sacred cause of the Theological Dialogue between our Churches.

The two respective Technical Theological Commissions appointed to prepare the Theological Dialogue are already busy with their task. This day last year we gave news of the Pan-Orthodox decision that the Inter-Orthodox Commission was to start work without delay. At the same time there came an announcement from ancient Rome that a corresponding Technical Commission of Roman Catholic theologians had been formed, and we were told the results of its first meeting. Now a whole year has passed by, and we have covered a long and important stretch of the road. During the next few days you and the members of our special Synodal Commission will bring yourselves up to date with the pertinent facts.

Considerable progress has been made by the Inter-Orthodox Technical Commission of Theologians, which has met twice this year, with questions of method and subject matter for the Dialogue. It is the doctrine of the sacraments that has been put forward for the first and principal round of discussions in the opening phase.

In our opinion it was a happy choice. It was obviously a prudent move to draw up the main outlines of the subject matter in distinct phases. We have absolutely no wish to see the discussions wander about aimlessly. On the contrary, the preparation for the dialogue must be serious, carefully delimited, and based on particular data. We declare unhesitatingly, then, that the wide and positive field of the sacraments is well adapted for the successful conduct of the dialogue.

We say this in view of the two following basic facts.

First, we have the same sacraments in common. We have a common Baptism, a common Eucharist, a common Priesthood that comes down to us through an unbroken apostolic succession. Further, we have a common teaching on the principal points of the other sacraments: Confirmation, Matrimony, Reconciliation of Sinners, and the Anointing of the Sick. All these are joined together in the one indubitable "Sacrament of the Church," which forms the One Body of Christ. He it is who is always "offering and being offered, who receives and who is shared out, Christ our true God . . . " Having in common, then, as we say, the "deposit of faith" in this matter, we are under an obligation to explore together the ways towards our unity in Christ in constructive dialogue.

We say with conviction that our Theological Dialogue should be developed from these common points, not from subjects that divide the Churches. On the other hand, it is quite a different matter to examine and accurately work out different nuances and emphases in the common sacramental teaching both in theology and practice. We recognize that in this field there is a variety, often well established, which is known in other words as "manifoldness" or "pluralism." But we say categorically that this does no injury to the essence of the dialogue; rather it builds up the unity which we seek and will keep on seeking throughout the multiplicity of liturgical, pastoral, historico-canonical and other details. This unity will not be in any case a dull uniformity or unyielding homogeneity of form and expression, but an identity of faith and doctrine, of grace and confession of Christ, with full respect for the traditional institutions, supported by the witness of history and theology, of either Church.

There is something else, too, which we should like to emphasize. In this new and hopeful phase of the dialogue it is completely beside the point for our Churches to become locked in discussion on matters that long ago led the two sides to confrontation and impasse. Rather what we should desire and hope for is, under conditions of full fidelity to the truth and utter sincerity, a theological quest ending in the discovery of new and more positive means of approaching the one indivisible truth.

We shall attempt to do this by entering into theological dialogue with one another. We shall not ignore the long standing differences, or overlook, naturally, the themes taken for discussion—however barren in results such discussions were—within the frames of reference of our "yesterday." But we shall nevertheless conduct the dialogue in a constructive and positive manner, in a God-fearing spirit, and with love of Christ. If a special effort and a boldness in resolving issues is a prerequisite for us both to get beyond the psychological or other difficulties that inhibit progress, neither of us should shirk this task.

Today East and West are living through new situations that give rise to wide reaching ecumenical hopes; we experience new theological tendencies and bearings; and at the heart of it all are mutual comprehension, recognition, and acceptance. Things that were beyond the bounds of hope become attainable; what was never looked for becomes the object of bold attempt—and this by "outsiders" to the Church. And we Christians, are we going to stand by idle? Certainly not! If we want to stay fixed in the methods of the past, our dialogue will be in vain, and vain, too, our preaching, and our words about reconciliation, unity, and ecumenism will ring hollow.

These, in short, brothers, are our thoughts. May the Lord give his blessing to everything that follows.

With these thoughts in our mind and heart, and borne on by these hopes, we embrace in spirit at this moment the Chief Pastor of ancient Rome, our dear brother in Christ, Pope Paul VI, and his Church, and we greet you, his worthy representatives, with love and esteem, as we say with the Prophet Isaiah: "How lovely on the mountains are the feet of the herald who comes to proclaim prosperity and bring good news" (Is 52:7).

360.   *7 December 1977*

Letter of Patriarch Dimitrios I handed to Pope Paul VI by Metropolitan Meliton**

To His Holiness Pope Paul VI, Bishop of ancient Rome, Dimitrios Bishop of Constantinople, greetings in the Lord.

The day before yesterday we welcomed to our Holy See the delegation of Your beloved Holiness led by your worthy repesentative, His Eminence Cardinal John Willebrands, who under the inspiration and guidance of Your Holiness excellently expounds the will of the Roman Catholic Church for Christian unity in general, and more especially your own desire and will that the great cause of Christian Unity should be founded on the solid ecclesiological unity of the Western and Eastern Churches.

We reply with the deepest joy to the message which you sent from the see of the Apostle Peter to that of his own brother Andrew—a message which greatly moved us and the Church of Constantinople because of its important content. We have commissioned the first member in rank of our Holy Synod, our dear and esteemed brother in Christ, Metropolitan Meliton, to visit you for this purpose in a special mission on our behalf. His task is in the first place to express our thanks and those of our Church for the continuation with all sincere brotherly understanding of the dialogue of charity, and also for the preparation with painstaking care, on your side as well as ours, of the theological dialogue between the two Churches. Moreover we should also like him to assure you that we are ready to cast down all the walls of division that have been erected between us for centuries past, so that we may together communicate in the Body and Blood of the Lord in a common Eucharistic Liturgy.

With this wish we send Your Holiness a humble sign of our love and brotherly regard, and our recognition that you, in your holy person, are the first Bishop of the Christian world. This is a lamp which was long kept in our private Patriarchal Chapel, and is meant to be placed now in your private Chapel, to show that "the light of Christ shines forth to all men."

We direct these expressions of our feelings to you with all charity and appreciation on the occasion of your eightieth birthday, on the twelfth anniversary of the lifting of the anathemas between our two Churches, and the tenth anniversary of the visit made by our celebrated predecessor, Patriarch Athenagoras, to you and your Church. We beg the Lord to bestow on Your most dear Holiness length of days in constant good health, and on the Church an ever increasing power to testify that we are all one in Christ, our only Lord.

361. *7 December 1977*

Inscription engraved in Greek on a silver plaque attached to the lamp presented by Patriarch Dimitrios I and handed to Pope Paul VI by Metropolitan Meliton**

ON THE FRONT

> "They light a lamp and put it on the lamp stand, and it shines to all in the house" (Mt 5:15).

ON THE BACK

> To the holy brother of Rome, Paul VI
> Dimitrios of Constantinople

On the 80th anniversary of his life on earth
And in recognition that he really
"shines to all in the house."

26 September 1897–26 September 1977

362.   *7 December 1977*

Address by Pope Paul VI during the audience with Metropolitan Meliton*

In the liturgical period of Advent, when the bracing wind of Messianic hope blows over the Christian Churches, and on this anniversary of the historic day of 7 December 1965, your visit takes on its whole significance. We thank God for these regular brotherly meetings between our Churches, and we congratulate Your Eminence on being, on your side, a convinced artisan in arranging them.

Yes, slowly but surely, our communities are moving towards complete meeting. At this moment, the formation of an Orthodox subcommission charged with keeping in contact with the similar Catholic subcommission, with a view to arriving at the creation of a joint commission for theological dialogue, is a step forward which we consider very important. And the dialogue between our Churches, based on the sacramental reality itself, benefits from a solid foundation which gives us reason to hope that the difficulties which do not yet permit a concelebration of the Eucharist can be overcome.

We ask you to express to His Holiness the Ecumenical Patriarch Dimitrios I our feelings of brotherly affection and our indomitable hope in the success of our joint efforts, humble and loyal, patient and repeated. May the Spirit of unity and holiness renew constantly the hearts of the pastors and faithful of the Orthodox and Catholic communities, and prepare them more and more for complete and definitive reconciliation "so that the world may believe."

363.   *23 December 1977*

Telegram from Patriarch Dimitrios I to Pope Paul VI for Christmas**

Once again we find ourselves sharing the same hopes and expectations before the mystery of the Incarnation of the Saviour Christ and the consolation that comes from the cave of Bethlehem, towards which the whole of mankind looks in these difficult days, as it celebrates the Christian feast *par excellence* of the appearance of the Lord in the world. During this feast we pray together with Your very dear Holiness, making supplication with you for the salvation of the world. May the newborn Lord keep you in health for a long time, and may he make the dawning New Year a promising and peaceful one for the Church and the whole world.

364.   *17 January 1978*

Letter of reply from Pope Paul VI to Patriarch Dimitrios I for Christmas*

We thank you warmly for the good wishes you sent us for the sacred celebration of the coming into this world of "our great God and Savior Jesus Christ" (Ti 2:13).

Yes indeed, in this season we are moved by our faith to say all over again in wondering adoration: "The Word was made flesh and dwelt among us" (Jn 1:14). Everything is given in him. He is the Way which leads us to the Father, the Truth which causes us to know the Father, and the Life of which we are made sharers here and now. It is quite true, "to all who have received him, he has given the power to become children of God" (Jn 1:12). With what tremendous love must the Father love us that we should become children of God (1 Jn 3:1)! But this places immense demands on us and our Churches. We have to testify before the world, through our brotherly love and our unity, to the mystery of the love of God revealed in the newborn Child of Bethlehem.

What we ask of him during these days for Your Holiness and all your people is that he give us this grace.

We assure you again of our feelings of fraternal charity and high regard.

365.   *23 March 1978*

Easter letter of Pope Paul VI to Patriarch Dimitrios I*

"We know that Christ has truly risen from the dead." From year to year the Church proclaims its faith in the glorious Resurrection of its Savior by this cry of the liturgy. Filled with joy and adoration before the wonderful kindness of God as his grace comes right down to us, and before the unforeseeable choice of his love, which saves us through the death and resurrection of his Son, we turn to you, most dear brother, to share our wonder with you: "Let the whole world recognize the marvelous truth: what was brought low is lifted up again, what had grown old is renewed, and everything recovers the integrity of its beginning in him who is the beginning and principle of all things, Jesus Christ" (*Roman Missal,* Easter Vigil).

It is a cause of happiness that we can make this fundamental affirmation of our Christian faith together with you. We whose task it is to continue in the world the mission of the Apostles, themselves witnesses of the Resurrection, are obliged more than ever to proclaim unceasingly: salvation is given us only in the Risen Christ, who reveals the meaning of our life and our death.

In this attitude of joy and thanksgiving, and inspired by the keen desire to see restored between us the full unity willed by our one and only Lord, we assure you again of the full extent of our fraternal charity.

366.   *24 March 1978*

Telegram from Patriarch Dimitrios I to Pope Paul VI for Easter**

On the great feast-day of Holy Easter we rejoice with Your dear and venerable Holiness. We would have every good thing deriving from the Risen Lord granted to yourself, your hierarchy, your holy clergy, and pious flock.

367.   *22 May 1978*

Letter of Patriarch Dimitrios I to Pope Paul VI for the Feast of Saints Peter and Paul**

Two years ago it was decided that we should make visits to one another, with renewed contacts, twice during the course of the year, on the feasts proper to the sees of our two Churches, testifying by this means among others to the community of love and honor existing between us. Following out this practice, we are happy to send a delegation to Your venerable Holiness for the feast of the leaders of the Apostles, Peter and Paul, whose praise is on everybody's lips. The group will be led by our dear brother in Christ, the Metropolitan Meliton of Chalcedon, and will include the Metropolitan Bartholomew of Philadelphia, and the Very Reverend Archimandrite Spyridon Papageorgiou.

We have given these representatives the responsibility, when they have reached the Eternal City, of assisting at the Mass to be celebrated by Your Holiness in the Basilica of the holy Apostle Peter on 29 June, and of conveying to you our brotherly greetings and warmest best wishes for your health and a long life. Afterwards they are to enter into communication with the Secretariat for Christian Unity and continue the series of exchanges which took place last year when your delegation visited us on the patronal feast of this see. They will, together with your representatives, pass in review and judge the worth of the steps so far taken, and will then make suggestions about what seems next indicated.

It is our hope and prayer that the Lord will add continually to our charity, and that he will give us strength and encouragement in the journey towards unity and full communion. We embrace Your Holiness with a holy kiss, and remain with appropriate special regards.

368.   *1 July 1978*

Address by Metropolitan Meliton at the papal audience of the delegation from the Ecumenical Patriarchate*

It is the glorious Apostles, or more precisely their leaders Peter and Paul, who have brought us here together, from the Old and the New Rome, in this city in which they met their martyrdom, and on the day when we celebrate their holy memory. We are here in the same place through the grace of the divinely ordered apostolic succession, a treasure which we carry in earthen vessels.

Our presence, that of the humble envoys of the Bishop of Constantinople, is meant to be understood in this light. This and the fact that we are here before Your Holiness, you who are the successor of St. Peter and bear the name of Paul, give our visit a significance that goes beyond the bounds of mere courtesy. This visit has its place within a different dimension, which is that of the Church.

If we see this visit from the appropriate point of view, then we can say that our sharing in the feast of the two leaders of the Apostles, and in the patronal feast of Your Holiness, is an ecclesial event—one belonging to the order of the Church. This visit binds the present again to the past of the undivided Church in a communion of love. And it looks, too, to the future, in other words to that unity which is expressed in the same confession of faith, and in full fellowship in the Holy Eucharist.

It is in this spirit, with this attitude, and in this hope, that we have the honor and joy of addressing Your Holiness today, and of giving you the kiss of peace in the Lord, on behalf of your brother, the successor of St. Andrew, St. Peter's own brother.

In the present circumstances this kiss of peace takes on a special meaning, because it follows so soon after the meeting at Chambésy, near Geneva, of the Inter-Orthodox Technical Theological Commission for the Preparation of the Theological Dialogue with the Roman Catholic Church. The work of this Commission, after its collaboration with the corresponding Theological Commission of your holy Church, has reached results which amount to a forward step on the road leading to the recovery of Christ's gift, namely the unity of the Church.

We are happy then because in this meeting here and now between Rome and the Phanar there is signified the greater meeting of the holy Roman Catholic Church with our Orthodox Church, at a very important stage of their common advance towards full unity.

May the Lord give Your Holiness, as the leading worker in this cause, the grace of seeing this holy advance reach its destination. Amen.

369.   *1 July 1978*

Address in reply by Pope Paul VI to the delegation from the Ecumenical Patriarchate*

We wish you a wholehearted welcome among us, venerable brothers, for this feast of the holy Apostles Peter and Paul which we have just celebrated. It is with affection and high regard that we receive you. We are glad that our Churches have decided to make these exchange visits each time they celebrate their patron saints. This is a new sign of the rediscovery of the profound ecclesial communion which already exists between our Churches.

These shared celebrations of the holy Apostles bring with them a demand for renewed fidelity. Fidelity to their faith, and fidelity to their mission, which continues throughout time in an unbroken succession for the purpose of proclaiming to the world the great good news that Christ has died for our sins and risen for our justification (Rom 4:26).

This annual exchange of visits also offers a favorable opportunity for fraternal discussions aimed at orchestrating our quest for full unity between our Churches. To fulfill the work we have begun it is quite clear that we must seek out our goal with an increasingly resolute collaboration. We must, too, have an unwavering determination to solve all the difficulties which still hold us back from the day when we will be able to commemorate all the Apostles and saints of the East and West in a great concelebration of the Eucharist which will express full and joyful unity.

Given these prospects, we are happy to hear that the two commissions responsible for preparing the theological dialogue in the Catholic and Orthodox Churches have already done good work. The fact that the coordinating committee made up of representatives of the two commissions has already met to work together is a clear indication of the progress made, and of the desire to reach the end of this preparatory phase quickly, and begin the Theological Dialogue proper.

May the Lord bless these endeavors, so that we can once and for all clear up all those points which in the past have produced tensions, collisions, and even the rupture of sacramental communion. May we achieve, in the fulness of a common faith, that complete unity which Christ asked for his disciples and for all who would believe in their words.

Your presence here at the celebration of the feast of Saints Peter and Paul has given fresh life to this joyful hope within us. We thank you for this, and we ask you to convey our feelings of fraternity, communion, and hope to our venerated and loved brother, Patriarch Dimitrios, and all his Holy Synod.

370.   *15 July 1978*

The last letter of Pope Paul VI to Patriarch Dimitrios I*

The presence in Rome of the delegation headed by His Eminence, Metropolitan Meliton of Chalcedon, and sent by Your beloved Holiness to share in the liturgical celebration of the feast of the Apostles Peter and Paul, has increased our joy on this blessed day.

We are very grateful to you for sending this delegation, and especially for the fraternal message of communion and charity which you kindly arranged for us to receive by this means. We are happy, too, to see that the contacts between our Churches are becoming wider in scope and are being reinforced by prayer in common and by the liturgy, two things which are at the very heart of the Church's life.

The participation of a delegation from the Roman Catholic

Church in the celebration for St. Andrew in your Patriarchal See, and that of a delegation from your Church in the celebrations for Saints Peter and Paul, strengthen and give practical form and shape to the spiritual ties that unite Catholics and Orthodox. These celebrations provide us with an opportunity for renewing in the presence of the Lord our common commitment to the search for full unity. For the people of God, and in the face of the world, they give a witness of charity, and are a pledge of the hope that inspires us that we shall celebrate together one day the single Eucharist of the Lord.

In this spirit of fraternity, and with this desire to bind ourselves to do everything possible to obey the Lord's commandment, we express, beloved brother, our affection in the Lord.

371.   *7 August 1978*

Telegram from Cardinal Carlo Confalonieri, Doyen of the Sacred College, to Patriarch Dimitrios I, on the death of Pope Paul VI*

His Holiness Pope Paul VI passed away the evening of August 6 feast of the Transfiguration of the Lord. The funeral will take place Saturday 12 August at 6 p.m. We recommend him to your prayers.

372.   *7 August 1978*

Message from the Holy Synod of the Ecumenical Patriarchate on the death of Pope Paul VI**

The Ecumenical Patriarchate was deeply moved and distressed by the news of the death of the leader of the Roman Catholic Church, Pope Paul VI.

As soon as this news arrived, His Holiness Dimitrios I called a special meeting of the Holy Synod.

At this special meeting His Holiness announced to the Holy Synod the sad news of His Holiness Pope Paul VI, and pronounced a panegyric of some length about this great and leading personality.

The Holy Synod, through its Doyen the Metropolitan Meliton of Chalcedon, associated itself with the feelings of the Ecumenical Patriarch.

After which His Holiness and the Holy Synod prayed for the repose of the soul of the late Pope Paul VI.

Further, the Holy Synod proceeded with the following resolutions:

a) that it should send a telegram of condolence to the *locum tenens* of the Papal See;

b) that His Holiness should make a declaration meant for the whole world on the death of the Pope;

c) that a delegation consisting of the Senior Metropolitan, Meliton of Chalcedon, and the Metropolitans Chrysostom of Myra and Bartholomew of Philadelphia should represent the Ecumenical Patriarchate at the funeral of His Holiness.

373.   *7 August 1978*

Telegram from Patriarch Dimitrios I to the Cardinal Chamberlain Jean Villot on the death of Pope Paul VI**

It is with the deepest distress, but also in expectation of the Resurrection, that we personally and as Ecumenical Patriarch have received the news of the departure to the Lord of His Holiness, our brother, Pope Paul VI. His holy personality will remain unique in the history of Christianity and humanity of our century. The Ecumenical Patriarchate as sister Church shares with its whole soul in the grief of the holy Roman Catholic Church and the entire Roman Catholic world. United with you in prayer, we make our petitions that the soul of our late brother Paul, Bishop of Rome, may rest in peace.

374.   *7 August 1978*

Declaration by Patriarch Dimitrios I on the death of Pope Paul VI**

The Ecumenical Patriarchate and we personally have been deeply distressed at the death of His Holiness Pope Paul VI, and we share with our whole soul in this grief of the Roman Catholic Church and the Roman Catholic world in general.

Pope Paul VI was one of the great Popes of our century. We can describe him without hesitation as the Pope of renewal in the Roman Catholic Church, of reconciliation between Christians, of understanding and cooperation with all religions; as one who maintained and worked for the dignity of the human person, with a special affection for neglected people on the margins of society; as the proclaimer of human rights and of the abolition of racial discrimination; as the champion of religious freedom, and as a leader in the struggle for peace in the world.

Pope Paul VI proved himself worthy of his historic responsibility at a critical time when a new order of things was emerging in the Roman Catholic Church and the inter-denominational Christian world, and there was confusion everywhere. He combined apostolic daring with an understanding and patience worthy of the Fathers, having as his fixed rule the Apostle Paul's recommendation: " . . . the greatest of these is charity" (1 Cor 13:13).

We, speaking for the Ecumenical Patriarchate and as Ecumenical Patriarch, at this sacred moment of his departure from this world, regard it as our duty to recall and give due prominence to five historic landmarks in the relations between the Ecumenical Patriarchate and the Vatican, and more generally in the reconciliation of the Orthodox and Roman Catholic Churches:

a) The meeting at Jerusalem between Pope Paul VI and our renowned predecessor Patriarch Athenagoras I, in the year 1964;

b) The lifting of the anathemas between the Churches of Rome and Constantinople, in the year 1965;

c) The visit of Pope Paul VI to the Ecumenical Patriarchate, in the year 1967;

d) The exchange visit made by our predecessor Athenagoras I, and his cordial welcome in the Vatican, in the year 1967;

e) The personal contribution of Pope Paul VI to the great enterprise of moving the exchanges between the Orthodox and the Roman Catholic Churches from the stage of the Dialogue of Charity to that of the Theological Dialogue.

We know that the swan-song of Pope Paul VI was his rejoicing at the fact that Orthodoxy and Roman Catholicism are entering upon the Theological Dialogue.

The Christian Church, all religions, the world and all humankind feel, and must feel, that the loss of this personality is a great one. The great contemporary evangelist of charity, reconciliation, and peace will be missing from our midst.

However, this evangelist leaves us a holy and great legacy, and one that we would even call onerous. We consider that as the Orthodox Ecumenical Patriarch we have responsibility for this legacy, but that a like responsibility falls simultaneously on the Roman Catholic Church and Paul VI's successor, whom this Church will elect.

After the departure of Paul VI we are all called upon to take up once again our responsibilities for reconciliation between Christians, for unity between the Churches, and for establishment of worldwide peace.

Speaking as Orthodox Ecumenical Patriarch, our last word is that for all mankind Paul VI will be an unforgettable memory.

375.   *8 August 1978*

Telegram from the Cardinal Chamberlain Jean Villot to Patriarch Dimitrios I*

We are very touched by the message of condolence and Christian hope sent by Your Holiness when His Holiness Pope Paul VI, who had at the heart of his ministry reconciliation between Christians, returned to his Father's house. We deeply appreciate your brotherly gesture, and assure you of our gratitude and charity.

PART IV

A Promising Beginning

Nos 376–384   **August 27, 1978–**
                                   September 30, 1978

Election of Pope John Paul I (376–377) ▪
Continuation of previous policy (378–381) ▪ Death of
Pope John Paul I (382–384)

376. *27 August 1978*

Telegram from Cardinal Jean Villot, Secretary of State, to Patriarch Dimitrios I, on the election of Pope John Paul I*

With joy I inform Your Holiness that Cardinal Albino Luciani[55] has been elected Bishop of Rome and Pope of the Catholic Church. He has taken the name John Paul the First. Sunday 3 September in the afternoon His Holiness will celebrate the beginning of his pontificate with a solemn Mass. With my fraternal respect and greetings.

377. *27 August 1978*

Telegram from Patriarch Dimitrios I to Pope John Paul I on his election to the See of Rome**

With joy, charity, and esteem, we hasten on the part of the Church of the Apostle Andrew to greet with an embrace Your beloved Holiness, appointed to preside over the Church of the Apostle Peter. We wholeheartedly congratulate Your most blessed Holiness on your well merited election to the most sacred and ancient see of Rome, and assure you that our Church and we personally are ready with all our hearts to continue our brotherly collaboration on behalf of Christian unity, and for the peace of the world, having as our final end the salvation of man made in the image of God.

378. *27 August 1978*

Declaration of Patriarch Dimitrios I on the election of Pope John Paul I**

It is with deep joy and great hope that we hail the election of the successor to Pope Paul VI, of blessed memory, the new Bishop of Rome Pope John Paul I.

---

55. Born in the Veneto of northern Italy in 1912 and ordained priest in 1935, Albino Luciani was rector and professor at the seminary in Belluno, then bishop of Vittorio Veneto (1958). In 1969 he was appointed Archbishop of Venice.

At the present stage of the relations between Old and New Rome, and more generally of the relations between the Orthodox and the Roman Catholic Churches, the election of a new Pope is not simply an event internal to the Roman Church, but has practical ecumenical implications. After Popes John XXIII and Paul VI, both of glorious memory, the Pope of Rome now possesses a new historical position, and a responsibility in the holy cause of Christian unity, which is the unity of the Church of Christ.

In this same spirit, in greeting the election of a new and venerated brother, the Bishop of Rome, we express not simply our joy at his succession to the Roman See, but in the same measure our hope that we will maintain the ecumenical Christian spirit of his two immediate predecessors.

We pray that our common Lord, the Head of the Church, may strengthen the new Pope in his historic responsibilities with regards to the Holy Roman Catholic Church, to Christianity, and to the human race.

Finally we proclaim from out the East that our hands will be always ready, with full brotherly collaboration, to hold the common Cross of the Lord.

379.   *1 September 1978*

Telegram in reply from Pope John Paul I to Patriarch Dimitrios I*

We are deeply touched by the feelings expressed by Your Holiness. At the moment when the Lord is entrusting us with this onerous mission in the service of his Church, we thank you and assure you that we are determined to advance unhesitatingly along the way that should lead to restoration of full communion between our Churches. Be assured of our fraternal charity.

380.   *2 September 1978*

Letter of Patriarch Dimitrios I to Pope John Paul I, to whom it was handed by the Delegation from the Ecumenical Patriarchate**

To the very holy and blessed Pope of ancient Rome, John Paul I, greetings in the Lord.

We hail the election of Your most blessed Holiness to the sacred and venerable See of Rome with heartfelt brotherly joy. We wish to lose no time in setting in clear relief the feelings of charity, esteem, and solidarity with which we should like to encompass, as it were, your venerable self and your lofty office, from the very beginnings of your pontificate.

At the moment when you take the helm of the holy Roman Catholic Church in your hands, our thought turns in prayer to our common Lord: it is our devout hope that, as you apply the holy sacrament of your pastoral charge to its sacred service, you may enjoy good health, spiritual strength, and peace.

Holy Brother,

You accede to the sacred See of Rome, which involves the greatest Christian responsibility, at a moment when the blessed spirit of unity is blowing through the Christian world, and when our two Churches, Roman Catholic and Orthodox, find themselves with charity and sincerity at a decisive point in the progressive approach they are making towards reconciliation with one another. May the Lord grant Your venerable Holiness the grace to carry on the constructive work.

For our part, we shall proffer you our wholehearted collaboration, and be of one mind with you in its pursuit, with all brotherly sincerity and readiness, so that we may accomplish the will of the Lord and justify the expectations of mankind, Christian and non-Christian, for the love of which Christ died and rose again.

In this first act of communion of charity with Your Holiness we are making our guiding rule and giving pride of place to the saying: "Christ was in our midst, he is there now, and will continue to be."

Wishing to give further prominence to this expression of the feelings and attitudes of our Church, and our own personally, we are sending you as envoys extraordinary their Eminences the Metropolitans, our dear brothers in Christ, Meliton of Chalcedon, Chrysostom of Myra, and Joachim of Melitene. Their instructions are to represent our Apostolic and Patriarchal See of Constantinople, and by word of mouth act as interpreters of our spirit. They are thus to give a fresh beginning, dealing directly with you in charity, to the fellowship of our holy Churches, as was done with your renowned and late lamented predecessors, John XXIII and Paul VI.

We would ask Your blessed Holiness to give these eminent delegates of our Church the welcome of your charity.

We embrace you in the Lord, and remain with brotherly love and special esteem.

> Your venerable Holiness's
> dear brother in Christ, . . .

381.   *2 September 1978*

Address by Metropolitan Meliton during the papal audience for the Delegation from the Ecumenical Patriarchate**

> "Weeping may tarry for the night,
> but joy comes with the morning"
> (Ps 29:6).

Your Holiness,

With joy together with the Psalmist, on the morrow that follows the evening, we from out of the lands of dawn hail the dawn of a new day in Rome, and one that has its part in the most holy sacrament of the Apostolic Succession.

We as humble envoys of the Bishop of Constantinople have the privilege, in accordance with his instructions, of bringing Your Holiness his greetings and congratulations, now that the Church of Rome has placed the cross of its Bishop in your holy hands. At the same time it is our wish and duty, at this first meeting with Your venerable Holiness, to be present, not simply as a formal act of protocol, but as giving expression to the ecclesial life of the East in its living reality. It is in this sense that we greet your canonical installation in the episcopal throne of the Lateran as a new dawn. Which is as much as to say that we bless God in that, throughout the Church as a whole, and in this particular instance in Rome, morning follows on evening and joy succeeds to sorrow.

Your Holiness,

The "ages" of the life of the Church Militant on earth succeed one another and pass by, leading to the consummation of things in the end-time. The only thing that remains permanently with us is the Age of Christ revealed.

Not as a mere theoretical proposition, but as something born out of living experience of the Cross, and our contemplation of God and his image, Man, and from a clear assessment of the overwhelming trials to which the human race is exposed today, we of the East tell you, and through you those of the West, of our sacred desire in this moment. It is this, that through the midst of the different ages we may come together, and give the whole world a visible expression and witness of the Age of Christ, who is the ultimate expectation and hope of the universe.

382.   *29 September 1978*

Telegram from Cardinal Carlo Confalonieri, Doyen of the Sacred College of Cardinals, to Patriarch Dimitrios I on the death of Pope John Paul I*

With sorrow we announce the unexpected death of His Holiness Pope John Paul I during the night of 28 September. We recommend him to your prayers. The funeral will take place Wednesday 4 October at 4:00 p.m. Fraternally.

383.   *29 September 1978*

Declaration of Patriarch Dimitrios I on the death of Pope John Paul I**

The unexpected death of our brother, who presided over the Church of Rome, has saddened us greatly.

The Ecumenical Patriarchate and we personally greeted the election of Pope John Paul I scarcely a month ago as a special grace from the Paraclete.

The memorable deceased, whether considered as a figure within the Church, as pastor and leader, or as a person of completely rounded out humanity, able to offer himself to his fellow man, and to dedicate his powers of service to the widest general good of the Church, the world, and humanity as a whole, emanated to everyone from the first day of his election a general sense of security, and we felt this ourselves. He gave every sign of being about to make a valuable contribution to the common cause of reconciliation within the human family and to the unity of our Churches.

The silence of death now seals off the keen hope which was enkindled on every side by that kindly, pleasant face, in which the light of inspiration shone.

But the Church of Christ lives and moves beyond our persons, beyond our intentions, plans, and outlooks, and indeed beyond our lives on earth.

The Paraclete remains, and will continue to remain in the Church of Christ. In him all things move, those of yesterday, today, and tomorrow.

At this moment we pray for the blessed soul of the celebrated Pope John I.

We share with all our hearts in the grief of our sister Church of Rome. We hope that the successor of Pope John Paul I of ancient Rome, now called to appear peacefully before the Lord, may be worthy of the great deeds of his two immediate predecessors, Popes John XXIII and Paul VI, as well as of the noble visions, expectations, and plans of action of the one who combined both these figures in his own name.

384.   *30 September 1978*

Telegram from Patriarch Dimitrios I to the Cardinal Chamberlain Jean Villot on the death of John Paul I**

The Ecumenical Patriarchate and we personally were greatly distressed by the unexpected death of our brother, Pope John Paul I. In the hope of the life to come in Christ for all who have lived and served in a way pleasing to God, we have prayed for the repose of his blessed soul. With the best hopes he was appointed Bishop of the Church that presides over charity. In peace he left the baton of charity and reconciliation to those who come after him. We share with all our soul in the grief of the venerable Roman Catholic Church and remain united with you all in the Spirit.

PART V

From Dialogue to Dialogue

385.   *17 October 1978*

Telegram from Cardinal Jean Villot to Patriarch Dimitrios I, on the election of Pope John Paul II*

With joy I inform Your Holiness that Cardinal Karol Wojtyla has been elected Bishop of Rome and Pope of the Catholic Church. He has taken the name of John Paul II.[56] Sunday 22 October His Holiness will celebrate the beginning of his pontificate with a Solemn Mass. With my fraternal respect and greetings.

386.   *17 October 1978*

Telegram from Patriarch Dimitrios I to Pope John Paul II on his election to the See of Rome**

With great joy we hail the fact that Rome has a Bishop, and that Your Holiness is taking up the first responsibility for charity in the Christian world. Your Holiness, you come from Eastern Europe and perhaps understand better than anyone else the need for yoking together the Christian East and West. We are making this yoke fellowship the key word of our interrelationship for the good of the whole of Christianity and the peace of the entire world.

387.   *30 November 1978*

Address by Bishop Ramon Torrella i Cascante, Vice-President of the Secretariat for Christian Unity, delivered in the Patriarchal Cathedral*

It is with joy that once again this year we are here in this Patriarchal Church, as representatives of the Roman Catholic Church, to cel-

---

56. Born in Wadowice (Poland) in 1920 and ordained priest in 1946, Karol Wojtyla was a parish pastor, then professor of philosophy at the Catholic University of Lublin. He became auxiliary bishop of Krakow (1958) and later its archbishop (1964). He became the first non-Italian pope in 455 years.

341

ebrate with Your Holiness, and your hierarchy, clergy, and faithful, the feast of St. Andrew the First-Called, the brother of St. Peter.

Our presence each year at this feast of St. Andrew, like that of the delegation from the Ecumenical Patriarchate at Rome for the feasts of Saints Peter and Paul, expresses our celebration in common of the two brother Apostles, and is a symbol of the quest by our Churches today to rediscover and translate into living fact their full fraternity in apostolic faith and holiness.

We bring you the cordial and fraternal greetings of the Church of Rome and the testimony of the growing communion between our Churches, which are called ever more urgently to full unity, the sign of perfect fidelity to the Lord.

I have the great honor and joy, Your Holiness, of bringing you a message from His Holiness Pope John Paul II.

388.   *30 November 1978*

Letter of Pope John Paul II to Patriarch Dimitrios I*

In the mysterious design of Divine Providence the Roman Catholic Church has passed through events in recent months of far reaching importance. The death of my venerated predecessor Pope Paul VI was followed by the election and sudden death of Pope John Paul I. Now God has called me to succeed them as Bishop of Rome and first Bishop of the Catholic Church.

During that time Your Holiness and the Ecumenical Patriarchate entered deeply into these important events in the life of our Church. By your messages, by the presence in Rome of eminent representatives of your Church, by your declarations and significant acts, you personally and publicly made it clear that you closely shared in the sorrow and joy of your Catholic brothers and sisters. I should like to tell you how thankful we are for this testimony of Christian love and solicitude, in which I see an expression of the close bond that already unites us in Our Lord Jesus Christ, in spite of the obstacles that unfortunately still exist between us.

Today I have the pleasure of sending you my representatives, who will convey this letter to you and express my gratitude for the good wishes which you sent me at the inauguration of my new ministry. They will present my message of good will for the patronal feast of your Church, and will tell you how much I am with you in prayer on this day. I want also to thank you for the letter which you sent my lamented predecessor John Paul I. He was called to the Lord before he had time to answer it. I want to assure Your Holiness that I am one with you in desiring that the Theological Dialogue between our Churches may begin at the first possible moment, and may unfold in an atmosphere of deep charity and trust, so that it may bear good fruit.

The special ministry which I am now assuming in the Church of God has for its foundation the profession of faith of the Apostle Peter: "Thou art the Christ, the Son of the living God" (Mt 16:16). Christ is the center of our faith; he has redeemed us by his Cross and Resurrection; he is the ultimate goal of all our striving. In and through his Spirit we share the very life of God, whose children we become, and hence we are brothers and sisters of one another.

To serve unity is an essential part of my new ministry. It is a service which answers to the will of Christ for his Church. It is also a response to the world of today, to which all Christians should give a single witness of their faith in Christ, who came "that they might have life, and have it more abundantly" (Jn 10:10). I pledge myself then resolutely to this work for the restoration of unity, in the spirit of the Second Vatican Council, and in harmony with the words and actions of my immediate predecessors.

Thank God, relations between the Church of Rome and the Ecumenical Patriarchate have developed and deepened over recent years. It is my sincere wish that we continue this progess, humbly and prudently, but also with the courage needed to follow the inspiration of the Holy Spirit, who continues to speak to the Churches (cf. Rv 2:7) and leads us towards a more perfect accomplishment of the mysterious design of God for his whole people.

It is with these thoughts in mind that I want to express all my brotherly affection to Your Holiness, and to assure you that in my prayers I shall ask the Lord to shed his blessing in rich measure on you, your clergy, and your faithful people.

389.   *30 November 1978*

Address in reply by Patriarch Dimitrios I in the Patriarchal Cathedral

Your Excellency Bishop Ramon Torella, and Very Reverend Fathers Pierre and Eleuterio, worthy representative of His Holiness Pope Paul II.

During this recent eventful period in the life of the Roman

Church, this see and we personally have had deeply brought home to us the meaning of the words of the Apostle Paul when he wrote in his First Epistle to the Corinthians: "If one member suffers, all suffer together; if one member is honored, all rejoice together" (1 Cor 12:26).

Indeed events in Rome followed hard on one another. The Church there passed from sorrow to joy and from joy to sorrow at an unforeseeably rapid rate in a whole succession of persons and situations. In the end she found relief with the election of her new Pastor, our worthy and dear brother, Pope John Paul II.

Two outstanding figures of the Western Church have gone to their rest in the Lord, Paul VI and John Paul I. The first after a long period of pastoral office, which was rich and constructive for the great common cause of the unity of Christians and reconciliation among men. The second after a brief ascent, fraught with hope, into the firmament of the Church. We sorrowed with the sorrow of our sister Church and rejoiced in her joy.

But above every other thought or feeling we have grasped the sublime meaning at the conclusion of St. Paul's passage, where he says with epigrammatic succinctness: "Now you are Christ's body, and each of you a limb or organ of it" (1 Cor 12:27). Indeed we felt more keenly then, as we still do, arising as it were out of the facts themselves, the extended applications to which this truth lends itself.

In this spirit, confessing with all the saints that "all of us who have been baptized in Christ have put on Christ" (Gal 3:27), and that all of us who "call upon the Lord Jesus" (Rom 10:13) have him in our midst (Mt 18:20), and that we all belong to him as to one Lord and God, we welcome you today, worthy representatives of His Holiness our brother the Bishop of Rome, as bearers of his first salutation and his first message of love, of his ardent confession of faith and hope in the one Lord Christ.

Everything, brothers, in our relations so far, and especially that task now firmly taken in hand of marching together in dialogue towards the unity of our Churches, presupposes absolutely that we come together in a desirable agreement in the one Lord, in whom we were baptized, on whom we call, and in whose word and grace we have our being.

No one can or wants to loosen these bonds or halt this march. That would be to deny the Lord and so to banish him from our midst. But who can deny Christ or take him from among us?

This being laid down, we declare, brothers, at solemn moment, that the common cause, begun under favorable auspices, will have its sequel, and by the grace of the Paraclete will one day reach its culmination, granted the good pleasure of God and the cooperation of the men and women of today and those of the generations to come. "For we are God's fellow workers; you are God's field, God's building" (1 Cor 3:9). The whole cause of unity and reconciliation is here involved.

Dear and distinguished Brothers,

Your visit here in our midst, the first since the election of the new head of the sister Church of Rome, is an important event for us, and we thank His Holiness and you personally for the joy it brings us. Your being here was meant also to determine, in a way, what happens next to the dialogue undertaken between our two worlds. We would like to mark your presence here today, at the see of the First-Called Apostle, in the queen of cities, on this patronal feast, with some positive statements about the future of the dialogue and of our relations. We make them from this see as a humble servant of Orthodoxy. And we say:

We ardently desire the dialogue and unity. We ardently desire these two highest good causes in the Church, as for that matter all who love the Church and the Lord ardently desire them too. We believe in the power of the word and of dialogue. We declare that we shall be prompt to do everything in our power to further the process of encounter and our common growth with you as we exchange thoughts with one another.

We have already by our common efforts travelled a long and laborious road in preparing for the Theological Dialogue, both from the Pan-Orthodox side and the equally representative Roman Catholic one.

God has graciously blessed the feast of this see today, as he has blessed the first days of the lofty mission, happily begun, of the new angel of the Church of Rome, by a very significant event. The Orthodox and Roman Catholic Churches are about to be called on to decide whether the preparatory work so far done by the respective Technical Theological Commissions is sufficient. They must then in the Lord's name, and with fear of God, select their Inter-Orthodox and Inter-Catholic Commissions, to which will be entrusted the responsibility of the Dialogue itself.

This is indeed a great moment. Great are the events which lie ahead. We know that there is a deep sense of responsibility on either side. In our opinion the time of the laying of foundations is over—that eventful period of charity, of grace, of shared Christian experience, which was lived to the full by the blessed predecessors of our brother in Rome and our own here. Already "it is towards evening, and the day is now far spent . . . Is not our heart burning" for the new day of the Lord, now on the point of dawning (cf. Lk 24:29,32; Mt 28:1)? The twilight of one evening must be followed by the dawn light of the next day, which we are called upon to usher in, and to render and display in all its crimson beauty, and indeed as being "rosy-fingered"[57] with hope and happy prospects. This on the one hand: on the other it must be full of grace and understanding, of wisdom and moderation, so that we do not force others to unsay their words, or have to unsay our own.

In all this we shall be both eager and vigilant. We shall always maintain agreement and cooperation with our sister Orthodox Churches, and our decisions and actions will run parallel, being taken in concert and on a basis of equality and reciprocity between both the West and the Orthodox East.

This, brothers, is what we have to say on our side. This is our message of love and honour to our elder brother in Rome, the much loved Pope John Paul II. We rejoice to find on his side a warm attitude answering to our own, one which we see clearly confirmed in the lines of his fine message which we received by your hands.

By way of conclusion to the foregoing, let us pray fervently as brothers. Let us pray to the Lord again and again. "For the peace of the whole world, for the good estate of the holy Churches of God, for the union of all, let us pray to the Lord." Amen

390.　*5 April 1979*

Easter letter of Pope John Paul II to Patriarch Dimitrios I*

At the moment when we are about to celebrate with joy and hope the Resurrection of the Lord, which is the central mystery of our faith, we meditate the Apostle's words: "For to this end Christ died and lived again, that he might be Lord both of the dead and the living" (Rom 14:9).

The Resurrection of Jesus gives a clear and overriding meaning to human life, and directs the course of the world and its history towards

---

57. The standard epithet for the dawn in the ancient Greek poets Homer and Hesiod.

the radical renewal which the spirit of the Lord brings about (Acts 2:33).

The new man who is born through participation in the death and Resurrection of Christ (cf. Rom 6:4) is destined to be a citizen of the new heaven and new earth, where there will be no more tears, or pain, or death (cf. Rv 21:1–4). From this faith spring forth our joy and the hope that does not deceive (cf. Rom 5:5). Forgiveness, purification, and renewal for each one of us and for all creation come forth from the Resurrection of Jesus Christ, who has become the Lord of the living and the dead (cf. Acts 2:36).

In this new world, born from the Easter of Christ, there is no room for division. Everything there should be true brotherhood, "unfeigned love" (Rom 12:9), and unity. It is for this reason, dearly beloved brother, that I so greatly desire that the relations between our Churches should grow stronger and stronger and cause us to advance to the full unity willed by Christ. We are called right from the present time to show clearly in the face of the world the deep communion which already unites us, and to do this by proclaiming together the mystery of the Risen Christ, by making it known that our redemption has inseparable divine and human aspects, by helping all to develop fully in themselves the new dignity with which they clad themselves in Christ, and to make real in everyday life the resurrection imparted in their Baptism.

With these thoughts in mind, and enlivened by this deep and joyful hope, I assure you again, my dear brother, of my fraternal charity and high regard.

391. *14 April 1979*

Telegram from Patriarch Dimitrios I to Pope John Paul II for Easter.*

On the bright shining feast of the victory over death, and gladdened by our common faith in the Resurrection, we send a cordial brotherly greeting to Your venerable Holiness. May the glorious Risen Christ grant you to remain in good health and to rejoice with the joy of Easter for many years to come. May he lead on apace the sacred endeavor for Christian unity and bring it to a successful conclusion, so that our joy and that of all men may be fulfilled.

392.   *18 June 1979*

Letter of Patriarch Dimitrios I to Pope John Paul II for the feast of Saints Peter and Paul.**

It is with the joy and hope of which Christ is the criterion that we greeted the call of Your very dear and venerable Holiness to the helm of the holy Church of Rome, a helm which bears the seal of Peter's cross. In prayer and thought and through our representatives we shared with the whole Roman Catholic Church and the other Christian Churches in the inauguration of your pontificate, which God himself urged forward. Since then we have seen on your part a brotherly attitude which matches ours, and so we have been in communion of charity with one another. Hence with persevering prayer and the utmost brotherly interest we have been following the progress of your holy and constructive work in the Church and the world.

Already with joy fulfilled we see that we have not hoped in vain. Because you, Your Holiness, helped by the intercession of the Mother of God, have with faith, hope and charity given us and the world a witness of strength in the Christ who strengthens you (cf. Phil 4:13). And this in the midst of a world which believes and hopes in the strength which draws its power from strength alone. All this you have done from the moment when you assumed your responsibility (in which again the lines of the Cross are etched) as Bishop of Rome, who presides over charity throughout the Christian world, which charity itself rests upon Christ's grace.

Today we are sending to Your Holiness and the Church of Rome a delegation from our own Church of Constantinople under the leadership of our dear brother in Christ Metropolitan Meliton of Chalcedon, and including the Metropolitan Damaskinos of Tranoupolis and the Very Reverend Archimandrite Spiridon Papageorgiou. They are to represent our Church and ourself personally at the celebration of the holy memory of our two common Apostolic leaders, Peter and Paul, both of whom you resemble in your zeal and mode of action. We are doing this of course in the first place in order to maintain and continue the pious tradition by which our two Churches take part and pray together in the Doxology of the Lord on the feast of their founding Apostles. This tradition was begun between our Churches by your great predecessor of happy memory, Paul VI, as something arising from the reality of our refound brotherhood. Its purpose was also to furnish a mutual testimony to the fact that we maintain, in continuous succession from the apostles, the service of apostolicity in the Church, both in the East and the West.

However, the presence of our delegation in Rome this year takes on a special significance, and for the following reason. It has the effect of confirming what we have achieved up till now by way of our common holy desire and endeavor, and by contributions made on both sides to the reconciliation in Christ of the Roman Catholic and Orthodox Churches, and to the search in Christ for ways of recovering their unity in him. Our delegation will give expression at the same time by the spoken word to the above mentioned joy at seeing our hopes fulfilled in the words and deeds of Your Holiness right up to this day.

Most holy and blessed brother,

In writing to you in this strain we have in mind your hope enkindling declarations and activities on behalf of Christian unity, and more particularly those in furtherance of the Theological Dialogue between us directed to this end. At the same time we have in view the welcome fact that the preparatory work on both sides have been completed, and that a common basis has been found by the two authorized Commissions for beginning this official dialogue. Here we are right now on the very eve of the opening. Invitations were issued from this see to the whole Orthodox world to begin this official Theological Dialogue as soon as possible, and we should like to tell Your Holiness that the replies contained a welcome acceptance.

In sending this news to Your Holiness, we wish to assure you and your Church that our Church of Constantinople, in its supreme responsibility within Orthodoxy, will do everything in its power to build up the holy edifice of unity on the foundations which have been laid. But we should also like to ask you, given the conviction which you have so far shown in favour of this holy cause, to encourage and reinforce from the side of your Church this sacred enterprise in which we are both engaged, so that in prayer, humility, patience, wisdom, but also with the daring and determination of the Fathers, we may speak the truth in love and unity, that we may love one another and become united in the truth (cf. Eph 4:15).

We ask Your Holiness kindly to accept our delegation in this spirit. We embrace you with a holy kiss and remain with deep love and esteem in Christ.

393.   *28 June 1979*

Address by Metropolitan Meliton during the papal audience with the Delegation from the Ecumenical Patriarchate**

"How unsearchable are his judgments and how inscrutable his ways!" (Rom 11:33). This is the testimony of the Apostle Paul, who underwent the experience of the Damascus road and ascended to the third heaven. Indeed the decrees of God *are* unsearchable and his ways inscrutable. It remains then for us to explore and find out how we are to conform our judgments and ways of action with the judgments and ways of God, and how we are to subordinate our wills to his will, so that his will may be done, his kingdom come, and his glory shine out over the earth.

Last year, at the great feast of the sacred memory of the leaders of the Apostles, Peter and Paul, we had the holy joy, as a delegation from the Ecumenical Patriarchate, of praying in the Basilica of St. Peter with your predecessor of happy memory, Pope Paul VI, who as you have often said and we too in the East hold, was really a great Pope. We were then received by him in audience in this very hall where we now have the privilege of being with Your Holiness, and of handing you the fraternal letter of our Ecumenical Patriarch Dimitrios I, and expressing by word of mouth his own feelings, thoughts, and good wishes, and those of the holy Church of Constantinople, towards you and the holy Roman Catholic Church.

The unsearchable judgments and inscrutable ways of God have decreed that we indeed should come back, but that instead of Pope Paul VI we should meet at the altar and the See of Rome Your Holiness Pope John Paul II, without there being in the interval any meeting or combined prayer at a liturgical feast with your immediate predecessor, Pope John Paul I of happy memory.

Why is there not a continuous series of meetings of the same sacred ministers of the same mystery? Herein lies the unsearchable and inscrutable nature of the judgments and ways of God, which forever abide. Those who minister to them, and to the mystery of the Church, can follow one another in succession. The decrees of God remain the same, the Church is the same, the sacred service of its mystery is one and the same in its continuity.

With this faith both in the inscrutable character of the judgments and ways of God and in the unbroken and successive ministry and service devoted to them, we continue here in Rome today the ecclesi-

astical communion between its Bishop and the Bishop of Constantinople. We do this in charity and prayer, close by the altar, while looking ahead to the consummation of this communion, which will take
place *on* the one altar shared by us both.

Persons pass, bishops are translated from the earthly to the heavenly altar, but the Church Militant of Christ continues its journey of
crucifixion until the day when, by means of martyrs who have won the
prize of victory, by means of many prayers, holy endeavours, and sacrifices in non-essentials, it comes upon the essential—until it comes,
that is to say, on unity of faith and its profession, and in this unity
discloses to all creation the full glory of the Body of Christ in its state
of Resurrection.

In this journey, Your Holiness, you have been assigned a position
by God as one who continues a line, and as one of the leaders who are
making the same journey together. In all your statements of policy,
from the effective beginning of your exceptionally important and
responsible work in Christianity and the world as chief pastor of the
Roman Catholic Church and first Bishop of Christendom, you have
given testimony till this very day that you are posted on the same road
as that which was opened and made straight by your predecessors of
happy memory, Popes John XXIII and Paul VI, on the one hand, and
Patriarch Athenagoras I, also of happy memory, together with the present Patriarch Dimitrios I, on the other. We may add that your immediate predecessor, Pope John Paul I, wished to render the same service.

In the East there is joy and hope that Your Holiness has succeeded
your three immediate predecessors, not only in the see of Rome, but
in the heritage of their ecumenical spirit, and that you will be the one
to continue and fulfil the desire we have in common to submit ourselves together, to submit our wills, that is to say, to the Lord's will,
which is that all should be one (Jn 17:11).

Your Holiness,

The joy and hope that spring from our presence here before you
are increased by the fact that today's meeting takes place at a decisive
turning point in the journey towards Christian reconciliation, and at a
specially important moment in the deployment of holy endeavours by
the Roman Catholic and Orthodox Churches to reach unity; in other
words, it takes place on the eve of the opening of the official Theological Dialogue between the two Churches.

At this important juncture we are called, as Churches of the East
and West, to take account of our responsibilities, which are now

greater and further reaching than before, and of our foreordained destiny as Churches in the whole plan of God's dispensation for the redemption of man.

As you began your holy work, you rightly discerned, drew attention to, and proclaimed, bold pastor and evangelist that you are, what lies at the very heart of the huge variety of demands, anxieties, and hopes of the world, namely that they are all summed up and brought to a head in the redemption which takes place in Christ Jesus, our common Lord.

In Christ the Redeemer, the unity, dignity and rights of the human person, and further, the unity of the world, its values and destiny, acquire their real worth and status.

The Church is the prolongation of the redeeming Christ. The Redeemer is one and indivisible. His Body, too, the Church, ought to be one and indivisible, as we see it to be in the common Creed of Faith. It was the human mind that divided the world and the human race, and it divided the Church, too.

Now at last it is the time for the Church in its united state to testify to the world and render that world redemptive service. And in doing this it must sound the signal to itself and the world of the return to "the depth of the riches and wisdom and knowledge of God" (Rom 11:34), so that all may know that "from him and through him and to him are all things. To him be glory for ever, Amen" (Rom 11:36).

394.   *28 June 1979*

Address in reply by Pope John Paul II to the Delegation from the Ecumenical Patriarchate*

Dear brothers, you come to associate yourselves with the Church of Rome in celebrating the holy Apostles Peter and Paul, and I bid you welcome. Because of what you represent and him whom you represent, your presence, while honouring the memory of the holy Apostles Peter and Paul, gives us an additional reason for gladness. I am deeply grateful to you.

The annual exchange of delegations between Rome and Constantinople for the feasts of the patron saints of each Church is not simply an occasion for the kind of meeting that could become a mere habit.

The sharing by a Catholic delegation in the feast of St. Andrew, brother of St. Peter, at the Ecumenical Patriarchate, and by an Orthodox delegation in the feast of Saints Peter and Paul at Rome—with either side participating in the liturgical celebration commemorating these patron saints of our Churches—are events richly fraught with meaning and hope. It is the Apostolic faith, the deposit they have handed down to us, which is the solid and stable basis of our dealings with one another.

These dealings are bringing us with quickening pace and growing importance ever closer to the full unity which we so greatly desire. In the past, difficult times, adverse circumstances, and human weaknesses and faults have driven our Churches into mutual ignorance and even hostility. Today, by God's grace, and through the good will of men who are keenly attuned to what the Lord is saying, both sides are firmly resolved to do their utmost to restore full unity. The contacts between our Churches, not merely between officials who bear some special responsibilities, but also between faithful lay members, are helping us to learn to live together in prayer, and to consult one another by way of reaching common solutions to the problems that face the Church today. These contacts, too are encouraging us to live like brothers, each helping the other. That is why I take such special pleasure in this meeting.

When opening the Week of prayer for Unity this year, I suggested that we also send up to God a prayer of thanksgiving. It was indeed God who aroused the desire for unity, and blessed our quest for it by making us more clearly aware of the deep communion already existing between our Churches. In this context the Theological Dialogue for which we are now holding ourselves ready, and which is soon to begin, will play a decisive part. We look to it to solve the doctrinal and canonical difficulties which up till now have impeded full unity. We must keep on asking light and strength from the Holy Spirit for the success of this dialogue: it is he who will give us the courage to take the necessary decisions.

I can assure you that the Catholic Church enters upon this dialogue fervently desiring to see full unity reestablished. It does so with complete candour and honesty towards its Orthodox brothers, and in a spirit of obedience to the Lord who founded his Church as one and one only, and who wants it to be fully united so that it may serve as sign and means of a close unity with God, and of the unity of humankind, and may be an effective agent for the preaching of the Kingdom of God among our fellow men and women.

I thank you once again for being here in Rome for these solemnities and in such significant circumstances. And looking beyond yourselves as individuals, I should like to send my cordial greetings to our revered brother, Patriarch Dimitrios. I would ask you to assure him of our affection and our sense of standing side by side with him.

395. *25 October 1979*

Telegram from Pope John Paul II to Patriarch Dimitrios I for his patronal feast-day.*

On the occasion of your feast-day, I offer you my warm good wishes, and assure you of my fervent prayer. May the Lord give Your Holiness the assistance of his strength and light for a fruitful pastoral ministry and for the good of your Church. With brotherly affection in the Lord.

396. *27 October 1979*

Telegram in reply from Patriarch Dimitrios I to Pope John Paul II**

In charity we received the brotherly good wishes of Your esteemed Holiness for our name-day, and warmly thank you for them. In our turn we wish you good health for long years ahead and a pontificate that will make you deservedly famous.

397. *18 November 1979*

Address by Pope John Paul II, preceding the Sunday Angelus, announcing his visit to Turkey***

Today I should like to give you the first inklings of an important piece of news: the Pope will soon make a journey to the East. At the end of this month I shall go to Turkey. First of all I shall go to Ankara, the capital of that great country, where I shall meet the authorities of that nation and give them my greetings and respects. Then I go to Istanbul to pay a visit to His Holiness Dimitrios I, and to take part in the celebration of the feast of the Apostle St. Andrew, brother of Peter. St. Andrew is the patron of the Church of Constantinople. In this way the brother replies to his brother's invitation: Peter replies to Andrew.

Both reply, in accordance with the numerous and various appeals of our time, to the Lord's invitation for the good of Christianity and of the Church, which is the Body of Christ.

This visit is an important one. It shows in a practical way the Pope's decision, already stated several times, to continue the endeavor to achieve the unity of all Christians. This was one of the main purposes of the Council. Today it is a more urgent demand than ever. Great progress has already been made, but we cannot rest content with this. We must carry out Christ's will fully. With the venerable Orthodox Churches we are on the eve of initiating a theological dialogue with a view to our both surmounting the differences that still divide us. By this visit I wish to show the importance that the Catholic Church attaches to this dialogue. I wish to express my respect and deep brotherly charity for all these Churches and their Patriarchs, but above all to the Ecumenical Patriarchate, to which the Church of Rome is bound by so many centuries old ties. These ties have taken on a new strength and relevance in the last few years, thanks to the wise and courageous action of the great and venerated Patriarch Athenagoras, and of my great and beloved predecessor Paul VI.

I shall also go to Ephesus, where in 431 the Third Ecumenical Council proclaimed the Virgin Mary *Theotokos,* Mother of God, and where she still receives the prayers and veneration of the faithful in an ancient sanctuary.

I should also like this journey to remind every one of you, and every faithful member of the Church, of the sacred duty of working for unity. Every Catholic must do so at least by means of prayer and interior conversion, as the Council asked.

I entrust this journey and its success to your prayers, to the prayers of each one of you.

398. *18 November 1979*

Announcement by the Ecumenical Patriarchate of the forthcoming visit by Pope John Paul II**

We release the news that His Holiness Pope John Paul II will be coming to our city 29 November, and will visit His Holiness the Ecumenical Patriarch Dimitrios I at the Ecumenical Patriarchate, where he is awaited with joy and honor within the setting of the warm brotherly relations existing between the Orthodox and Roman Catholic Churches.

399.   *28 November 1979*

Speech by Pope John Paul II at Rome's Fiumicino airport, on his departure for Turkey**

I sincerely thank the venerable Cardinals, the Bishops, the Doyen of the diplomatic corps to the Holy See, the Minister Adolfo Sarti, and the other Italian authorities, as well as the rest of you who have been so kind as to offer me your greetings and good wishes at the beginning of my short journey to the East.

This new pilgrimage of mine follows in the wake of my predecessor Pope Paul VI, who went to Turkey at the end of July 1967. As I have already said when making the first announcement of my journey, I am going to that nation for the following reasons. First, to give renewed commitment and take further action in the effort for the unity of all Christians, in accordance with one of the primary aims of the Second Vatican Council. Then, further, I wish to show, as a theological dialogue draws near, the importance which the Catholic Church attaches to its relationship with the venerable Orthodox Churches. Finally I wish to express my deep affection and sincere charity for all those Churches and their Patriarchs, and in a special way towards the Ecumenical Patriarchate.

Therefore, after paying my due respects to the authorities of the Republic of Turkey at Ankara, I shall go to Istanbul to meet His Holiness the Ecumenical Patriarch Dimitrios I, and to take part in the annual liturgical celebrations in honor of St. Andrew. From there I shall go to Ephesus, the city in which the Third Ecumenical Council took place in 431, when the Virgin Mary was proclaimed *Theotokos,* that is to say, "Mother of God." I shall also pay a visit to Izmir.

May the Lord God, through the motherly intercession of the Blessed Virgin, accompany my steps with his grace along this way of great hope, which represents another important stage towards the full and perfect unity of all Christians.

For these great religious and ecumenical purposes, I ask at this moment the earnest prayer of all the members of the Church, and would bid them keep themselves peacefully ready to harken to the voice of the Spirit.

400.   *29 November 1979*

Welcoming address by Patriarch Dimitrios I to Pope John Paul II in the Patriarchal Church of St. George at the Phanar**

Most Holy Brother,

We give glory to God as we welcome you today to this city of the Mother of God, and within it to the Church of her Son, our common Lord and Savior Jesus Christ. For centuries the Church of Constaninople has been a sacred centre in which the Christian faith has been formulated, preserved intact, proclaimed, and its good tidings spread abroad.

Your visit to us, full of Christian charity and simplicity as it is, has a significance far in excess of a meeting between two bishops of particular sees: we look on it as a meeting of the Western and Eastern Churches.

Hence the joy felt over this important and historic visit is not simply a local matter, or one that just lasts for a day or two: our meeting finds its due place within the universality and eternity of the redemption of the human race.

The meeting does take place locally, but, on the one hand, in terms of ecclesiastical definition it is linked geographically with the entire East and the entire West; and on the other, in terms of the contemporary geographical definition of the inhabited world, it is linked with the North and the South.

The meeting does take place today, but it is bound up with a far off "yesterday," that of the Apostles, the Fathers, the Martyrs and Confessors whom we have in common, that of the Ecumenical Councils which we both recognize, and that of concelebration at the same altar, and of fellowship deriving from the one holy chalice. But it is bound up, too, with a recent "yesterday," the "yesterday" of our two great predecessors, Pope Paul VI and Patriarch Athenagoras I. This meeting of today, moreover, is predestined for the "tomorrow" of God—the "tomorrow" when there will be unity again, when there will be a common profession of faith again, when there will be full communion again in the Holy Eucharist.

If we make a due appreciation of this historic visit against the background of space and time, we recognize the splendor and importance of the action you have taken, and we thank you for it.

It is our belief that the Lord is present at this moment in our midst, and that the Paraclete is upon us, that the two brothers Peter and Andrew are rejoicing with us, that the spirits of our common Fathers and Martyrs are moving among us and urging us onwards. Present to our minds and making claims on our responsibility are the anxious expectations of divided Christians, the anguish of man without God and without Christ, the misery of a whole world of men and women deprived of human rights, of freedom, of justice, of people without bread, without medicine, without education, with no security and no peace.

With all this in view, we regard the blessed presence of Your Holiness and our meeting here as the will of God, and as a challenge and invitation which the world issues and to which we must reply. For this reason our Church, which is given over to the glory of God, welcomes you at this Doxology.

"Glory be to God in the highest, and peace on earth; good will among men" (Lk 2:14).

Welcome, holy brother!

401.   *29 November 1979*

Reply by Pope John Paul II to Patriarch Dimitrios I*

"Blessed be the name of the Lord" [said in Greek].

Your Holiness,

Blessed be the Lord, who has granted us the grace and the joy of this meeting here, at your Patriarchal See.

It is with deep affection and brotherly esteem that I greet you, Your Holiness, as well as the Holy Synod gathered about you, and through your person I greet all the Churches that you represent.

I cannot hide my joy at being in this land of very ancient Christian traditions, and in this city rich in history, civilization and art, which make it stand forth among the most beautiful in the world, and this today as yesterday. For Christians of the whole world used to reading and pondering the New Testament writings, these places are familiar, and so too are the names of the first Christian communities of many cities which today are in the territory of modern Turkey.

Christ "is our peace," St. Paul writes to the first Christians of Ephesus (Eph 2:14). And he adds: "God, who is rich in mercy, out of the great love with which he loved us, even when we were dead through our trespasses, made us alive together with Christ—by grace you have been saved—and raised us up with him . . ." (Eph 2:4–6).

This proclamation of faith in the divine dispensation for the salvation of men rings out over this land, and reverberates and is renewed from generation to generation. And it is destined to spread to the ends of the earth.

The fundamental dogmas of Christian faith, of the Trinity and of the Incarnate Word of God born of the Virgin Mary, were defined by the Ecumenical Councils which were held in this or in neighboring cities (cf. *Unitatis Redintegratio,* N. 14). The very formulation of our profession of faith, the *Credo,* took place in those first Councils celebrated together by the East and the West. Nicaea, Constantinople, Ephesus, Chalcedon, are names known to all Christians. They are particularly familiar to those who pray, study, and work in different ways for full unity between our sister Churches.

Not only have we had in common these decisive Councils, prolonged organ notes, as it were, in the life of the Church, but for a millennium these two sister Churches were able to grow together and give detailed and developed expression to their great vital traditions.

The visit I am paying today is meant as a meeting in the common Apostolic faith, so that we can walk together towards that full unity which suffered injury from sad historical circumstances, especially in the course of the second millennium. It would be impossible for me not to express our firm hope in God for the dawn of a new era.

For all these reasons I am happy, Your Holiness, to be here to give utterance to the deep feeling of the Catholic Church for the Eastern Orthodox Churches, and its sense of brotherly solidarity with them.

I thank you here and now for your warm welcome.

402. *30 November 1979*

Address by Pope John Paul II in the Patriarchal Church of St. George at the Phanar at the conclusion of the Patriarchal and Synodal Liturgy*

Your Holiness, my very dear brother: "Behold, how good and pleasant it is when brothers dwell in unity" (Ps 133:1). [*These opening words were spoken in Greek.*]

These words of the Psalmist spring from my heart on this day when I am in your company. Yes, how good it is, how pleasant, to be all brothers together.

We are gathered to celebrate St. Andrew, the First-Called among the Apostles, and brother of Peter, the leader of their group. This fact emphasizes the ecclesial meaning of our meeting today. Andrew was an Apostle, that is to say one of those men chosen by Christ to be transformed by his Spirit and sent into the world, as he himself had been sent into the world by his Father (cf. Jn 17:18). They were sent to announce the good news of the reconciliation given in Christ (cf. 2 Cor 2:18–20), to call men and women to enter by Christ into communion with the Father in the Holy Spirit (cf. 1 Jn 1:1–3), and thus to gather them, now become children of God, into a great people in which all are brothers and sisters. To gather all things together in Christ in praise of God's glory (cf. Eph 1:10–12): this is the mission of the Apostles, this is the mission of those who, in their wake, were also chosen and sent, and this is the vocation of the Church.

This Apostle, patron of the renowned Church of Constantinople, is Peter's brother. It is true that all the Apostles are bound together by the new brotherhood which unites those whose hearts have been renewed by the spirit of the Son (cf. Rom 8:15), and to whom the ministry of reconciliation has been confided (cf. 2 Cor 5:18); but this does not cancel out—far from it—the special ties created by birth and upbringing in the same family. Andrew and Peter were brothers, and within the Apostolic circle they must have been bound by a greater intimacy and united in a closer collaboration in the Apostolic task.

Here again today's celebration reminds us that special bonds of brotherhood and intimacy exist between the Church of Rome and that of Constantinople, and that a closer collaboration is natural between these Churches.

Peter, Andrew's brother, is the leader of the Apostles. Thanks to the inspiration of the Father, he fully recognized in Jesus Christ the Son of the living God (cf. Mt 16:16); owing to this faith, he received the name of Peter, so that the Church might rest on this Rock (cf. Mt 16:18). He had the task of seeing to the apostolic preaching. A brother among brothers, he received the mission of strengthening them in the faith (cf. Lk 22:32); he in the first place has the responsibility of watching over the union of all, of seeing that there is a symphony of the holy Churches of God in fidelity to "the faith which was once for all delivered to the saints" (Jude 3).

It is in this spirit, urged on by these feelings, that Peter's successor wanted on this day to visit the Church whose patron saint is Andrew, to visit its venerated pastor, its hierarchy and all its faithful. He wanted to come and take part in its prayer. This visit to the first see of the Orthodox Church shows clearly the will of the whole Catholic Church to go forward in the march towards the unity of all. It also shows its conviction that the reestablishment of full communion with the Orthodox Church is a fundamental stage in the decisive progress of the whole ecumenical movement. The division between us may not, perhaps, have been without an influence on the other and later divisions.

The new step I have taken fits in with the gesture of openness by John XXIII. It takes up and continues the memorable initiatives of my predecessor Paul VI. To begin with, that which took him in the first place to Jerusalem, where for the first time there was a moving embrace with the Ecumenical Patriarch of Constantinople, and the first exchanges by word of mouth were made in the very place where the mystery of Redemption to unite the dispersed children of God was enacted. Then there was the meeting which took place here, just over twelve years ago, anticipating the visit of Patriarch Athenagoras who came in his turn to visit Paul VI in the Roman see. These two great figures have left us to join God: they have completed their ministry, in which they were both straining towards full communion and almost impatient to bring it about in their lifetime. As for me, I did not want to delay any longer in coming to pray with you, in your country. Among my apostolic journeys, already carried out or planned, this one had special importance and urgency in my eyes. I venture to hope that Patriarch Dimitrios and I will be able to pray together again, and this time on the tomb of the Apostle Peter. Such actions express our impatience for unity before God and before the whole people of God.

For nearly a whole millennium, the two sister Churches grew side by side, as two great vital and complementary traditions of the same Church of Christ, keeping not only peaceful and fruitful relations, but also concern for the indispensable communion in faith, prayer and charity, which they did not at any cost want to imperil, despite their different kinds of sensibility. The second millennium, on the contrary, was darkened, apart from some fleeting bright intervals, by the sense of estrangement which the two Churches felt toward each other, with all the fatal consequences of this. The wound is not yet healed. But the Lord can cure it and he bids us do our best to help the process. Here we are now at the end of the second millennium. Surely it is time to quicken our pace towards perfect brotherly reconciliation, so that the dawn of the third millennium may find us standing side by side, in full communion, witnessing together to salvation before the world, which needs this sign of unity if it is to be evangelized.

On the practical plain, today's visit also shows the importance that the Catholic Church attaches to the Theological Dialogue which is about to begin with the Orthodox Church. With realism and wisdom, in conformity with the wish of the Apostolic See of Rome and also with the desire of the Pan-Orthodox Conferences, it had been decided to renew relations and contacts between the Catholic Church and the Orthodox Churches which would enable them to recognize one another and create the atmosphere required for a fruitful theological dialogue. It was necessary to create the context again before trying together to rewrite the texts.

This period has rightly been called the dialogue of charity. This dialogue has allowed us to become aware again of the deep communion that already unites us, and enables us to consider and treat each other as sister Churches. A great deal has already been done, but this effort must be continued. It is necessary to draw the consequences of this mutual theological rediscovery, wherever Catholics and Orthodox live together. Habits of isolation must be overcome so that we may collaborate in all fields of pastoral action in which this collaboration is possible, given the almost complete communion that already exists between us.

We must not be afraid to reconsider, on both sides, and in consultation with one another, canonical rules established when awareness of our communion—now close even if it is still incomplete—was still dimmed. These rules perhaps no longer correspond to the results of the dialogue of charity and to the new and promising openings which have been thus created. It is important that the faithful on both sides should realize the progress that has been made, and it would be desirable that those who are to be responsible for the dialogue should keep in mind the consequences for the life of the faithful of the kinds of progress still to come.

This Theological Dialogue which is about to begin now will have the task of overcoming the misunderstandings and disagreements which still exist between us, if not at the level of faith, at least at the level of theological formulation. It should take place not only in the atmosphere of the dialogue of charity, which must be developed and intensified, but also in an atmosphere of worship and openness of mind and will.

It is only in worship, with a keen sense of the transcendence of the inexpressible mystery "which surpasses knowledge" (Eph 3:19), that we will be able to see our divergences in their proper setting and "to lay . . . no greater burden than these necessary things" (Acts 15:28), so as to reestablish communion (cf. *Unitatis Redintegratio,* 18). It seems to me, in fact, that the question we must ask ourselves is not so much whether we can reestablish full communion, but rather whether we still have the right to remain separated. We must ask ourselves this question in the very name of our faithfulness to Christ's will for his Church, for which constant prayer must make us both increasingly open and ready in the course of the Theological Dialogue.

If the Church is called to gather men in praise of God, St. Irenaeus, the great Doctor of the East and of the West, reminds us that "the glory of God is living man" (*Adv. Haer.* IV, 20, 7). Everything in the Church is ordered to allowing man to live really in this full freedom which comes from his communion with the Father through the Son in the Spirit. St. Irenaeus indeed immediately continues: " and man's life is the vision of God"—the vision of the Father manifested in the Word.

The Church can respond fully to this vocation only by bearing witness through her unity to the newness of this life given in Christ: "I in them and you in me, that they may become perfectly one, so that the world may know that you have sent me and have loved them even as you have loved me" (Jn 17:23).

In the certainty that our hope cannot be disappointed (cf. Rom 5:5), I repeat, beloved brothers, how glad I am to be among you, and with you I give thanks to the Father from whom every perfect gift comes (cf. Jas 1:17).

403.   *30 November 1979*

Address in reply by Patriarch Dimitrios I to Pope John Paul II**

> "How beautiful are the feet of those who
> proclaim peace, who announce good news"
> (Rom 10:15).

Most Holy Brother,

With these words, which are those both of the Prophet and the Apostle, we greet Your venerable Holiness as you make your historic visit to the holy Church of Constantinople, which serves the Orthodox East, and we hail your presence, which is full of significance, at this feast commemorating the glorious Apostle Andrew the First-Called, and at the Eucharistic Liturgy celebrated upon his altar.

Your journey to us from Rome is indeed that of a messenger of peace and good things, and of one who comes, we are convinced, not only to us and our Holy Orthodox Church, but to this great country of ours, and much further still afield. It is the expression of a new journey of Your Holiness to man made in the image of God, whose worth as a person is so sorely tried today. This journey has been undertaken because of those threatened values and good things which are intrinsic to the very being of humanity, and determine the deepest reason for our existence on earth.

Looking at your visit and giving it its true worth in this wide and extended setting, seeing it as one made to this country, which is a bridge between East and West, and to this city which is the cradle of great civilizations, of important religious developments and Christian forms of culture, we remain convinced that we are formulating the outlook of the Church of Christ about the world and man. At the same time, we acknowledge the fact that, from the time of your accession to the Roman see, all the measures you have adopted and the journeys you have made—and these also concern causes and peoples external to your see—have the same meaning as what we express. Thus you are putting to use, in accordance with the inscrutable decrees of the Lord, the talent of liberty which was given you, and make your way forth out of walls of every sort to bring glad tidings of peace and good things to all men without distinction.

So, "how beautiful are the feet of those who publish peace, who preach good news."

Most holy brother,

From yesterday we have welcomed you to our humble see as one who brings glad tidings of peace, of the peace of Christ and of the good things that go with it, and as one who was moved to do this by sheer goodness.

We, too, long for and seek out peace for both the Church and the world. It is in the pursuit of this common aim that we come together. It was with this same holy purpose that our two great and renowned predecessors met in Jerusalem, here at Constantinople, and at Rome. It was with this aim in mind that our two Churches issued forth from their state of isolation and mutual alienation, not to say their hostility, and took the road towards fresh encounter and reconciliation. For this purpose the anathemas between us were lifted. With faith in the will of the Lord, the Ruler and Father of peace, who would have us be one (Jn 17:21), but also drawing upon courage, patience, wisdom, and hope, and holding exchanges with one another in charity, we have both covered a long road in a relatively short time, and have reached the position where we stand today. Throughout this journey the Risen Christ was with us, accompanying us on our way, indeed guiding us along it, leading us to the breaking of the Bread.

So it was with our gaze fixed on this full communion in the breaking of the Bread that we made our way together up till today. As from today we are inaugurating a new and most important stage through your presence, symbolic and significant in so many ways as it is, at the liturgical assembly of the Church of Constantinople.

Most holy brother,

The two Churches which we represent at this moment, the Roman Catholic and the Orthodox, and the other Christian Churches and Confessions, the other religions, and the world in general, are waiting to learn what particular stage in our journey towards Christian unity has been reached by our meeting today, which was brought about at the cost of so much effort on your part.

Thanks be to God, we are both able to answer today by saying that we are entering on a new phase of the attainment of brotherhood, indeed a serious and important phase, of which the issue will be decisive for the goal to which we look, namely unity.

We are entering on the phase of the official Theological Dialogue between the two Churches, Roman Catholic and Orthodox.

We prepared the ground through the "dialogue of charity" by means of mutual endeavors, not to mention ecclesiastical declarations and acts, and we made the prior arrangements for the Theological Dialogue through the work done on either side by the commissions appointed for this purpose. Given these facts, we the Roman Catholic and Orthodox Churches are happy to announce that we have officially set up two Theological Commissions, which, under the form of a single Joint Theological Commission will soon engage in the first phase of the Dialogue following the daily program arranged and approved by the two Churches acting together.

Our meeting here today makes it possible then to announce this definite practical fact.

Perhaps Christians of other Churches and Confessions will be wondering whether this dialogue between the Roman Catholic and the Orthodox Churches whose beginnings we applaud today, is as far as we aim to go.

To this question we are both able to answer No. And we would both go on immediately to say that our ultimate and crowning aim is not merely the union of our two Churches, but total Christian unity in the same Lord and a common sharing of the one holy Chalice.

And to those non-Christians who might be wondering what Christian unity really means—whether it represents an alliance or common front against non-Christians—our reply would be this. The Christian unity which we are trying to achieve is not aimed against anyone. It represents rather a positive contribution and service to all, regardless of sex, or race, or religion, or social class, in keeping with the fundamental Christian principle: "there is neither Jew nor Greek, there is neither slave nor free, there is neither male nor female" (Gal 3:28).

Most holy brother,

It is in such a divine-human embrace of humankind by the Church of Christ that we embrace you and the Roman Catholic Church today in this holy center of Orthodoxy.

Doubtless various obstacles loom up before us. In the first place we have to reckon with serious theological problems which concern essential points of the Christian faith; it is to solve these that we are arranging the Theological Dialogue. At the same time there are the obstacles arising from distrust, from irresponsibility, from the non-theological factors in the differences between Christians, from intolerance and fanaticism, whether between Christians or members of different religions—in short all those pointed weapons that belong to Lucifer's armory. From Lucifer, for that matter, come all the heresies and divisions and the various forms of opposition of man to God and man to his fellow man.

We live and endeavor to fulfil the will of God and to spread the Gospel of love, unity, and peace at a critical hour for the human race, when Lucifer, the one who in his person is opposed to God and is the spirit of evil, is tempting humankind beyond its strength.

Indeed, Your Holiness, we find ourselves before a heightened state of temptation and of the action of the evil one in the world, in every sphere, the religious, social, cultural, political, to such a degree that before us we see the single victim of all of this: man who was made in the image of God. We are in the presence of a phenomenon, a sign of the times, which could be described as a return to the age of religious fanaticism, of "holy wars," of the mutual shattering of men and faiths, and all this constantly done in the name of God. Before this picture of humanity stretching out before us in all its naked and tragic reality, and with the thread of Satanic anarchy on every side, Your Holiness comes to us, so that we may together proclaim the Gospel of peace and goodness, looking to every quarter of the globe.

According to a very ancient and pious tradition of the Church, the Apostle Andrew the First-Called, brother of Peter, the leader of the Apostolic group, was crucified upon a cross having the shape of the Greek letter X, which means that he was crucified upon the monogram of Christ. From that time onwards that cross is his throne and the throne of his successors. From it we greet you, and together with you bear testimony to love, peace, and salvation, before the whole world.

404.　*30 November 1979*

Joint Declaration by Pope John Paul II and Patriarch Dimitrios I*

We, Pope John Paul II, and the Ecumenical Patriarch Dimitrios I, give thanks to God who has granted us to meet and celebrate together the feast of the Apostle Andrew, the First-Called and brother of the Apostle Peter. "Blessed be the God and Father of our Lord Jesus Christ, who has blessed us in Christ with every spiritual blessing in the heavenly places" (Eph 1:3).

Seeking only the glory of God through the accomplishment of his will, we state anew our resolute determination to do everything possible to hasten the day when full communion will be reestablished between the Catholic Church and the Orthodox Church, and when we will at last be able to concelebrate the divine Eucharist.

We are grateful to our predecessors, Pope Paul VI and Patriarch Athenagoras I, for everything they did to reconcile our Churches and cause them to progress in unity.

The progress made in the preparatory stage enables us to announce that the Theological Dialogue is about to begin and to make public the list of the members of the Joint Catholic-Orthodox Commission which will take it in hand.

This Theological Dialogue envisages not only an advance towards the reestablishment of full communion between the Catholic and Orthodox sister Churches, but also a contribution to the multiple dialogues that are pursuing their course in the Christian world as it seeks its unity.

The dialogue of charity (cf. Jn 13:34; Eph 4:1–7), rooted in complete faithfulness to the one Lord Jesus Christ and to his overriding will for his Church (cf. Jn 17:21), has opened up the way to better understanding of our respective theological positions and thereby to new approaches to theological work, and to a new attitude with regard to the common past of our Churches. This purification of the collective memory of our Churches is an important outcome of the dialogue of charity and an indispensable condition for future progress. The dialogue of charity itself must continue with might and main in the complex situation which we have inherited from the past, and which forms the real order of things in which our enterprise must be conducted today.

We want the progress in unity to create new openings for dialogue and collaboration with believers of other religions, and with all those of goodwill, so that love and brotherhood may prevail over hatred and opposition among men. We hope to contribute in this way to the advent of a true peace in the world. We implore this gift of him who was, who is, and who will be, Christ our one Savior and our real peace.

405.　*30 November 1979*

List of Catholic members of the Joint Catholic-Orthodox Commission for the Theological Dialogue (to be held in Rhodes 1980)*

- Cardinal John G. M. WILLEBRANDS
  Archbishop of Utrecht
  President of the Secretariat for Christian Unity
- Cardinal William Wakefield BAUM
  Prefect of the Sacred Congregation for Catholic Education
- Cardinal Joseph RATZINGER
  Archbishop of Munich and Freising
- Most Reverend Mario BRINI
  Titular Archbishop of Algiza
  Secretary of the Sacred Congregation for the Eastern Churches
- Most Reverend Nicolas PHOSCOLOS
  Catholic Archbishop of Athens
- Most Reverend Habib BACHA
  Metropolitan of Beirut and Byblos for the Catholic Melkites
- Most Reverend Mariano MAGRASSI
  Archbishop of Bari (Italy)
- Most Reverend Alfred PICHLER
  Bishop of Banjaluka (Yugoslavia)
- Most Reverend Ramon TORRELLA
  Vice-President of the Secretariat for Christian Unity
- Most Reverend Antal JACAB
  Bishop of Alba Julia (Rumania)

- Most Reverend Miroslav MARUSYN
  Vice-President of the Pontifical Commission for the Revision of the Oriental Code of Canon Law
- Most Reverend Georges ABI-SADER
  Bishop of Lattaquié of the Maronites (Syria)
- Most Reverend Alfons NOSSOL
  Bishop of Opole (Poland)
- Monsignor Michele MACCARONE
  President of the Pontifical Committee of Historical Studies
- Father Jean CORBON
  Secretary of the Ecumenical Commission of the Assembly of the Patriarchs and Catholic Bishops of Lebanon
- Father Frederic McMANUS
  Professor in Canon Law at the Catholic Univerisity of America
- Father Dimitri SALACHAS
  of the clergy of Athens,
  Professor in Canon Law in the Pontifical University of St. Thomas Aquinas (Rome)
- Father Ernst SUTTNER
  Professor in Patrology and Oriental Theology in the University of Vienna
- Father Harmon VOGT
  Professor in Patrology in the University of Tübingen
- Father Emmanuel LANNE, O.S.B.
  of the Monastery of Chevetogne (Belgium)
- Father Jean M. R. TILLARD, O.P.
  Professor in the Dominican Faculty of Theology at Ottawa
- Father André de HALLEUX, O.F.M.
  Professor in Patrology and Oriental Theology in the University of Louvain
- Father Miguel ARRANZ, S.J.
  Professor in Liturgy at the Pontifical Oriental Institute (Rome)
- Father Peter-Hans KOLVENBACH, S.J.
  Provincial for the Middle East (Beirut)
- Father Louis BOUYER
  Priest of the Oratory of France
- Father Waclaw HRYNIEWICZ, O.M.I.
  University of Lublin (Poland)

- Father Patrick van der AALST
  Professor in Oriental Theology in the University of Nijmegen (Netherlands)
- Dr. Vittorio PERI
  of the Apostolic Vatican Library
- Father Pierre DUPREY
  Under-Secretary of the Secretariat for Christian Unity

406. *30 November 1979*

List of Orthodox members of the Joint Catholic-Orthodox Commission for the Theological Dialogue**

Ecumenical Patriarchate
Most Reverend STYLIANOS (Harkianakis)
Greek Orthodox Archbishop of Australia

Professor John ZIZIOULAS
University of Glasgow

Patriarchate of Alexandria
Most Reverend PARTHENIOS
Metropolitan of Carthage

Professor Stylianos PAPADOPOULOS
Faculty of Theology, University of Athens

Patriarchate of Antioch
Most Reverend Georges KHODR
Metropolitan of Byblos and Botrys (Lebanon)

Reverend Father Georges ATTIE', Tripoli

Patriarchate of Jerusalem
Most Reverend GERMANOS
Metropolitan of Petra (Israel)

Professor Georges Galitis

Patriarchate of Moscow
Most Reverend KIRILL
Archbishop of Vyborg

Reverend Professor Liveri VORONOF
Theological Academy, Leningrad

Patriarchate of Belgrade
Most Reverend SAVA
Bishop of Sumadija

Professor Stoyan GOSCHEVITCH, Belgrade

Church of Bucharest
Most Reverend NICHOLAS (Corneanu)
Metropolitan of Banat

Reverend Professor Stefan ALEXE

Church of Sofia
Most Reverend JOAN
Bishop of Dragovitza

Reverend Professor Nikolai CHIVAROV

Church of Cyprus
Most Reverend CHRYSANTHOS (Sariyannis)
Metropolitan of Morphou

Professor Makarios PAPACHRISTOPHOROU
Galata-Soleas

Church of Greece
Most Reverend CHRYSOSTOMOS
Metropolitan of Peristeriou

Professor Megas PHARANDOS
Faculty of Theology, University of Athens

Church of Poland
Most Reverend SAVVAS
Bishop of Lodz and Posnan

Most Reverend SIMON
Bishop of Lublin

Church of Georgia
Most Reverend NICKOLOSI (Guenton)
Archbishop of Sukhumi and Abkhazia

Monsignor DAVID (Tchkadua)
Bishop of Batumi and Schemokmeḑi

Church of Czechoslovakia
Reverend Professor Pavel ALES

Church of Finland
Reverend Protopresbyteros Matti SIDOROFF
Reverend AMBROSIUS of Valamo

407.   *30 November 1979*

Address by Pope John Paul II upon his return to Rome**

With a heart unable to contain its keen feelings and my mind full of unforgettable pictures of places made dear to us by venerable traditions, I set foot again on Italian soil.

I am grateful to the Lord for the assistance he gave me throughout this pilgrimage, which took place under the banner of two special "notes" of the Church, *apostolicity* and *unity*. I have in fact been to visit His Holiness Patriarch Dimitrios I, to pay tribute, together with him, to the brother of the Apostle Peter and to confirm in this way that the apostolic origin remains indelibly imprinted on the face of the Church as one of her outstanding characteristics. By this journey I also intended to bear witness to my firm resolution to go forward along the way that leads to the full unity of all Christians, and at the same time do something to bring people closer to one another in their respect for what is essentially and deeply human.

My thought now turns with gratitude to the Turkish authorities who were so very courteous to me during my stay in that nation; to my dear brother His Holiness Dimitrios I; to the metropolitans, bishops, clergy and faithful of the Ecumenical Patriarchate of Constantinople, with whom I had the joy of experiencing a brief but significant time of communion in faith and in charity; to my venerated brothers in the episcopate, together with the priests and the people of God of the Catholic Church in Turkey; and to the whole Turkish population, who with spontaneous signs of fellow-feeling made me understand what a desire for understanding and brotherhood there is in every man's heart. . . .

408. *1 December 1979*

Telegram from Pope John Paul II to Patriarch Dimitrios I*

When I had only just reached Rome again, and was still feeling moved by my experience of the celebration in your Cathedral, I paid a visit to the tomb of the Apostle Peter to thank God for our brotherly encounter, and to ask the Apostle to guide us in this new and decisive stage of our advance towards unity.

I should also like to thank Your Holiness and your Holy Synod wholeheartedly for the very warm welcome given me, and to assure you that I am firmly resolved to work closely with you, and that my feelings are those of unfailing fraternal charity.

409. *2 December 1979*

Address by Pope John Paul II before the recitation of the Sunday midday Angelus****

1. In the first place I wish to express again my joy at the visit I was enabled to make to the Sister Church of Constantinople and to Patriarch Dimitrios I on the solemnity of St. Andrew the Apostle, who is the patron saint of that Church.

The tradition of Andrew, who was Peter's brother, brings back to my mind the image of the Church, which is ever being built and takes its growth on the cornerstone Jesus Christ, and at the same time on the foundation of the Apostles and the Prophets (cf. Eph 2:20). This process is continued with the strength of her original unity, and at the same time is accompanied by the *desire* for that perfect unity, which in a time known only to God must be reached by the operation of the Holy Spirit, because he is the Spirit of truth and love. The Church, in her bimillenary history, has developed from what we might call the cradle of her early days along the way of great and distinct traditions, the Eastern and the Western. For many centuries these two traditions displayed the common riches of the Body of Christ, completing one another in the heart of the people of God and also in hierarchical institutions, in liturgical rites and in the doctrine of the Fathers and the theologians.

2. The Second Vatican Council reminded us that these riches and this tradition do not cease to be a common possession of the whole of

Christianity and that on this basis and under the action of the Holy Spirit, we must put behind us the division that has oppressed us since the eleventh century and seek mutual agreement and union again.

. In this connection I am happy to recall what the Council Fathers recognized when they noted that "from their very origins the Churches of the East have had a treasury from which the Church of the West has drawn many elements of its liturgy, spiritual tradition, and its body of law" (*Unitatis Redintegratio,* 14). It has drawn hence especially in the matter of devotion to the Blessed Virgin, to whom "the Eastern Christians pay high tribute in beautiful hymns of praise" and in that of Eastern monastic spirituality, "which became, so to speak, the source from which Latin monastic life took its rise" (*U.R.,* 15).

The Eastern Churches, therefore, the Council Father concluded authoritatively, "although separated from us, yet possess true sacraments, above all—by apostolic succession—the Priesthood and the Eucharist, whereby they are still joined to us in closest intimacy" (*U.R.,* 15).

It is a pleasure for me to recall here how well deserving the Church of Constantinople was in the conversion of the Slavs. It was this Church which took up the invitation of Prince Rastilav, and sent the brothers Cyril and Methodius to Greater Moravia, where they initiated a work of thorough evangelization, continued by their disciples.

It was in this same spirit of communion that I formed the idea of my recent pilgrimage, and with the help of God carried it out. I hope that it will yield abundant fruit for the ecumenical cause. I call upon you all to pray for this intention.

3. Deep gratitude is the keenest feeling in my heart at this moment. I feel the need to thank above all Christ the Lord and his Holy Mother, who were specially close to me in this pilgrimage. I must then thank my beloved brother, His Holiness Dimitrios I, the metropolitans, bishops, clergy and the faithful of the Eucumenical Patriarchate, who treated me with exquisite and moving charity. With them I wish to thank also Patriarch Shnorhk Kalustian and the Christians of the Armenian Community, who remain courageously faithful to authentic traditions. I want to say "thank you," too, to my venerable brothers in the Episcopate, and to the priests and people of the various Catholic rites in Turkey, for their repeated proofs of brotherly communion and sincere homage.

I sent respectful and grateful greetings also to the rulers of the noble Turkish nation, whose fine courtesy and thoughtful attentions I appreciated in the way they prepared my welcome and made sure that my stay was comfortable and untroubled.

At Ankara I delivered a special address on the relations between the Catholic Church and Islam, taking my stand on the statements in the declaration *Nostra Aetate* of the Second Vatican Council.

I would ask you all to thank the Blessed Virgin for watching over me throughout this journey by now reciting the Angelus.

410. *10 December 1979*

Address by Pope John Paul II, in his public audience, on his journey to Turkey****

1. The Lord Jesus called Andrew in the first place among all the Apostles. "He first found his brother Simon, and said to him, 'We have found the Messiah' (which means Christ). He brought him to Jesus. Jesus looked at him, and said, 'So you are Simon, the son of John? You shall be called Cephas' (which means Peter)" (Jn 1:41f.).

This incident, reported in the Gospel according to St. John, made it inevitable for some time past that I should pay a visit to the ancient see of the Patriarchs at Constantinople, which venerates St. Andrew the Apostle in a special manner; and that I should do so on the very day of 30 November, which is that linked by the liturgical calendar of the Western and Eastern Churches with the memory of the one whom the Lord Jesus first called. Today I wish to thank Divine Providence for this visit, which I so longed for under a special breath of influence from that eternal Wisdom which was worshipped for so many centuries in the Church on the Bosphorus. This visit had as its result that both the Ecumenical Patriarch and I were further strengthened as we walk those ways on which Patriarch Athenagoras I and my great predecessors, Pope John XXIII and Paul VI, set forth.

If then I may be allowed to appeal to the analogy arising from the Gospel event, the successor of Peter in the Roman See wishes today to express his satisfaction at having heard the call coming from the East, from the see which makes Andrew, the brother of Peter the center of special veneration because he followed the call. Thanks to that, he found himself once more in the presence of Christ, who confirmed the vocation of Simon Peter in making use of the brotherly tie with Andrew.

2. As I thank Divine Providence which shortly before the beginning of Advent turned my steps towards the East, I wish at the same time to thank all those who, in the service of that Providence, shouldered the many human tasks which made this important visit possible.

I am thinking particularly of the Turkish authorities, beginning with His Excellency the President of the Republic, the Government, and the Foreign Minister. This visit gave me the opportunity to meet them and to make a very useful exchange of experiences and ideas on subjects which are very important for the coexistence of nations and countries all over the world, and particularly in that important point of the globe which is practically a gateway between Europe and Asia. Thus the alacrity and readiness in welcoming the guest from Rome, as well as the great concern shown that the journey should run its whole course safely and well deserve my particular gratitude, which I wish to express again at this moment.

3. Although my principal purpose was to visit the Phanar, the see of the Ecumenical Patriarchate at Istanbul, at the same time the recent journey also gave me the opportunity of meeting the Armenian community in the persons of its Patriarch Kalustian and the Catholic Archbishop Tcholakian. The Armenian Church represented by the former is engaged in an earnest dialogue with the Catholic Church, particularly since the memorable visit to Rome of Vasken I, who is the head, or "Catholicos" of that Church, which has its center at Etchmiadzin. The visit took place in May 1970.

The Armenian Catholic Church, which on the other hand is in full communion with the Apostolic See of Rome, has about 150,000 faithful all over the world. My thought and my gratitude go also to the Armenian community as a whole. I also wish to recall the representatives of the Jewish community, whom I was able to meet on the occasion of the liturgy in the Latin Catholic cathedral dedicated to the Holy Spirit in Istanbul.

4. I consider the meeting with Patriarch Dimitrios I a fruit of the particular action of the Spirit of Christ, who is the Spirit of unity and love. It was really in such a spirit that this meeting took place, and it was to such a spirit that it bore witness. Its culminating moment was the common prayer through mutual participation in the Eucharistic Liturgy, even though we were not yet able to break the Bread together and drink from the same Chalice. This same kind of participation took place beforehand on the vigil of St. Andrew's day, in the evening, in the Latin cathedral of the Holy Spirit. Here Patriarch Dimitrios I was with us (as well as the Armenian Patriarch), and we solemnly exchanged the brotherly kiss of peace, imparting the blessing together at the end. And it took place again later, on the solemnity of the Apostle in the Patriarchal church, where it was my privilege and that of the whole delegation of the Apostolic See, to assist at the splendid liturgy of St. John Chrysostom, to renew the kiss of peace with my brother of

the see in the East with the same as those there assembled, to speak and above all listen to his address.

What deep love he manifested for the Church and for her unity, which Christ continues to desire. At the same time, what loving solicitude for man in the modern world. The great mystery of "the godhead and humanity," meditated upon so deeply and marvelously by the whole Eastern patristic and theological tradition, is the greatest source of this concern.

The Patriarch said: "It is peace and goodness that we, too, desire and seek, both for the Church and for the world, and we meet for the purpose of pursuing this holy aim together . . . during this process the Risen Christ was present, walking with us . . . this is why, looking towards full communion and the breaking of bread, we have walked together right up to this day."

5. If, therefore, we have the right to say after St. Paul, "the love of God urges us on" (2 Cor 5:14), then today this love of Christ assumes the particular form of solicitude for man and for his vocation in the modern world, a world full both of promise and alarm. Therefore, together with the Theological Dialogue, certainly so necessary, which is to begin in the near future between the Catholic Church and the Orthodox Church as a whole (that is to say, with all the Orthodox autocephalous Churches), we continue to need the dialogue of brotherly love and *rapprochement*. This has already been going on for some years, that is, since the times of the Second Vatican Council, but there is no doubt this dialogue must be given greater impetus and depth. It must, in a certain sense, become an integral part of pastoral programmes on both sides. Union can be only the fruit of the knowledge of truth in love. They must both operate together; one apart from the other is not enough, because truth without love is not yet the full truth, just as love does not exist without truth.

A great deal can be hoped from this new stage of our ecumenical initiatives, especially after the proof of the good will and support which, when I recently visited Constantinople, all the Orthodox Patriarchs gave to Patriarch Dimitrios, who as "Ecumenical" Patriarch is first among the others.

6. In the framework of this happy meeting gifts that were eloquent in meaning were also exchanged. The Ecumenical Patriarch offered his guest an ancient episcopal stole, thinking of that Eucharist which the merciful God will perhaps permit us to celebrate together— something that Pope Paul and Patriarch Athenagoras desired so ardently before us. The gift that I left at Constantinople was an icon of the Mother of God, she with whom I became familiar at Jasna Gora

and Czestochowa from my earliest youth. In making this gift, I was guided not only by reasons of a personal nature, but above all by the special eloquence of history. The Icon of the Bright Mountain, Jasna Gora, contains the symptomatic features which speak to the soul of the Christian whether of the East or the West. It also comes from that land in which the meeting of those two great traditions of the Church took place, in the whole course of her history. My country, it is true, received Christianity from Rome and at the same time also the great heritage of Latin culture, but Constantinople, too, became the source of Christianity and of culture, in their Eastern form, for many Slav peoples and nations.

I expressed these ideas already in the course of my pilgrimage to Poland in June last. To sum up, our meeting at the Phanar, Istanbul, was full of great problems and deep matters. When questioned by one of the journalists about my "impressions," I said that it was difficult to speak on this subject. And it really is difficult. We are in another dimension. We are and must remain with our eyes fixed on that image of Wisdom, which speaks to us from the top of the great monument at the Bosphorus. It is an image of Advent. And we, too, serve the great cause of the Advent of the Lord.

Blessed are we if the Lord finds us watchful on his arrival (cf. Mt 24:46).

I prayed particularly for this intention amid the ruins of Ephesus, where the Virgin Mary, obedient to the Holy Spirit in the deepest and most simple way, was solemnly proclaimed by the Church *Theotokos,* that is "Mother of God."

411.   *16 December 1979*

Statement made by Patriarch Dimitrios I to the paper, *Ekklesias- tiki Alithia* (16 December 1979), of the Church of Greece, after the visit of Pope John Paul II. Followed by an interview given by Met- ropolitan Meliton of Chalcedon*

What are the results of the visit of Pope John Paul II to the Phanar?

The historic visit to the Ecumenical Patriarchate of my brother, Pope John Paul II has contributed to the advancement of the ecumen- ical spirit, since he has shown that ecumenical responsibility is not a matter of words and theories, but of works and deeds inspired by humility and Christian courage. Ecclesiastical acts which are made authentic by the humility willed by Christ can only have as their effect the opening of heaven. From now on it is these acts which make theology. St. Gregory the Theologian puts it exactly when he says: "the road which climbs towards theory (i.e. contemplation) is laid down by action." Ecclesiastical acts broke the communion between the East and West. Ecclesiastical acts can gather the single flock of Christ into full unity. We are praying and hoping.

How do you regard the work of ministering to the ideal of "the union of all" from the point of view of the see of the Great Church of Constantinople?

Orthodoxy must contribute to the strengthening of the authentic ecumenical spirit in the Christian world, and indeed in the whole world, by its rich spiritual treasures and the true ecumenism of its Fathers, who must always be our rule in inter-Church relationships. The Ecumenical Patriarchate never departs in the slightest way from the ecumenical spirit of the Fathers, and it strives to give testimony always and everywhere to the Orthodox faith, but also to freedom in Christ. We serve the holy cause of the unity of the Body of Christ with full responsibility. We are working and building.

What are the aims of the Joint Commission for the dialogue between the two churches, of which news has been released?

What we expect from the Joint Commission set up for the dialogue between the Roman Catholic and the Orthodox Churches is that it should resolve the present difference one after the other, so that the day which we so much desire, when there is full union and we are able to communicate from the same holy chalice, may be brought closer. Perhaps the work of the Commission will be long and difficult, but nothing is impossible for God. Faith in the truth will set us free.

INTERVIEW WITH METROPOLITAN MELITON OF CHALCEDON

Your Eminence, how do you sum up the results of the meeting between the Ecumenical Patriarch and the Pope?

It is a "miracle" in the true sense of the word, and I say this without hesitation. It opens the way to further progress in the relations between the two Churches, since with the publication of the names of the members of the two Commissions which are to examine the points of difference between the two Churches, this meeting marks the beginning of dialogue which from now on becomes a theological one. It must be emphasized that after his visits to Mexico, to Poland, to Ireland, and to the United States (where he spoke directly mainly to Roman Catholics and gave addresses on charity and brotherhood for humankind in general), the Pope chose the Ecumenical Patriarchate for his first ecumenical visit. This shows the significance which the Pope attaches to unity with Orthodoxy. It is thus that I would sum up the importance of this visit. The results flowing from it will of course be matter for future evaluation. But, to be sincere, I must tell you that I foresee them as being of happy omen.

It is said that the two Churches were separated mainly by prejudices. Do you think that the dogmas that separated them, namely the primacy and infallibility of the Pope, are such that the theological dialogue can get beyond them? Or will there be concessions made on both sides?

As far as the division and separation of the Churches go, prejudices did not play a decisive role. And for prejudices, there are a certain number about today! At the time of the separation, it was love that was missing. But to be honest and frank with you, there were a certain number of disagreements touching the faith of Christianity and its formulation.

The ecclesial dialogue is now beginning. There will be no concessions on essential matters, but only a search for a common basis. We Orthodox do not accept any sacrifice of truth. All we are doing is to seek an interpretation of the truth with love as a criterion. In this dialogue there will be no compromise; there will be no agreements of a political sort that are signed today and rescinded tomorrow. We are dealing here with a reality that enters into living experience.

But is it not a fact that the search for truth will be conducted within the domain of the sacraments which are common to both Churches?

That is so. The two Churches have a common theology in what concerns the sacraments. And since these sacraments are for the most part the same, we have chosen, for the first phase of the Theological Dialogue, to clarify this subject, and more particularly the subject of the Holy Eucharist.

The Theological Dialogue aims at finding what is right for the

Christian Church. This is something so sacred, so great and important, that it obviously calls for a new spirit which is purely Christian, a spirit of humility and earnestness, a spirit of freedom and not of fanaticism. It calls also for a spirit of perseverance in the truth and in the faith of the undivided Church.

What about the likelihood of political conversations between the two Church heads?

Perhaps as a head of State the Pope has had political conversations here in Turkey. But with us the dialogue was purely on religious and Church matters. I must remind you that as an Ecumenical Patriarchate we are a non-political, a purely religious institution. Of course, in the past, and even the recent past, the Church did get mixed up with politics. But history never repeats itself in the same form; it is not a static phenomenon, but a dynamic action, and its events should become lessons for the peoples of the world. What I wish to say is that the various peoples should not fall into a sentimental sleep, like prisoners of legends, but should adapt themselves to reality and choose the practical best in that reality.

It has been said that this journey of the Pope has heightened the prestige of the Ecumenical Patriarchate.

It is not for me to comment on what people say. The fact is that the Pope came to meet the other head of Christians as equal to equal. What I mean by that is that we acknowledge the Pope's primacy of honor, just as the other Orthodox Churches recognize a similar primacy in the Ecumenical Patriarchate.

Roman Catholic prelates have further indicated that the Patriarch has found the Pope the person he can speak to best.

That is quite true. I realized myself how enthusiastic the Patriarch was about his conversation with the Pope. I think that the earlier and outstanding pastoral activity of the Pope in Poland, a matter in which we have a special interest, had its part to play in this enthusiasm. We believe that the other courses of action that the Pope is adopting will be constructive both for Christian mankind and for the whole world, especially his endeavours to strengthen respect for the human personality.

412. *Christmas 1979*

Christmas letter from Patriarch Dimitrios I to Pope John Paul II**

We are celebrating together the supernatural mystery of the visitation to us of our God from on high, in which the Day Spring of all the dawns rose upon our world, and the unapproachable Light came and was apparent to us.

Illuminated by this light, we contemplate the utter condescension of our God and his love for man, and together with the angels we give glory because of what has come to pass, that there has been born to us a Savior. We go further and acknowledge that the Savior who was born in the flesh from Mary, the ever-virgin Mother of God, is the one Redeemer of us all, and that all of us who are Christians take our origin from him.

In this spirit we begin a journey in our mind to Bethlehem, and we desire to make our way in the company of Your blessed Holiness to the cave of the Nativity, and in a common action with you, and indeed together with the shepherds and the Magi, to adore him who "has broken down the dividing wall that kept us apart" (Eph 2:14), and reconciled us to the Father (cf. Rom 5:20). For this reason we hasten to hold communion with you by means of this brotherly letter on the occasion of the feast.

And first of all, as we impart an embrace of greeting to Your venerable Holiness on this great feast of Christianity, we send up a prayer to the Lord from the depths of our heart for you and for the holy Roman Catholic Church in your parts. Next we join you in an expression of our lowliness before the Son of God who emptied himself and became poor for our sake, and in an expression too of our submission to his holy will, by way of seeking divine enlightenment from him that we may continue and urge forward the holy cause of the full unity of our Churches, and not only that but the assembly of all Christians into one in Christ Jesus.

We consider that an important contribution to this holy cause was furnished by the recent journey which Your venerable Holiness made to our Church, a journey that was full of Christian charity, courage, and good will. We should like to assure you that we still remain deeply moved by the meeting with you before the Lord, and this to such an extent that the joy and hope for the Christian future that spring from this event give added richness to our celebration of Christmas this year. For this reason we thank you once more, most holy brother, in that following closely the love shown by John and the readiness for self-offering of Paul, you came from the Church of Peter to that of Andrew, and stood in its liturgical assembly, so that we might give joint testimony that we are brothers, and that we want all on earth to be brothers and sisters, since peace and God's good pleasure have been given them from Bethlehem.

In sending Your most blessed Holiness this festive message, we greet you again with a holy kiss, and remain with brotherly charity and special esteem.

413. *17 January 1980*

Letter in reply of Pope John Paul II to Patriarch Dimitrios I*

The celebration of the day on which the goodness of God our Savior and his love for men were revealed (cf. Ti 2:13) has renewed in us a fervent expectation "of the blessed hope, the appearing of our great God and Saviour Jesus Christ" (Ti 2:13).

As our heart overflows with gratitude before the mystery of the divine plan which is revealed to us in all its wonder, and we are filled with joy springing from the sure ground of our hope, we realize more clearly than ever how necessary it is to proclaim this message to all those of our time. They too should be able to enter into and advance within this light which shows them their life, their destiny, and what they are. This is the task which today more than ever rests squarely on our shoulders, and which also more than ever requires our unity.

Our meeting and our prayer together have given a clear indication to the whole world that we are firmly agreed that the dialogue about to begin between the Catholic and Orthodox Churches is to be a decisive stage in our common enterprise. This is to establish full communion between our Churches, so that they can, acting together in perfect harmony, minister to the coming of God's kingdom.

I give thanks once more to the Lord who has allowed me to feel at first hand both your own charity and that of your whole Church, and I confide to him the good wishes and hopes that I entertain for Your Holiness, the hierarchy, and all the Christian people round about you. In doing this I earnestly ask him to grant us to make great progress along the way that leads to that unity which he wishes to see reigning among his disciples.

I thank you for the kind and thoughtful good wishes which you sent me, and I give renewed expression, dear brother, to my feelings of deep and utterly fraternal charity.

PART VI

The Dialogue of Charity
in Its Supporting Role

414. *28 May 1980*

Address by the envoy extraordinary of the Patriarch, Metropolitan Meliton of Chalcedon, to the members of the Joint International Commission for the Theological Dialogue between the Catholic and Orthodox Churches. Given at the official opening of the dialogue during the doxology celebrated in the Patriarchal Church of St. John the Theologian at Patmos**

Reverend and dear Brothers,

I am very happy to welcome you to this sacred site on behalf of the Bishop of this island, His Holiness the Ecumenical Patriarch Dimitrios I, and I convey his greeting, which is one of love and peace, to each of you. All hail then, and let us rejoice in one another's company so that there may be joy piled upon joy.

Reverend Members of this Commission,

We are gathered here for a reason [*logos*] that goes beyond human considerations [*logos*]; it is because of the divine Word [*Logos*] which was in the beginning, and which brought John the Theologian [*Theologos*], the "disciple whom Jesus loved," to this island called Patmos.[58]

At first sight the conditions under which he and we came may well appear quite different, but with deeper discernment it dawns upon us that they have a certain similarity.

In his *Apocalypse* (Book of Revelation) John says: "I John, your brother, who share with you in Jesus the tribulation and the kingdom and the patient endurance, was on the island called Patmos on account of the word of the Lord and the testimony of Jesus. I was in the Spirit on the Lord's day" (Rv 1:9–10).

---

58. Patmos, one of the group of twelve Greek islands (the Dodecanese) off the Coast of Asia Minor, was in St. John's time used as an imperial penal colony, and today remains barren except for the monastery of St. John. It was to Patmos that John, the author of the *Apocalypse (Revelation),* was banished.

A long-standing tradition common to both Eastern and Western traditions identified the John of the *Apocalypse* with St. John the Evangelist, author of the Fourth Gospel and sometimes called "The Theologian." The Greek word *logos,* which moves through a spectrum of meanings, occurs prominently in the prologue of St. John's Gospel, and again in Rv 1:9; hence its thematic recurrence in Meliton's speech.

Tradition has it that John the Apostle and Evangelist came to Patmos at the order of the Emperor Diocletian, an exile and in bonds. Such were the conditions under which *he* came. Outwardly, and from the world's point of view, we have come to Patmos in a different manner, free and unbound. In spite of that, if we look at the basic realities, we too have come as exiles and in bonds.

Let me make myself clear. We too have come as exiles, not as the victims of any worldly ruler, but as exiles from the peace that existed between the Churches of the East and the West and was destroyed. We come in bonds, not at the dictate of an emperor, but because of our own divisions. At the same time we have come, as John did, "on account of the word of God and the testimony of Jesus." And there are further basic similarities between his case and ours. John came to Patmos as a "brother" to those who formed the local Churches, but he also came as one who shared with them "in the tribulation and the kingdom and the patient endurance" of Jesus. Tribulation and patient endurance are together involved with God's kingdom in the Church, even if they bear different features now from those of John's time.

It is out of the question that we should have come here together other than the way John came. We too have come as brothers, brothers who have become strangers to one another, not for geographical reasons or by the decree of an emperor, but through a spiritual estrangement and because of human excesses. Nevertheless we have come together once more "in the tribulation and the kingdom and the patient endurance [which we share] in Jesus."

It is irrelevant that the tribulation and patient endurance of the Church in the West is different from that of the Church in the East; it is still the tribulation and patient endurance of the Church which is united in the kingdom of Jesus, that kingdom which is one and indivisible throughout the centuries.

Over and beyond these outwardly different but fundamentally similar conditions the fact remains that John came to Patmos "in the Spirit" and "on account of the word of God and the testimony of Jesus."

I would ask you, what power could possibly have brought us together at Patmos, Roman Catholics and Orthodox who are in schism with one another, and were until quite recently even enemies—what power could have done this except the Spirit? I believe that we have come together at Patmos "in the Spirit," as John did, and we must believe that we have come for the same reason [*logos*] as he did, "on account of the word [*logos*] of God and the testimony of Jesus."

We are here on account of the word of God and the testimony of

Jesus. Our foregathering in this spot, our presence, our work have as their aim the conduct of a theological dialogue between the Roman Catholic and the Orthodox Churches, which represent the two great sections of the divided Christianity of East and West.

The spiritual atmosphere of Patmos gives our dialogue an atmosphere of its own, and this for Christianity and the world must belong to the order of revelation and prophecy. The driving force of our dialogue is supplied in John's words: "on account of the word of God and the witness of Jesus."

Brothers, we have come to Patmos, this place marked in the highest degree as the site of apostolic theology; and we have come first and foremost to listen, not to make speeches. We have come to discover once more the theology of the Apostles and the Fathers of the undivided Church, and thereby return, all of us, to "the word of God and the testimony of Jesus." Only by making a fresh discovery of ourselves and one another will we be able to give a decisive "testimony of Jesus."

We meet one another again, after centuries of schism and separation, within a framework set up by our Churches and as giving them a voice—we are not assembling in mere academic guise. Moreover, we pursue our theological dialogue with the aim of reaching a happy conclusion, under God, in mutual agreement and a common profession of faith. None of this means, however, as you will all agree, that we are looking for a Christian unity between Roman Catholics and Orthodox which would be an end in itself and limited to them. Rather our dialogue is "on account of the word of God" which applies to the one Church of Christ in its entirety. And we can add without further ado— for these two things are bound up inseparably with one another—that it is "on account of the testimony of Jesus."

Our Theological Dialogue which is being blessed and opened today is and must be a "testimony of Jesus" within Christendom and beyond it, to all the nations, to the whole world and the entire creation. It must be a renewed proclamation of the good news as well as that proclamation pure and simple.

The Church of Constantinople, and I am sure the combined whole of Orthodoxy, take the view in the Spirit of Christ that this is the Lord's will, the need of the Church, the demand of our times, and the expectation of Christians and non-Christians, namely that we should give "testimony" in the light of the revealed fact that the Church is one.

In addition then to other reasons, we are under pressure of the demands made on us by the men and women of today, and these are anguished demands to which the One who beyond all others lends a ready ear is he who founded the Church for the world's salvation. Which means that we are being called on by the Lord and the world to give "the testimony of Jesus" here from Patmos.

The message of revelation and prophecy—one which moreover concerns the last things—comes to us at Patmos, and it is this that sets forth the scope of our responsibility both in the ecclesial and the theological sense.

My brothers, there is still one thing missing from our meeting at Patmos, the one quite essential thing whose absence makes the situation as we come so different from John's, thereby bringing out the tragic nature of the sin of division, and increasing our responsibility as Churches and as theologians engaged in dialogue.

What I have in mind is this. John came to Patmos "on the Lord's day." Although he was an exile and in bonds, still it was on the Lord's day that he came, in other words at that great and holy interval in time of the Eucharistic fellowship, which has been and remains throughout the centuries the expression of the One, Holy, Catholic and Apostolic Church. It is this expression in a universal Eucharistic fellowship which gives living reality to the theology of the Word and "the testimony of Jesus."

We, my brothers, have come to Patmos, but not "on the Lord's day," that is to say, not in Eucharistic fellowship. Nevertheless we have come in our true identities, and in one another's company, so that we may make ready for "the Lord's day," and this "on account of the testimony of Jesus" which we must give to the world.

These are the things that the Church of Constantinople has to say to the holy local Churches of God in the West and the East.

Brothers, the sacred aim that we have in mind is and must be the "Lord's day," meaning full Eucharistic fellowship "in simplicity of heart" and "oneness of mind" (Acts 2:46).

So, in so far as I am able to express the spirit of the East, [I would say that] we, the two larger parts of the Christian world of West and East, are called upon here at Patmos to conform ourselves to the Word of God, as this Word has been expressed and defined by the undivided Church. That is why in the very first place we are going back in mind to the primal meeting of the Word with humanity, in which it took flesh. It is on this ground that we meet one another.

Let me carry my explanation a step further. The Word of God met humanity in that situation in which it actually was at the time of his incarnation. We are meeting one another in the respective situations ecclesiastical and theological, in which we actually are right now. Such a meeting is dictated by and is an extension of the meeting of the divine and human, from which fundamentally the Church derives its institution and its final orientation.

The redeeming Word of God did not make his encounter with us away from the Synagogue and the Forum.[59] He came to meet us all where we are, Jews and Gentiles, *within* the Synagogue and Forum. We in our turn are called to imitate closely the divine-human mode of action of God the Word by meeting one another where we are and as we are today, so that we may make our way side by side toward the Lord of peace and glory.

Imbued by the spirit of love and theological insight of St. John we all fully realize—while being subject to presuppositions and outlooks which will make their presence felt—that this moment of our encounter for theological dialogue is an historic and decisive one, bringing with it a heavy responsibility for all taking part.

It is with these considerations and in sole obedience to the Lord's will that in his presence we dedicate and open today the theological dialogue unanimously decided on by our two Churches. This dialogue was announced from the Phanar by Pope John Paul II and the Ecumenical Patriarch Dimitrios I, on the feast of the Apostle Andrew, as being directed to the unity of the Church and as a reaffirmation of its unbreakable bond with its divine Founder and Head, Our Lord Jesus Christ. We are gathered here to give glory to him, with the Father and the Holy Spirit, and to beg his mercy, through the prayers of the most holy Mother of God Mary, his mother and the adoptive mother of John the Theologian, and those of all the saints.

Brothers, let us pray to the Lord. Come, Lord, you "who are and were and are to come." Amen.

415.   *28 May 1980*

Address by Cardinal John Willebrands during the doxology to celebrate the opening of the meeting at Patmos*

Dear Brothers in Christ,

"To him who loves us and freed us from our sins by his own blood, who has made us a royal nation of priests in the service of his

---

59. The Forum (Latin) or Agora (Greek) was the market-place, the venue for popular gatherings and the site of legal tribunals and often religious temples or shrines. It represents the Gentile world of the Graeco-Roman civilization, as distinct from the Synagogue which stands for Judaic life and worship. The combination represents total humanity.

God and Father—to him be glory and power forever. Amen!" (Rv 1:5–6).

As we begin the first meeting of the Joint Commission of the Catholic and Orthodox Churches with a combined ceremony of prayer on the Isle of Patmos, this doxology of the first chapter of St. John's *Apocalypse* springs to my mind of its own accord and fills my heart with joy and adoration. It sheds light on our meeting and indicates the spirit which should inspire it.

After all it is to the Lord that we are all now turning together, to the Lord who frees and unites us, the Lord who brings us here together to find the means of reestablishing full communion between our Churches.

Our meeting begins here at Patmos, the island to which the Apostle John was banished for the sake of the Gospel, and where he was told to write a book to be sent to the seven Churches of Asia Minor (cf. Rv 1:9–11). The Johannine vision of the renewal of all things thus hovers on the horizon of our meeting: "The One who sat on the throne said to me: 'See, I make all things new!'" (Rv 21:5). The reestablishment of full communion between our Churches is of a piece with this final renewal which derives from the heralding of the Gospel and the fulfilment of its demands.

The communion of all men and women gathered before God will be the culmination of our history: "I heard a loud voice from the throne cry out: 'This is God's dwelling among men. He shall be with them and they shall be his people and he shall be their God who is always with them. He shall wipe away every tear from their eyes.'" (Rv 21:3–4a) The unity of the Church, itself the universal sacrament of salvation, is the beginning, the germinal source, and the means of bringing about this greater and final unity. So it was that Jesus, the High Priest and Head of the Church, made his prayer, "that all may be one, as you, Father, are in me, and I in you, that the world may believe that you have sent me" (Jn 17:21). The accomplishment in human history of what is contained in this call has met with the counter forces of sin, with its perpetual pull towards division.

In the letters to the seven Churches the author of the *Apocalypse* strongly exhorts these to purity of faith and a life that goes hand in hand with this faith they have received. While he praises them all singly for their fidelity and the good they have done, he also calls them in turn to repentance and conversion: "I find that the sum of your deeds is less than complete in the sight of my God. Call to mind how you accepted what you heard; keep to it and repent." Each of the seven letters has a concluding sentence that rings out like a refrain, reminding us of the fundamental need to be watchful and open to guidance: "Let him who has ears heed the Spirit's word to the Churches" (Rv 2:7,11,17,29;3:6,13,22).

Over the last few decades our Churches have been alert to these promptings of the Spirit, and with quickened awareness have taken the way indicated by his call, which amounts to a strenuous striving to reestablish full communion.

It was by the operation of the Holy Spirit, as the Vatican Council reminded Catholics, that the movement for unity was born (*Unitatis Redintegratio,* 1). The process of purification of heart and memory, bringing Catholics and Orthodox to a fresh realization that over and beyond their differences they are members of the same family and brothers, must have been due to the Spirit of God—from what other source could it have come? The Spirit of God raised up in our Churches personalities of great stature, men who with conviction and perseverance worked to lessen the gap between our Churches, while looking to the restoration of full unity. To mention only a few who are now with the Lord, how could we fail here to recall Patriarch Athenagoras, Pope John XXIII, Metropolitan Nicodemus of Leningrad, Pope Paul VI, and Cardinal Bea?

It was through the action of the Holy Spirit that we resumed contact with each other, hesitantly at first, and then saw these relations develop slowly but surely to the point where they have brought us today. Now we have an official meeting of the Churches seeking to clear up their differences so as to achieve full unity. Moreover they are doing this with no other aim than to obey their one Lord, and so preach his Gospel to greater effect, and with stronger claims to credence, to the people of our own time.

Our meeting occurs just after we have celebrated Pentecost, the day on which the Holy Spirit came down on each of the disciples, when they were "all filled with the Holy Spirit" (Acts 2:3–4). This event is fundamental to the Church and continues in its life, and it remains the model according to which Christian life is meant to pursue its course: all of us filled with the Holy Spirit, each of us receiving his or her own gift.

Speaking to the Christians of Corinth St. Paul says: "There are different gifts but the same Spirit." And he goes on to say: "To each person the manifestation of the Spirit is given for the common good" (1 Cor 12:4,7). Clearly this is true not only as regards individuals, but must apply also to the life of our Churches, which have been called to live in conditions formed by different kinds of history and culture. While our Churches received the same faith, they developed this

Christian patrimony in different ways: "the heritage handed down by the Apostles was received in different forms and ways, so that from the very beginnings of the Church it has had a varied development in various places, thanks to a similar variety of natural gifts and conditions of life" (*U.R.*, 14).

We find these different developments in every realm of the Church's life, in spiritual and liturgical traditions, in discipline, in ways of expressing, presenting, and organizing reflection on the mysteries of faith. "It is hardly surprising, then, that sometimes one tradition has come nearer than the other to an apt appreciation of certain aspects of a revealed mystery, or has expressed them in a clearer manner. As a result, these various theological formulations are often to be considered as complementary rather than conflicting" (*U.R.*, 17).

It is within this setting that we should see what direction our work should take, keeping in view perfect communion in faith, while at the same time making proper allowance for the manifold and diverse elements which are necessary for expressing the infinite richness of God and his gifts. Let us bend low in adoration of the incomprehensible and inexpressible splendour of God, praising and thanking him for the self-disclosure he has made in calling us to share in his life. By so doing we will be able to enrich one another and put ourselves in a position to be guided by the Spirit towards the truth in its fulness.

In this way we shall be able to set about a genuine work of theology, and by loving one another succeed in professing with one mind and heart all the truth that has been revealed to us.

Dear Brothers in the Lord,

How wonderful it is to be here together in this island, this part of the world sanctified by the presence and preaching of the Apostles, and to sail these seas just off the shores where they evangelized the people and suffered for the Gospel of the Lord. Here in this island the Apostle John left us his earliest testimony, the *Apocalypse*. It is a meditation on the message and mystery of Christ, on the Spirit and the Bride. This book does not take as its subject the earthly life of Jesus, as the Gospels do, it looks rather to his appearance in glory. Unlike the *Acts of the Apostles* it does not describe the Church in its first years, but gives us a vision of its forward journey through the centuries, and interprets and explains the meaning of its mission. It has taken the measure of suffering and persecution and sees them as the way to victory.

Through persecution and suffering the Church follows in the wake of Christ, who passed through death to resurrection and glory. Having entered into his glory and taken his seat at the Father's right hand, the

Lord sent the Spirit on the Church of God, which the Spirit continually leads to the God who is love, and to the celebration of the truth in love. At the decisive hour of his earthly life the Lord prayed: "Father . . . give glory to your son that your son may give glory to you" (Jn 17:1). He did not keep this glory for himself, but as he goes on to say: "I have given them (i.e. those who believe) the glory you gave me, that they may be one as we are one" (Jn 17:29).

The glory of Christ is the manifestation to the human race of his perfect communion with the Father. Those who know by faith this glory of Christ are drawn towards his communion with the Father; they are one in Christ and with one another, and so themselves come to be the manifestation of Christ's glory.

Is the hour ripe for the Church to pray with the Lord: "Father, the time has come, give glory to those who are now sons in the Son"? The Church follows the example of her Lord in passing through sufferings, through persecution. But what stops her from fully manifesting to the world the glory of Christ is the lack of communion and the division resulting from it.

The Church of God is always on its journey: the Lord shows us the way and opens our eyes as he did with the disciples going to Emmaus. The Spirit leads us to the truth in faith and love through the thick and thin of difficulties and errors so that we may finally come to show forth his glory to the world.

Today's meeting, for all its limitations and imperfections, should be a manifestation of the glory of Christ. The eyes of our Churches are upon us, but above all it is under the gaze of God that we stand, and his ears harken to our prayers. This meeting should mark a moment in divine history, a moment of grace which manifests the Lord's presence among us. We are here, we bishops and theologians, priests and laymen, as sent by our Churches. You theologians are not here in your scholarly capacity, but as men of the Church, and for an event in the life of the Church, for our meeting is an ecclesial one. The dialogue which we are now beginning is at one and the same time a dialogue between our Churches and a dialogue within the Church, in other words an ecclesial dialogue.

The Church is the icon of God, Father, Son and Holy Spirit. The Holy Trinity is not only its exemplar, but the source of its existence and life. As we look over the history of the Church we have to admit that it has not always drawn from this pure and inexhaustible source. If we take God's plan for the Church and begin from the time of Abel, we recognize that at various times it made mistakes, wandered from the path, and was unfaithful. It had to be born from the water and blood of the Lamb. It was chosen in the Father's plan and sanctified by the Holy Spirit to obey Jesus Christ, but it will always need to be sprinkled with his blood (cf. 1 Pt 1:2), if it is to be an icon without spot.

Within these vistas the direction which our meeting must take is clear: we must live out the truth in love, and thus grow towards him who is the Head, towards Christ (cf. Eph 4:15), and so manifest his glory to the world, being one body in one Spirit (cf. Eph 4:4).[60]

416.   *17 June 1980*

Message of Patriarch Dimitrios I to Pope John Paul II for the feast of Saints Peter and Paul**

To the most blessed and holy Pope John Paul II, greetings in the Lord.

The honor fell to us to commemorate with our brothers the Apostle Andrew in our Church's see, with Your Holiness in great charity unforgettably present; and now we have a like holy occasion for commemorating together the leaders of the Apostles, Saints Peter and Paul, and of paying honor to them.

We would have liked this celebration, which is being held in its turn at your own venerable see, to be observed under equivalent circumstances, but since it is impossible for us to be present in person, we are sending to Rome, by Synodal decision, a delegation led by our dear brother in the Lord, His Eminence Metropolitan Meliton of Chalcedon, Doyen of the Holy Synod, accompanied by His Grace Bishop Jeremiah of Sasima and the Very Reverend Archimandrite Spyridon Papageorgiou. We have charged this delegation to bring the festive greetings of our Church to yours, and to convey to Your Holiness an embrace of love, peace and honor in Christ.

Blessed be God the Father of our Lord Jesus Christ who has granted our two sister Churches to commemorate and honor together the holy Apostles who are their patron saints by the taking of two decisive and historic steps in their common journey towards unity. The

---

60. On 30 May the Joint Commission of sixty bishops and theologians moved to the nearby island of Rhodes. The commission chose its co-presidents: Archbishop Stylianos of Melbourne and Cardinal Willebrands. It accepted the plan for the Dialogue which had been drafted by a preparatory commission of theologians, and set up a coordinating committee and three sub-commissions to prepare a draft for the next plenary session (Munich, July, 1982). The topic chosen was "The Mystery of the Church and the Eucharist in the Light of the Mystery of the Holy Trinity."

first of these was the formation and promulgation of the Joint Commission for the conduct of the Theological Dialogue between yours and the Orthodox Churches; and the second was the promising consecration and opening of this dialogue.

In this important new phase of our reconciliation in Christ we are moving into a fellowship of theological thought, in the service, with fidelity to the truth, of the sacred cause of unity. As we do this we are called all the more to cultivate and deepen our fellowship in charity, so that we may work with surer aim and ampler effect to meet the Lord's sacred will. Thus we shall hasten the coming of that holy and illustrious day which we all desire, when in full communion we shall celebrate together the mystery of the Church in the mystery of the divine Eucharist, to the glory of the mystery of the Holy Trinity.

With such thoughts and this desire we visit your dear and venerable Holiness in prayer; we embrace you on this feast with a holy kiss, and remain with deep fraternal charity in the Lord and special esteem.

417. *28 June 1980*

Address by Metropolitan Meliton of Chalcedon when the Delegation from the Ecumenical Patriarch was received by Pope John Paul II for the feast of Saints Peter and Paul**

It is just and fitting that we should give glory to the holy, consubstantial and life-giving Trinity, since this year again the Churches of Rome and Constantinople are privileged to commemorate together as sister Churches the leading Apostles Peter and Paul, to whom we both look, and to do so close by the tomb of your predecessor Peter, in the same eternal city in which they were martyred.

This joint celebration of their feast cannot be aligned with the conventions of the world. It is a joint churchly celebration, indicated as such by the churchly presence of our humble selves as representatives of the Patriarch of Constantinople.

The joint commemoration of Andrew, Peter's brother, in his own Church on 30 November last year, belonged to the same order of things: it was mutual in a churchly sense and conducted in a brotherly spirit through your own dignifying presence.

There is something more than custom in these joint celebrations of our common Apostles as we religiously carry them out in one another's sees. The fact is that Jesus, the beginner and ender of our faith and that of the Church, has led us to this state of things in which we embrace one another as did Peter and Paul.

When this takes place our churchly meeting at the joint celebration of the Apostles turns into a holy act of dedicated service, and plays its part in reuniting the Church, which means carrying out the Lord's will that we should be one, and vindicating the injunction of the Apostles and our common Church Fathers.

The Apostle Paul bids the Philippians and through them bids us: "Make my joy complete by your unanimity, possessing the one love, united in spirit and ideals. Never act out of rivalry or conceit; rather let all parties think humbly of others as superior to themselves, each of you looking to others' interests rather than his own" (Phil 2:2–4). St. Basil the Great in his letter to the priests of Tarsus adds some timely words: "The age tends strongly towards the destruction of the Churches, and this is something that has been brought home to us for a long time. For building up the Church, for correcting errors, for entering into the sufferings of the sick brethren and protecting the sound, there is no one. . . . As far then as this age is concerned there is a crying need for rendering good service to the Church with concern and care: to unite what was hitherto broken is such a service."[61]

Your Holiness,

Our two Churches of Peter and Andrew, inspired by the apostolic and patristic spirit just referred to, at a certain definite point in the history of the second millennium of Christianity, felt the movement of the Holy Spirit and offered themselves to it. It is a movement towards Christian renewal and unity, for the purpose of evangelizing the world. It was in this way that our Churches came to the realization of their responsibility for the division of the Church and for restoring it to its integral state. For the last twenty years now they have been working with daring and patience, in obedience to the divine will, to this end.

And see, the Lord has blessed the enterprise to such a degree that we have reached this important stage of our journey to unity, namely the beginning of the Theological Dialogue between the Roman Catholic and Orthodox Churches.

Our churchly meeting of today, falling on the morrow of our return from Patmos and the Cave of the Apocalypse, endows the Dialogue now begun with its most significant dimension, the churchly one. In this Dialogue it is not purely and simply theologians who are

---

61. The reference given is to the Greek patristic collection, BEPPES (55, Letter 113, 20–30), corresponding to Migne, *Patrologia graeca,* 32, c. 526.

exchanging views, it is our Churches. Consequently this Dialogue is of a quite distinct ecclesial nature, which renders it more greatly responsible before Christianity and the world. The capacity of the churches for meeting the appeal of the Lord, the appeal of the people of God, and the dire need of the world, will be judged by the course which this Dialogue takes.

For this reason we must give the Dialogue a central place in our affection and vigilant attention, and while it is under way intensify the [other] dialogue of ecclesial interrelationships and charity by such generous gestures and acts as fit into the tradition, held by us both, of the undivided Church. We are summoned to clear the air more thoroughly of negative elements, psychological and other, by means of Christian sincerity and simplicity—to rid ourselves of such things as stand by the heavy legacy of history as obstacles in our path.

We meet and conduct our Dialogue before the whole world, a world which is about to enter into the third thousand years of Christianity, which in Your Holiness's vision is to be a millennium of Christian unity.

It is devoutly to be wished that the Theological Dialogue now begun will be a decisive factor in building up the unity of Christ's Church, so that she may give more effective witness to the world and work salvation there. Let us then entrust ourselves on both sides to the Paraclete who brings the entire institution of the Church into a compact whole.

With this wish on our lips we address Your blessed Holiness, and communicate the festive greetings of our Church and the embrace of your brother the Ecumenical Patriarch Dimitrios I.

418.   *28 June 1980*

Address in reply by Pope John Paul II to the Delegation*

I am happier than ever to meet the Delegation sent by my brother Dimitrios I and his Synod from the Ecumenical Patriarchate to the Church of Rome for the feast of the holy Apostles Peter and Paul.

My happiness is indeed all the greater because this year we have had a more thoroughgoing experience of the things that bind us together, and because we have more clearly and decisively adopted the course of together living out in practice the communion of faith already existing between us. As a result we shall be able to make a further advance towards complete unity in utter truth and all charity.

By sharing on both sides year by year in the feasts of the patron saints of the Churches of Rome and Constantinople, we have opportunities for meeting in prayer and asking and receiving help from the Lord— from him who lights up before us the way we must go, and gives us strength to advance in accordance with his will. More and more in our meetings as brothers we discern the influence shed by his presence: "know that I am present with you always, until the end of the world" (Mt 28:20).

I should like to see these meetings take place in the same spirit, allowing for differences of place and circumstance, wherever Catholics and Orthodox live together, so as gradually to create the conditions required for full unity. The dialogue of charity must go on and on, reaching out through the entire membership of our Churches. In the combined declaration with Patriarch Dimitrios which was the crowning point of my visit to the Ecumenical Patriarchate, we explicitly stated: "The dialogue of charity itself must continue with might and main in the complex situation which we have inherited from the past, and which forms the real order of things in which our enterprise must be conducted today."

The Theological Dialogue which was officially opened on the Isle of Patmos is an important event: in Catholic-Orthodox relations it is the greatest thing that has happened not merely this year but for centuries past. We are entering into a new phase of our relations, since the Theological Dialogue is an essential element in a wider exchange between our Churches. In this Dialogue both the Catholic and Orthodox Churches are involved as a whole. As a result we have found the general framework, and within it the effective means, by which we can pin-point in their real context—beyond the range of preliminary prejudices and reservations—the various kinds of difficulties which still stand in the way of full communion.

The subject chosen for the first phase of the Dialogue is "The Mystery of the Church and the Eucharist in the light of the mystery of the holy Trinity." This subject deserves the deepest consideration, since it takes us to the very core of what it means to be a Christian. The proposal made by both the Catholic and Orthodox preparatory commissions that the Theological Dialogue should begin from what we have in common was given a welcome acceptance—a fact which offers this Dialogue a solid basis and puts it in the most promising perspective.

The programme of work settled on by a common agreement of the Joint Commission at its first meeting, the distribution of tasks among the sub-commissions, and the coordinating role assigned to a combined committee will certainly make it possible for the theological work to develop effectively in a direction agreed upon by both.

For all this we give thanks to God, for it is he who is guiding us. We shall continue to ask his help day by day, since we shall always need this to overcome the difficulties which will be inevitably met along the way to unity. We are praying all the more fervently for this reason.

On our side we shall listen closely to what the Spirit chooses to say, and you can be sure that we shall spare no effort in the quest for full unity. At the end of the vista on which the Theological Dialogue opens (and this is no less true of our meetings for the feast of St. Andrew at the Ecumenical Patriarchate and of Saints Peter and Paul at Rome), stands one and the same thing: the [combined] celebration of the Eucharist. And this must come when the difficulties which today still cause our two Churches to fall short of full and perfect communion have been surmounted.

I thank you, beloved brothers in the Lord, for your visit and presence here and the feelings which you kindly expressed.

I would ask you to bear my cordial and brotherly greeting to Patriarch Dimitrios and his Synod, together with my warm thanks for his message of fellowship and charity and his commitment to the search for full unity.

May the Lord be always with us.

419.   *12 July 1980*

Letter of Pope John Paul II to Patriarch Dimitrios I, concerning the opening stages of the Catholic-Orthodox Theological Dialogue at Patmos and Rhodes*

We greatly rejoiced when the Delegation came to Rome for the celebration of the feast of Saints Peter and Paul, bringing with it the greetings of Your Holiness and the Holy Synod of your Church, and bearing your warm hearted letter: we received the delegates with much brotherly affection.

I thank Your Holiness with all my heart. The delegates by their presence here in Rome stirred in me memories of my visit to the Ecumenical Patriarchate for the feast of St. Andrew—I felt this particularly when they joined us in prayer, and again when they exchanged the kiss of peace with us. This latter was in earnest of our celebrating the Eucharist together in full unity when God so wills it, an event towards which we have bound ourselves to work with full determination. The warm applause which broke forth spontaneously from the throng of lay folk in St. Peter's in sign of their support for this fraternal liturgical gesture shows clearly how the Christian people today are taking ever more to heart the call to unity, understanding, and cooperation between our Churches.

This confirms our desire to do everything possible to hasten the day of full unity, with all due prudence but also with the courage which God asks of us. That day, as I reminded the people present in St. Peter's when I welcomed the delegates, will be a day of sheer joy.

Given these prospects, the new stage initiated at Patmos and Rhodes by the opening of the Theological Dialogue warrants our full attention. The endeavors of the Joint Commission are nourished and sustained by the prayers of the faithful people of our Churches. I have in fact asked all the Catholics of the world to take part in this Dialogue by prayer. It is a decisive moment in the interrelationships of our Churches. The issues are these: doing away with the residue of the centuries when we were at cross purposes, getting beyond the kinds of [real] incomprehension which we have inherited from the past, and finally resolving the questions still pending in controversy between our Churches. This is all indispensable if we are to attain to a stable unity by which we shall be gathered together in full communion praising God with one heart and mind, and bearing a common witness before the world.

It is with these feelings of gladness, of brotherly love, of hope in the power of God, and with a firm determination of advance towards full communion, that the Church of Rome received the Delegation sent by you, much loved Brother in the Lord, and by your Holy Synod.

420. *25 October 1980*

Telegram from Pope John Paul II to Patriarch Dimitrios I for the feast of St. Demetrius*

The feast of Saint Demetrius gives me the opportunity of offering Your Holiness my warm and cordial best wishes. I pray that the Lord may give you strength and light to pursue your fruitful pastoral ministry and the mutual search for the full communion of our Churches. I express once more my complete fraternal charity.

421. *28 October 1980*

Letter in reply of Patriarch Dimitrios I to Pope John Paul II**

The brotherly good wishes and greetings conveyed by telegram on 25th of this month from Your much loved, venerable, and very dear Holiness on the anniversary of our patronal feast-day reached us amid the rejoicing of our devout local flock and the children of our Church throughout the world, and deeply stirred our heart with feelings of joy difficult to express.

We thank Your blessed Holiness then from the bottom of our heart for thus displaying your brotherly feelings, and we pray the Lord to grant both of us and all the clergy and laity of our Churches health and strength to go straight forward along the ways that lead to the fulfilment of his holy will.

With these feelings we greet Your Holiness with a holy kiss, and remain with brotherly love and special esteem.

422. *24 November 1980*

Letter of Pope John Paul II to Patriarch Dimitrios I*

Last year we celebrated together the feast of St. Andrew, the First-Called Apostle and brother of Peter. Prayer was at the centre of this warm and fraternal meeting. The time that has passed since has not weakened the feelings we felt then or the memory of this event; on the contrary, it has deepened and revived them. This year, the celebration of the holy Patron of your Church gives me again the opportunity to send you a delegation, presided over by our dear brother Cardinal Willebrands; he will convey to Your Holiness, to your Holy Synod, to the clergy and to the whole faithful people, my affectionate greeting and that of the Church of Rome. "The grace of the Lord Jesus Christ and the love of God and the fellowship of the Holy Spirit be with you all" (2 Cor 13:14).

It is with a joy and hope renewed every year that we celebrate the feasts of the two brothers, the holy Apostles Peter and Andrew. I am convinced, in fact, that this union in prayer will help our sister Churches to hasten the day when full communion is reestablished between them. The joy of this joint celebration is, as it were, a foretaste of what we will feel when we give testimony together of our faithfulness to the Lord, and in so doing give the world an example of true reconciliation and make a contribution to peace among men.

The Theological Dialogue that the Joint Commission between the Catholic and Orthodox Churches initiated this year on the Island of Patmos—a place so rich in apostolic memories and prophetic promptings—is an event of the highest importance for relations between our Churches. The atmosphere of warm fraternal charity that characterized this meeting, as well as the commitment taken before the Lord to work for the reestablishment of unity, enable us to catch a glimpse of the substantial progress that will be made. The old differences that led the Eastern and Western Churches to cease celebrating the Eucharist together are going to be tackled in a new and constructive way. Both the subject chosen for the first phase of the dialogue and the general orientation give a clear indication of this.

Our prayer will accompany the Theological Dialogue that it may be more and more deeply rooted in the truth, carried out in sincerity and a fidelity on both sides freed from shadows [of the past], animated by the Spirit of God, and therefore fruitful for the life of the Church. For this purpose I have requested the prayer of all the Catholic faithful, and in order that we may grow together in Christ, I have expressed the wish that where Catholic and Orthodox live side by side they should be involved in fraternal relations and an un-self-seeking collaboration which will prepare step by step for our full linking up together.

Beloved Brother, these are some of the thoughts, some of the hopes and feelings that fill my heart and which I was anxious to tell you about in these lines. In these I should like to assure you again of my firm resolution to be faithful to all the Lord's demands, and of my very deep and fraternal charity.

423.   *30 November 1980*

Address by Cardinal John Willebrands in the Church of St. George at the Phanar for the feast of St. Andrew*

The Apostle Paul, writing to the Romans, gives free rein to the joy he feels at the prospect of soon visiting their Church. He tells them: "I long to see you . . . that we may be mutually encouraged by our common faith" (Rom 1:11–12). What Paul felt as he was preparing to visit the Church of Rome is very much what I feel today as I come from Rome to pay a visit to your Church. It is with a heart full of gratitude and thanksgiving to God the Father, from whom every good gift descends, that I find myself among you, my brothers in the Lord, to share in your jubilation for the feast of St. Andrew the Apostle, the "First-Called" by Christ, the one whom you honor as going back to the beginnings of the Apostolic preaching in these parts. The celebration of the feast of St. Andrew gives us the opportunity of a further meeting with Your Holiness, with the Holy Synod, and your clergy and faithful people. At this solemn celebration of the holy Eucharist we come together in this city which calls to mind the testimony given to the Apostolic faith by the proclamations of various Ecumenical Councils. A meeting corresponding to this takes place each year at Rome for the feast of the Apostles Peter and Paul, with a delegation present from the Ecumenical Patriarchate.

The fact that we experience and appreciate together the spiritual happiness arising from the feasts of these Apostles who form the foundation of the Church which has Christ as the corner stone takes on an ecclesial importance, i.e. one which goes beyond ourselves as individuals and affects the whole Church. As we remember the Apostles, we are led back again to communion in prayer, to an encounter as between brothers, to the dialogue of charity that we have undertaken with a view to surmounting the difficulties which still stop us from celebrating the Lord's Eucharist in full fellowship.

The picture which the Acts of the Apostles gives us of the life of the first Christians opens up a bright vista ahead: They devoted themselves to the Apostles' instructions and communal life, to the breaking of bread and the significant link between our Churches, but keeps on reminding them of the urgent need of restoring and expressing their full communion in the total truth and full charity of Christ, the Head of the Church. I am anxious to reassure you, dear brothers, that with attention and receptiveness to what the Spirit of the Lord asks of his Church today, we are resolved to spare no effort, whether in the area of study or action, to reach the object of our hope and steady aspiration (cf. Rom 8:25).

Last year your Church received Pope John Paul II for the feast of St. Andrew with warm brotherly charity. He came from ancient Rome to express the esteem and love of that Church for the leading see of the Orthodox world, and through it for all the Orthodox Churches. This visit furnished the occasion for the announcement that a Joint Commission for Theological Dialogue between the Catholic Church and the entire Orthodox Church had been set up. This Theological Dialogue was something that we accepted as a gift from the Lord. It was in it that the dialogue of charity in which Pope Paul VI and Patriarch Athenagoras recognized and embraced one another as brothers in Christ grew and came to fruition. Through this commission a suitable means was created for carrying out the dialogue to which our Churches have seriously pledged themselves. The time which has passed since then has been put to good use.

The Theological Dialogue has begun in a climate created by charitable exchanges of views and by a sense of the responsibility undertaken before the Lord and his Church. In the isle of Patmos, where St. John the Apostle was caught up in the spirit and had the revelation of "what must happen very soon" (Rv 1:1), we recited together the priestly, Paschal prayer of Jesus, in which he asks his Father to bring those who belong to him into perfect unity (Jn 17:23). We ended our prayer with a solemn doxology, giving glory to God and begging his grace for the work which was to begin at Rhodes and to continue with the bishops and theologians of the Commission. The study sub-commissions have already been busy with the work allotted to them. Yes, we have quite a number of reasons for thanking the Lord for the help he has given us this year.

We look to the future then with confidence and hope. As our fellowship in faith and love increases and becomes the source of added strength, we shall be in a position in the course of the dialogue to face the series of questions which have been handed down over the centuries. It seems to me likely that, for all my hopes to the contrary, the dialogue will, as it goes on, pass through some difficult moments, whether these derive from circumstances or from human sources, or from the spirit of evil which is always on the watch for what can divide. Should such circumstances arise, we must "conduct ourselves in a way worthy of the gospel of Christ . . . standing firm in unity of spirit and exerting ourselves with one accord for the faith of the gospel" (Phil 1:27), being ready also to suffer for Christ (cf. Phil 1:29).

The whole pattern of relations built up through the grace of God in these last twenty years with the Orthodox Churches in their totality and with each in particular gives us reason to hope for decisive progress along the way to unity. The same is true of the constructive work of the committees preparing for the Theological Dialogue. Our confidence is all the stronger when we think of the spirit in which Catholics and Orthodox are approaching the Dialogue. It is God himself who is working within us to build his Church in unity. Taking this outlook, it seems to me that special mention should be made of the subject chosen by the Joint Commission for the first phase of the Theological Dialogue: "The Mystery of the Church and the Eucharist in the light of the Holy Trinity." The Church's love and the Son's adoration of the

Father in the Spirit are indeed the inexhaustible sources of Christian joy. May we be granted to sing this joy with a single voice in the Eucharistic assembly.

The fact that the Churches of the East and the West at a certain moment of their history reached the tragic and scandalous situation of ceasing to celebrate the Lord's Eucharist together means that they considered the differences then existing between them to be grave. That this was so calls for the greatest attention on everybody's part, both those who are directly involved in the Dialogue, and the whole Church as it follows it with prayer, charity and hope.

Historical, cultural and political factors have certainly played a decisive part in bringing about the present situation. Pope Paul VI has always emphasized the fact that we are only looking for one thing: to give effect to the Lord's will for his Church in obedience to the requirements of faith and charity. It was simply by the conviction of his faith that Pope Paul VI felt moved to come to your venerable Church. The very subject matter which has been chosen makes the Dialogue free from concerns and systematic problems that have already been put behind us or at least seen within a new and larger context. What we are trying to do is in fact to find again in our own times—and this with strict regard for all that the truth of faith requires—full communion between our Churches.

If on the one hand the Church inevitably undergoes historical conditioning, on the other hand she has the mission of transfiguring history by building, through the preaching of the Gospel and sacramental life, a new community ordered to a new history of brotherhood and communion. The seer of Revelation contemplated this new community in the innumerable host of those invited to celebrate the wedding of the Lamb.

Never in history, it seems to me, has the pursuit of unity between East and West been so free and sincere as in these times in which the Lord gives us the grace of living.

While the Theological Dialogue follows its course our Churches will continue to make their fraternal relations closer in the "dialogue of charity," as Patriarch Athenagoras of venerable memory liked to call it. To this dialogue we can apply St. Paul's words: "There are in the end three things that last: faith, hope, and love, and the greatest of these is love" (1 Cor 13:13). The ultimate aim of the Theological Dialogue is in fact to make more brotherly and warm the factors that bring our Churches and their members together in full communion of faith and life, "speaking the truth in love" (Eph 4:15).

With this spirit of brotherhood and this deep commitment to the search for full communion, we have been sent to celebrate with you, Your Holiness, and with your Church, the feast of the Apostle Andrew. On this official occasion I am happy and honored to hand Your Holiness a message from His Holiness Pope John Paul II.

424. *30 November 1980*

Address in reply by Patriarch Dimitrios I to Cardinal Willebrands*

It is with very deep joy and very great esteem that St. Andrew's Church greets your presence here today for the celebration of the Apostle who was called first. We see this presence as a brotherly presence of the Church of the Apostle Peter, the brother of the Apostle Andrew, as a presence of the worthy representatives of our brother in Christ, our venerated and beloved brother, the Bishop of Rome Pope John Paul II; but we also see it as your own presence, you worthy and fervent artisans of the [mutual] rediscoveries of our two Churches. It is you moreover, Eminent Cardinal, who preside over this delegation, you who are the worthy successor of Cardinal Bea, of unforgettable memory, and who have been right from the beginning one of the pioneers of the reconciliation of the Christian East and West—of the unity of the Church.

We welcome you and we meet you during liturgical prayer in this venerable church where there is still preserved the spiritual presence of the one who sends you, the holy Pope John Paul II, who was present here in person [as it were] "yesterday." So "yesterday" and "today" unite and become one "today."

This event becomes the symbol of the aim of our relations and our meetings in Rome, here, and elsewhere. For in fact, our aim is the meeting and union of the Church's "yesterday" and "today" in a permanent "today" spreading over centuries, as is the nature and the destiny of the Church according to the will of our common Lord Jesus Christ, her Founder and her Head, he who is "the same yesterday and today and for ever" (Heb 13:8).

The new history of the rediscovery of our common yesterday, of the common realization of the tragedy of our division today, but at the same time of the awareness of responsibilities, obligations and the necessity of making yesterday and today an eternal today of the

Church, this new history, I say, began as a dialogue, as was the case with the creation of the world and its salvation, the foundation of the Church and her purpose.

This year we met in Rome and we meet here, today, in this new phase—the theological one—of the dialogue now under way.

In this fact, in the development of this new period of the history of the life of the Church, in the evolution of the dialogue between you and us, we see clearly the action and the presence of the Holy Spirit who gives firmness and cohesion to the whole institution of the Church, and repeats his gift.

This new history, this new dialogue, is not man's work. It is the work of the Holy Spirit with the Father and the Son. The men who have left us and those of today, those who worked and are working for this purpose, were and are instruments of the Holy Spirit, as were the evangelists and in general the Apostles and the Fathers of the Church.

We have, therefore, to glorify and thank the holy and life-giving Trinity, consubstantial and indivisible.

The meeting of our two Churches in Rome for the feast of the holy Apostles Peter and Paul took place immediately after the inauguration and organization of the Theological Dialogue between the Roman Catholic Church and the Orthodox Church, at Patmos and at Rhodes. Our solemn meeting here today occurs immediately after the early steps of this dialogue in its effort to penetrate the mystery of the divine unity of the Church, with the meeting of the first sub-commission and its promising work.

But the Church of Christ and the holy cause of its unity is not simply and only theology. Beyond that it is a mystery, it is a liturgical experience lived by the Body of Christ, an experience which culminates and is accomplished in the common celebration of the Holy Eucharist and in communion in this Eucharist.

That is why we do not confine or limit the dialogue of the two Churches to theological studies and workshops, valuable though they certainly are, but we conduct it within the wider reach of the love and life of our Churches.

That is also why we make exchanges at the various levels of the life of our Churches and we look on both sides for opportunities for various meetings. That is why we are here together today.

So let us progress together in the Theological Dialogue; let us continue together along the way of charity, ecclesial relations and Christian solidarity up to the moment when together we will proclaim Christ's one and undivided truth, the one faith, and when it will be granted us to celebrate the divine Eucharist together, to receive Holy Communion together in the same Body of Christ, shared but not divided.

With these thoughts, these hopes and these wishes, we address you, worthy and dear representatives of Rome.

Christ was, is, and will be among us.

425.   *24 December 1980*

Telegram from Patriarch Dimitrios I to Pope John Paul II for Christmas**

With feelings of brotherly honor and love we embrace Your dear and cherished Holiness in this happy season of the Incarnation and Epiphany of Christ our Savior. We rejoice with you and ask the Savior who was laid in a cave to grant you health and to support your steps in our common endeavors for the restoration of the full unity of our Churches and for the peace desired in the world.

426.   *17 January 1981*

Telegram of reply from Pope John Paul II to Patriarch Dimitrios I*

I thank Your Holiness for your good wishes, and, united with you in the joy and the hope that cannot be confounded, I ask our Savior to grant you peace and health during this year, and to hasten the day when our Churches are able to discover themselves fully once more in a concelebration of his Eucharist.

427.   *28 January 1981*

Letter of Patriarch Dimitrios I to Pope John Paul II, inviting him to send a representative for the celebration of the 16th centenary of the First Council of Constantinople**

To the holy and blessed Pope of the Senior Rome, John Paul II, greetings in the Lord.

The Church in these parts is desirous of taking steps to give prominence to the great ecclesiastical event constituted by the summoning and meeting in this city of the Second Ecumenical Council, of which the sixteenth centenary occurs this year. Having regard to the importance of this event, and taking its stand on the notification issued in our Patriarchal declaration at Christmas, it has reached the decision that this year 1981 should be proclaimed as dedicated exclusively to this Council, and will proceed on the occasion of this happy anniversary to celebrate the dedication with appropriate and important displays of many kinds.

Since our Church wishes to give this celebration an inter-Orthodox and inter-Christian dimension, it has decided to include an invitation to this effect to Your Holiness, so that through your representative you may share in the celebration here, which will take place 5–7 of next June in our city.

We are happy to inform Your Holiness that as part of the more detailed commemorative programme taken in hand by our Church we have decided to issue a Patriarchal and Synodal Encyclical emphasizing the importance of the event, and that we have sanctioned the insertion in the calendar of our Orthodox Church of the feast of the holy Fathers of the Second Ecumenical Council, held here in Constantinople, their memory being kept up henceforth on the first Sunday of June each year with a special sung office. We also intimate that the hierarchy in the exarchates abroad that fall under our jurisdiction have been urged to arrange events befitting the occasion in the areas that fall to them by divine lot, and that we have decided to organize theological symposia and seminars in our own Patriarchal centers, that is to say in the Center for Patristic Studies in the Patriarchal Stavropegiac Monastery of Vlatadon in Thessalonica, and our center at Chambésy near Geneva. Finally, we are going to publish two commemorative volumes containing worthwhile scholarly studies by our own and other theologians, to bring out the significance and importance on the theological side of this holy Second Ecumenical Council.

In writing then to Your Holiness and telling you about our plans and decisions, we present our invitation to take part in the coming celebration, and would ask you to appoint your representative at an opportune time, letting us know his name and office and providing for him to be in our city at the dates mentioned above. We further indicate that the agency responsible for all exchange of information about the details of the celebration will be the chief Secretariat of the Holy Synod.

We communicate the foregoing to Your Holiness by a Synodal decision for use by you, and in expectation of your reply we remain with much love and special esteem.

428.   *8 April 1981*

Letter of Pope John Paul II to Patriarch Dimitrios I, telling him that a delegation would take part in the celebrations for the 16th centenary of the Council of Constantinople, and informing him that the Catholic Church also would be commemorating the First Council of Constantinople as well as the 1550th anniversary of the Council of Ephesus, in celebrations to be held at Rome on the feast of Pentecost, 7 June 1981*

It was with great pleasure that I received the letter from Your Holiness informing me that the Ecumenical Patriarchate has organized a solemn celebration of the sixteenth centenary of the First Ecumenical Council of Constantinople, and I wholeheartedly thank you for inviting the Catholic Church to take part by sending a representative. In this invitation I see a sign of our common concern to help on the growth of communion between our Churches, and at the same time I welcome it as a deep and sincere expression of the brotherhood which was consolidated between us at our meeting on the feast of St. Andrew.

I have asked Cardinal Maxmilian de Fürstenburg to represent the Church of Rome at these festivities. He will be accompanied by Monsignor Eleuterio F. Fortino.

The teaching of the First Council of Constantinople is the expression of our common faith. The series of celebrations this year will certainly help to emphasize the importance of this common faith in the Holy Spirit who continues to fill the Church with life and lead it along the ways of holiness and love.

For these reasons, and acting in the same spirit, the Catholic Church too will commemorate the First Council of Constantinople. I have had the idea of linking with this Council a commemoration of the fifteen and a half centuries that have passed since the Council of Ephesus. The celebrations will take place at Rome on 7 June, the feast of Pentecost. This date was suggested to me by the fact that the feast coincides this year, according to the calendar of our Church, with the day originally fixed on for the beginning of the Council of Ephesus.

For the purpose of this commemoration I have invited the various episcopal conferences of the Catholic Church to send representatives to Rome for the feast of Pentecost, when we will conduct two celebrations, one in the morning in St. Peter's Basilica, and one in the afternoon in the Basilica of St. Mary Major (which was built to commemorate the Council [of Ephesus] and in honour of the Mother of God).

I should be happy if Your Holiness agreed to send a delegation from your Church to join us in the commemoration of these Councils and thus bring out the unity of the two celebrations, in which thanksgiving for what we have been allowed to achieve together in the past will be coupled with a fervent prayer to the Holy Spirit, asking him to lead us once more to this unity in the profession of our faith, whole and entire.

With this hope, I am happy, dear brother in Christ, to give renewed expression to my feelings of deep and fraternal charity.

429.   *11 April 1981*

Easter letter of Pope John Paul II to Patriarch Dimitrios I*

"This is the Jesus God has raised up, and we are his witnesses. Exalted at God's right hand, he first received the promised Holy Spirit from the Father, then poured this Spirit out on us" (Acts 2:32–33).

I should like to repeat, dear brother, this announcement of the Apostle Peter, which is a radiant summary of the very core of our faith, at this time when we are celebrating the Resurrection of Jesus by which he was "proclaimed, in the order of the spirit, the spirit of holiness that was in him, Son of God in all his power" (Rom 1:4).

By faith we know that he who has raised Jesus Christ from the dead will also give life to our mortal bodies through his Spirit living in us (cf. Rom 8:11). By believing in the Resurrection of Christ we are in fact making discovery of the mysterious destiny of the human race. We all ought to be witnesses in the power of the Spirit of this mystery of the Resurrection of Jesus in all its depth and breadth and height (cf. Acts 1:8).

The celebration this year of the sixteenth centenary of the First Council of Constantinople gives us an opportunity of rendering testimony to our faith in this Spirit poured out by the Risen Christ; and the exchange of representatives which we have in mind for this occasion should enable us to show forth the unity of our testimony. To avoid the risk of obscuring the unity of this single celebration in two different places, I decided not to invite a delegation from each of the Orthodox Churches.

We shall all of us be brought together on that day in a single act of supplication, and we shall all in like fashion make ourselves open and available to the Spirit communicated to the Church by the Risen Christ, so that we may hear and understand what he is saying to the Church today, and draw strength from him to translate this faithfully into action.

In the glad light of Easter, dear brother, I express anew my deep and fraternal charity in all its fulness.

430. *17 April 1981*

Telegram of reply from Patriarch Dimitrios I to Pope John Paul II**

As dawn rises on the first day of the week, we embrace Your dear and venerable Holiness as brother to brother. We rejoice with you and jointly pray that new life may be given to the hope of the human race. We always celebrate with you God's saving Easter.

431. *15 May 1981*

On learning of the attempt made on the life of Pope John Paul II, the Ecumenical Patriarch Dimitrios I immediately sent His Eminence Metropolitan Meliton of Chalcedon, Doyen of the Sacred Synod of the Patriarchate and official responsible for relations with other Churches, to Rome. Metropolitan Meliton arrived just in time to take part in the vigil of prayer for the Pope in St. Peter's Square. His statement was broadcast in English on Vatican Radio.

I was in Athens when I heard the sorrowful news of the attempted assassination of His Holiness Pope John Paul II.[62] We, like everyone else, only more so, were greatly upset. His Holiness Patriarch Dimitrios immediately got in touch with me and asked me—charged me— to go to Rome straightway to express his deep grief, his sympathy, and his solidarity in this situation. He also sent me a telegram entrusting

---

62. Mehmet Ali Agca shot and seriously wounded the Pope during the Wednesday general audience in St. Peter's Square, 13 May.

me with this mission. I came yesterday evening. I took the first plane available and arrived to carry out the Patriarch's orders.

I made a statement at Athens [and said], as I did this morning during the prayers to the Blessed Virgin which we recited in the Orthodox Church of St. Andrew in Rome, that this moment—this sacred and anxious moment when His Holiness lies on his bed of pain—is not the time for many words. It is a time for recollection and above all prayer.

We Orthodox, who are united with you in love, sympathize fully with the Pope in his suffering, and with the holy Roman Catholic Church, and we share with you in prayer. What I can say is that from the beginning of his pontificate Pope John Paul II adopted an "existential" attitude in carrying out his ministry. He has shown himself the defender *par excellence* of the human person, and of the dignity, rights, and moral and spiritual values that make a person truly human. Now Pope John Paul II has a new experience of suffering in his own very body, an experience which is more "existential" than the mere *idea* of sharing in human suffering.

We pray that this trial may pass by quickly, that His Holiness may recover as soon as possible. My own belief is that after this experience the Pope will return to the midst of the world to give a new witness to the Gospel.

432. *20 May 1981*

Telegram from the Secretary of State, Cardinal Agostino Casaroli, to Patriarch Dimitrios I, thanking him for the visit made in his name by Metropolitan Meliton to Pope John Paul II**

His Holiness Pope John Paul II is deeply touched by the visit of the Metropolitan of Chalcedon and the feelings expressed in the name of the Ecumenical Patriarchate, and bids me convey his gratitude to you, and thankfulness for the prayers offered on his behalf. With my respectful and fraternal sentiments.

433. *4 June 1981*

Letter of Pope John Paul II to Patriarch Dimitrios I for the ceremonies marking the sixteenth centenary of the First Council of Constantinople*

The sixteenth centenary of the First Council of Constantinople (381), which all Christian Churches hold in common as the second great Ecumenical Council, is a pressing invitation to believing hearts to meditate on the present relevance of the astonishing mystery which is the revelation of the living God, of the holy and indivisible Trinity, in human history. This history, which is the wonderful and dramatic working out of the plan of salvation, is brought to a head in Christ Jesus under the powerful action of this same Spirit which enables us believers to announce, in the diversity and inadequacy of our human tongues, "the great things God has done" (Acts 2:11).

The truth has been revealed in its entirety once and for all in Christ the Lord. The Spirit of truth, who gives form and life to the Church, continues his assistance, continues to be its living memory, inspiring it with what it must say and the way to say it, so that it may "guard the deposit" (2 Tm 1:12;14) of "the faith delivered once for all to the saints" (Jude 3), and both denounce heresies and speak of the unfathomable richness of Christ.

This is exactly what took place between the first Ecumenical Council, of Nicea in 325, and the second, that of Constantinople in 381. After the definition of the authentic faith in the divinity of the Son, consubstantial with the Father, heresies began to spread calling in doubt the divinity of the Holy Spirit. Great doctors of the Church like St. Athanasius of Alexandria, St. Ambrose of Milan, the Cappadocian Fathers, Epiphanius of Salamis in the baptismal creed of the Church of Cyprus, and our great predecessor Pope Damasus, gradually drew up terminology which gave sharpened expression to the common faith of the Churches. It was in their teaching that the Council of 381 found inspiration when it filled out the creed professed at Nicea. This [resultant] creed was solemnly recognized as having the status that goes with an Ecumenical Council, and so as regulative and irrevocable, by the Council of Chalcedon during its fifth session, October 451, and since then it has been accepted by all the Churches.

The Creed, henceforth called the Niceno-Constantinopolitan, is thus the outstanding expression of the fellowship in faith of the Churches of Christ in this mystery of the Holy Spirit "who is Lord and giver of life." "He proceeds from the Father. With the Father and the Son he is worshipped and glorified. He has spoken through the prophets."

The creeds of the Ecumenical Council express the Christian faith in unalterable fashion. As I wrote when announcing the celebration to mark its sixteenth centenary: "The teaching of the First Council of Constantinople is still, as ever, the expression of the one common faith of the Church and all Christianity" (Letter *A Concilio Constantinopolitano* I, I, 1).[63]

Naturally I am not unaware that in the course of history controversies occurred between our Churches about the doctrine of the Holy Spirit, especially with regard to the eternal relation of Son and Spirit.

This question, like all those which have not yet been wholly cleared up between our Churches, will have to be matter for the dialogue which has so happily begun. We all expect this dialogue to help hasten the longed for day when in the clear light and without misgivings we will be able to proclaim our faith together by a concelebration of the holy Eucharist.

I shall say no more on this subject. You are acquainted, Venerated Brother, with the situation in which I find myself as the result of recent events. The designs of God's Providence pass all understanding, but we know that they are always inspired by divine mercy. Personally, I am happy to offer my sufferings for the Body of Christ which is the Church (Col 1:24), so that the day may be brought nearer for the Lord's prayer to take effect: "that they may be one" (Jn 17:21).

It is with this hope, dear Brother, that I wanted to express these thoughts as we celebrate today's centenary. The fact that this celebration is one and the same is brought out by the presence of my dear brother Cardinal Maximilian de Fürstenberg with you and that of your eminent envoy with us.

Together we give thanks to the Father of lights (Jas 1:17), and we ask him to make us ever more faithfully open and responsive to what "the Spirit says to the Churches" (Rv 2:7).

Be assured dear Brother of all my fraternal charity.

434.   *6 June 1981*

Homily by Metropolitan Damaskinos of Tranoupolis, leader of the delegation from the Ecumenical Patriarchate at the celebration in Rome of the 16th centenary of the First Council of Constantinople and the 1550th anniversary of the Council of Ephesus, during the First Vespers of Pentecost in the Basilica of St. Peter*

In the midst of this mood diffused by evening meditation and the prayers of Vespers, themselves pierced through and through by love

---

63. Cf. *AAS* 73 (1981), 513–527.

and the vision of spiritual beauty, the words of St. Paul addressed to the Romans and to all of us here gathered in the grace of the Holy Spirit, ring out loud and clear.

They are words about the Holy Spirit, "giver of life," words about the Spirit of God, "the Spirit of truth who proceeds from the Father" (Jn 15:26), "straightforward Spirit;" "Spirit who rules and leads" (Ps 50:12–14), "source of sanctification," "intelligible light . . ."[a] "Simple in essence," the Spirit "manifests his power by different kinds of wonderful works, present in his entirety to each being and entirely present everywhere;" "without inroads on his being he is portioned out," "without loss of integrity he gives himself to others by way of participation."[b]

They are words about him "by whom hearts are lifted, the weak are led by the hand, those who are making progress become perfect. It is he who by shining on those who have purified themselves from all stain makes them 'spiritual' through communion with him."[c]

Words about him from whom all these wholly derive: "foreknowledge of the future, understanding of mysteries, comprehension of things hidden, distribution of the gifts of God; heavenly citizenship, union with the angelic chorus, endless joy, continuous dwelling in God, resemblance to God, and the highest object of desire, which is "to become God."[d]

"For all who are led by the Spirit of God are sons of God. For you did not receive the spirit of slavery to fall back into fear, but you have received the spirit of sonship. When we cry, 'Abba! Father!,' it is the Spirit himself bearing witness with our spirit that we are children of God, and if children, then heirs, heirs of God and fellow heirs with Christ, provided we suffer with him in order that we may also be glorified with him" (Rom 8:14–17).

To be adopted sons and daughters of God means becoming like Christ himself, "not by nature and the real truth of things," as Athanasius the Great said, but "by a disposing act and divine grace, by participation in his Spirit . . . and imitation."[e] This means sharing in his sufferings, and thus being able to share in his glory, being conformed

---

a. St. Basil the Great, *Treatise on the Holy Spirit* IX; Sources Chrétiennes, 17, p. 325. [To save the slight distortions that sometimes occur during a journey through two languages, the frequent patristic citations in this homily have been translated directly from the original texts.]

b. *Ibid,* p. 329.

c. *Ibid.* p. 329.

d. *Ibid.*

e. St. Athanasius the Great, *Contra Arianos* III, 19; P.G. 26, cc. 361, 364.

to the image of the Son "so that he may be the first-born among many brethren" (Rom 8:29).

God, becoming incarnate in Christ, is humanized, draws close to men and women, without derogation from his own nature. "The Spirit descended on the Son of God, made the Son of man, becoming accustomed in fellowship with him to dwell in the human race, to rest with human beings, and to dwell in the workmanship of God, working the will of the Father in them, renewing them from their old habits into the newness of Christ."[f]

It is the Holy Spirit that brings about this communion between God and his creature. Since the Son became man, the Spirit of the Father makes us sons and daughters of God in Christ. What we are concerned with here is a filial relationship and a fraternity deified in communion with God. In this communion, "the glory of God is living man and woman, and the life of man and woman is the vision of God."[g] It is a deep life in God which is brought about through the Spirit of the Son; this holy and brotherly life is life in the Church, One, Holy, Catholic and Apostolic. In the Creed of Constantinople, the article on the Holy Spirit is inseparably linked with faith in the One, Holy, Catholic and Apostolic Church. Because it is the Holy Spirit who gives the Church her existence and keeps her in a communion of brothers and sisters.

It is the Church which makes manifest this communion of brothers and sisters that does not know fear and slavery. "Sons and daughters are those who neither from fear of threats nor desire of things promised, but out of character and the habitual and voluntary tendency and disposition of the soul towards good, are never separated from God, like that son to whom it was said: 'My son, you are always with me, and everything I have is yours.' They are as far as can be, by adoption in grace, what God is and is believed to be by nature and cause. Let us then not forsake the holy Church of God which contains in the sacred order of the divine symbols celebrated in her such great mysteries of our salvation. Through them, in making each of us who leads his or her life well in the respective proper measure to be like Christ, she brings to light the grace of adoption which was given through baptism in the Holy Spirit, with each living according to Christ."[h]

This way of filial life presupposes a dynamic movement in the

---

f. Irenaeus of Lyons, *Adv. Haer.* III, 17, 7; SC 34, p. 303.

g. *Idem*, IV, 20, 7; SC 100, p. 649.

h. Maximus the Confessor, *Mystagogia*, P.G. 91, 712.

Spirit by which men and women are glorified. "Through this order and process," St. Irenaeus says, "and with such a directing force, man and woman, first created and fashioned, come to exist in the image and likeness of the uncreated God: the Father sees fit and commands, the Son does his ministering and fashioning work, the Spirit nourishes and gives increase, and man and woman gradually go forward to reach perfection, that is to say, they draw near to the uncreated One—this being God. First they had to be multiplied, thus multiplied to become strong, so strengthened to be glorified, and having been glorified to see their Lord."[i]

Here we have the possibility of salvation offered to the whole world by the Father in his Son, in the gift he made of his life even for those who showed their hatred for him to the extent of delivering him up to death. Christ is always present, through the Holy Spirit, in the Church which is a community of the Son of God glorified, the body of Christ—crucified and risen again—of the first-born of a multitude of brothers and sisters, who keep the identity of their personal being, while opening themselves to others.

That means that all, without distinction, if they are guided by the Holy Spirit of God, can be incorporated into the one family of the Son of God, and this in spite of their differences in race, language, morals and habits, sex, age, social rank, fortune, way of life, character and outward bearing.

Participating in the life of the Church, they are reborn and transfigured by her in the Spirit.

This family, the "body of Christ," is called the Church. This Church, which we ourselves are as members of this body, does not exist for herself, or to assert herself, but for the world. Precisely because she represents the body of him who "through his humanity becomes identical with us" and who shares in the life of the Church and of history, the Church exists only as an incarnation of the Lord in the world and in history. She has an organic relationship with the world.

This relationship lived out in the Eucharist, by which the mysteries are accomplished, is the sacramental event in which renewed communion with God is celebrated and made real in the Holy Spirit. So that there is no renewal within the essential historical continuity without the Holy Spirit and, conversely, there is no continuity without

---

i. Irenaeus of Lyons, *Adv. Haer.* IV, 38, 3; SC 100, p. 955–957.

faithfulness to origins combined with availability towards the Holy Spirit. It is in and by the Eucharist that the Church "sends her sons and daughters into their Father's presence."[j] Men and women are placed in a community, and created for it. If they should lose this community, their whole relationship with their fellows and their milieu is upset. The center of this communion is the Man-God, the salvation of the world, the divine humanity of Jesus, the vision of the new man and woman, the new society, which is characterized by two movements which are mutually involved and inseparable: from the altar towards the world and from the world towards the altar, contemplation and action, the service of the human family and the service of God, liturgy and *diaconia,* the spiritual and the temporal.

As ecclesial communion in the Holy Spirit is not juridical, it is characterized by the grace of our Lord Jesus Christ, the love of God the Father, and the Spirit of truth. Truth and love form an inseparable whole in the communion of the Holy Spirit. It is in and through love for their neighbor that men and women, becoming imitators of God— that is, servants of the weak, the hungry and prisoners—truly become sons and daughters of God, led by the Spirit. Heresy consists not only in rejecting one or other truth of faith concerning our salvation. Since this faith refers to Christ himself—he who is "the way, and the truth, and the life" (Jn 14:6), and who identifies himself with the neighbor— every attitude which consists in saying that Christ acts today, but which excludes our neighbor, is only mere ideology and a form of heresy.

Maximus the Confessor, dealing with the central subject of the *Ascetic Dialogue,* the love of one's neighbor, says: "Believe me, my children, nothing else has caused schisms and heresies in the Church but the fact that we do not love God and our neighbor."[k]

These are the conditions for all ecclesial communion in the Holy Spirit, communion of faith and love which overcomes all divisions. This saving communion is effected within each ecclesial community by the Eucharist, which visibly expresses our unity and painfully our division.

Today the Holy Spirit imposes on us a great task: to reestablish the unity of divided Christendom.

---

j. Irenaeus of Lyons, *Adv. Haer.* IV, 1, 3; SC 100, p. 795.

k. The quotation given (with reference) is from the *Pratum Spirituale (Spiritual Meadow)* by John Moschus and Sophronius, P.G. 87, 2925. Cf. J. M. Garrigues, *Maxime le Confesseur,* Paris 1976, p. 44.

As we experience in our lives today the tragedy of separation and the need to put it right, we are particularly called—in this year when we celebrate the 1600th anniversary of the meeting of the Second Ecumenical Council at Constantinople—to make a deeper study of the creed of faith of this Council, which constitutes the basis of ecumenical dialogue for the reestablishment of unity.

This year should be for all the Churches and Confessions the year of an urgent invitation to examine in common—through bilateral and multilateral dialogues—to what extent they are obliged, in fidelity to their origins and to their faith, to reestablish unity or not.

This appeal and this invitation apply particularly to those among the Churches which claim to continue exclusively the One, Holy, Catholic and Apostolic Church. They must seek and recognize as being Church, in the full sense of the term "Church"—outside their own canonical frontiers, with which they identify the One, Holy, Catholic and Apostolic Church—the Churches with which they will be called to eucharistic communion (naturally, all this if and as far as possible).

My brothers and sisters,

"Let us love one another, in order that, in the same spirit and the same heart, we may all be able to confess together our faith in the Father, the Son and the Holy Spirit, the consubstantial and indivisible Trinity."[l]

Let us not forget that "in unshakable faithfulness to truth," to quote Gregory Palamas, "God grants us all to be really the image of this supreme and mysterious love which the Holy Spirit is in the life of the Trinity."[m]

And I conclude by quoting a personal avowal made by the Rev. Fr. Yves Congar at the theological seminar held a few days ago in the Orthodox Center of the Ecumenical Patriarchate at Chambésy, in words which I make my own:

"Brothers, I love, you, I love you just as you are and for what you are. I would like, one day, to receive Communion with you at the same cup of Jesus's Blood, full of the fire of the Spirit!"[n]

---

l. Invitation to the recitation of the Confession of Faith in the Liturgy of St. John Chrysostom.

m. Cf. Gregory Palamas, *Capita Physica* 36, 37: P.G. 150, 1144–1145.

n. Yves Congar, O.P., *Synthèse générale de la problématique pneumatologique— Réflexions et perspectives;* lecture given at the Orthodox Centre on 26 May 1981.

435.   *7 June 1981*

Address by Patriarch Dimitrios I at the liturgy celebrated in the Patriarchal Cathedral of the Phanar in celebration of the 16th centenary of the First Ecumenical Council of Constantinople*

My dear Brothers in Christ,

Our local Church here at Constantinople, mystically typifying the Cherubim and singing to the life-giving Trinity of the hymn "Holy, Holy, Holy," as it casts aside all earthly care, has received the King of all, invisibly accompanied by the legions of angels. And from this sacred altar of the Apostle Andrew, through the humble prayers of its unworthy bishop, surrounded by our brothers in the episcopate who are concelebrating, it has offered to the all-powerful God, who alone is holy and who receives sacrifices of praise, the spiritual and unbloody worship of the divine Eucharist, and has prayed for the descent of the Holy Spirit. And the Lord who is the lover of humankind, the One who is holy and all-holy (he and his Son and his Holy Spirit), magnified in glory, has received the prayers and gifts offered by us sinners and has made the bread the precious Body of his Christ, has made what is in the chalice the precious Blood of his Christ.[64]

We have celebrated this divine and sacred sacrament, commemorating the whole Orthodox episcopate which faithfully dispenses the word of truth, the whole presbyterate and the diaconate in Christ, and all the holy orders. But, further, we have offered this spiritual worship for the good of the whole world, for the Holy, Catholic and Apostolic Church.

In this ecumenical celebration and offering of the Divine Eucharist by the local bishop for the good of the Holy Catholic and Apostolic Church, you are all included, you Christians, dear and honored brothers, who have gathered from West and East, from North and South, for this liturgical blessing: "May the grace of Our Lord Jesus Christ, and the love of God, and the fellowship of the Holy Spirit be with you all."

We would depart from the spirit and the teaching of the great and holy Second Ecumenical Council were we to seek its heart anywhere than at the altar of the Divine Eucharist celebrated by a canonical bishop of that place on behalf of the whole.

---

64. This paragraph employs the language of the Liturgy, with special references to the Cherubic Hymn, the Anaphora, and the Epiclesis.

The Council assembled in one place on behalf of the whole. And as from one place and for the good of the whole it professed doctrines and canons, in the concelebration of the Divine Eucharist, in the common profession of the faith by the one and unique Symbol of Faith of the One, Holy, Catholic and Apostolic Church, universally accepted as the Creed of Nicaea-Constantinople.

Today, sixteen hundred years later, we Christians are again gathered on the soil of the undivided Church in the fellowship of the Holy Spirit; but also—through sins known only to God, but largely because of reasons that derive from non-theological, linguistic and general cultural factors—we return here in a state of division, as pilgrims homesick for the ecumenical Christian unity, for the undivided Church, for the One, Holy, Catholic and Apostolic Church of our common Symbol of Faith.

The holy Ecumenical Councils of the undivided Christian Church, which constitute the supreme ecumenical authority of the Church of Christ on earth—among them the Second holy and great Council celebrated here—were the divine instruments for the uninterrupted continuity of the one Body of Christ until the end of time. Consequently, they were not meant solely for the past; they looked towards today; they envisaged the future. It is in this catholic consideration of the holy Ecumenical Councils—in their twofold dimension as temporal and transtemporal—that we consider the holy and great Second Ecumenical Council as we reverence and celebrate this great anniversary.

And so, from the episcopal chair of Gregory the Theologian and of Nectarius, Bishops of Constantinople,[65] we proclaim this anniversary as a sign of the Lord who unites the past of the Church with the present and the future until the end of time; and this for the affirmation and formulation of the eternal and living expression of the presence and the witness in the world of the One, Holy, Catholic and Apostolic Church of Christ.

Such is the will of the Lord. Such is the reason for the existence of his Church. This is what the whole world has need of.

God, his Church and his Universe all call us to our responsibility. May this anniversary be for us not only an expression of our duty to our Fathers but also a new starting point for a witness to the love for the whole world and for the salvation of all on earth. Amen.

---

65. St. Gregory of Nazianzus, called the Theologian because of the brilliance of his doctrinal discourses; Nectarius presided after him at the First Council of Constantinople, 381.

436.   *7 June 1981*

Address by Cardinal Maxmilian de Fürstenburg[66] in the Patriarchal church of the Phanar, for the celebration of the 16th centenary of the First Council of Constantinople*

Your Holiness,

I have the honor and joy of finding myself among you all today as an envoy of His Holiness Pope John Paul II, thus showing that the Church of Rome joins you in thanking God for what he did for his Church here sixteen hundred years ago, and for what he does not cease doing to maintain and cause us to progress in the right faith in his Spirit and in submissiveness to his action upon us.

It is an honor and joy for me to express at this moment the feeling of the other Churches here represented. We thank you, Your Holiness, for having taken the initiative of celebrating the First Council of Constantinople in this city.

[The next three paragraphs repeat what is already contained in Pope John Paul's letter of 4 June, see above, N. 433]

It is on this common basis that Christians of today continue to proclaim the very same Gospel of salvation, and that the Churches seek to reestablish full communion through a sincere dialogue in charity and truth, in order to resolve all the differences which came to the fore in the past. This dialogue, on this day of commemoration, has turned into prayer.

[The following continues to repeat largely *verbatim* the Papal text]

437.   *25 June 1981*

Letter of Patriarch Dimitrios I to Pope John Paul II for the feast of Saints Peter and Paul**

We having living experience of the mystery of apostolicity through the treasure which was mercifully committed to us, vessels of

---

66. Then Prefect of the Congregation for Eastern Churches.

clay though we are, and we are as men sorrowing but always rejoicing (2 Cor 6:4–10). It is thus that we celebrate and honor the memory of the two foremost Apostles, Peter and Paul, and with them of all the Twelve; and it is with this outlook that we view the feast of the holy Church's see of Rome and send you the embrace of the Church of Constantinople. In keeping with the above, we should like to share in that blend of opposite elements made up by suffering and holy joy as we enter into communication with Your Holiness, the reverend Bishop of Rome, our dear and esteemed elder brother.

And so, following the custom which has obtained in recent years, and which has God's blessing and is expressive of the rediscovered brotherhood between our Churches—the custom, that is, of celebrating together the feasts of our patronal saints—we have recognized in Synod that we should send Your Holiness and your Church a delegation from our Patriarchate. This will be under the leadership of our Doyen, the senior Metropolitan, Meliton of Chalcedon, our beloved brother in Christ, who will be accompanied by His Excellency Bishop Gennadios of Krateia and the Very Reverend Archimandrite Spyridon Papageorgiou. By the fact of their presence and by word of mouth they will convey our sentiments at this particular juncture.

Holy and dear Brother in Christ, we take this opportunity of joining with you and the Roman Catholic Church, our sister, in giving glory once again to the Holy Trinity for allowing us both to feel its presence more intensely in the life of the Church this year, and letting us move towards one another and meet more closely under the strong breath of the Holy Spirit.

The celebration here, in the very place where it was convened, of the Second Ecumenical Council on its 1600th anniversary, together with the joint celebration in Rome and the exchange of delegations, but above all the spirit of reverence and obedience which was shown by all to the teaching of that holy Ecumenical Council, have gone beyond the commemoration and honoring of an event of capital importance in the history of the Christian Church: they have made the feast a manifestation of the action of the Holy Spirit.

East and West, we have met on what was the soil of the undivided Church, and have had a fresh trial of the truth that the nearer we draw to that sacred space and to the spirit of the Fathers the healthier will be our interchange and the more effective for building up of full fellowship in full unity.

We are led in all reverence to signalize this year as an interval in time in which the Holy Spirit was moving in a special way, leading us to the region of the Ecumenical Councils, and this moreover in such a way that we might live them afresh and go forward in continuity with their spirit and character.

Hence we thank you for the contents of your much appreciated letters of 8 April and 4 June, in which you expound the universal value of the teaching of the Second Ecumenical Council. We thank you also in a more general sense for the way in which you look forward, in a spirit of reconciliation and with reverence towards the Fathers of the Church, to the much desired hour of full unity.

Furthermore, we attribute to the same movement of the Holy Spirit the indications we have had so far that those who are conducting the theological Dialogue between our two Churches are acting in conformity with the spirit of the Fathers and the teaching of the undivided Church. We pray that under the breath and enlightenment of the Paraclete who leads us into all truth, not only the dialogue, but also the other exchanges in charity between our Churches may be impelled strongly forward.

It is with these sentiments, thoughts and desires, that we visit Your Holiness through our delegation on the feast of the holy Apostles Peter and Paul, as you lie on your bed of pain. We pray very specially that the severe sufferings which you are bearing with such faith, perseverance and hope, may prove to be an acceptable sacrifice at the heavenly altar, and that the Lord may grant you in return a full restoration to health, so that you may continue the precious service which you render to Christ's Gospel.

In conclusion we greet Your Holiness with a loving kiss, and remain with brotherly love and special regard.

438.   *27 June 1981*

Metropolitan Meliton of Chalcedon, leader of the delegation sent by the Ecumenical Patriarch for the feast of Saints Peter and Paul, wrote in the open book at the Gemelli Hospital in Rome**

We bear the greetings of the Church of Constantinople to the Church of Rome on the feast of Saints Peter and Paul, and also the warmest good wishes of Patriarch Dimitrios I and the Holy Synod to His Holiness Pope John Paul II for his complete restoration to health, on which we set much store.

[*The Metropolitan was then received by the Holy Father in his room in the hospital*]

439. *8 August 1981*

Telegram from Patriarch Dimitrios I to Pope John Paul II, expressing prayerful concern for the second surgical operation undergone by the Holy Father**

We accompanied Your Holiness with anxiety and prayer through the second surgical operation which you underwent, and have glorified God with joy for its successful outcome. Once again we tell you of the deepest sympathy of our Church, and we pray the Lord, Healer of bodies and souls, that this recent suffering may be the final phase of a full cure and the entire restoration of your health, for the joyful relief and good of the whole Christian Church and the whole human world [whose members are] children of God.

440. *11 August 1981*

Telegram of reply from Cardinal Agostino Casaroli, Secretary of State, to Patriarch Dimitrios I*

His Holiness Pope John Paul II was deeply moved by your message of sympathy. He thanks Your Holiness with all his heart, and expresses his warm brotherly affection in the Lord.

441. *15 October 1981*

Telegram from Patriarch Dimitrios I to Pope John Paul II for the anniversary of his election to the Papacy ****

God who chose you as Bishop and Pope of the holy Roman Catholic Church, our sister, has preserved you and enabled you to celebrate the third anniversary of your election, for which we are now able to congratulate you. On this anniversary we come in spirit to visit Your Holiness. With all our heart we rejoice with you, and with brotherly affection pray that with health and the strength of God you may continue, for many years still of life and office, your great mission in the Church and the world.

442. *23 October 1981*

Telegram from Pope John Paul II to Patriarch Dimitrios I for the latter's feast-day*

As your feast comes round I should like to offer Your Holiness my warmest good wishes. I ask the Lord to grant you his plentiful gifts, and assure you again of my fraternal charity.

443. *27 October 1981*

Letter in reply from Patriarch Dimitrios I to Pope John Paul II**

The almighty and all-merciful God who holds all things in his power has granted us in his grace to celebrate the anniversary of our name-day once more this year. It was with the greatest pleasure that we received from Your dear and esteemed Holiness the brotherly good wishes and greetings for this event sent us in your telegram of the 24th of this month.

We warmly thank you for the contents, and in return ask God to grant you his greatest blessings. We embrace you with a holy kiss, and remain with great charity in the Lord and special regard.

444. *31 October 1981*

Letter in reply of Pope John Paul II (signed in his own hand) to Partiarch Dimitrios I, thanking him for the good wishes sent for the anniversary of the Pope's election (cf. N. 441)*

I was deeply touched by your warm message for the anniversary of my pontifical ministry as Bishop of Rome. I thank Your Holiness wholeheartedly for your good wishes and above all for your prayers. I assure you once more of my fraternal affection in the Lord.

445. *30 November 1981*

Letter of Pope John Paul II to Patriarch Dimitrios I for the feast of St. Andrew*

"The grace of the Lord Jesus Christ and the love of God and the fellowship of the Holy Spirit be with you" (2 Cor 13:13). And with us all!

Our delegation presided over by our dear brother Cardinal John Willebrands, President of the Secretariat for the Unity of Christians brings the greeting of the Church of Rome to Your Holiness and your Church (cf. Rom 16:16) and says by its presence, as in so many words, how united I am with you in prayer on this day of the celebration of the feast of the Apostle Andrew.

These annual meetings, at the see of your Church and in Rome on the occasion of the feast of the Apostles Peter and Paul, not only permit common fervent and renewed prayer, but also give us the opportunity to intensify and harmonize our efforts regularly in pursuit of unity.

Through the celebration this year of the sixteenth centenary of the second Ecumenical Council, the First Council of Constantinople, our Churches have endeavored to renew and deepen in the mind and hearts of the faithful the traditional certainties, still valid today, of our common faith in the Holy Spirit. At the same time they have insistently recalled the necessity for continual prayer, imploring the quickening action of this same Spirit and our readiness to accept it with souls eager to learn.

This new awareness of the common faith expressed by this Council should help us, I hope with all my heart, to overcome the doctrinal difficulties which still arise on the way that leads to the rediscovery of full unity. Two years ago, on the occasion of our unforgettable brotherly meeting in your Patriarchate, we had the joy of announcing together the creation of the Joint Commission for Theological Dialogue. Today I rejoice to see that this Commission has used means which have enabled it to achieve the goals it set for itself after its first meeting, and this with eagerness, competence, and with deep love of the Church and of the unity willed by the Lord.

Our march forward must not indeed be slowed down or dispersed. Both the necessities of the Christian world and, more generally, the choices proposed to the men and women of today, choices on which their future existence depends, demand that the dialogue between our Churches should not be scattered over secondary questions, but be concentrated on what is essential in order to reach as soon as possible this full unity which can be an important contribution to the reconciliation in the human race. And what is essential is unity in faith, in this faith rooted in the Word of God which comes to us in Holy Scripture, which was preached by the Apostles, which has been defended against all distortion and forcefully proclaimed by the Ecumenical Councils in the different ages.

Your Holiness, I wish to assure you again of the full readiness of the Catholic Church, in a spirit of loyal understanding and brotherly solidarity, for such new steps as are considered possible and opportune, both in the field of study and in that of action. I refer to steps which might deepen and strengthen the growing brotherhood between our Churches. May the intercession of the holy brothers the Apostles Andrew and Peter, obtain for us vigilant, obedient and energetic responsiveness to all the inspirations of the Holy Spirit.

In these sentiments, I repeat to you, beloved Brother, my deep charity in our one Lord.

446. *30 November 1981*

Address by Patriarch Dimitrios I to the Delegation from the Church of Rome for the patronal feast of the Church of Constantinople*

Dear Brothers,

It is with love and deep joy that we greet you, worthy representatives of the venerated Church of Rome and its holy leader Pope John Paul II, you who are present here in this city and our Church (a fact we much appreciate) for the commemoration of the glorious Apostle St. Andrew the First-Called, founder and protector of our Church.

Your presence during this sacred feast takes on a special meaning, because it represents an abiding reality which is prolonged through love and dialogue. For love, when one comes to think of it, cannot be love unless it continues and is consistent with itself. And dialogue cannot be truly dialogue, unless the partners actually meet one another and take their exchanges lovingly further. However, we on both sides, Constantinople and Rome, have learnt from the Word that we must serve God's plan, which takes effect and is followed through in a divine-human dialogue, as we reflect and work together. This is why we pursue our dialogue, here and in Rome. It is to this indeed that we are called: we are to take part in working out, or rather in ministering to the divine plan, which is for the salvation of humankind.

The Church of Christ the Savior, the Church of those who believe in him, is responsible, according to the teaching of the Sacred Scriptures, of our common holy Fathers and Doctors, and the decisions of

the undivided Church, for the unity which the Lord wills and the salvation of the race.

We of the East, with full understanding and lowliness, aim in
every step we take and every effort we make, at nothing else than the
salvation of humankind in the Church.

In the East we feel more and more with the passing of the days
that what the whole Church of God wills must never be neglected.
That will was imparted to us by the Lord through the Apostles; it was
confirmed and proclaimed by our common Fathers who gathered of
old in Ecumenical Councils; and it was attested above all by the saints,
confessors and martyrs. What is willed is that the Church should conform to the divine plan which would have us all one, and that we
should, so united, give continuous effect to the work of our divine Savior until the end of time.

Worthy brothers of Rome, we welcome you in this spirit which
goes with the divine plan for the One Holy Catholic and Apostolic
Church, a plan always in our mind. We wish to assure you that the
venerable elder Church of Rome will receive from our Orthodox
Church of the East all the collaboration conceivable within the setting
of what is warranted by the whole undivided Church in what concerns
the common profession of faith and basic canonical order. It will also
find full understanding on our part in what has to do with *theologoumena,*[67] though we shall always have as the fundamental model, in all
that bears upon the capital and essential items of our faith, the mind
of our common Fathers and Doctors and Ecumenical Councils, that is
to say, the mind of the Church of Christ before the division.

Dear delegates from the Church of Rome, your presence here
today, over and above the reasons already cited, gives us in our own
person as well as our Church the opportunity of expressing our joy,
and with this joy of giving thanks to our common Father who is in
heaven, since we receive you as representatives of our dear brother in
Christ, the holy Bishop of Rome, Pope John Paul II, who by the grace
of God has survived the danger that threatened his life.

We emphasize this point, because we received the news of the
attempted assassination of His Holiness the Pope with horror and distress, and we followed with anxiety and a sense of complete involvement the whole series of dramatic incidents which enabled him to
escape death, to receive medical attention, and to recover his health—

---

67. *Theologoumena,* a name given to those theological interpretations which have
high status but are not normative for faith, as are clearly declared dogmatic
pronouncements.

which is of such value not merely for the Roman Catholic Church, but also for the whole of Christianity and the world.

God brings it about that today, from this place, we can express our joy that His Holiness, with health restored, is fully exercising his sacred duties, and is in a foremost position to carry out his task for the unity of Christ's Church.

Venerated and dear representatives of the Bishop of Rome, see, we are celebrating together the memory of the Apostle Andrew, Peter's brother. We are carrying out this celebration in loving brotherhood, and are looking forward to a concelebration in the common chalice.

Today, for reasons known to God, we do not have a common profession of faith. But yes, we do love one another, and our mutual love should lead us to a profession of faith in which we agree. Perhaps the official Theological Dialogue which is under way, and to which both our Churches look for a solution of the theological problems between us, will lead us (as we hope from the bottom of our heart) to the next stage—to a commonly accepted profession of faith, and thence to full communion in the same holy sacrament of the Eucharist, where we share the one chalice.

In this spirit, and with this outlook on the future, we have the conviction that the Holy Spirit will supply what we lack and lead us to the common profession of faith of the One Holy Catholic and Apostolic Church, as it was held, following on the time of our common Apostles Peter and Andrew, by our common martyrs, and Fathers, and the common Ecumenical Councils which they assembled. In this spirit then we greet you, and regard your presence, representatives of our venerated elder brother the Bishop of Rome, as a promise filled with hope that we shall work closely together, making our way with one heart towards the common profession of faith, and from this to the common chalice, so that our Lord and Savior may be glorified in his one Church, and through her in the salvation of the whole world.

447.   *30 November 1981*

Address by Cardinal John Willebrands to Patriarch Dimitrios I at the celebration of the feast of St. Andrew at the Phanar*

"We have seen the true light, we have received the heavenly Spirit, we have found the true faith, as we worshipped the undivided Trinity which has saved us." This hymn, which has just been sung as the liturgy was ending, sums up for us, and I would be inclined to say presents today a composite pattern of our feelings, our faith, and our mission, as well as the task which rests on all of us of restoring full unity. Enlightened by the one true light, Jesus Christ, we are gathered here in adoration of the undivided Trinity, sharing our certainty that it has saved us; and we do so quickened by the same Spirit, prompted by the same faith.

The feast of the Apostle St. Andrew the First-Called, who in his turn bore the ultimate witness to the Lord by martyrdom, brings us together again this year to adore the most Holy Trinity in the mystery of the Eucharistic celebration, just as the feast of St. Peter and St. Paul brought us together at Rome through the now traditional participation by a delegation from your Church.

And so each year the Apostles Andrew and Peter summon our Churches and invite them to unity, to the profession of the same faith in the bond of peace, by giving them the great joy of this meeting, and at the same time by making them feel the sting and spur of disappointment of not yet being able to celebrate side by side the one Eucharist of the Lord.

This year which marked the sixteenth centenary of the Council held in this city—the Second Ecumenical Council—has been an occasion for both East and West to meditate at length on the one and undivided Trinity, and on the Creed which takes its name from Nicaea and Constantinople and still expresses today the one single faith to which all Christians adhere.

The ecumenical solemnity which Your Holiness chose to give this centenary, and the corresponding solemnity which Pope John Paul II, in close conjunction with the Ecumenical Patriarchate, gave it in Rome has drawn attention to the fundamental importance of the Creed for the restoration of full unity. Naturally the Church has the pastoral duty, today as in every phase of its history, of professing its faith in such a way as to make it understood by different mentalities and in different cultures. It has the same duty to defend that faith against the counterfeit versions which may creep in, or on the other hand to express a unity regained after a time of division.

The Council of Chalcedon explains that this is precisely what the Fathers of the First Council of Constantinople did with regard to the faith professed by the Council of Nicaea. In declaring that the faith proclaimed at Nicaea was inviolable, the Council of 451 confirms "the doctrine on the nature of the Spirit subsequently transmitted by the Fathers assembled in the imperial city ... this doctrine which they proclaimed to all, not indeed to supply something thought to be missing in what was earlier taught, but with the support of Scripture to set forth their mind on the Holy Spirit against those who sought to deny his sovereignty" (Denz. Sch. 300). This way of seeing things of the Council of Chalcedon can be of considerable help to Christians in their search for unity, and to the Church itself in its proclamation of salvation to the men and women of our own time. And indeed for the Church of today, concerned no less that that of yesterday to maintain the integrity of faith in the midst of many different pastoral needs, the Creed of Nicaea-Constantinople remains the necessary criterion of orthodoxy: every new expression of this faith must inevitably be made with reference to this Creed, with each statement fitting in evenly and being of a piece with it.

What is more, in proclaiming our faith in "the Spirit who is Lord and giver of life," the Creed keeps on reminding us that if God manifests himself to us, it is to make a covenant with us; if he reveals his inner mystery to us, it is to bring us to share in it; if he enlightens us with the true light, it is to save us. This Creed is continually forcing us to face a fundamental challenge: there is no truly faithful response to revelation except by a life led more and more in communion with the Father through the Son in the Holy Spirit, and thereby in communion with all those who, like ourselves, are born anew of the Spirit and for that reason are our brothers and sisters. It is only by loving one another that we can profess the same faith. It is only through a deep and continuous dialogue of charity that the Theological Dialogue can develop and reach fruition. This is the conviction of our Churches, and it is the conviction of all who, with a keen awareness of their responsibility, are committed to the Theological Dialogue between our Churches.

Now that the three sub-commissions and the coordinating committee have finished the work entrusted to them, we are on our way towards the Second Plenary Meeting of the Joint Commission for Dialogue.[68] The fact that the work of each of the three sub-commissions ended with a complete agreement of all members augurs well for the meeting of the Commission and for the transition to a new phase of our quest.

Thus we are training ourselves in a knowledge of one another in truth and in a growth in charity. Today we have prayed together—and prayer is at the heart of the whole search for unity. May the Lord hear

---

68. The three sub-commissions had met at Chevetogne in Belgium (5–9 October, 1980); Rome (27–30 October, 1980); and Belgrade (29 April–1 May, 1981). The coordinating committee, in Venice (25–30 May, 1981), prepared a unified report for the next plenary session in Munich.

our prayer, and enable us who have seen the true light, together and in the unity of the Spirit to proclaim it to others, so that all may believe in the one and undivided Trinity, and thus have life and be saved.

448. *24 December 1981*

Telegram from Patriarch Dimitrios I to Pope John Paul II for Christmas**

As we celebrate once more the great mystery of our religion, the Incarnation and Epiphany of the divine Word, we greet Your dear Holiness with feelings of deep brotherly love and honor, and rejoice with you. We pray that for you, for the Church of Christ itself, and for the whole world, the new year now approaching may be health giving, favorable, peaceful, and of saving effect.

449. *2 January 1982*

Telegram in reply from Pope John Paul II to Patriarch Dimitrios I*

In these days when we celebrate with thanksgiving the manifestation of God's goodness and his love for mankind, I wish Your Holiness a new year filled with joy and the peace of which the new born Savior is the only true source. I assure you once more of all fraternal charity.

450. *3 April 1982*

Easter letter of Pope John Paul II to Patriarch Dimitrios I*

During these days the Church endeavors to contemplate with greater fervor the redemption wrought by Christ, who by giving up his life for his brethren has shown the love which is greater than all other (cf. Jn 15:13). And if darkness came upon the whole land at the moment when Jesus committed his spirit to his Father (Jn 19:30), we know that it was followed by the radiant splendor of the Resurrection, and that for the eyes of faith it is this which remains the great light, ever giving rise to hope.

Even in those periods of history when all is dark and gloomy, the definitive victory won by Christ gives us the assurance that the day will come when everything will be renewed and brought to a head in him (Eph 1:10), when sin and death will be finally conquered, and God will be all in all (cf. 1 Cor 15:28).

The Easter celebration re-enkindles in Christians this certainty, this hope and joy. And it gives me, beloved Brother, the consoling opportunity of sharing these feelings with you. Together with you I give thanks to the Lord and strengthen my prayers and strivings for the coming of that full communion of faith and charity which, according to the divine plan, must accompany our testimony to the Resurrection of Christ, which now lights up the vocation of man and the world and shows us the way we must go.

With the joy that comes from the Risen Christ, I assure you, dear Brother, once again of my deep charity.

451.　*9 April 1982*

Telegram from Patriarch Dimitrios I to Pope John Paul II for Easter**

We embrace Your beloved Holiness as brother to brother on the great feast of the light-bearing Resurrection of the Lord, which is the source of joy and hope for the whole world. We pray that you may enjoy this feast in health with your faithful people. With you we pray that peace may come upon the world.

452.　*28 June 1982*

Letter of Patriarch Dimitrios I to Pope John Paul II for the feast of Saints Peter and Paul**

In pursuit of the tradition approved by God by which our Churches celebrate together in love, peace and brotherhood the memory of their respective Apostle protectors—and this by sharing in each other's celebrations—we are sending a delegation again this year from our Church and from us personally to our sister Church of Rome for the feast of the leading Apostles Peter and Paul. It will be headed by the Doyen of our Holy Synod, His Eminence Metropolitan Meliton of Chalcedon, our dear brother in Christ, who will have as fellow members His Excellency Bishop Kallistos of Diocleia and the Very Reverend Archimandrite Spyridon Papageorgiou. The delegation will convey our salutation for the happy occasion, and will furnish an expression of the spirit of unity in brotherly love which exists between us.

The fact that this year's feast gives us an opportunity for getting in touch with one another is a matter for special rejoicing, since before our very eyes we behold the triumph over evil of the all-powerful and gracious working of the God of all goodness. This is evident in that the danger to the invaluable life of Your venerable Holiness has yielded place, and with it the whole painful experience by which your physical state was sorely tried. Now you have your full health and strength back again, and while it is true that you bear the marks of your portion in the sufferings of Christ and the martyrdom of those Apostles whose feast we are keeping, you have been brought to the point where you are able to officiate at the memorial ceremony. Last year you went through the experience of suffering in patience; this year you are letting it be known what a grace it is in God's sight to endure patiently for his sake—as the Apostle Peter says: "If you put up with suffering for doing what is right, this is acceptable in God's eyes" (1 Pt 2:20).

Holy Brother, not only the tradition of communicating with each other for feast-days, but in a more general way the development and continual cultivation of brotherly relations, and the mutual sharing in each other's sorrow and joy—these things, in so far as they are the fruit of love, have clearly proved to be the really sound Christian way leading to the sacred goal envisaged, which is unity not only in love but in truth and faith.

We thank the Lord that he gives us immeasurably more than we ask or imagine (Eph 3:20), and that he has so far blessed the enterprises and endeavors undertaken in his name by the two Churches in the direction indicated. It is an important fact that the Theological Dialogue between the Roman Catholic and Orthodox Churches, whose inception we announced together during your unforgettable stay in our city and participation in the feast of the Apostle St. Andrew, is going steadily ahead. Within the next few days the second general assembly of the Joint Theological Commission will be held in Munich. We look to this assembly and more generally to the development of this Dialogue with the highest hopes, without disregarding the obstacles and difficulties. We believe that in spite of such things the Holy Spirit will enlighten everyone's minds and hearts, so that the truth may shine forth, and agreement and unity be grounded in it.

For this reason we would ask Your Holiness's help, so that on both sides we may lend our support as Churches to those conducting the Dialogue, and this by our loving concern and by encouraging the growth of a climate of brotherly closeness. Let us take care not to make existing differences and problems more acute, or create new ones, but rather try as hard as we can to remedy the causes of the division. Above all, let us be united in prayer, especially during the days when the Commission is in session. Let us ask the Paraclete to watch over its work, leading it into all truth (cf. Jn 16:13), so that the Lord's will be fulfilled, and that he may be glorified with his Father and the Holy Spirit in his unified Church, to the end that his kingdom may prevail and the world be brought to salvation.

We write in this strain from the Church of the Apostle Andrew to the Church of his own brother Peter, and to Your Holiness its Bishop, at the same time as we recall the sacred memory of the Apostles Peter and Paul, and so doing greet you with a holy kiss, and remain with brotherly love and special esteem.

453. *28 June 1982*

Address by Metropolitan Meliton at the audience given to the Patriarchal Delegation for the feast of Saints Peter and Paul**

"Glory be to God for all things!" These words of praise of the holy Father St. John Chrysostom, Archbishop of Constantinople,[69] springs to our lips at this moment when we are privileged, as representatives of his sucessor Dimitrios I, to bring the greetings of our Church and the embrace of our Patriarch to the holy Church of Rome and Your blessed Holiness, for the memorial celebration of the Apostles Saints Peter and Paul, and to meet you again in your see presiding over the feast-day ceremonies.

These words of praise fit Your Holiness's case more especially at the present time. St. John Chrysostom uttered them in his hour of ordeal; we are repeating them at the moment when, together with the ordeal, we see the happy outcome which the Lord has given it. For, after a marathon contest with death, Your Holiness, under the protection of the holy Mother of God and with the grace of her Son Our

---

69. St. John Chrysostom ("Golden-mouthed"), Archbishop of Constantinople (398–407) and famous preacher and Doctor of the Chruch, was exiled from his see and harried in a long journey into Pontus, on the Black Sea. He uttered these words as he was dying of exposure, exhaustion, and fever.

Lord, has been made to stand forth as champion of life, to be the defender of the life of others, and to be the herald and bringer of good news to the world of the One who "came that we may have life and have it abundantly" (Jn. 10:10).

Your Holiness, afflictions, severe sufferings, persecutions, martyrdom—these are among the essential elements that make up the mission and forward movement of the Church in the world, and which take their origin from Golgotha, from the Apostles, and the martyrs and confessors of our Christian faith. These elements continue, under different forms, right up to this moment, at every point of the globe, even as the dialogue itself between life and death helps to make up the paradoxical mystery of apostolicity. Often it is the lot and privilege of God's servants to experience this mystery in their own lives, just as the Apostle Paul experienced it in his and gave it expression: "dying we still live on, disciplined by suffering, we are not done to death" (2 Cor 6:9).

With this experience as Churches in particular places and as bearers of apostolicity, we are enabled to carry out our service perseveringly and to enter with deeper insight and keener personal feeling into the sufferings of the human race.

These are the spiritual thoughts which this year's meeting with Your Holiness has suggested to me.

But our exchanges today, over and above their feast-day character, and beyond what I have just said, assume a special meaning for the relations of our Roman Catholic and Orthodox Churches. And this by reason of the fact that they occur on the very eve of the second general assembly of the Joint Commission for the official Theological Dialogue between the two Churches.

When we met on the same occasion two years ago, it was the immediate aftermath of the consecration and inauguration of the Dialogue in the Cave of the Apocalypse in Patmos. Your Holiness and I spoke of our joy over the Dialogue and the course we hoped it would take, while admitting that difficulties were inevitable and that the Church would need to encompass the dialogue with its loving concern and make the way smooth for it, so that it could be one in which truth was sought and unity built up. We also recognized the need for prayer if this sacred historical undertaking was to proceed to a happy issue.

Today then, as we meet in this same hall on the eve of a further installment of the Dialogue in plenary session, we see hopeful signs in the progress already made through the positive work and findings of the three sub-commissions and the coordinating committee, but above all through the prevalent spirit of cooperation and the fine, sincere attitude of those engaged on either side in the working parties.

At the same time, keeping in view the inevitable difficulties, let us renew our consecration of this devout work to the Holy Spirit and his directing influence, and let us hope that the labors of the Second Plenary Session at Munich will be brought to a successful conclusion. May it thus prove to be an important stage in the progress of the Dialogue, and from this may we be led step by step to full unity, and be so favored from on high that the meetings of our Churches may not be merely mutual dealings in brotherly love, but may turn into full Eucharistic communion.

Addressing Your Holiness in this spirit and holding forth these hopes, we congratulate you again on this great and sacred feast, and we implore the glorious Apostles Peter and Paul to watch over and protect the Church of Rome and Your Holiness, the whole Church of Christ on earth, and the world in all its fulness.

454.   *28 June 1982*

Address in reply by Pope John Paul II to the Delegation from the Ecumenical Patriarchate*

Dear Brothers in Christ,

It is indeed a matter of great spiritual joy to meet you on these feast-days. Through you I thank the Ecumenical Patriarch Dimitrios I and the Holy Synod for having sent you as messengers of reconciliation and ecclesial closeness. Your presence in Rome when we celebrate the holy Apostles Peter and Paul becomes each time a further sign of brotherhood and communion between our Churches. Likewise when we send a delegation from the Catholic Church to the Phanar for the feast of St. Andrew, as we do now each year, this betokens the same mutual affection and brings out the same deep link with the first body of the Apostles. These visits to and fro give grounds for a gladness that grows each year. The fact is that personal meetings nearly always take on a sense of vivid flesh and blood reality which exchanges of letters, valuable as they are, cannot adequately match. The experience of speaking to one another personally, as we are doing now, with the Holy Spirit re-enkindling our prayer, gives rise each time to new hope.

These encounters do indeed make it clearer than ever that full unity must be set up again between our Churches. It is owing to the deep and mysterious communion which gathers us together round Our Lord that such meetings can happen. He is present in his Church according to his promise (Mt 28:20), and he incorporates us into himself in a unity which belongs to the order of mystery, and which no hostile power can destroy. We are familiar with the great texts on this subject: "We were all brought into one body by baptism in the one Spirit" (1 Cor 12:13); and then a few verses later on: "You are Christ's body and each of you a member of it" (*ibid.* 27).

It is therefore a matter of urgency that we should rise above the divisions inherited from the past, which have obscured and at times even completely hidden this deep reality. The fact that you are here on such a significant day shows clearly that this movement towards full reconciliation, blessed as it is by God, is making headway throughout our Churches. Let us praise the Lord for raising up personalities of spiritual distinction to take in hand this important but delicate work. I think very naturally of Popes John XXIII and Paul VI, but I should like to mention in the same breath Patriarch Athenagoras, whose memory we hold in veneration, especially about this time which marks the tenth anniversary of his return to God.

Today, as we find ourselves on the eve of the second assembly of the Joint Catholic-Orthodox Commission for the Theological Dialogue, the thoughts of both of us turn to this important event. Our prayers mount together to the Father of lights, begging him to shed the wisdom of his Spirit plentifully on all those taking part in this theological interchange, so that it may help in a new advance towards that unity which Christ willed for those who believe in him. There is no need to emphasize the great importance which the Catholic Church attaches to the work of this Commission. In a climate of serenity and courage may it pick out every obstacle to a full agreement in faith, and see what it really amounts to. The experience of the Fathers of the Church has taught us that the agreement we have in mind must allow for a rich variety in self-consistent expressions of the one faith (cf. *Tomos Agapis* no. 172). So "let us profess the truth in love and grow to the full maturity of Christ the head" (Eph 4:15).

The Joint Commission has arranged the *agenda* of its theological work in a positive and constructive way, allowing us to look forward with hope. It is a sign of realism to take as a starting point the whole body of things in which the Orthodox and Catholics are at one, even if the riches we share have been experienced under particular forms deriving from diverse cultural features and somewhat different types of religious feeling. But at the same time this Commission is concerned to isolate the real points of divergence, in other words the differences which are incompatible with full communion, so as to face them clearly in the light of the Sacred Scriptures and the great tradition of the Church. We all suffer particularly from not being able to celebrate the Eucharist together. Would that we could clear up the reasons for this situation, which is quite opposed to the Lord's will, so that we could put an end to it by getting at the causes and setting them right.

These then are the demanding tasks to which the Joint Commission will devote itself with utmost care. But it needs continual support from the fervent prayer of our Churches, who owe it to themselves to send up strong entreaties to Christ "through whom the whole body grows, and with the proper functioning of the members joined firmly together by each supporting ligament, builds itself up in love" (Eph 4:16).

It is with these feelings of gladness and love, of gratefulness and deep respect towards the Ecumenical Patriarchate, that I welcome you today. May the blessed hope of seeing our Churches make real progress towards full unity take hold of our hearts more and more.

455.   *17 October 1982*

Telegram from Pope John Paul II to Patriarch Dimitrios I, who is undergoing treatment in the Swiss cantonal hospital at Basel*

I am anxious to assure Your Holiness of my deep sympathy, and of my prayers to the Lord asking for your rapid and complete recovery. With my enkindled and unstinted charity.

456.   *21 October 1982*

Telegram in reply from Patriarch Dimitrios I to Pope John Paul II**

I am deeply moved and much fortified by the brotherly sympathy and solidarity of Your Holiness, and above all your prayers. I thank you warmly for this fresh proof of the fraternal charity which binds us together, and in which I continue in the One who is our common Lord.

457.   *25 October 1982*

Telegram from Pope John Paul II to Patriarch Dimitrios I in Swiss hospital with good wishes for his feast-day*

On this feast of St. Demetrius I should like to express once more my warmest wishes for your prompt recovery, and to assure you again of my complete and very brotherly charity.

458.   *27 October 1982*

Telegram in reply from Patriarch Dimitrios I to Pope John Paul II**

Holy brother, I am grateful for your renewed prayers on my behalf, and for the brotherly love which joins us. St. Demetrius was a man who struggled on behalf of the faith of the Lord, and on his holy nameday I want to assure you that I am one with you in desiring to give a common testimony to the world of our struggle for Christ.

459.   *24 November 1982*

Letter of Pope John Paul II to Patriarch Dimitrios I given by the papal delegation at the Phanar for the celebration of the feast of St. Andrew**

"May God the Father and the Lord Jesus Christ grant the brothers peace and love and faith" (Eph 6:23).

The feast of the Apostle Andrew, with its accompanying celebration, comes round again this year to strengthen the ties of charity and faith that bind us together. The celebration comes to add new life to the feelings of reconciliation and peace which we experience within the rediscovered brotherhood of our Churches. The liturgical year very appositely brings these feasts freshly before us, not only as a memory of the past but as an opportunity for our Churches to meet in prayer before and with the Lord.

It may be that Your Holiness is not yet well enough to preside over this year's liturgical celebration, but all the same our two Churches must not miss this chance to meet one another in thanksgiving and petition. For this reason I thought it right to send the now traditional delegation, which will be led by Cardinal John Willebrands, Archbishop of Utrecht and President of the Secretariat for Christian Unity. It will have an additional reason for joining in the liturgy celebrated in the Cathedral of St. George at the Phanar, for it will appeal to the Lord for the full recovery of your health, enabling you to take up your pastoral ministry again with renewed energy. I can assure Your Holiness that I am praying personally for this intention, and I offer you my warm good wishes.

The feast of St. Andrew, as it is kept up this year, sees our two Churches more committed than ever to the Theological Dialogue, and to a course of action which we hope will lead to full unity and so to a concelebration of the Eucharist.

A Joint Commission had been given the task of finding the most suitable pathways to this goal, and of clearing them of all hindrances. It has already produced its first results by reaching agreement on the basic statements of the apostolic faith with regard to the mystery of the Church. Those who are taking part in this Dialogue, while fully conscious of their responsibility and anxious only to obey their Lord, hope that it will be able to bring a clear cut and durable solution to all the difficulties which have prevented full communion between our Churches for centuries. This very important and delicate work must be continually supported by the prayers of all the faithful, Catholic and Orthodox. In this way the Spirit of truth will enlighten the minds and warm the hearts of all. He will allow this newly refound communion to expand and encompass the whole people of God.

This exchange of delegations between our two Churches—that at Rome for the feast of Saints Peter and Paul and that at the Phanar for the feast of St. Andrew—ought to spur on all Catholics and Orthodox, wherever they live in proximity, to pray harder, and to involve themselves on the appropriate levels in some such dialogue in which the truth is sought out in love. Every celebration in which we both take part marks some progress in the purification of hearts by charity found afresh, and brings us closer to the time when we can together announce the Gospel of our one Lord to the human race, to which we owe no greater or prior service.

I constantly keep fresh in memory the brotherly and prayerful meeting which I had had with Your beloved Holiness three years ago on this same occasion, when the feast of St. Andrew was being celebrated; and I now want to voice the hope that we will be able to meet again, this time by the tomb of Andrew's brother, Peter.

With these thoughts in mind, I assure Your Holiness of my prayer and of my deep charity in the Lord.

460.   *30 November 1982*

Address by the Metropolitan of Chalcedon at the end of the liturgical celebration for the feast of St. Andrew**

Dear Brothers in the Lord,

We honor you as representatives of the holy Roman Catholic Church, and of His Holiness Pope John Paul II who presides over it, as you take your place in our Church of the Apostle Andrew. The fact that you are here on the very day on which we celebrate the sacred memory of this Apostle who was crucified like Christ, and indeed that you are present at this heavenly time of the Liturgy—all this fills our hearts with great spiritual joy. With this feeling we cordially greet you and embrace you as brothers in the name of the Church of Constantinople and its Bishop, His Holiness the Ecumenical Patriarch Dimitrios I, for whom I act as humble office bearer. Further, we warmly thank both His Holiness the Pope for sending you, and we thank you personally—each cherished one of you—for taking the trouble involved in carrying out this responsible mission.

Speaking on this site, and out of the depths of our hearts, we would especially like to say "Thank you" for the keen concern and brotherly sympathy which His Holiness the Pope showed recently when our Patriarch underwent an operation in Switzerland. Involved with each other as they are in joy and sorrow, our two Churches find themselves standing shoulder to shoulder in every changing situation.

See how we met "yesterday" in Rome and meet again today in this city for the same purpose—to celebrate together the Apostles to whom we trace our origins, and from whom we receive succession (carried it is true in our vessels of clay), and whose work we are called upon to continue in today's world.

These meetings of ours here and in Rome are not of an academic nature, they belong to the churchly order. They are conducted in church, before the Holy Table, before the real presence of the Lord of the Church in the Holy Eucharist—that real presence which we believe in and worship.

Of course the natural meeting place, the natural situation, would be one in which we stood together in concelebration round the Holy Table, as in the early days of the undivided Church. That would be fellowship brought to fulness, including a unity in the faith and its profession, and in the way in which we experience the nature of the Church in our own lives.

By judgments known only to God this unity has been broken, so that we cannot be together with one mind, forming a circle round the Table of the Eucharist. But we do come together in our refound brotherhood, and in front of that Table we stand round the other table—that of the Theological Dialogue. We ache for the loss of the divine good gift of the full fellowship enjoyed by the Apostles and Fathers, and we sorely yearn with holy desire for its restoration. Thus we are seeking again, with truth and fidelity to the teaching which was lived out by the undivided Church, some way in which we can relive that unity and full communion.

Already, by the grace of God, we have had blessings bestowed upon us as we advance in our common pilgrimage towards the Church as it was in its primordial unity. The progress to date of the work of the Joint Theological Commission with its sub-commissions and coordinating committee gives us courage and hope. And this not merely with regard to the positive points arising from agreements and overlapping views carefully worked out in common, but also with regard to the negative points, where divergences either of dogmatic teaching or ecclesial practice are brought to light. Because the negative points, too, when submitted sincerely and with upright minds to the test of truth—as this was put into dogmatic form and lived out in the experience of the undivided Church—are capable of being transformed into something positive.

For this reason, at the very serious, responsible, and delicate stage of the official Theological Dialogue through which we are now passing, there is one thing that must be constantly kept in mind by those on either side who are officially conducting the Dialogue, and more generally by the two Churches with their theological institutions and personnel and the whole body of their faithful. This Table of Dialogue is not one for negotiations that follow an ideological or a more broadly secular pattern, where compromises or new types of theological formulations are looked for, other than those drawn up by our common holy Fathers, "bearers of the divine."

The world watches our Theological Dialogue from the standpoint of its own standards, and is on the wait for sensational and rapid results. It must realize that this is not a case of arranging some improvised and temporary agreement which could be repudiated by either side under certain conditions. What we are dealing with here touches on the very existence of the Church of Christ.

In view of all this, we must glorify God for the progress already made, and renew our hope of being led to a happy conclusion. At the same time we must continually fortify ourselves with a pure faith in this holy work, combined with patience and understanding, and above all with prayer. And this that we may attend to any kind of criticism, whatever its source, of the findings reached stage by stage in the Dialogue. Then, secondly, that we may apply ourselves to the thorny dogmatic and ecclesiological subjects which divide us. These of course will be laid explicitly and in due order on the Table of Dialogue, but they will also inevitably crop up during the examination of those matters on which there is greater agreement between the two Churches, and to which we have given priority at the outset.

Hence we must not regard the Table of Dialogue (which has

already been serving its initial role) as a kind of rendezvous for the discussion of theological ideas, or as something like a battle-field on which theological attitudes and propositions face one another in unyielding array—attitudes and propositions which are uppermost in different ways in the one or other Church, and which either derive from non-theological factors or come within the category of *theologoumena*.

Instead we should consider the important Table of the Theological Dialogue, which was laid out, over and above our humble efforts, by the Holy Spirit, as an anticipation and ante-chamber of the holy Eucharistic Table. It is from this Table that the Dialogue is in a position to receive its theology, its depth, its perspective, its sacramental texture in which the divine and human are both present. And it is towards this Eucharistic Table that the Table of Dialogue, like that of the rite of preparation,[70] must look—in other words, to consecration and transubstantiation. And this is so that the brightness of the Church's mystery may shine forth to the world in the mystery of the Holy Eucharist, which itself is embedded in the mystery of the Holy Trinity, and that this may take place to the glory of the same Trinity.

It is with these thoughts which were inspired by this meeting at the holy Eucharistic celebration that we greet you again as brothers, as you stand near the altar of the Apostle Andrew, brother of the Apostle Peter. We embrace you in the love and peace of Christ, and with you we beg him to grant us see that great day in which we shall share like our common Fathers in the same Bread and the same Chalice. Then united once more we shall give a common witness, and together proclaim that Christ is the salvation and peace of the world.

461.   *30 November 1982*

Address by Cardinal John Willebrands at the conclusion of the liturgical celebration for the feast of St. Andrew*

Your Eminence, dear Brother in Christ,

We meet once again for the eucharistic celebration of the feast of St. Andrew, who has been the protector of this illustrious see throughout the course of the Church's history.

---

70. In Churches of the Byzantine rite, on this table of the *prothesis* are prepared and laid out the gifts and sacred vessels before they are brought out in procession to the altar.

I am very happy to be appointed once again as the bearer of brotherly greetings from the Church of Rome, and to bring you with this greeting the mark of our communion in faith, charity, and Christian "togetherness." His Holiness Pope John Paul II asked me to carry his own personal greeting in the Lord: he retains a vivid and happy memory of his meeting with each one of you, and particularly with Patriarch Dimitrios, in this very Church, celebrating the very same feast.

Today, for reasons of health, Patriarch Dimitrios is not presiding at the Liturgy. His absence dims our joy with a hint of sadness, which however is lessened by the hope of seeing him soon resuming his pastoral activity. We have joined our fervent prayers to yours, and with our whole heart we said together: "Remember first, O Lord, your holy Patriarch Dimitrios, and grant him to live in peace, in safety and honor, in health and length of days, faithfully dispensing the word of your truth."[71]

A common prayer to this effect has mounted to the Lord today, not only from those of us assembled in this church, but also from the many Orthodox and Catholic faithful far beyond the limits of this city and country who are one in spirit with us at this celebration. The Lord "in whom we live and move and have our being" (Acts 17:28) will certainly give ear to this prayer coming from so many of his own who have joined together in his name and for his service.

The double annual encounter, here at the Ecumenical Patriarchate for the feast of St. Andrew and for that of Saints Peter and Paul at Rome, provides us with a heaven-sent opportunity for doing two things. In the first place we can join together in prayer and so purify and strengthen our intentions and resolution. And then we can make a combined examination of what has been done, and at the same time integrate the necessary further endeavors for the full communion of our Churches. This year we have very good reasons for thanking the Lord for what he has enabled us to achieve along the road to unity.

A particularly important event was the issue of the document drawn up together by the Joint Catholic-Orthodox Commission on the mystery of the Church and the Eucharist.[72] This document contains fundamental statements exhibiting a common sacramental conception of the Church, together with the same understanding of the local Church and the role of the Bishop in it, and of the communion

---

71. From the commemoration of the living, in the Liturgy of St. John Chrysostom.
72. The "Munich Statement" was issued at the end of the second plenary session, 30 June–6 July, 1982. English text in SPCU *Information Service* 49 (1982), II/III, 107–112; *Origins* 12(1982), 6(July 24), 91–96.

between sister churches in the universal symphony of the holy Church of God.

Thus this first common document makes an affirmative statement about a whole cluster of essential elements of the ecclesiology of communion—elements which guarantee a real progress in the relations between our Churches. The document leaves various questions open, e.g. the way in which conciliar life, as a traditional expression of ecclesial life, is to be conceived and put into practice; or again the role of the Church of Rome in the symphony of the Churches. But the general outlook of the document and the theological quality of its content, and the fact that it was given unanimous approval, provide good reason to hope for further progress. We want to go together along the whole road that leads to unity. The Lord will be with us and will help us; he will speak to us along the way and cause us to understand the Scriptures (cf. Lk 24:32), and he will guide us up to the moment when we can take part together in the breaking of the bread.

In order to go further along this way the sub-commissions have already resumed their work. They aim to study the subjects which were assigned them by the Joint Commission for the second phase of the Dialogue: "faith and communion in the sacraments in relation to unity." The sacramental conception of the Church which was asserted in the first phase of the Dialogue calls for this further working out in depth. We hope that the new phase into which we are now entering will be marked by new progress.

The document published after the Munich meeting is set within a perspective which made a genuine agreement possible. "In composing this document we intend to show that in doing so we express together a faith which is a continuation of that of the Apostles." This setting implies a distinction between the faith and the various expressions or theological formulations of which it is susceptible, and furthermore makes it positively clear that it is linked with the faith of the Apostles. This should be the setting, in our opinion, for all the following stages of the Dialogue as well. More than that, it seems to be the only one which admits of true progress in mutual understanding, and is capable of leading us to a true unity while fully respecting the diversity of our traditions. The Joint Commission, however productive of good things it may be, does not express the whole variety and richness of the interplay between our Churches. This is being carried further and developed in an atmosphere of trust on which we can increasingly count at the different levels of the Church's life. The Theological Dialogue is evolving in the midst of the Dialogue of Charity, and the two interact with each other as they go forward.

We must not fail to explore any area of possible pastoral cooperation between us. The whole people of God must be actively involved as we make our way together towards unity. Those who are engaged in theological dialogues ought to be alert to the possiblity of practical consequences which could be suggested to Church authorities as theological agreement comes more and more to expression. This is absolutely required if the Dialogue is to be a living reality, and not something isolated in the realm of theory. Wherever such things are possible, common prayer, combined study, and cultural collaboration will make it easier to spell out again, item by item, that unity which would make the Church's life a sign of the Gospel message. These hopes nestling in our hearts are transformed into real expectation as we confide them in prayer to our one Lord.

I have the honor, Your Eminence, of handing you the message which His Holiness John Paul II has addressed to the Church of Constantinople and its Patriarch for the feast of St. Andrew.

462.   *24 December 1982*

Telegram from Patriarch Dimitrios I to Pope John Paul II for Christmas**

In evil days, behold once again light comes from holy Bethlehem to illuminate the world, to teach the peace [so much] desired, to give understanding to mankind, to encourage those who hunger and thirst for justice. On this holy day which is *par excellence* bearer of hope, we embrace Your beloved Holiness with brotherly longing. We rejoice with you, and ask the newly born Christ to strengthen you in your much appreciated efforts for the relief of members of the human race. May the coming year be a blessed one for you and your holy Church, and may it be a saving effect for the whole world.

463.   *29 December 1982*

Letter in reply of Pope John Paul II to Patriarch Dimitrios I*

During these days when we are celebrating the birth of him who said, "I am the light of the world" (Jn 8:12), our mind goes back to the shepherds of Bethlehem "around whom shone the glory of the Lord" (Lk 2:10). The light shone in the night of Bethlehem, and it shone in the night of human history. The Truth was made flesh so that flesh could shine out in the world with the beauty of the Truth. This is a great mystery, which fills the mind that contemplates it with delight and amazement, an amazement which runs through the whole Gospel. The light of Bethlehem's night shines and will keep on shining in all its radiance in the Church, the Bride of Christ, whose vocation it is to gather members of the human race into the light of truth.

I thank Your Holiness for the good wishes you sent me, and I confide mine for you to the Lord, asking him that our ministry may be filled with every blessing, and that during the coming year our Churches may draw closer together, and go ahead along the way of unity which the Lord wills.

May the light of Bethlehem triumph over darkness everywhere; may it shine forth from the face of men and women, made in the image of their creator; may it shine forth from every family united by love; may it shine out in the midst of human relationships where tensions have been resolved into a higher harmony.

In this spirit I assure Your Holiness again of my fraternal charity in our one Lord.

464.   *1 April 1983*

Easter letter of Pope John Paul II to Patriarch Dimitrios I*

During these days when we are celebrating the Paschal Feast of the Lord with common faith in the Risen One, I feel sure that both Your Holiness and I share the same anxiety with regard to those of the human race who flee from God. But I feel more particularly that we share the same hope that they will return to the Father who is waiting for them (cf. Lk 15:11–32), and that we share too the wonderful joy of being certain that God *is* waiting for them, that he is waiting for every man and woman.

With these feelings strong upon me, my thought reaches out to those who are more intimately involved in the Paschal mystery, even without knowing it, even perhaps while denying it. I think of all the victims of war and violence, of those who suffer hunger and are out of work, of parents who have gnawing worries about their children's future in an unstable world, of young people who try to slake their thirst for life with drugs.

To be true to ourselves we have to proclaim, more emphatically than ever, the deep meaning behind the joy of Easter—the certainty that Christ has risen from the dead, the first-born of a multitude of brothers and sisters (cf. Col 1:18; Rom 8:29).

With this joy and this hope, I assure you once more, Your Holiness, of my deep and brotherly charity.

465. *1 April 1983*

Telegram from Patriarch Dimitrios I to Pope John Paul II for Easter**

Fervently desiring that we may both soon be granted to proclaim to the world with one voice and one heart the world saving tidings of the Resurrection of the Lord, with brotherly feeling we embrace Your Holiness on the occasion of this year's feast. Once again we rejoice with you, and wish you all strength arising from the life-bearing message [of Easter] for the continuation of your great peaceful journeys to meet struggling humanity along the pathways of the world.

466. *21 June 1983*

Letter of Patriarch Dimitrios I to Pope John Paul II sent with the Delegation from the Ecumenical Patriarchate which came to Rome for the feast of Saints Peter and Paul**

To the blessed and holy Pope of Rome, John Paul II, greetings in the Lord.

Now once again the commemoration of the two leading Apostles Peter and Paul bids us celebrate their feast with charity and in brotherly partnership.

We would like to come personally to your venerable see, Holy Brother, to honor the memory of the Apostles with you, and generally to enjoy your company at first hand. But it is impossible to do this, deeply as we desire it. Instead, by a decision taken in Synod, I am sending to you and the sister Church of Rome a delegation from our Church led by His Eminence, our dear brother in Christ and first in rank of our Synod, Metropolitan Meliton of Chalcedon. Taking part with him will be his Excellency Bishop Gennadios of Krateia, and the Very Reverend Archimandrite Spyridon Papageorgiou, head of the Greek Orthodox community in Rome. This delegation will convey the greetings of our Church, that of the Apostle Andrew.

This new occasion for bringing our two sister Churches into contact to honor the memory of the two holy Apostles also gives us an opportunity on both sides to confirm our steady purpose, which is to go on cultivating close fraternal relations by mutual love and persistent efforts, and to search in the Dialogue sincerely and with fidelity to the truth the common expression of that truth, which should be such as was professed by the united Church of ancient times. All this that we may make the journey to full unity and communion in the divine Eucharist, and together proclaim the Gospel of our one and undivided Lord.

The contributions made so far in all good will by our two Churches, as they worked together with corresponding views, have by the grace of God produced suitable results, and progress has been made towards unity. For these things let us glorify the Lord of the Church.

The progress so far made, while it strengthens us and fills the two churches with hope, also spurs them on to greater efforts, and calls on us for spiritual vigilance and for an increased sense of Christian responsibility. And this so that in our journey to unity we may not rest with easily won conclusions, but may carefully seek to uncover the real foundation of the truth and proceed to build the solid structure of unity on it. Neither, on the other hand, should we lose heart in the face of the difficulties and disappointments which will inevitably appear; instead, we should confront this phase of things with Christian courage and humility, and serve the Lord and his designs.

We hope that the meeting of our two Churches for the feast of the Apostles this year will bring new progress in our journey towards holy unity, and make the kingdom of God prevail more and more on earth—that kingdom which the world waits and thirsts for.

With this wish we embrace Your venerable Holiness; we assure you of our prayers for your health and important work, and remain with deep brotherly love and special esteem.

467.   *30 June 1983*

Address by Metropolitan Meliton of Chalcedon during the audience of the Delegation from the Ecumenical Patriarchate with Pope John Paul II on the occasion of the feast of Saints Peter and Paul**

We have come again this year to Your Holiness and the sister Church of Rome in this eternal city as envoys from the Church of St. Andrew and His Holiness our Patriarch Dimitrios I who presides over it, to celebrate with you the commemoration of our common Apostles Peter and Paul, in the very place of their martyrdom.

We have already felt what a good thing it is to be spiritually united with you in charity and to make a prayerful offering towards the all-good God, as we did just a short time ago at the Eucharistic Liturgy. Now we have the happy privilege of appearing before Your Holiness, and of transmitting to you and through you to the Church of Rome the greeting and embrace of the Church of Constantinople, and of the Ecumenical Patriarch and his Holy Synod.

We glorify the Holy Trinity, source of all good, for graciously bringing about this blessed meeting at a common liturgical feast, and we thank Your Holiness for the welcome, cordial as always, which you have given us.

The continuation of this beautiful sacred custom which was initiated and hallowed by the two Churches in a spirit of reconciliation as they rediscovered their brotherhood—the custom that is of celebrating together twice a year the holy founder Apostles whom they both recognize—is certainly not a static repetition of the same thing. Each time it is a new instalment, a dynamic forward thrust, a growth in depth with regard to the mystery of the Church as it moves stage by stage towards the final reality.

When we take into account that this liturgical practice is carried out within the setting of the new and blessed state of the relations between the Roman Catholic and Orthodox Churches, and that it runs parallel to the Theological Dialogue between them, we gain a deeper insight into its value. We can say that by being and worshipping together in fellowship we fill out and cast light on the Theological Dialogue and all the other outward signs of our fraternal relations, because such actions introduce the divine dimension into the whole enterprise for unity.

Last year we celebrated this great feast together on the eve of the Second Plenary Session of our Joint Theological Commission, and our prayers for the success of its work were heard in his kindness by God. This year we come together again for the feast just after the meeting of the coordinating committee for the Dialogue.[73] And in both cases we were greeted with good fruit. What excellent coincidences! How wonderfully the Lord in his watchful care over for his Church arranges

---

73. Convening in Nicosia, Cyprus (12–17 June, 1983), the coordinating committee drew together the subcommission reports on faith and communion in the sacraments and on the relation of the sacraments of initiation to the unity of the Church. The text was to be submitted to the fourth plenary session (Crete, 30 May–8 June, 1984).

events, and brings love, prayer and sincere theological discussion into a coherent whole which he uses for the fulfilment of his holy will that we should be one.

Moreover, this year our ecclesial meeting in Rome takes place during the liturgical period following Pentecost, thereby emphasizing and reminding us of two things: first that the Holy Spirit is present and operative within the life and forward movement of the Church, and second that, if he was able to bring the Church into actual existence, then much more is he able to bring it back into unity and the beauty of its origins.

In the hymnody of the Eastern Church the *kontakion* sung for the feast of Pentecost runs: " . . . when he distributed the tongues of fire he called all into unity."

The distribution and variety of languages, spiritual gifts, of particular local forms, does not signify fragmentation and division. Transcending such things is the fire of the Holy Spirit, which enlightens, purifies, consumes, warms, and summons into unity.

Let us commit ourselves then to the power and guidance of the Holy Spirit, and let us ask him to enlighten the hearts and minds of all, Roman Catholic and Orthodox, so that we may realize more deeply and clearly that the Church of Christ is one, just as the truth which it is called to attest and proclaim is one. May that fire of the Holy Spirit burn away all those human seeds of division, and summon everyone to unity, so that in a new Pentecost we may confess and herald the primordial common faith, and with one voice glorify the All-Holy Spirit (*Kontakion* of Pentecost). Amen.

468. *30 June 1983*

Address in reply by Pope John Paul II to the Delegation from the Ecumenical Patriarchate*

On this day when we keep up the feast of the holy Apostles Peter and Paul, the presence of a delegation from our sister Church of Constantinople gives us added reason to be glad. I should like to tell you how really grateful I am that you are here. This recent tradition of celebrating together Saints Peter and Paul at Rome, and Peter's brother Andrew at the Ecumenical Patriarchate, to some extent fills the gap created by the incomplete communion between our Churches. It does so by the desire it expresses and the hope it stirs of reaching the day when we are finally able to celebrate the Eucharist together, like faithful disciples round their one Lord. By sharing each in turn in the feast of the Apostles, we are both expressly committing ourselves to prepare in unity and charity for the Supper-in-communion which the Lord wants us to celebrate as a memorial of his death and Resurrection, and as a pledge of eternal life.

Today's celebration reminds us of the calling of the first disciples. "As Jesus was walking along the Sea of Galilee he watched two brothers, Simon now known as Peter, and his brother Andrew, casting a net into the sea. They were fishermen. He said to them, 'Come after me and I will make you fishers of men.' They immediately abandoned their nets and became his followers" (Mt 4:18–20). After that Peter and Andrew became united more deeply than by ties of blood in a vocation that goes beyond the needs of the moment, pressing though they may be, of their daily work.

In calling them to follow him the Lord gave them a mission to the human race: they were to make all nations disciples of the Lord (cf. Mt 28:19). This is the vocation and permanent mission in our time, too, of all who appeal to the Apostles and look on themselves as their successors in an unbroken line across the centuries. Although the time in which we live is rife with various powers and energies and with unforeseen conquests of the human mind, it is also one in which people are oppressed from within by severe anxieties and tried by tragic temptations that lead to death. Such a society needs more than ever a living assurance of faith, unity, and love, and for this assurance it looks to us who believe in him who gave his life for the salvation of the world. In point of fact, the unity which in obedience to the Lord's will we are trying to set up again between our Churches is directed to the proclamation of the good news to the whole human race, "so that the world may believe" (Jn 17:21), so that it may have peace and its joy be full. The unity of Christians in Christ is a condition for the credibility of the Gospel as we announce it in our own time.

Obviously each year our combined celebration of the Apostles allows us to deepen our knowledge of one another, and of the brotherly love which is working within us. But it also brings the opportunity for joining in thanks to the Lord who is causing us to go forward slowly but surely towards full ecclesial communion.

A sense of expectant "togetherness" is developing between our Churches, and this comes from a feeling of fellowship which goes out between Catholics and Orthodox at all levels. These feelings ought to take practical form more and more in joint work within the study area, and also in certain sectors of pastoral activity, where Catholics and Orthodox are living in the same locality.

As part of the series of new moves which tend to recreate between us the spirit proper to brothers, the Theological Dialogue is making its way. I learn with joy that since the Second Plenary Session of the Joint Commission for Dialogue, which was held exactly a year ago, the study sub-commissions have finished their work, and that the joint coordinating committee has already met to prepare for the calling of the Third Session. Fired by the same zeal Catholics and Orthodox bishops and specialists have thrown themselves into the Dialogue with devotion and professional skill, drawing on all the resources of their mind and heart. Several times I have asked everyone to pray that the Lord may make this Dialogue productive, for it is he "who gives the growth" (1 Cor 3:7). Prayer on every side is required to banish those vague misgivings which may linger here and there, and above all to overcome the doctrinal difficulties which the Dialogue will have inevitably to face.

With these feelings of joy and fellowship, of earnest involvement and hope, we welcome you, Your Eminence, and the delegation which Patriarch Dimitrios has kindly sent to Rome again this year.

I would ask you to convey my brotherly gratitude to His Holiness, and tell him that I retain a vivid memory of my visit to him, which occurred appropriately for the feast of St. Andrew. May God grant us to come together again and recite a combined prayer. Both the Church of Rome and I would be extremely grateful if this could take place over the tombs of the holy Apostles Peter and Paul.

469.　　*13 October 1983*

Telegram from Patriarch Dimitrios I to Pope John Paul II for the fifth anniversary of his election**

The fifth anniversary of the election of Your venerable Holiness to the see of the Bishop of Rome and to the high office of Pope and Patriarch of the West is hailed by our Church of Constantinople and ourselves personally as recalling an event of great importance for the Church, and one that concerns the position and future of Christianity in the world. In saying this we are convinced that we are interpreting the spirit of our Christian Church of the East in general. For the service rendered in these five years by Your blessed Holiness as Pope of Rome has given an extremely important witness on a worldwide scale of a Christian bishop, an office of grace that you have borne for twenty-five years. In celebrating these two important anniversaries which are bound together and complement one another (since "bishop" explains "pope," and "pope" expresses [the meaning of] "bishop" with greater force),[74] with deep brotherly love and joy we send our cordial congratulations for the occasion. We pray that Christ the Head of the Church may grant Your Holiness and myself to celebrate other such anniversaries of the holy Church of Rome and its Bishop in the near future together, in conjunction with anniversaries of Christian unity arising from blessed events.

470.   *22 October 1983*

Telegram from Pope John Paul II to Patriarch Dimitrios I for the latter's feast-day*

As the feast-day of Your Holiness comes round I send my warmest good wishes. With the memory of our meeting still present to me, I assure you of my fervent prayer and deep and brotherly charity.

471.   *28 October 1983*

Letter in reply by Patriarch Dimitrios I**

To the holy and blessed Pope of elder Rome, John Paul II, greetings in the Lord.

Amid the usual laborious succession of the days of our life we feel a singular pleasure as we come to certain fixed dates on which the custom obtains between brothers in the Lord to exchange good wishes and embrace one another in him.

Such then was the pleasure we felt when we received the greetings and prayers of Your dear and esteemed Holiness on the feast-day of the saint after whom we are named, as it occurred again this year.

We warmly thank you for this, and once again embracing you with a holy kiss, we remain with brotherly love and especial esteem in the Lord.

---

74. *Pope* is from *pápas* (Greek) and *papa* (Latin), meaning *father*. It was applied to bishops from the third to the fifth centuries, and thereafter more especially to the Bishop of Rome.

472. *22 November 1983*

Letter of Pope John Paul II to Patriarch Dimitrios I for the feast of St. Andrew*

"May grace and peace be yours in abundance"

(1 Pt 1:2)

This was the greeting sent by the Apostle Peter to the first Christians of Pontus, Galatia, Cappadocia, Asia, and Bithynia, "chosen according to the foreknowledge of God the Father, consecrated by the Spirit to a life of obedience to Jesus Christ and purification with his blood" (1 Pt 1, 2).

I send you, venerable Brother, the same greeting of fellowship, in the same spirit of faith, for the feast of the Apostle Andrew, Peter's brother.

The delegation which I am sending you, led by Cardinal John Willebrands, will unite itself with the prayer of your Church in thanking and blessing the Lord, who "in his great mercy gave us new birth; a birth unto hope which draws its life from the resurrection of Jesus Christ from the dead; a birth to an imperishable inheritance, incapable of fading or defilement" (1 Pt 1:3–4).

I should like to make a point of uniting myself personally with this prayer.

Given this occasion, I should like to thank Your Holiness warmly for the brotherly message which you sent me for the fifth anniversary of my ministry as Bishop of Rome and the twenty-fifth of my episcopate. What you had to say about the part played by a bishop in the life of the Church brings out an essential element in the structure of the Church, and one intended by Christ for the sake of its unity.

In the Catholic Church, the Second Vatican Council has once again insisted very clearly on the importance of this matter. In point of fact our Churches share "true sacraments, and above all, in virtue of the apostolic succession, priesthood and the Eucharist." Thus, in spite of the changing events of history and the obstacles which arose between them in the past, our Churches remain united by ties that reach deeply down (cf. *Unitatis Redintegratio*, 15). Neither differences in the liturgy surrounding these sacraments or in the canonical rules governing their administration bring this fundamental identity into question.

The apostolic succession of the bishops acts, through the assistance of the Holy Spirit, to keep the Christian community faithful to the truth of the Gospel as preached by the Apostles and handed down to us without interruption.

Every time the feast of an Apostle is celebrated our attention is drawn once more to this mysterious reach in depth and extension of the Church and the Church's mission, which is to preach the Gospel of salvation in every age to all nations, teaching them what the Lord has given to its charge, baptizing them in the name of the Holy Trinity (cf. Mt 28:19–20), and thus making them members of the one Body of Christ.

This mission can only be completely carried out if our Churches, by the fact of their unity, allow the Gospel message to be seen with all its powerful claims on belief.

For this reason we rejoice that the Theological Dialogue between the Catholic Church and all the Orthodox Churches is making progress, slowly indeed but surely, and that at each step efforts are being made to see that the basis is secure.

I should like to take the opportunity presented today to repeat my statement that the Catholic Church is ready to do everything possible to smooth the way for this progress, and to contribute to it both by prayer and study.

May Saints Peter and Andrew, brother Apostles and martyrs for the faith in Jesus Christ our one Savior, intercede with the Lord to give us light and strength to do his will.

With these feelings of joy, fellowship, and hope, I assure Your Holiness of my deep brotherly affection in Christ Jesus.

473. *30 November 1983*

Address by Patriarch Dimitrios I to the Catholic Delegation present at the Phanar for the feast of St. Andrew*

Eminent Cardinal and dear members of the Delegation,

On this holy day of the commemoration of St. Andrew the Apostle, the "First-Called," the founder of our Church of Constantinople, we here and now welcome you, worthy representatives of our sister Church of Rome and its revered head, our dear brother Pope John Paul II. At such a time then the first word that springs to our lips is one of thanksgiving to our common Lord Jesus Christ that he has allowed us to come together in his name once again this year to pay combined honor to his Apostle.

After thanking the Lord we voice our gratitude to His Holiness the Pope of Rome, who has been so kind as to send you as his representatives, messengers of peace and good things.

But we also thank each one of you personally, dear brothers, for undertaking this exalted mission—you who are zealous workers and fellow builders in the great cause of the unity of our Churches. We embrace you in the love of Christ, and wish to tell you forthwith that we—that is to say, the Church of the Apostle Andrew and we personally—receive you, not as strangers, but as belonging to us—our brothers.

Truly blessed was the moment when the idea was conceived, like a divine inspiration, of establishing a combined commemoration of our Patron Apostles here and at Rome.

This pious custom was decided upon here in 1976 by the delegations of our Churches in concert with one another, and then approved by the two Churches themselves. It was initiated that year by the first visit of the delegation from Rome for the feast of St. Andrew, and by the grace of God it has continued since then without a break for eight years already.

The tradition is a recent one. Every good and pious tradition in the life of the Church began of course at a certain moment and passed through the period of its youth. But being an expression of the love of God in the spirit of the Gospel, such a tradition came to take on a value deriving from eternity, and by preserving its Gospel purity remained and became with time an ancient one.

This new tradition of feast-day ecclesial gatherings bears within itself a certain eternal value. Because it is an evangelical act of love and prayer, it has a character of purity and Christian authenticity. We of Rome and Constantinople meet in each city in turn, and we meet on the brink of the mystery of the Holy Eucharist, on the brink of the mystery of the Church, we ourselves being humble servants of these mysteries. We meet that we may feel more deeply the sin of division and our responsibility before God and man to make our way out of this scandal and work for further reconciliation, looking towards the final reestablishment of the fulness and visible integrity of the spotless Body of Christ in this world, and within view of the world.

But even more, during these ecclesial meetings of ours, with humility and nostalgia for the undivided state of the early Church, not putting "our confidence in ourselves" (2 Cor 1:9), we ask the Founder and Lord of the Church, of that Church "which he has acquired at the price of his own blood" (Acts 20:28), to have pity and guide us to do his will, and so be one (cf. Jn 17:20). These feast-day meetings of ours take place against the background of the overall willingness of the

Roman Catholic and Orthodox Churches to reestablish unity between themselves, and in the setting of their combined decision to foster fraternal relations for this purpose.

In this spirit we meet one another again this year. We meet to further the advance towards the holy goal of unity which we desire. We meet to confirm the will of our two Churches to go ahead without faltering in this direction, despite all difficulties and obstacles. We meet to compare our experience of what has been so far achieved and taken into our lives in our joint efforts for progress in reconciliation, for drawing together, and finally for unity. We meet to strengthen the love and brotherhood between us, to renew our hope, to exchange information, and to alert one another to dangers from the Evil One who watches balefully to sap our efforts, but we meet also to support one another in the conviction that in the end it is Christ and his will that will prevail.

We strengthen ourselves in this conviction by signs that are already present in our midst. These signs which reveal the development of both the Dialogue of Charity and the Theological Dialogue are, according to the best judgments available, happy ones. They are positive, constructive, and promising signs, far removed from those that point only to negation.

In line with this we would mention more particularly as a positive point the progress made so far in the official Theological Dialogue.

We hope that our meeting and personal contacts this year again will, by the Lord's grace, form a further step towards full communion between us both.

Dear Brothers,

During this fraternal meeting of ours, while naturally concerning ourselves in the first place with the holy cause of the relations between our two Churches, and with the progress of the unity which we seek between them, we must at the same time remember that this unity which we seek to foster is not and ought not to be an end in itself. It is a stage, and a very important one of course, towards the greater and holy goal of complete Christian unity. But our duty and responsibility do not stop even there.

Certainly we consider Christian unity as a natural situation in conformity to the Lord's will, as the natural situation of the One Holy Catholic and Apostolic Church, both in prospect and in practice. But this second, pan-Christian goal, though greater than the first, does not constitute an end in itself either. Our design is not only to bring about the unity of those who are already Christian, but through this unity to witness to the world in a convincing manner that Jesus Christ is its Saviour, and through this same unity to have the world transformed and integrated into the Church of Christ, so that his kingdom may be established on earth.

On this point also we agree with the opinion expressed by our brother Pope John Paul II in his speech to our delegation last June in Rome.

Just as God the Father of Our Lord Jesus Christ became linked in solidarity, through the redemption wrought by his Son, with humanity in its entirety, so we, in so far as we make up the Church and prolong through time the saving work of the Lord, are linked in solidarity with the human race, with every man and woman, with the whole of humanity on this earth.

In saying all this we wish to make it clear that we cannot at this moment ignore the reality of the world that surrounds us. Nor can we exclude from our immediate concern, from our duty and responsibility, men and women of today who suffer and find themselves seriously threatened—men and women of today independently of their religion, race and color, who live on this earth: they are creatures of the one God, made in his image and likeness.

Consequently, as we look at the present picture—the situation of the real world, from the vantage point of this very ancient see of the East, which has been put to the test in grandeur and humility, we note that all the evidence, the signs from every quarter, all the technological achievements of our age which were first invented for human prosperity, point or lead in fact towards worldwide destruction, and this under the influence and control of self-seeking and ultimately nihilistic forces.

Before the threat of universal destruction we join forces with Pope John Paul II in his fight for the avoidance of this disaster, and in league with him we make our appeal to the powerful ones of the earth to halt the arms race, to resolve their subjects of dispute by peaceful means, to protect the sacred human person and fundamental human rights, to seek some kind of balance between the well developed countries and those in course of development, so that liberty with justice and peace with love may prevail on earth, in place of disaster and the imbalance between excess and famine, between domination and servitude.

With such thoughts and sentiments towards the holy Roman Catholic Church, and His Holiness who is its head, towards the Christian world and all humanity, we greet you again dear brothers here present, and thank you.

474. *30 November 1983*

Address by Cardinal John Willebrands at the conclusion of the liturgy held at the Phanar for the feast of St. Andrew*

"Again and again let us pray to the Lord"

This call to prayer which recurs in the Liturgy like a refrain, is made to every Christian, not only while the Eucharist is being celebrated, but at every moment of his or her life. But I would say that it is made particularly to those who are engaged in the quest for full unity between the Churches, for full unity between the Churches of the East and West.

We have just striven with you to answer this call. It was with great joy that I came once again from Rome with my companions, to associate ourselves in prayer with you, Your Holiness, with the prayers of your Holy Synod, and those of the clergy and the faithful here present, so that we could all celebrate together the feast of St. Andrew the "First-Called," who was the brother of Peter, leader of the Apostles. Our presence is symbolic of a wider sharing, a further reaching fellowship. We bring you the brotherly greetings of His Holiness Pope John Paul II, and greetings, too, from the Church of Rome, and also, I am sure, from the faithful far and wide within the Catholic Church. The desire for full unity between our Churches has become common among Catholics. Is it not highly likely that prayer, this meeting in the presence of God, is responsible for all the progress we have made in this matter, particularly for the fact that our minds are cleansed of the prejudices which pervaded them not long ago, and that our hearts are free of the tendency to say No to one another. Our union in prayer has caused us to rediscover what is really required of us by the fact of the unity of the people of God—that people redeemed by Jesus Christ, united by the Holy Spirit, and made coordinate members of a single Body.

These reflections on the meaning of our presence here with you today bring vividly back to mind the unforgettable meeting in prayer which took place twenty years ago, 5 January 1964, on the Mount of Olives at Jerusalem, between Patriarch Athenagoras and Pope Paul VI, now in one another's company in the kingdom of the just. Their pilgrimage from different points to meet at the place where our redemption was wrought—a pilgrimage which they both carried out in a spirit of conversion—their encounter as they recited the earnest prayer made by Jesus to his Father before he died for us—all this remains for us an exemplary series of events indicating the way in which further progress can be made. The kiss of peace exchanged between these two great representatives in this particular spot marked in itself an important step forward in the ecclesial order. In point of fact this kiss was in itself an act of reconciliation. It was reconciliation between our Churches and reconciliation in the Lord, who before his Passion and Resurrection prayed for the unity of his disciples and for all those who through their word would believe in him, and over the course of the centuries make up the community of the Church. This act of reconciliation initiated the dialogue of charity, which must find its fulfilment in the perfect charity of a common celebration of the Eucharist, so that the Lord's joy may be in us and our joy be full (cf. Jn 15:11; 17:13). Today we discover in practice how this meeting and prayer were mysteriously productive. Since that time the relationships between our Churches have been filled out in extent and depth to a degree unhoped for. The dialogue of charity brought us to the very centre of the Gospel message: "I give you a new commandment: Such as my love has been for you, so must your love be for one another. This is how all will know you for my disciples: your love for one another" (Jn 13:34–35).

This new attitude, this new way of looking at one another, this openness of heart towards one another, gradually introduced a new quality into Catholic-Orthodox relations, and created conditions for a fruitful theological dialogue.

Following on the meeting at Jerusalem the way was opened for other historic meetings, those between Pope Paul VI and Patriarch Athenagoras here at the Ecumenical Patriarchate and in Rome at St. Peter's Basilica, and the one when Pope John Paul II visited Your Holiness on the very feast which we are celebrating again today.

The meeting at Jerusalem was close to the origins of an unprecedented development in the encounter of Catholics and Orthodox, and also of prayer and mutual awareness, and a deep movement on either side to unity.

This movement has not yet reached its term. It is one that goes straining towards the goal, which is the reestablishment of full communion, as clearly stated in the document preliminary to the Theological Dialogue.

Today, twenty years further on, the providential meeting at Jerusalem is still able to inspire us. And perhaps it can do this in a very special way, now that the Theological Dialogue is preparing to face those questions which in past times brought about an alienation on both sides ending in division. Indeed it is precisely now that we need this coming together in prayer, from which every inspiration springs. It is now, right now, that we must learn to get beyond the limits of our own historical and cultural habits and go out to meet one another in the faith.

That meeting at Jerusalem also reminds us that the dialogue between our Churches ought not to be subjected to conditions which are external or foreign to the Church, or even opposed to the overriding demands of obedience to the will of Jesus Christ, who for us and our salvation died on the Cross. The Cross of Jesus Christ—nothing less than that—is calling us to unity. He in fact died "to gather into one all the dispersed children of God" (Jn 11:52).

Whatever may be the difficulties we may have to face, whether they come from the matter of the dialogue itself, or the circumstances in which we live today or will be living tomorrow, we are summoned to follow out our vocation with practical effect: to be one, that the world may believe (cf. Jn 17:21).

May today's celebration presided over by Your Holiness, and our prayer together make us still firmer in our fidelity and unshakable in perseverance.

The Lord who is present where two or three are gathered in his name is present in a special way in the Eucharistic liturgy in which we have just taken part: he will remain with us and help us to march forward together, as in his name we have bound ourselves to do.

So it is with our wills strengthened by the presence of the Lord that we gladly accept the bidding at the end of this Liturgy: "*en irini proelthomen,*" "let us go forward in peace."

Your Holiness, it is my honor and special pleasure to hand you a brotherly message from His Holiness John Paul II, who is spiritually united with you and us today in prayer and in the desire to pursue the forward journey towards full unity and concelebration of the one Eucharist of the Lord.

475. *24 December 1983*

Christmas letter of Patriarch Dimitrios I to Pope John Paul II**

The angels, the shepherds, the cave and the manger call us once again to listen to the good tidings of great joy: "Today there has been born to you a Savior, who is Christ the Lord." They call us to go and adore Christ our Savior, born of the Virgin, singing the while: "Glory to God in the highest, and peace on earth."

As we adore and glorify the coming Prince, whom the prophets announced long ago, on the occasion of this imminent great feast and the New Year soon to dawn, with brotherly love we send Your dear esteemed Holiness and your Church our own and our Church's warm greeting. We pray that God who was born in Bethlehem may always heap his rich grace on you, and grant that the coming new year of our salvation may be full of every gift from above.

We embrace Your Holiness with a brotherly kiss, and remain with much love and special esteem.

476.   *16 January 1984*

Letter in reply of Pope John Paul II to Patriarch Dimitrios I*

I thank you wholeheartedly for the good wishes which you sent me, and I offer my own during these days when we want to communicate the feelings of joy, praise and thanksgiving which fill our hearts, as we contemplate the mystery of the infinite love of God coming amongst us to reconcile us to himself. May the Lord cause everyone in the whole world to hear the message of Christmas and share the joy felt by the shepherds of Bethlehem. As we celebrated the Lord's birth we meditated once again on the mystery of man, who by grace is born to the life of God; before the human tears of God as an infant we came to understand that the tears of mankind can turn into a prayer.

With these feelings we turn our gaze towards the year now beginning. May the Lord who induces men to transform "their swords into plowshares, their spears into pruning hooks" (cf. Is 2:4) hasten the fulfilment of his promise, and grant us to be united as we give witness to the world of our hope. May he cause men and women to open their ears to the message of Christmas, become newly aware of their vocation, and devote themselves to the building of a more human world.

Very soon Christians will be united all over the world in raising a prayer to the Lord for the unity of his disciples, on the occasion of the Week of Prayer for Christian Unity, which we will be holding from 18 to 25 January. At this juncture I shall ask the Lord to increase the reality of our brotherly ties and hasten our progress towards full communion.

With these thoughts and feelings, I assure you, Your Holiness, of my deep charity in the Lord.

477.   *12 April 1984*

Easter letter of Pope John Paul II to Patriarch Dimitrios I*

"Grace and peace from God our Father and the Lord Jesus Christ" (1 Cor 1:3)

The celebration of the coming feast of Easter will be the climax of the meditation on the mystery of the Redemption which has been central to the Holy Year just ending in the Catholic Church. Indeed the Paschal mystery is at the heart of revelation; it is the supreme factual expression of the divine mercy for all men and women of all times.

By the sacrifice and Resurrection of Christ the individual receives the gift of reconciliation with God and the pledge of eternal life. He or she is called to become part of the one community of faith of those who are saved.

"Yes, God so loved the world that he gave his only Son, that whoever believes in him may not die but may have eternal life" (Jn 3:16).

This one faith and this common hope gather into an indestructible unity, in spite of remaining divisions, all the members of our Churches who, through the sacraments, share in the death and Resurrection of Christ so as to rise again into the new life (cf Rom 6:4). This is why our Churches are called to witness together to faith in the Resurrection of the One who gives human existence its fullest meaning. This year we rejoice to see that the dates for our celebration of Easter coincide. This happy conjunction will manifest more clearly our common faith. It so happens that our Churches and all other Christians will together announce the death of the Lord for the salvation of all, and will proclaim eternal life given in the Risen Christ.

This Good News answers the great need of our world, which is to find the complete meaning of life in its being a gift of God. Such tidings ought to help humanity overcome the temptations to death which assail it today, and to restore and consolidate peace and fraternity among all.

In every age the main mission of the Church is to announce the Resurrection. Whence it follows that this vocation and the urgent needs of our time bid us strive anew for full reconciliation between Christians, so that we may proclaim the Resurrection with one voice and in a convincing way. It was in this way indeed that the Apostles, who had seen the Lord and touched him with their hands, proclaimed him, so that all might be in communion with the Father and the Risen Son (cf. 1 Jn 1:2–3) through the Spirit given us.

In communion with you in our faith in this mystery, I renew the determination to do everything to deepen the brotherhood between our Churches. Hoping one day to be able to share the Bread of Life with Your Holiness, after the fashion of the disciples at Emmaus, I would ask you to believe in my warm brotherly charity in the Risen Lord.

478. *Easter 1984*

Easter letter of Patriarch Dimitrios I to Pope John Paul II**

Early this morning, the day of the Resurrection, as we carried out the Liturgy with the holy Metropolitans who stand round about us, we offered on the sacred altar of our hallowed Patriarchal Cathedral the bloodless sacrifice for the faithful living and dead. Rejoicing in heart and soul, and united with our devout local flock and with all who believe in Christ-God everywhere on earth, we celebrate in festival the glorious Resurrection from the life-endowed tomb of the One who conquered death, Jesus Christ our Lord.

On this chosen and holy day, we enter into communion in brotherly love with Your esteemed Holiness, and in an Easter embrace we greet you with the lovely traditional *Christos anesti* ("Christ has risen"). We express with all our heart the hope that the Lord who has risen from the tomb will grant you to celebrate the Holy Pasch of the New Testament in good health for very many years to come.

We embrace Your Holiness fraternally in the Risen Christ, and remain with brotherly charity and especial esteem.

479. *28 June 1984*

Letter of Patriarch Dimitrios I to Pope John Paul II brought to Rome by the Patriarchal Delegation for the feast of Saints Peter and Paul*

This year's sacred commemoration of the holy leaders among the Apostles, Peter and Paul, brings us once more closer together, so that we may jointly celebrate and glorify our common Lord, our God and Savior Jesus Christ, "through whom we both have access in one Spirit to the Father" (Eph 2:18).

As we celebrate together this patronal feast of the holy Church of Rome "which presides over charity," we become more aware of the sacred fact that, in spite of our separation by a judgment known only to God, we are both built up "on the foundation of the apostles and prophets, with Christ Jesus as the cornerstone" (Eph 2:20)—he who is *par excellence* "the apostle and high priest whom we acknowledge in faith" (Heb 3:1).

In truth, Holy Father, through the Apostles the Church has a full and authentic knowledge of its founder, and is called today as ever to preserve and communicate without error the tradition of the faith and of the apostolic preaching, so that it may give effect to its divine mission, the salvation of those for whom Christ died.

This mission will be more effectively carried out by a Church of Christ which is united on earth; it is for this reason that we both pray and work to remove divisions and schisms. We are grateful to Christ, for he is blessing this sacred endeavor, and is causing brotherhood, love and understanding to grow ever more between us. This is shown among other things by the steady and healthy advance of the Theological Dialogue which is going on between our sister Churches (and this augurs well for the future).

These sentiments, thoughts and expectations will be presented to you at greater length by the delegation which comes to you from the Church of Constantinople and from us personally, for the patronal feast of your holy Church of Rome. This delegation is led by His Eminence the Primate of Australia, Archbishop Stylianos, who is the Orthodox co-president of the Joint Commission which is conducting our Dialogue. With him are the Very Reverend Archimandrite Spyridon Papageorgiou and the under-secretary of our Holy Synod, the deacon Meliton Karas.

Let us ask the holy Apostles Peter and Paul whose feast we are celebrating to protect the Church of Rome and the whole Church of Christ. Let us ask them to bless our common efforts so that the unity of the Church in the apostolic faith may be rendered visible. We congratulate Your Holiness and the sister Church of which you are the head, as this feast comes round. We embrace you with a holy kiss, and remain with deep charity and special reverence in the Lord Your Holiness's dear brother in Christ.

480.   *28 June 1984*

Address by Archbishop Stylianos[75] during the audience with the Holy Father of the Delegation from the Ecumenical Patriarchate for the feast of Saints Peter and Paul [in English]

Your Holiness,

It is for my humble person a great honor and a deep spiritual pleasure to be able to pay Your Holiness a visit on behalf of the Patriarch of Constantinople, especially on this most official day of the patronal feast of the Church of Rome, on the commemoration of the first among the Apostles, Peter and Paul.

Along with the other two members of the Patriarchal Delegation we are sent to bring to Your Holiness and to the Church of Rome the brotherly regards and the warm congratulations of the Patriarch and of the Church of Constantinople on this occasion.

Such an exchange of official congratulatory visits between our two sister Churches on the occasion of the patronal feast of each is, of course, by no means a matter of simple protocol. On the contrary, despite the annual regular repetition, it is not a matter of routine, but indeed constitutes a warm manifestation of mutual love, reverence and fidelity. Equally, the daily repetition of sun rising does not degrade the value of this daily miracle of the Divine Providence.

We come to you, Your Holiness, immediately after the third successful plenary meeting of the Mixed Theological Commission on the Dialogue between our two Churches.[76] I have the high privilege and honor to co-preside, on behalf of the Orthodox, along with His Eminence Cardinal Willebrands, in this Commission. Therefore I can with joy assure you also—as I recently did at the Phanar—that this sacred task is with God's help progressing, in rhythm and in results, in a very satisfactory way. However, we must stress that we do not expect spectacular results, nor do we seek them.

---

75. Born in 1935, Archbishop Stylianos (Harkianakis) since 1975 is the Primate of the Greek Orthodox Church of Australia and Exarch of Oceania, and co-chairman of the International Roman Catholic-Orthodox Commission for Theological Dialogue.

76. The third plenary session of the Joint Commission convened in Crete, 30 May–8 June, 1984. The redrafting of "Faith, Sacraments and the Unity of the Church" was too late for final approval, and an improved text was submitted to the fourth plenary session, in Bari (Italy), 29 May–1 June, 1986. The Bari meeting began discussions on "The Sacrament of Order in the Sacramental Structure of the Church," and continued them at Bari in June 1987.

Spectacular things are the target of the world. The Church is always interested not in spectacles, but in miracles. And it is indeed a miracle, Your Holiness, that bishops and theologians of both Churches are learning again—cooperating with each other in dialogue—to humble themselves together, to search together, to confess together and, thus purified to be enlightened by the common Holy Spirit. Perhaps it is not possible to know exactly how much we have become mature to love each other through the Dialogue of love.

Yet we know that in the theological dialogue, "'speaking the truth in love" (Eph 4:15), we shall not run in vain (cf. Gal 2:2), since we love God and His Church. For "all things work together for good to them that love God" (Rom 8:28).

Pray, Your Holiness, as you did until this day with all the Heads of the Orthodox Autocephalous Churches, that our dialogue may continue to progress according to God's will, in order that gradually it may bring together again all that which the Devil divided and scattered. The task of the Dialogue will not be successful, unless it develops in a directly reverse course to that of the Devil.

Wishing with the other two members of the Patriarchal Delegation—through the supplications of the Apostles celebrated—that your course in the Church and in the world may be long, honorable and apostolic until the very end, I have the honor to hand over to Your Holiness this precious letter of your brother Patriarch Dimitrios, along with his small gift to you. It is a copy of a tray of the 16th century representing the figures of the whole sacred college of the Apostles, a brotherly reminder of our common apostolic descent and at the same time of our common apostolic responsibility in the world.

Ad multos annos, Your Holiness.

481. *28 June 1984*

Address in reply by Pope John Paul II to Archbishop Stylianos [in English]

1. To yourself and to those who are with you I say: you are most welcome. Receiving you with brotherly affection and great joy, I wish of course to do honor to those who have sent you: His Holiness Patriarch Dimitrios I and the Holy Synod of the Church of Constantinople. But I am particularly happy to receive you personally, since I know of

your work as pastor of the Greek Orthodox in Australia, and also that you share with Cardinal Willebrands the presidency of the Commission for the Theological Dialogue between the Catholic Church and the Orthodox Church. Your coming amongst us for the feast of Saints Peter and Paul is a reason for great rejoicing: I am profoundly convinced that personal acquaintance between the pastors of our Churches is a decisive factor for progress in our joint search for full unity. Still more decisive is joint prayer by those pastors for the People of God. Welcome then, in the name of the Lord. May he always bless your steps, and prosper your work.

2. Once again the Feast of Saints Peter and Paul is an occasion for us to meet and celebrate together their memory, just as each year at the Ecumenical Patriarchate there is a common celebration of the memory of Saint Andrew, brother of Peter. Today the words of the Gospel come to our minds: "As he walked by the Sea of Galilee, (Jesus) saw two brothers, Simon who is called Peter and Andrew his brother, casting a net into the sea; for they were fishermen" (Mt 4:18). These two brothers from the beginning live in daily communion, do the same work, collaborate for the same family community, have the same place of work: the lake, now quiet, now stormy (cf. Mt 8:24), now yielding no fish, now an abundant catch (cf. Lk 5:4–7); they experience the same pains and the same joys.

To this common origin succeeds a common vocation: "Follow me, and I will make you fishers of men" (Mt 4:19).

To this common vocation they give an identical answer: "Immediately they left their nets and followed him" (Mt 4:20).

They followed him all their lives, to the final point of martydom. They listened carefully to the Lord's teaching and put it into practice. They heard and carried out the mandate of the risen Lord: "Go therefore and make disciples of all nations . . . teaching them to observe all that I have commanded you" (Mt 28:19–20).

Their preaching has reached us, the Christians of the West and of the East, uniting us in a common vocation to a single mission: to make all peoples into one family established in the acceptance of the teaching which Jesus Christ entrusted to his disciples.

It is by way of uninterrupted apostolic succession that the truth of Christ has come down to us.

The celebration of the Apostles beckons us again in our time to this vocation. Humanity today is like a stormy sea, swept by whirling currents: of unrest, of anxiety, of fear for its uncertain future. But it also feels gentle and calm breezes which induce hope and trust, which call for faith that the Lord is with us "always, even to the close of the age" (Mt 28:19), and which call too for a harmonious witness of faith, of mutual love and joint action.

3. It is for this reason that, in obedience to the Lord's will, our joint attention is concentrated on prayer, on theological dialogue and deeper study. This unity that the community of the baptized needs today should be untarnished; it should be full and perfect. Hence we need to clear up all the questions which hinder full communion in faith. It seems therefore that the Joint Commission for Dialogue chose aptly when it took as a starting point the study of the sacramentality of the Church, and her sacraments. The shared conception of the sacramentality of the Church will give positive support to the whole dialogue. Certainly, the search for unity will in no way mean a search for uniformity. The life of the Church is many sided. It has aimed—in the course of centuries—to answer as fully as possible to different cultural and spiritual needs, giving full value to the patrimony of the various peoples.

This variety has permeated even liturgical life. When such diversity expresses the same faith, not only is it no obstacle to unity, but it is a valuable complementary manifestation of the inexhaustible Christian mystery.

All this enriches dialogue, emphasizing everything that is compatible with unity, the better to face and resolve any doctrinal difficulty.

Such an aim calls for the participation of everybody, especially in prayer which should be fervent and unceasing. Many times we have called for the prayers of all Catholics for this dialogue. I am sure that the same call has been made to the Orthodox faithful.

4. A sound and really fruitful continuation of the theological dialogue will need to be supported by that wider dialogue which we call the dialogue of charity. Fraternal relations between our Churches are being intensified, and so also should be encounters between our respective faithful, as well as practical collaboration and, in certain circumstances, mutual pastoral care, disinterested and open hearted. Mutual love, candid dialogue to bring out the whole truth, and steadily closer contacts, will bring Catholics and Orthodox to full communion of faith within a variety of liturgical, disciplinary, spiritual and theological traditions.

Those holy Apostles, the brothers Peter and Andrew, sustain us by their intercession. They have given us a decisive example: "Immediately they left their nets and followed him." To listen to the Word of God is the decisive factor in our journey together towards full unity.

This joint prayer for the Feast of Saints Peter and Paul and this fraternal encounter are signs of our shared will to follow the Lord in the present and the future. "To him be the glory both now and to the day of eternity. Amen" (2 Pt 3:18).

APPENDIX I

Pope Paul VI and Patriarch Athenagoras I at Jerusalem** *

N. 47   4–6 January 1964

PROTOCOL FOR RECEPTION

1. The Patriarch, escorted by Metropolitans and other clergy, will arrive by car at the Apostolic Delegation.

   A number of Cardinals and Archbishop Dell'Acqua will receive him at the gate. The Holy Father will receive him at the entrance to the building.

2. The Pope and the Patriarch will each deliver a short address when they visit one another. The scripts of these addresses will be exchanged beforehand, but will remain secret until the two visits have taken place, after which they will be made public. On the occasion of the Pope's visit to the Patriarch of Constantinople, the Ecumenical Patriarch will speak in ancient Greek and the Pope in Latin.

3. The Pope and the Patriarch will remain alone at the beginning of the visits which they make to one another. Then the members of the retinues of the Pope and the Patriarch will be brought in, but not other persons.

4. When the Patriarch visits the Pope, Chapter 17 of St. John's Gospel will be read, partly in Greek and partly in Latin.

5. During the Pope's visit to the Patriarch the same ceremonial will be followed, but this time the Lord's Prayer, in Latin and Greek, will be recited.

ATHENAGORAS, METROPOLITAN OF THYATEIRA

A. DELL'ACQUA
Under-Secretary
Rome, 30 December 1963

MEETINGS OF THE POPE AND THE PATRIARCHS

4 January

At Amman: The Holy Father will arrive by air at the Amman airport. Two Archbishops representing the Patriarch of Jerusalem will be at the airport to welcome him. They will take their places immediately after the King [Hussein of Jordania] and the Catholic Patriarchs. Should they wish to go to Jerusalem with the Pontifical cortège, their car will come immediately after that of the Catholic Patriarchs.

At Jerusalem: At the Damascus Gate another delegation from the Greek Orthodox Patriarchate, consisting of Archbishops and other clergy, will be present, and will be assigned a place immediately after the Catholic Patriarchs. After Mass at the Holy Sepulchre, the Holy Father will pass in front of the Greek Orthodox Patriarchate on his way to Bab al Qalil. Patriarch Benediktos has signified his wish to stand at the entrance and wish the Holy Father welcome.

At 7:00 p.m. the Holy Father will receive a visit from the Greek Orthodox Patriarch of Jerusalem, Benediktos, at the Apostolic Delegation.

At 8:00 p.m. the Holy Father will return the visit of the Greek Orthodox Patriarch of Jerusalem, Benediktos, in the Patriarch's summer residence on the Mount of Olives.

5 January

On his return from Nazareth, about 8:30 p.m., the Holy Father will receive the visit of the Patriarch of Constantinople, Athenagoras I.

6 January

On his return from Bethlehem the Holy Father will pay a return visit to the Ecumenical Patriarch Athenagoras I in the Patriarchal residence on the Mount of Olives at about 10:00 a.m.

ATHENAGORAS, METROPOLITAN OF THYATEIRA

A. DELL'ACQUA
Under-Secretary
Rome, 30 December 1963

APPENDIX II

The Prayer Service for Reception of Pope Paul VI at the Ecumenical Patriarchate**

N. 174   25 July 1967

As His Holiness the Pope and His Holiness the Ecumenical Patriarch enter the Patriarchal Cathedral, the choir begins singing:

1. Behold how good it is and how pleasant, where brethren dwell at one!
   For there the Lord has pronounced his blessing, life forever (Ps 132:1.3).†

2. O Lord, our Lord, how glorious is thy name over all the earth (Ps 8:9).

3. The precepts of the Lord are right, rejoicing the heart; the command of the Lord is clear, enlightening the eye (Ps 18:9).

4. The Lord will give strength to his people; the Lord will bless his people with peace (Ps 28:10).

5. Be extolled, O Lord, in thy strength! We will sing, chant the praise of thy might (Ps 28:10).

6. Behold how good it is and how pleasant, where brethren dwell at one! For there the Lord has pronounced his blessing, life for ever (Ps 132:3).

First Deacon: Sir, give the blessing.
Priest: Blessed be the kingdom of the Father, the Son, and the Holy Spirit now and for ever, world without end.
Choir: Amen. *Then the Troparia*

1. Blessed be thou, Christ our God, who hast made simple fishermen full of wisdom by sending them the Holy Spirit, and through them hast taken the whole world in thy net. Glory be to thee, lover of mankind!

---

† The numbering of the Psalms in this and the following liturgies is that of the Greek Septuagint and Latin Vulgate versions, which from the second part of Ps 9 are usually one behind the Hebrew arrangement followed in most modern Bibles.

2. Princes of the Apostles and teachers of the world, plead with the Master of all things that he may bestow peace on the world and show great mercy on our souls.

3. Protectress of Christians, never confounded, enduring mediatrix with the Creator, fail not to regard the voice of sinners as they make their suppliant prayer, but in thy kindness hasten to our aid as with faith we cry to thee: "Be prompt to intercede for us, be our speedy supplicant, O Mother of God, thou who dost always protect those who honor thee!"

Then four verses from the Great Doxology

1. Glory to thee, who dost show us the light. Glory be to God in the highest; peace on earth and good will to men.

2. Thou who sittest at the right hand of the Father, receive our prayer, and have mercy on us.

3. Blessed be thou Lord, the God of our fathers, and praised and glorified be thy name for ever. Amen.

4. Stretch forth thy mercy to all who know thee. Holy God, Holy Strong One, Holy Immortal One, have mercy on us.

First Deacon:	Have mercy on us, God, according to thy great mercy; we beseech thee, hear us and have mercy on us.
Choir:	Lord have mercy (thrice). (The same is said after each of the following prayers.)
Second Deacon:	Again we pray thee for the most holy Pope of Rome, Paul, and for our Archbishop and Patriarch Athenagoras, that their steps may be guided to every good work.
First Deacon:	Again let us pray for rulers and those in authority, that the Lord God may speak good things to their hearts.
Second Deacon:	Again let us pray for the good estate of the holy Churches of God and for the union of all.
First Deacon:	Again let us pray for the peace and good condition of the whole world.

Second Deacon:	Again let us pray that the Lord God may hear the voice of our supplication and have mercy on us.
The Patriarch:	Hear us, O God our Savior, hope of all the ends of the earth and of those who are far off at sea, and thou who art a gracious Master be gracious to us in our sins, and have mercy on us. For thou art a God of pity and lover of man, and to thee do we offer glory, to the Father, Son, and Holy Spirit, now and for all ages.
Choir:	Amen.
First Deacon:	Let us pray to the Lord.
His Holiness the Pope and His Holiness the Patriarch, together:	Our Father . . . For thine is the kingdom, the power, and the glory, now and for ever, Amen.
Choir:	Glory be to thee, Lord, glory to thee.

The addresses by His Holiness the Pope and His Holiness the Patriarch (see NN. 172, 173).

Then His Holiness the Pope gives a blessing (in Latin):
> May the grace of our Lord Jesus Christ, and the love of God, and the fellowship of the Holy Spirit be with you all.

Similarly His Holiness the Patriarch gives a blessing:
> May the blessing of the Lord and his mercy come upon you, by his divine grace and love for man, always, now, and for all ages. Amen.

The Choir sings the **Polychronion** *of His Holiness the Pope:*
> May the Lord God give a long life to the very holy and blessed Pope of Rome, Paul VI. Lord, keep him for many years, for many years, for many years.

And the **Polychronion** *of His Holiness the Patriarch:*
> May the Lord God give a long life to our most holy Head and Master, the Ecumenical Patriarch, Athenagoras I. Lord, keep him for many years, for many years, for many years.

The Priest: Lord Jesus Christ our God, through the prayers of our holy Fathers have mercy on us and save us.

Choir: Amen.

As His Holiness the Pope and His Holiness the Patriarch are making their way out of the Cathedral, the choir sings the same Psalms as those used at the beginning.

APPENDIX III

The Prayer Service at the Cathedral of the Holy Spirit in the Presence of Pope Paul VI and of Patriarch Athenagoras I*** *

N. 177   25 July 1967

Veni, Creator Spiritus,
Mentes tuorum visita:
Imple superna gratia
Quae tu creasti pectora.

All rise and sing in Latin:

Qui diceris Paraclitus,
Altissimum donum Dei,
Fons vivus, ignis, caritas,
Et spiritalis unctio.

Tu septiformis munere,
Digitus paternae dexterae,
Tu rite promissum Patris,
Sermone ditans guttura.

Accende lumen sensibus,
Infunde amorem cordibus,
Infirma nostri corporis
Virtute firmans perpeti.

Hostem repellas longius,
Pacemque dones protinus,
Ductore sic te praevio,
Vitemus omne noxium.

Per te sciamus da Patrem,
Noscamus atque Filium:
Teque utriusque Spiritum
Credamus omni tempore.

Deo Patri sit gloria,
Et Filio, qui a mortuis
Surrexit, ac Paraclito,
In saeculorum saecula. Amen.

The Holy Father: Emitte Spritium tuum et creabuntur.
All: Et renovabis faciem terrae.
The Holy Father: Deus, qui corda fidelium Sancti Spiritus illustra-
                   tione docuisti; da nobis in eodem Spiritu recta sap-
                   ere, et de eius semper consolatione gaudere. Per
                   Christum Dominum nostrum.
All: Amen.

First Reading (Eph 3:8–21)

To me, the least of all believers, was given the grace to preach to the Gentiles the unfathomable riches of Christ and to enlighten all men on the mysterious design which for ages was hidden in God, the Creator of all. Now, therefore, through the Church, God's manifold wisdom is made known to the principalities and powers of heaven, in accordance with his age old purpose, carried out in Christ Jesus our Lord. In Christ and through faith in him we can speak freely to God, drawing near him with confidence. Hence, I beg you not to be disheartened by the trials I endure for you; they are your glory.

That is why I kneel before the Father from whom every family in heaven and on earth takes its name; and I pray he will bestow on you gifts in keeping with the riches of his glory. May he strengthen you inwardly through the working of his Spirit. May Christ dwell in your-hearts through faith, and may charity be the root and foundation of your life. Thus you will be able to grasp fully, with all the holy ones, the breadth and length and height and depth of Christ's love, and experience this love which surpasses all knowledge, so that you may attain to the fulness of God himself.

To him whose power now at work in us can do immeasurably more than we can ask or imagine—to him be glory in the Church and in Christ Jesus through all generations, world without end. Amen.

Hymn: "Ubi caritas et amor" ("Where there is charity and love"),
           in Latin.
Cantors: Ubi caritas et amor, Deus ibi est.
Others: Ubi caritas et amor, Deus ibi est.
Cantors: Congregavit nos in unum Christi amor.
           Exultemus et in ipso iucundemur.
           Timeamus et amemus Deum vivum.
           Et ex corde diligamus nos sincero.
All: Ubi caritas et amor, Deus ibi est.
Cantors: Simul ergo cum in unum congregamur,
           Ne nos mente dividamur, caveamus.

Cessent iurgia maligna, cessent lites.
Et in medio nostri sit Christus Deus.
All: Ubi caritas et amor, Deus ibi est.
Cantors: Simul ergo cum in unum congregamur,
Ne nos mente dividamur, caveamus,
Cessent iurgia maligna, cessent lites.
Et in medio nostri sit Christus Deus.
All: Ubi caritas et amor, Deus ibi est.
Cantors: Simul quoque cum beatis videamus
Glorianter vultum tuum, Christe Deus:
Gaudium, quod est immensum atque probum.
Saecula per infinita saeculorum.
All: Amen.

Second Reading (Jn 14:23–30)

Anyone who loves me will be true to my word, and my Father will love him; we will come to him and make our dwelling place with him. He who does not love me does not keep my words. Yet the word you hear is not mine; it comes from the Father who sent me. This much have I told you while I was still with you; the Paraclete, the Holy Spirit, whom the Father will send in my name, will instruct you in everything, and remind you of all that I told you. "Peace" is my farewell to you, my peace is my gift to you; I do not give it to you as the world gives peace. Do not be distressed or fearful. You have heard me say, "I go away for a while, and I come back to you." If you truly loved me, you would rejoice to have me go to the Father, for the Father is greater than I. I tell you this now before it takes place, so that when it takes place you may believe. I shall not go on speaking to you longer; the Prince of this world is at hand. He has no hold on me, but the world must know that I love the Father and do as the Father has commanded me.

Litany

Dear brethren, let us beseech the God of our fathers that he may deign to preserve in his Church the wonders of his power and mercy, and that he may give to the nations and to mankind peace based on charity and justice.

a) That all those who believe in Christ may be preserved from all evil and made perfect in his love, let us pray to the Lord.

Response: Kyrie eleison.

b) That his Holiness Pope Paul VI, His Holiness the Ecumenical Patriarch Athenagoras I, and the pastors of all the Christian communions may be faithful servants of the Gospel of Christ, let us pray to the Lord.

Response: Kryie eleison.

c) That the Lord's word may be fulfilled in all those who bear the name of Christ, and that they may have perfect unity, let us pray to the Lord.

Response: Kyrie eleison.

d) That those who are here assembled, and those who throughout the world are praying with us, may be workers for peace, love and justice, let us pray to the Lord.

Response: Kyrie eleison.

e) That those who are in positions of government in this country, and those who rule or exercise authority in the world may be blessed and enlightened in their work, so that there may be true peace and concord between men and nations, let us pray to the Lord.

Response: Kyrie eleison.

f) For every soul undergoing trial and affliction, for all who need the mercy of God and the help of their brother men, for all who are looking for the light of Christ, let us pray to the Lord.

Response: Kryie eleison.

The Holy Father:
Deliver us, Lord, from every evil, past, present and to come, and by the intercession of the blessed and glorious ever-virgin Mother of God, Mary, of your holy Apostles Peter and Paul, and of all the saints, grant us peace in our day, so that through the help of your loving-kindness we may be ever free from all sin, and safe from all anxiety. Through Jesus Christ your Son, Our Lord, who lives and reigns with you in the unity of the Holy Spirit, one God for ever and ever.

At this point the Brief Anno Ineunte *is read aloud* (cf. N.176).

Final Invocation: The grace of Our Lord Jesus Christ, the love of God, and the fellowship of the Holy Spirit be with you all.

The Magnificat sung in Latin
Magnificat anima mea Dominum:
Et exultavit spiritus meas in Deo salutari meo.
Quia respexit humilitatem ancillae suae: ecce enim ex hoc
　　beatam me dicent omnes generationes.
Quia fecit mihi magna qui potens est: et sanctum nomen eius.
Et misericordia eius a progenie in progenies timentibus eum.
Fecit potentiam in brachio suo: dispersit superbos mente cordis sui.
Desposuit potentes de sede, et exaltavit humiles.
Esurientes implevit bonis: et divites dimisit inanes.
Suscepit Israel, puerum suum, recordatus misericordiae suae.
Sicut locutus est ad patres nostros, Abraham, et semini eius in saecula.
Gloria Patri et Filio et Spiritui Sancto, sicut erat in principio et nunc
　　et semper: et in saecula saeculorum.
　　Amen.

APPENDIX IV

Liturgical Celebration at St. Peter's Basilica, Rome, for Reception of Patriarch Athenagoras I*** ** *

N. 191   26 October 1967

1. ENTRANCE

The Patriarch will be welcomed by the Holy Father on the porch of St. Peter's. The procession will pass by the Chapel of the Blessed Sacrament and the altar of the Blessed Virgin on its way to the altar of the Confessio [the main altar over the site of the early shrine called Confessio Petri]. Meanwhile the entrance Psalm is sung.

Choir:
A new commandment I give you:
that you love one another, as I have loved you,
says the Lord.

All:
A new commandment I give you:
that you love one another, as I have loved you,
says the Lord.

Psalm 118

1. Ah, how happy those of blameless life,
   who walk in the law of the Lord.

   Antiphon: A new commandment . . .

2. I will meditate on your precepts
   and consider your ways.

   Ant.

3. I run the way of your commandments,
   since you have set me free.

   Ant.

4. Look how I yearn for your precepts:
   give me life by your righteousness.

   Ant.

497

5. So, having sought your precepts,
   I shall walk in all freedom.

   Ant.

6. Your commandments fill me with delight,
   I love them deeply.

   Ant.

7. Meditating all day on your Law,
   how have I come to love it!

   Ant.

8. Your promise, how sweet to my palate!
   Sweeter than honey to my mouth!

   Ant.

9. Now your word is a lamp to my feet,
   a light on my path.

   Ant.

10. Your decrees are so wonderful
    my soul cannot but respect them.

    Ant.

    Glory be to the Father, the Son, and the Holy Spirit, as it was in
    the beginning, is now, and ever shall be, world without end. Amen.

2. INTRODUCTORY PRAYER

The Holy Father:
Let us pray.
All remain silent for a moment in prayer.

   God our Father, you bring many nations together to unite in praising your name. Make us able and willing to do what you ask. May the
people you call to your kingdom be one in faith and love. We ask this

through our Lord Jesus Christ, your Son, who lives and reigns with you and the Holy Spirit, one God for ever and ever.

All: Amen.

3. READINGS

After the prayer all sit down for the first reading.

A Reading from the Epistle of St. Paul to the Philippians (2:1–11).

In the name of the encouragement you owe me in Christ, in the name of the solace that love can give, of fellowship in spirit, compassion, and pity, I beg you: may my joy complete by your unanimity, possessing the one love, united in spirit and ideals. Never act out of rivalry or conceit; rather, let all parties think humbly of others as superior to themselves, each of you looking to others interests rather than his own. Your attitude must be that of Christ. Though he was in the form of God, he did not deem equality with God something to be grasped at. Rather, he emptied himself and took the form of a slave, being born in the likeness of men. He was known to be of human estate, and it was thus that he humbled himself, obediently accepting even death, death on a cross. Because of this, God highly exalted him and bestowed on him the name above every other name. So that at Jesus' name every knee must bend, in the heavens, on the earth and under the earth, and every tongue proclaim to the glory of God the Father: JESUS CHRIST IS LORD'.

Responsorial Song in Latin:

"Ubi caritas et amor, Deus ibi est" (for Latin text see the prayer service in the Cathedral of the Holy Spirit, Istanbul, Appendix III).

Antiphon: Where there is charity and love, there the God of love abides.

The love of Christ has gathered us as one;
Rejoice in him with joy which he imparts:
Let us revere and love the living God,
And love each other with unfailing hearts.

Ant.

And so, when we are gathered here as one,
Let quarrels die, and envious rancour cease;

Be our resolve all bitterness to shun,
And in our midst be Christ, his love and peace.

Ant.

O lead us, Master, by your saving grace,
To where the Blessed glory in your sight;
There let us see and love you, face to face,
Gathered once more in everlasting light.

Ant.

(The following section, leading up to and including the Gospel, will be sung in Greek.)

Deacon:	Wisdom! Let us arise and listen to the Holy Gospel.
The Patriarch:	Peace be with you.
Choir:	And with your spirit.
Deacon:	A reading from the holy Gospel according to St. John.
Choir:	Glory be to you, Lord, glory to you.
Deacon:	Let us pay close attention.

St. John 13:1–15

Before the feast of Passover, Jesus realized that the hour had come for him to pass from this world to the Father. He had loved his own in this world, and would show his love for them to the end. The devil had already induced Judas, son of Simon Iscariot, to hand him over; and so, during the supper, Jesus—fully aware that he had come from God and was going to God, the Father who had handed everything over to him—rose from the meal and took off his cloak. He picked up a towel and tied it round himself. Then he poured water into a basin and began to wash his disciples' feet and dry them with the towel he had around him. Thus he came to Simon Peter, who said to him, "Lord, are you going to wash my feet?" Jesus answered, "You may not realize now what I am doing but later you will understand." Peter replied, "You shall never wash my feet!" "If I do not wash you," Jesus answered, "you will have no share in my heritage." "Lord," Simon Peter said to him, "then not only my feet, but my hands and head as well." Jesus told him, "The man who has bathed has no need to wash; he is entirely cleansed, just as you are; though not all." (The reason he said, "Not all are washed clean," was that he knew his betrayer.) After he had washed their feet, he put his cloak back on and reclined at table once more. He said to them: "Do you understand what I just did for you? You address me as 'Teacher' and 'Lord,' and fittingly enough, for that is what I am. But if I washed your feet—I who am Teacher and Lord—then you must wash each other's feet. What I just did was to give you an example: as I have done, so you must do."

4. PRAYER OF THE FAITHFUL

(In Italian) Dear brethren, let us ardently implore the mercy of our Lord Jesus Christ: as he came into the world to bring the Good News to the poor and to heal the contrite of heart, so may he bring salvation today to all who are in need.

   a) *(In Italian)* That all who believe in Christ may be preserved from every evil and may be made perfect in his love: let us pray to the Lord.

   Response: Kyrie eleison, Kyrie eleison, Kyrie eleison.

   b) *(In Greek)* Again let us pray for His Holiness the Pope of Rome, Paul, and for the Archbishop and Patriarch Athenagoras, that their steps may be guided to every good work.

   Response: Kyrie eleison, etc.

   c) *(In French)* That the word of the Lord may be fulfilled in all those who bear the name of Christ, and that their unity may be perfect: let us pray to the Lord.

   Response: Kyrie eleison, etc.

   d) *(In English)* For all who are gathered here, for those from all over the world who pray with us, that we may devote ourselves to the words of peace, of love and of justice: let us pray to the Lord.

   Response: Kyrie eleison, etc.

   e) *(In German)* That the Lord may bless and enlighten all those who rule and exercise power in the world in their endeavors for peace and concord between men and nations: let us pray.

   Response: Kyrie eleison, etc.

f) *(In Spanish)* For all Christian souls who are undergoing trial and affliction, for all those who stand in need of the mercy and help of God, and for all who are seeking the light of Christ: let us pray to the Lord.

Response: Kyrie eleison, etc.

The Holy Father (in Latin)
O God, you who have made love for you and our neighbour the fulfilment of all the commandments, hear and grant the prayers that out of love for your Name we have brought before you. Through Christ Our Lord.
All: Amen.

5. THANKSGIVING

The Holy Father
The Lord be with you.
R. And with your spirit.
V. Lift up your hearts.
R. We lift them up to the Lord.
V. Let us give thanks to the Lord our God.
R. It is right to give them thanks and praise.

Father all powerful and ever living God,
we do well always and everywhere to give you thanks.
Through your only begotten Son,
Jesus Christ our Lord,
you have brought us to the recognition
of your truth,
so that linked by one faith and baptism
we may become his Body.
Through him you have poured forth on all nations
your Holy Spirit,
who brings about wonders
in gifts of every kind,
and distributes different graces;
who enables tongues
to preach your word,
and makes unity arise;
who has his abode in all believers,
and fills and governs the whole Church.
And so the whole wide world

exults and rejoices,
while the powers above
and all the angels of heaven
sing for ever to your glory:

(All take up the "Sanctus" in Latin)
Holy, holy, holy Lord,
God of power and might,
heaven and earth are full of your glory.
Hosanna in the highest.
Blessed is he who comes in the name of the Lord.
Hosanna in the highest.

The Holy Father
You are indeed holy,
King of the ages and source of unity;
you have gathered the different nations into one
to proclaim with faith your name.
Holy is your only begotten Son,
who on the night he was betrayed
prayed that all who believed should be one,
and gave up his body and blood
as a sacrament of unity.
Holy too is your Spirit,
through whom it was your will
to call and bring together
the people of the new covenant,
in a unity of faith, hope, and charity.
Through him, too, you have awakened the minds of Christians,
so that, in a penitent spirit,
they should spend themselves in devoted toil,
seeking to bring to perfection
the unity of the Body of Christ.
All of us indeed who are united
in the same proclamation of the Gospel
and the same baptism,
and are sharers in the same sacraments and gifts of the Spirit
and together enjoy the protection
of Mary, the most holy Mother of God and ever-virgin,
and are thoroughly instructed by the example
of Apostles and Saints,
feel deep distress that for centuries
through the tragedy of division we have gone our separate ways

and have been held back from that full fellowship
which would be a witness to the world.
Look down then on us, your servants,
who, enlightened by the grace of your Spirit,
and led by brotherly love,
are sorry for our sins against unity,
and humbly ask pardon from you and our brothers,
as with one voice we implore you
to grant perfect unity among all who believe in you.
We beseech you then Lord, lover of man,
to grant us today a new and fuller
outpouring of the grace of your Spirit.
Cause us to lead a life
worthy of the calling to which we have been called,
with all lowliness and meekness,
with patience bearing with one another in love,
eager to maintain the unity of the Spirit
in the bond of peace,
so that, recognizing the signs of the times,
and redeeming our past mistakes
by an unwearied pursuit of unselfishness,
we may deserve to reach the hour
of that perfect communion
for which we have so longed.
Hear us favorably then, O Lord,
and manifest in our regard
the fulness of your ancient mercies.
By the power of your Spirit as he comes upon us,
put an end to division among the Churches,
renew the beauty of the Bride of Christ,
pour out in abundance your love and your peace,
so that the Church may shine with greater brilliance
as a sign lifted up among the nations,
and the world, enlightened by your Spirit,
may attain to faith in the Christ whom you have sent.
Make us, all of us, sons of light and peace,
and grant that, having here and now some presage of eternity,
we may, with one heart and voice,
glorify your mysterious name,
Father, Son, and Holy Spirit,
now and for ever through the ages to come.

All: Amen.

6. THE LORD'S PRAYER

The whole congregation will sing the Pater Noster in Latin

The Holy Father:
Oremus. Praeceptis salutaribus moniti et divina institutione formati, audemus dicere:
    All:
Pater noster, qui es in caelis, santificetur nomen tuum; adveniat regnum tuum; fiat voluntas tua sicut in caelo et in terra. Panem nostrum quotidianum da nobis hodie; et dimitte nobis debita nostra sicut et nos dimittimus debitoribus nostris; et ne nos inducas in tentationem, sed libera nos a malo.

    The Holy Father:
Deliver us, Lord, from every evil, past present and to come, and by the intercession of the blessed and glorious ever-virgin Mother of God, Mary, of your holy Apostles Peter and Paul, and of all the saints, grant us peace in our day, so that through the help of your loving-kindness we may be ever free from all sin, and safe from all anxiety. Through Jesus Christ your Son, Our Lord, who lives and reigns with you in the unity of the Holy Spirit, one God for ever and ever.

7. ADDRESS BY THE PATRIARCH
(SEE N. 198)

8. ADDRESS BY THE HOLY FATHER
(SEE N. 190)

9. KISS OF PEACE

The Holy Father and the Patriarch exchange the kiss of peace. Then the Holy Father exchanges the kiss of peace with the four Metropolitans of the Patriarch's retinue, while the Patriarch does the same with the three Cardinals from the Papal escort and the Cardinal Arch-Priest of the Basilica. The senior Cardinal and the first of the Metropolitans then communicate the kiss of peace to the Synod of Bishops and the members of the Patriarch's retinue respectively.

10. FINAL PRAYER BY THE PATRIARCH

The Patriarch (in Greek):

Master rich in mercy, our Lord and God Jesus Christ, you have given us to make these prayers together and in harmony, and you have promised to grant the entreaties of two or three who come together in concord in your name; fulfil now the supplications of your servants as they pray for what is to their good; give peace to the Church and the world, and enable us to do your holy will in the knowledge of your truth. For you are the King of Peace and Savior of our souls, and to you we render glory, to the Father, Son, and Holy Spirit, now and for ever, world without end.

All: Amen.

11. BENEDICTION

The Holy Father (in Latin):

May the blessing of almighty God, Father, Son, and Holy Spirit, descend upon you and remain for ever.

All: Amen.

The Patriarch (in Greek):

May the blessing and mercy of the Lord come upon you, by his grace and love of man, now and for ever, world without end.

All: Amen.

The ceremony ends with the singing of Psalm 97, during which time the Holy Father and the Patriarch make their way out of the Basilica.

Choir:

Sing to the Lord a new song: from the ends of the earth is his praise, alleluia.

All:

Sing to the Lord a new song: from the ends of the earth is his praise, alleluia.

Psalm 97(98)

1. His right hand has won victory for him,
   his holy arm.

   Ant. Sing to the Lord . . .

2. The Lord has made his salvation known:
   in the sight of the nations he has revealed his justice.

   Ant.

3. He has rememberd his kindness and his faithfulness
   toward the house of Israel.

   Ant.

4. All the ends of the earth have seen the salvation by
   our God.

   Ant.

5. Sing joyfully to the Lord, all you lands;
   break into song, sing praise.

   Ant.

6. Sing praise to the Lord with the harp,
   with the harp and melodious song,
   with trumpets and the sound of the horn.

   Ant.

7. Sing joyfully before the king, the Lord,
   Let the sea and what fills it resound,
   the world and those who dwell in it.

   Ant.

8. Let the rivers clap their hands,
   the mountains shout with them for joy,
   before the Lord, for he comes to rule the earth.

   Ant.

9. He will rule the earth with justice
   and the peoples with equity.

   Ant.

10. Glory be to the Father, and to the Son, and to the Holy
    Spirit, as it was in the beginning, is now, and ever
    shall be, world without end.

   Ant.

CHRONOLOGICAL TABLE OF DOCUMENTS

1962:

8. 27 February 1962 — Letter of Monsignor John Willebrands to Patriarch Athenagoras, thanking him for the Monsignor's first visit to the Phanar

9. 28 February 1962 — Letter of Cardinal Bea to Patriarch Athenagoras, thanking him for the welcome given to Monsignor Willebrands

10. 12 April 1962 — Reply of the Patriarch Athenagoras to Cardinal Bea

11. 12 April 1962 — Reply of the Patriarch Athenagoras to Monsignor John Willebrands

12. 18 April 1962 — Letter of Monsignor Willebrands to Patriarch Athenagoras about contacts with other Christian bodies to examine the possibility of having observers sent to the Second Vatican Council

13. 21 April 1962 — Telegram from Metropolitan Maximos to Cardinal Bea, asking him to convey to the Pope the Easter wishes of the Patriarch

14. 5 May 1962 — Telegram from Cardinal Bea to Metropolitan Maximos, conveying the thanks and good wishes of Pope John to Patriarch Athenagoras

15. 18 June 1962 — Letter of Cardinal Bea to Patriarch Athenagoras thanking him for the welcome which he gave to Monsignor Willebrands

16. 29 June 1962 — Letter of Patriarch Athenagoras to Cardinal Bea

		sympathy and good wishes for the recovery of the Pope's health
25.	1 June 1963	Telegram from Cardinal Amleto Cicognani, Secretary of State, to Patriarch Athenagoras, thanking him on behalf of the Pope
26.	4 June 1963	Statement of Patriarch Athenagoras at a meeting of the Holy Synod on the death of Pope John XXIII
27.	5 June 1963	Telegram from Archimandrite Symeon, Chief Secretary of the Holy Synod, to Cardinal Cicognani, expressing the condolence of the Patriarch and the Synod on the death of Pope John XXIII
28.	7 June 1963	Telegram from Cardinal Aloisi Masella, Chamberlain, to Archimandrite Symeon, thanking the Patriarch and the Holy Synod for their sympathy and prayers
29.	25 June 1963	Letter of Cardinal Bea to the Patriarch Athenagoras, announcing the election of Pope Paul VI
30.	8 July 1963	Letter of Cardinal Bea to the Patriarch Athenagoras, conveying Pope Paul's invitation to send observers to the Second Session of Vatican Council II
31.	22 August 1963	Letter of Patriarch Athenagoras to Cardinal Bea, acknowledging receipt of the invitation
32.	9 September 1963	Letter of Metropolitan Maximos to Pope Paul VI, conveying the congratulations of the Patriarch on his election to the See of Rome

42. 27 December 1963   Telegram from Pope Paul VI to the
                            Patriarch Athenagoras, conveying his
                            best wishes for the Christmas season

43. 28 December 1963   Telegram from Cardinal Bea, sending
                            his good wishes to the Patriarch

44. 28 December 1963   Address by the Metropolitan Athena-
                            goras of Thyateira, on the occasion of
                            his visit to Pope Paul VI

45. 30 December 1963   Telegram from Pope Paul VI to Patri-
                            arch Athenagoras, expressing joy at the
                            prospect of their coming encounter

46. 30 December 1963   Letter of Pope Paul VI to Patriarch
                            Athenagoras, thanking him for sending
                            the Metropolitan Athenagoras of
                            Thyateira

47. 30 December 1963   Procedural arrangements for the meet-
                            ing of the Pope and the Patriarch,
                            signed by Metropolitan Athenagoras of
                            Thyateira and Archbishop Angelo
                            dell'Acqua, Deputy Secretary of State
                            (see Appendix I)

                            1964:

48. 5 January 1964   Address of Patriarch Athenagoras to
                            Pope Paul VI in the Apostolic Delega-
                            tion on the Mount of Olives in
                            Jerusalem

49. 6 January 1964   Allocution of Pope Paul VI to Patri-
                            arch Athenagoras, delivered in the
                            Patriarchal residence on the Mount of
                            Olives in Jerusalem

50. 6 January 1964   Common communiqué of the Pope
                            and Patriarch, published after their
                            meeting

61.	18 April 1964	Letter of Pope Paul VI to Patriarch Athenagoras, introducing the Papal delegation
62.	19 April 1964	Telegram from Patriarch Athenagoras to Pope Paul VI, thanking him for his telegram of 2 March
63.	23 April 1964	Telegram from Patriarch Athenagoras to Cardinal Bea thanking him for the visit of the Papal delegation
64.	29 April 1964	Telegram from Cardinal Bea to Patriarch Athenagoras, thanking him for the welcome given to the Papal delegation
65.	19 May 1964	Letter of Patriarch Athenagoras to Pope Paul VI, thanking him for the visit of the Papal representatives and for the letter brought by Archbishop Martin of Rouen
66.	20 June 1964	Letter of Cardinal Bea to Patriarch Athenagoras, informing him of the Pope's decision to restore the relic of St. Andrew to the Church of Patras
67.	27 June 1964	Telegram from Patriarch Athenagoras to Pope Paul VI, thanking him for the transference of the relic of St. Andrew
68.	27 June 1964	Telegram from Patriarch Athenagoras to Bishop Willebrands on the occasion of his episcopal ordination
69.	28 June 1964	Telegram from Patriarch Athenagoras to Pope Paul VI for the feast of his patron saint
70.	29 June 1964	Telegram from Pope Paul VI to Patriarch Athenagoras, thanking him for the two preceding telegrams

71. 3 July 1964   Letter of Cardinal Bea to Patriarch
                                   Athenagoras, sending him a copy of the
                                   letter addressed to the heads of the
                                   Orthodox Churches, inviting them to
                                   send observers to the Third Session of
                                   the Vatican Council

72. 8 September 1964   Telegram from Patriarch Athenagoras
                                   to Cardinal Bea, telling him of the
                                   decision of the Holy Synod to send
                                   three observers to the Third Session of
                                   the Council

73. 10 September 1964   Telegram from Patriarch Athenagoras
                                   to Cardinal Bea, giving the names of
                                   two delegated observers to the Council

74. 11 September 1964   Telegram from Cardinal Bea to Patri-
                                   arch Athenagoras, thanking him for
                                   sending delegated observers

75. 24 October 1964   Telegram from Patriarch Athenagoras
                                   to Cardinal Bea, giving the name of a
                                   third observer for the Vatican Council

76. 29 October 1964   Message from Pope Paul VI to the
                                   Third Pan-Orthodox Conference of
                                   Rhodes

77. 5 November 1964   Telegram from Metropolitan Meliton
                                   to Pope Paul VI, thanking him for his
                                   message

78. 19 November 1964   Letter of Pope Paul VI to Patriarch
                                   Athenagoras, sending him an episcopal
                                   ring which had belonged to Pope John
                                   XXIII

79. 28 November 1964   Telegram from Patriarch Athenagoras
                                   to Pope Paul VI on the occasion of his
                                   journey to Bombay

80. 1 December 1964   Telegram in reply from Pope Paul VI to Patriarch Athenagoras

81. 21 December 1964   Telegram from Pope Paul VI to Patriarch Athenagoras, sending him good wishes for the feasts of Christmas and New Year

82. 23 December 1964   Telegram from Patriarch Athenagoras to Pope Paul VI sending his good wishes in return

83. 24 December 1964   Telegram from Patriarch Athenagoras to Pope Paul VI, thanking him for his letter of 19 November

1965:

84. 2 January 1965   Telegram from Patriarch Athenagoras to Pope Paul VI, recalling the first anniversary of their meeting in Jerusalem

85. 5 January 1965   Telegram in reply from Pope Paul VI to Patriarch Athenagoras

86. 25 January 1965   Letter of Patriarch Athenagoras to Pope Paul VI, announcing the coming to Rome of a Patriarchal delegation with instructions to communicate the decisions of the Third Pan-Orthodox Conference of Rhodes

87. 16 February 1965   Address of the Metropolitan Meliton of Helioupolis and Theira to Pope Paul VI

88. 16 February 1965   Reply of Pope Paul VI on his reception of the Metropolitans Meliton of Helioupolis and Theira and Chrysostom of Myra

89. 23 February 1965   Letter of Cardinal Bea to Patriarch Athenagoras, thanking him for the visit of the Patriarchal delegation

90. 8 March 1965   Letter from Patriarch Athenagoras to Cardinal Bea, thanking him for his letter of 23 February

91. 11 March 1965   Telegram from Patriarch Athenagoras to Pope Paul VI, thanking him for the welcome given to the Patriarchal delegation

92. 31 March 1965   Letter of Pope Paul VI to Patriarch Athenagoras telling him that a Papal delegation headed by Cardinal Bea will be coming, and emphasizing the harmony between the decisions of the Third Pan-Orthodox Conference and the Decree of the Vatican Council, *"Unitatis Redintegratio"*

93. 3 April 1965   Address delivered by Cardinal Bea during his visit to Patriarch Athenagoras

94. 3 April 1965   Address of Patriarch Athenagoras in welcoming Cardinal Bea

95. 4 April 1965   Address of welcome to Cardinal Bea at the Theological College of Halki, given by Bishop Andrew of Claudioupolis on behalf of the Rector

96. 4 April 1965   Address of Cardinal Bea at the Theological College of Halki

97. 10 April 1965   Letter of Cardinal Bea to Patriarch Athenagoras, thanking him for the welcome

98. 15 April 1965   Telegram from Patriarch Athenagoras to Pope Paul VI, sending him Easter greetings

99. 18 April 1965

Telegram from Pope Paul VI to Patriarch Athenagoras sending him Easter greetings

100. 31 May 1965

Letter of Cardinal Bea to Patriarch Athenagoras, inviting him to send observers to the Fourth Session of the Vatican Council

101. 10 June 1965

Letter of Patriarch Athenagoras to Cardinal Bea, assuring him that the names of the observers will soon be forwarded

102. 13 June 1965

Letter to Pope Paul VI from Patriarch Athenagoras, brought by Metropolitan Meliton, in reply to the Pope's letter of 31 March

103. 18 June 1965

Telegram from Patriarch Athenagoras to Pope Paul VI on the second anniversary of his election to the See of Rome

104. 21 June 1965

Telegram from Pope Paul VI to Patriarch Athenagoras, thanking him for his good wishes

105. 23 June 1965

Telegram from Patriarch Athenagoras to Pope Paul VI on his patronal feast

106. 27 June 1965

Telegram from Pope Paul VI to Patriarch Athenagoras, thanking him for his good wishes

107. 9 July 1965

Letter of Cardinal Bea to Patriarch Athenagoras in reply to the Patriarch's letter of 12 June

108. 10 July 1965

Letter of Pope Paul VI to Patriarch Athenagoras, thanking him for the presence in Rome of Metropolitan Meliton, and for the gift of an icon of

118. 2 October 1965   Telegram from Pope Paul VI to Patriarch Athenagoras, thanking him for his good wishes on the occasion of his last journey

119. 18 October 1965   Letter of Cardinal Bea to Patriarch Athenagoras about the anathemas of 1054

120. 12 November 1965   Letter of Pope Paul VI to Patriarch Athenagoras thanking him for his prayer for the success of the Council

121. 16 November 1965   Letter of Cardinal Bea to Patriarch Athenagoras, giving him the names of the Catholic members of the Joint Commission appointed to study the anathemas of 1054

122. 22 November 1965   Address of Metropolitan Meliton of Helioupolis and Theira, Co-President of the Joint Commission, at the inception of its work

123. 22 November 1965   Address of Bishop John Willebrands, Co-President of the Joint Commission, in reply to the address of Metropolitan Meliton (a summary based on notes taken during the speech)

124. 23 November 1965   Minutes of the proceedings of the Joint Commission

125. 2 December 1965   Letter of Patriarch Athenagoras, thanking Pope Paul VI for his letter of 12 November

126. 2 December 1965   Letter of Patriarch Athenagoras to Cardinal Bea on the work of the Joint Commission

136. 23 June 1966   Telegram from Patriarch Athenagoras to Pope Paul VI on the occasion of his patronal feast

137. 25 June 1966   Telegram in reply from the Pope to Patriarch Athenagoras

138. 29 June 1966   Telegram from Patriarch Athenagoras to Pope Paul for the feast of St. Paul

139. 2 July 1966   Telegram from Pope Paul VI in reply to Patriarch Athenagoras

140. 28 July 1966   Telegram from Pope Paul VI to Patriarch Athenagoras, thanking him for the welcome given to the Pope's brother

141. 7 December 1966   Telegram from Patriarch Athenagoras to Pope Paul VI on the first anniversary of the mutual lifting of the anathemas

142. 7 December 1966   Declaration of Patriarch Athenagoras on the first anniversary of the mutual lifting of the anathemas

143. 10 December 1966   Telegram in reply from Pope Paul VI to Patriarch Athenagoras

144. 14 December 1966   Letter of Bishop Willebrands to Patriarch Athenagoras, thanking him for the welcome given him on his recent visit to the Phanar

1967:

145. 20 February 1967   Telegram from Patriarch Athenagoras to Pope Paul VI, congratulating him on his efforts for peace

215. 8 April 1968   Easter letter of Pope Paul VI to Patriarch Athenagoras

216. Easter 1968   Easter letter of Patriarch Athenagoras to Pope Paul VI

217. 13 April 1968   Telegram from Patriarch Athenagoras to Pope Paul VI, thanking him for his 8 April letter

218. 30 May 1968   Letter of Cardinal Bea to Patriarch Athenagoras on the date of Easter

219. 12 June 1968   Letter of Patriarch Athenagoras to Cardinal Bea on the date of Easter

220. 23 June 1968   Telegram from Patriarch Athenagoras to Pope Paul VI, congratulating him on the anniversary of his enthronement

221. 24 June 1968   Telegram from Patriarch Athenagoras to Pope Paul VI for the feast of his patron saint

222. 30 June 1968   Telegram in reply from Pope Paul VI to Patriarch Athenagoras

223. 25 July 1968   Telegram from Pope Paul VI to Patriarch Athenagoras on the anniversary of his visit to the Phanar

224. 25 July 1968   Telegram from Patriarch Athenagoras to Pope Paul VI on the anniversary of the Pope's visit

225. 9 August 1968   Telegram from Patriarch Athenagoras to Pope Paul VI, expressing the Patriarch's agreement with the encyclical *Humanae Vitae*

226. 21 August 1968   Telegram in reply from Pope Paul VI to Patriarch Athenagoras

arch Athenagoras, thanking him for the welcome given him at the Phanar

239. 16 December 1968   Letter of Bishop Willebrands to Patriarch Athenagoras, thanking him for condolences on the death of Cardinal Bea

240. 23 December 1968   Telegram of good wishes from Patriarch Athenagoras to Pope Paul VI for Christmas

241. 24 December 1968   Telegram from Pope Paul VI to Patriarch Athenagoras for Christmas

242. Christmas 1968   Christmas letter of Patriarch Athenagoras to Pope Paul VI

1969:

243. 7 January 1969   Letter in reply of Pope Paul VI to Patriarch Athenagoras

244. 10 January 1969   Letter of Pope Paul VI to Patriarch Athenagoras on the development of relations between the Churches of Rome and Constantinople

245. 19 January 1969   Letter of Bishop Willebrands on the discussions during his recent visit

246. 24 January 1969   Telegram from Pope Paul VI to Patriarch Athenagoras on the twentieth anniversary of the Patriarch's enthronement

247. 13 February 1969   Letter of Patriarch Athenagoras to Bishop Willebrands, thanking him for the souvenir of Cardinal Bea

248. 1 April 1969   Easter letter of Pope Paul VI to Patriarch Athenagoras

249. 4 April 1969
Telegram from Patriarch Athenagoras to Pope Paul VI for Easter

250. 22 April 1969
Telegram from Patriarch Athenagoras to Cardinal Willebrands to congratulate him on his appointment

251. 26 April 1969
Telegram in reply from Cardinal Willebrands to Patriarch Athenagoras

252. 6 May 1969
Telegram from Patriarch Athenagoras to Pope Paul VI on the occasion of the appointment of thirty-five new Cardinals

253. 12 May 1969
Telegram in reply from Pope Paul VI to Patriarch Athenagoras

254. 12 June 1969
Telegram from Patriarch Athenagoras to Pope Paul VI on the Pope's journey to Geneva

255. 21 June 1969
Telegram in reply from Pope Paul VI to Patriarch Athenagoras

256. 20 June 1969
Telegram from Patriarch Athenagoras, congratulating Pope Paul VI on the anniversary of his election to the See of Rome

257. 24 June 1969
Telegram from Patriarch Athenagoras to Pope Paul VI on the feast-day of his patron saint

258. 8 July 1969
Telegram in reply from Pope Paul VI to Patriarch Athenagoras

259. 8 July 1969
Letter of Patriarch Athenagoras to Cardinal Willebrands on a joint commission for the publication of the communications between the Churches of Rome and Constantinople

280. 24 December 1969   Telegram from Patriarch Athenagoras to Pope Paul VI, presenting his Christmas wishes

281. Christmas 1969   Letter from Patriarch Athenagoras to Pope Paul VI, sending his Christmas wishes.

1970:

282. 13 January 1970   Letter in reply from Pope Paul VI to Patriarch Athenagoras

283. Easter 1970   Easter letter of Pope Paul VI to Patriarch Athenagoras

284. 28 March 1970   Telegram from Patriarch Athenagoras to Pope Paul VI on the feast of Easter

1971:

285. 8 February 1971   Letter of Pope Paul VI to Patriarch Athenagoras on the development of relations between the two Churches

286. 21 March 1971   Letter in reply of Patriarch Athenagoras to Pope Paul VI

287. 2 April 1971   Easter letter of Pope Paul VI to Patriarch Athenagoras

288. 8 April 1971   Telegram from Patriarch Athenagoras to Pope Paul VI for Easter

289. 7 December 1971   Address by Cardinal Willebrands at the Phanar for the sixth anniversary of the lifting of the anathemas, and for the presentation of the *Tomos Agapis* to Patriarch Athenagoras

1972:

290. 24 January 1972

Address by Metropolitan Meliton on the occasion of his presentation of the *Tomos Agapis* to Pope Paul VI

291. 24 January 1972

Dedication of the copy of the *Tomos Agapis* presented by Patriarch Athenagoras to Pope Paul VI

292. 24 January 1972

Dedication inscribed inside the casket containing the precious cross presented by Patriarch Athenagoras to Pope Paul VI

293. 24 January 1972

Address in reply by Pope Paul VI to Metropolitan Meliton

294. 24 January 1972

Address by Pope Paul VI at the prayer service in the Lateran Basilica, held on the arrival of the delegation from the Ecumenical Patriarch

295. 25 January 1972

Press conference by Metropolitan Damaskinos of Tranoupolis and Father Pierre Duprey at the presentation of the *Tomos Agapis*

296. 24 March 1972

Easter letter from Pope Paul VI to Patriarch Athenagoras

297. 30 March 1972

Telegram from Patriarch Athenagoras to Pope Paul VI for Easter

298. 7 July 1972

Telegram from Pope Paul VI to the Holy Synod of the Eucumenical Patriarchate, upon the death of Patriarch Athenagoras

299. 9 July 1972

Tribute by Pope Paul VI to Patriarch Athenagoras in his speech before the recitation of the Angelus, Sunday 9 July

323. 30 November 1974   Letter of Pope Paul VI to Patriarch
                           Dimitrios I concerning the transfer of a
                           relic of St. Cyril to Thessalonica

324. 30 November 1974   Address in reply by Patriarch Dimi-
                           trios I to Father Duprey

325. 24 December 1974   Telegram from Patriarch Dimitrios I to
                           Pope Paul VI for the opening of the
                           Holy Year

1975:

326. 26 March 1975   Easter letter of Pope Paul VI to Patri-
                           arch Dimitrios I

327. 27 March 1975   Easter letter of Patriarch Dimitrios I to
                           Pope Paul VI

328. 18 May 1975   Letter of Cardinal Willebrands to
                           Patriarch Dimitrios I on the possibility
                           of arriving at a fixed date for Easter

329. 19 June 1975   Letter in reply of Patriarch Dimitrios I
                           to Cardinal Willebrands

330. 14 December 1975   Address by Metropolitan Meliton in
                           the Sistine Chapel at the end of the lit-
                           urgy celebrated by Pope Paul VI on the
                           tenth anniversary of the lifting of the
                           anathemas

331. 14 December 1975   Letter of Patriarch Dimitrios I to Pope
                           Paul VI on the tenth anniversary of the
                           lifting of the anathemas

332. 14 December 1975   Address by Pope Paul VI in the Sistine
                           Chapel after the reading of the letter
                           from Patriarch Dimitrios I

1978:

441. 15 October 1981   Telegram from Patriarch Dimitrios I to Pope John Paul II for the anniversary of his election to the Papacy

442. 23 October 1981   Telegram from Pope John Paul II to Patriarch Dimitrios I for the latter's feast-day

443. 27 October 1981   Letter in reply from Patriarch Dimitrios I to Pope John Paul II

444. 31 October 1981   Letter in reply of Pope John Paul II (signed in his own hand) to Patriarch Dimitrios I, thanking him for the good wishes sent for the anniversary of the Pope's election

445. 30 November 1981   Letter of Pope John Paul II to Patriarch Dimitrios I for the feast of St. Andrew

446. 30 November 1981   Address by Patriarch Dimitrios I to the Delegation from the Church of Rome for the patronal feast of the Church of Constantinople

447. 30 November 1981   Address by Cardinal Willebrands to Patriarch Dimitrios I at the celebration of the feast of St. Andrew at the Phanar

448. 24 December 1981   Telegram from Patriarch Dimitrios I to Pope John Paul II for Christmas

1982:

449. 2 January 1982   Telegram in reply from Pope John Paul II to Patriarch Dimitrios I

450. 3 April 1982   Easter letter of Pope John Paul II to Patriarch Dimitrios I

Ecumenical Documents Series

Volume I: Doing the Truth in Charity, eds. Thomas F. Stransky and John B. Sheerin

Contents

The Decree on Ecumenism and other Vatican II texts • The two-part Directory concerning ecumenical matters and ecumenism in higher education • Ecumenical collaboration at the regional, national and local levels • Sacramental sharing • Marriages between Catholics and other Christians • Reception of adult baptized Christians into the Catholic Church • Principles for interconfessional cooperation in bible translations • Common calendar and fixed Easter date • Relations with the Orthodox Churches, and with the Anglican and Protestant Communions • Extracts from papal letters, sermons, etc. • Relations with the Jews

Volume II: Growth in Agreement, eds. Harding Meyer and Lukas Vischer

Contents

Anglican conversations with Lutherans, with Old Catholics, with Orthodox, with Roman Catholics • Baptist-Reformed • Disciples-Roman Catholic • Lutheran-Roman Catholic • Lutheran-Reformed-Roman Catholic • Methodist-Roman Catholic • Old Catholic-Orthodox • Pentecostal-Roman Catholic • Reformed-Roman Catholic • WCC Faith and Order Report on Baptism, Eucharist and Ministry

Volume IV: Building Unity, eds. Jeffrey Gros and Joseph Burgess

Contents

Roman Catholic dialogues in the U.S.A. with Anglicans, with Southern Baptists, with Disciples of Christ, with Lutherans, with United Methodists, with Eastern Orthodox, with Oriental Orthodox, and with Presbyterian and Reformed • The Group of Dombes (European) statements on eucharistic faith, on reconciliation of ministries, and on episcopal ministry • National Council of Churches (U.S.A.) on responsible debate concerning abortion and homosexuality, and on conciliar fellowship ● International congress of theology on basic Christian communities ● Caribbean Conference of Churches, Latin American Council of Churches and Ecuadoran Episcopal Conference on contemporary religious movements